88-1203

Bridging
the Gap Between
Rich and Poor

Recent Titles in
Contributions in Economics and Economic History
Series Editor: Robert Sobel

Off the Track: The Decline of the Intercity Passenger Train in the United States
Donald M. Itzkoff

The Crash and Its Aftermath: A History of Securities Markets in the United
States, 1929-1933
Barrie A. Wigmore

Synthetic Rubber: A Project That Had to Succeed
Vernon Herbert and Attilio Bisio

Military Spending and Industrial Decline: A Study of the American
Machine Tool Industry
Anthony Di Filippo

Famine in Peasant Societies
Ronald E. Seavoy

Workforce Management in the Arabian Peninsula: Forces Affecting Development
George S. Roukis and Patrick J. Montana, editors

A Prologue to National Development Planning
Jamshid Gharajedaghi

Lost Initiatives: Canada's Forest Industries, Forest Policy
and Forest Conservation
R. Peter Gillis and Thomas R. Roach

Friedrich A. Sorge's *Labor Movement in the United States:*
A History of the American Working Class from 1890 to 1896
Kai Schoenhals, translator

The Coming of Age of Political Economy, 1815-1825
Gary F. Langer

The Reconstruction of Economics: An Analysis of the Fundamentals
of Institutional Economics
Allan G. Gruchy

Development Finance and the Development Process
Kempe Ronald Hope

Bridging the Gap Between Rich and Poor

American Economic Development
Policy Toward the Arab East, 1942-1949

Nathan Godfried

Contributions in Economics and Economic History, Number 75

G
P

MURDOCK LEARNING RESOURCE CTR.
George Fox College
Newberg, Oregon 97132
WITHDRAWN

Greenwood Press
New York • Westport, Connecticut • London

HC
415 .15
.G 63
1987
X

Library of Congress Cataloging-in-Publication Data

Godfried, Nathan.
   Bridging the gap between rich and poor.

   (Contributions in economics and economic history,
ISSN 0084-9235 ; no. 75)
   Bibliography: p.
   Includes index.
   1. Economic assistance, American—Middle East.
2. United States—Foreign economic relations—Middle
East.   3. Middle East—Foreign economic relations—
United States.   4. United States—Foreign economic
relations—Developing countries.   5. Developing countries
—Foreign economic relations—United States.   I. Title.
II. Series.
HC415.15.G63   1987   338.91'73'056   87-8471
ISBN 0-313-25648-9 (lib. bdg. : alk. paper)

British Library Cataloguing in Publication Data is available.

Copyright © 1987 by Nathan Godfried

All rights reserved. No portion of this book may be
reproduced, by any process or technique, without the
express written consent of the publisher.

Library of Congress Catalog Card Number: 87-8471
ISBN: 0-313-25648-9
ISSN: 0084-9235

First published in 1987

Greenwood Press, Inc.
88 Post Road West, Westport, Connecticut 06881

Printed in the United States of America

The paper used in this book complies with the
Permanent Paper Standard issued by the National
Information Standards Organization (Z39.48-1984).

10 9 8 7 6 5 4 3 2 1

Copyright Acknowledgment

Portions of Chapter 4 first appeared in the article, "Economic Development and Regionalism:
United States Foreign Relations in the Middle East, 1942-1945," in the *Journal of Contemporary
History* 22 (July 1987): 481-500. I am grateful to the *Journal* for permission to incorporate
material from this article into the present work.

DEDICATED TO

MY FATHER AND THE MEMORY OF MY MOTHER

Contents

Abbreviations   ix

Preface   xi

Acknowledgments   xiii

Prologue   1

1. Economic Development as a Postwar Goal   28

2. Reconstruction versus Development: 1946-1949   62

3. Reconstruction versus Development: Financial and
      Technical Aid   96

4. America's Development Policy and the Arab East:
      1942-1949   121

5. Arab East Development and the United States,
      1942-1949: Case Studies   149

    Epilogue: The United States and Third World
                Development   185

    Appendix   199

    Select Bibliography   205

    Index   217

Abbreviations

AEMME	American Economic Mission to the Middle East
AFL	American Federation of Labor
API	American Palestine Institute
Aramco	Arabian American Oil Company
BEW	Board of Economic Warfare
CCP	Conciliation Commission on Palestine (UN)
CED	Committee for Economic Development
CFR	Council on Foreign Relations
CIO	Congress of Industrial Organizations
CTAL	Confederacion de Trabajadores de America Latina
ECA	Economic Cooperation Administration
ECEFP	Executive Committee on Economic Foreign Policy
ECLA	Economic Commission for Latin America (UN)
ECME	Economic Commission for Middle East (UN)
ECOSOC	Economic and Social Council (UN)
ERP	European Recovery Program
Eximbank	Export-Import Bank
FEA	Foreign Economic Administration
FRUS	Foreign Relations of the United States
FSOs	Foreign Service Officers
FTUC	Free Trade Union Committee
IBEC	International Basic Economy Corporation
IBRD	International Bank for Reconstruction and Development
IDAB	International Development Advisory Board
ILO	International Labor Organization
IMF	International Monetary Fund
ITO	International Trade Organization
JVA	Jordan Valley Authority
MESC	Middle East Supply Centre
NAC	National Advisory Council on International Monetary and Financial Problems
NAM	National Association of Manufacturers
NEA	Near East Division/Near Eastern and African Affairs (Department of State)
NFTC	National Foreign Trade Council
NIEO	New International Economic Order
OEA	Overseas Economic Administration
OIAA	Office of Inter-American Affairs
PEC	Palestine Economic Corporation
PPS	Policy Planning Staff (Department of State)

x   ABBREVIATIONS

REA   Rural Electrification Administration
TVA   Tennessee Valley Authority
UNCTAD   United Nations Conference on Trade and Development
UNSCOP   United Nations Special Committee on Palestine
ZOA   Zionist Organization of America

Preface

Inequality defines the world order. "Collective disparities
of wealth and power," argued Robert W. Tucker, "determine the
structure of the international system."* Throughout the
twentieth century, and especially since World War II, the gap
between rich and powerful states and poor, weak areas has
widened. A debate has evolved between industrially advanced
nations and those of the underdeveloped world. Third World
nations have accused the United States and other advanced
capitalist states of nurturing an international system which
serves the interests of the rich at the expense of the poor.
The United States contends that the existing capitalist world-
economy is the best of all possible worlds.

The basic issues comprising this conflict between the
developed countries of the Northern Hemisphere and the
relatively impoverished nations of the Southern Hemisphere
took distinctive form during the 1940s. The decade began with
a destructive world conflict and ended with a potentially
fatal Cold War. It encompassed the end of a global depression, the reconstruction of war-devastated industrial societies, and the discontent and hope of poor, agrarian nations.
During the 1940s the United States emerged as the supreme
productive, commercial, and financial power in the world.
American policymakers recognized and seized the opportunity to
create an American order. They actively sought global
political leadership for the United States. An important
ingredient of Pax Americana was the stabilization, integration, and development of the Third World. The issue of
economic development became an essential element of American
postwar policy toward the nations of Asia, Latin America, the
Middle East, and Africa.

This study examines the development component of United
States-Third World relations during the 1940s. By outlining
both the internal and external American discussions concerning
development and the international debates over the issue, the
study identifies and analyzes those policies that have come to
dominate the American approach toward Third World economic
development during the last half of the twentieth century.

---

* Robert W. Tucker, The Inequality of Nations (New York:
Basic Books, 1977), p. 171.

The study includes the views of corporate, labor, and political leaders and focuses on the thoughts and actions of the state's executive branch, where economic development policies were formulated and implemented.

The Prologue and chapters 1, 2, and 3 describe steps along the development path traversed by American policymakers. The Prologue outlines the world-economy in which the United States and the Third World confronted each other. It explains where and why policymakers stood on the issue of development by the early 1940s. Chapter 1 describes how development became a postwar goal of the United States. Chapter 2 analyzes the refining and hardening of the development framework and the challenges posed by Third World nations during the postwar years. Chapter 3 explores the specific issues of financial and technical aid that comprised key elements in the overall development policy.

The issues raised in these chapters are then examined in the context of American development policy toward the Arab East (Egypt, Jordan, Palestine/Israel, Lebanon, Syria, Saudi Arabia, Kuwait, and the small states of the Arabian peninsula). Chapter 4 surveys America's policy toward the region as a whole, while Chapter 5 describes American economic relations with Egypt, Saudi Arabia, and Israel. The Epilogue briefly analyzes American policies since 1950.

When compared to Latin America and East Asia, the Middle East prior to World War II was an area of minor concern to American policymakers. Yet by 1950 the United States considered the region vital to its national interests. This change reflected, in part, the developing Cold War and the growing importance of Middle East oil to the economic recovery of Europe. Economic development issues helped to link policy decisions concerning the Cold War and oil production.

It is problematic whether Arab East development was typical of other areas. A proper reply requires a comparative history including the Middle East, Latin America, Africa, and Asia. Unique aspects of the Arab East's history, economy, politics, and culture make generalizations for the entire Third World hazardous. Nevertheless it is safe to say that the countries of the Arab East faced domestic and foreign pressures and political and socioeconomic problems similar to those of other developing countries. The region's countries displayed a variety of circumstances (mineral rich to dirt poor) and policies (laissez-faire to state planning), which makes the Arab East's experiences with the United States a suitable microcosm of American development relations with the Third World.

Acknowledgments

Many individuals have contributed to the completion of this work. John A. DeNovo was particularly helpful in the preparation of an earlier version of this study. His intelligence and prudence are appreciated. William Borden shared with me his considerable knowledge of international trade and world economic integration. Manjunath Pendakur has impressed upon me his unique understanding of political economy. Conversations with Bill and Manji have sharpened my analysis of Third World economic development and American policy. Robert Wiebe read an earlier draft of this work and offered useful suggestions; as did the anonymous reviewer for Greenwood Press. I am deeply indebted to Thomas J. McCormick, who read various drafts of the manuscript and provided invaluable criticisms. Tom's invigorating teaching, insightful scholarship, and warm friendship are deeply cherished. I am, of course, solely responsible for the contents of the study.

My intellectual debts do not equal what I owe to my family and friends. Their understanding and companionship helped me survive this ordeal. In no particular order I wish to thank Randy Roediger, the Pendakurs, Tom McCormick, Henry Binford, Mark Tolstedt, Ron and Marge Schildknecht, Bill Borden, Ira and Lynn Basen, Jim Schwoch, Pat Hearden, the softball gang, and all the others who are not mentioned, but are in my heart and memory. One final thanks to Beth McKillen who has assisted me in innumerable and intangible ways.

Prologue

The demand for, and the corresponding debate over, economic development of poor areas took recognizable shape during the 1940s. Most foreign policy histories of the 1940s and the Cold War era plunge into the decade's crises and great power conflicts.(1)   Obsession with the "horizontal dimension of rivalry among the most powerful states" (e.g., the American-Soviet confrontation) obscures the vertical dimension of power--that is, "the domination and subordination of metropole over hinterland, centre over periphery, in a world political economy."(2)   Also lost in the morass of big power politics is an understanding of the "reciprocal and dynamic interaction" of polity and economy.(3)   A political economy perspective avoids these pitfalls and thus illuminates U.S.-Third World relations and the issue of economic development during the 1940s.

POLITICAL ECONOMY: CAPITALISM, CORPORATISM, AND THE WORLD SYSTEM

Taking a political economy approach to American foreign relations involves examining events on several planes and dimensions simultaneously.   American policies toward the Third World derived from the internal needs of a capitalist and corporatist nation.   Those policies also represented the demands and responsibilities of a hegemonic power in a capitalist world-economy.   The following sections examine separately the internal and external determinants of American foreign relations.   In practice these levels of analysis intersect and overlap.

A political economy perspective recognizes a reciprocal relationship between socioeconomic structures and political superstructures. An economic structure is a mode of production.   It consists of a set of productive forces or means of production--for example, raw materials, tools, technology, skills, energy, and so forth.   It also entails the ways people relate to one another in producing, distributing, and exchanging goods.   These social relations of production describe who owns and/or controls the means of production, the division of labor, and the network of exchange relations. Social relations of production define class structure and class struggle within a particular setting. Productive forces and the corresponding relations of production shape the superstructure of political and intellectual ideas and institutions. The superstructure, in turn, affects the operation of the economic system.(4)

The capitalist mode of production--the economic structure that shapes and defines American society--rests upon a profit orientation and private ownership of productive forces. Capitalists own and control the means of production and the process of production itself. Wage-workers, divorced from the productive forces, sell their capacity to work (i.e., their labor power) to those who own the means of production. Capitalist production is sold on a market for maximum profit. Goods are made for exchange, not for direct use by the producer. Both labor power and the means of production become commodities to be bought and sold to the highest bidder. Expansion, the continual drive for capital accumulation, is at the heart of the capitalist system. "Capitalists must constantly expand in order to remain capitalists, for if they did not they would be destroyed by competitors; they would be consumers and not capitalists."(5)

Capitalism produces and sustains wealth and poverty. The two are inexorably linked together. Wealth in a capitalist nation means "a concentration of much of society's production (its means and its product) in relatively few hands, and there is no way for that to occur without the simultaneous creation of its opposite--poverty, the material deprivation of the many, at least in relative terms."(6)   Inequality is merely one of many severe and inherent problems in capitalism. Endemic imbalances in capitalism derive from the fundamental separation between those who own and control the means of production and those who do not. Conflict between the capitalist class and the working class determines the economic and political life of capitalist society. "In fact, the political process in these societies is mainly **about** the confrontation of these forces, and is intended to sanction the terms of the relationship between them."(7)

The relationship between "civil society" and "political society," or class and state, is complex and open to debate. The state includes "not only the apparatus of government," but all the institutions (e.g., education, media, foundations) that help create within the population the behavioral patterns and expectations consistent with the prevailing social order. Every state attempts to "reproduce" the society in which it develops. If it fails in this task, the state disintegrates and dies. State "intervention in the affairs of society is crucial, constant, and pervasive; and that intervention is closely conditioned by the most fundamental of the state's characteristics, namely that it **is** a means of class domination."(8)

In the capitalist mode of production the state reproduces capitalist economic structures and political superstructures. By definition, therefore, the state assists the capitalist class in maintaining its control over the means of production and in accumulating capital. The capitalist state performs several crucial functions. It actively or passively aids in the process of capital accumulation. In the United States during the twentieth century this has meant state encouragement of corporate concentration and cooperation, management of the business cycle, and financing of infrastructural services.

The state   also maintains   law and   order within its sovereign
borders.   It contains or represses intra-class and inter-class
struggles that threaten the prevailing mode of production.   In
an ideological realm the state promotes consensus in regard to
the   existing   order.   Legitimizing the inherent inequalities
within the socioeconomic system   involves concessions   to certain groups   and cooptation   of others.   It requires a general
mystification and obfuscation of the benefits and costs of the
system so   that the   policies which serve the capitalist class
appear to contribute to the   general   welfare.   Finally, the
capitalist state   advances the   "national interest" in the international arena.   It   performs   its   internal/external functions on   a global level--aiding in the worldwide accumulation
of capital, the maintenance of   international   stability, and
the formulation of global or universal principles and laws.(9)

Although the state serves the interests of the capitalist
class, it "enjoys a high degree   of autonomy   and independence
in the manner of its operation as a class state."   Intra-class
differences and inter-class challenges necessitate a relatively autonomous   state.   Individual firms or industries, for example, may   push for   policies that   maximize their short-term
profits, but threaten the long-term profitability of the capitalist class as a whole.   At other   times, working   class demands   and capitalist   class   intransigence   may endanger the
entire functioning of the capitalist mode of production.   The
state   thus   must   engage   in those compromises and sacrifices
that will   maintain   the   long-range   interests of   the whole
capitalist class.(10)

By the early 1900s in the United States, capitalist class
elites had recognized the important role of the state in regulating political   structures and manipulating power alignments
in order to minimize class conflicts and maximize   capital accumulation.   During the closing decades of the nineteenth century the capitalist class   faced   severe   economic   crises and
potential class   war.   The most class conscious capitalists--
those representing   the   largest,   most   concentrated corpora-
tions--advocated   order,   social   cohesion, and a rationalized
political economy.   They   believed that   long-range stability,
"class harmony and organic unity were essential to society and
could be secured if the various   functional groups,   and especially the   organizations of   capital and   labour, were imbued
with a conception of mutual rights and obligations."(11)   Responding to   this challenge, leading corporate and state officials began to develop a theory of social   order and political
structure that historians have labelled "corporatism."

Corporatism proposed   to wed the elites of large, hierar-
chical, functional groups--capital,   labor,   and agriculture--
and the   elites of   the state   into an informal and, at times,
formal "public-private power-sharing arrangement."   Corporate
elites argued   that a community of interests, aims, and ideals
united labor, capital, and   the   state.   In   particular, increased production   and the   concomitant expansion of markets,
sources of raw materials,   and investment   outlets would bring
prosperity and   full employment to all Americans and an end to
the possibility of class war at home.   Organized labor leaders
such as   Samuel Gompers and William Green embraced the productionist policies of the capitalist class   and the   state; they
favored   policies   designed   to   increase the absolute size of
America's economic pie, while keeping the   individual portions
the same.   They rejected concepts of class struggle, abandoned

demands for democracy in the workplace, and ignored distribu-
tionist strategies aimed at reallocating wealth and power in
American society. Trade union elites promised a responsible,
predictable, and peaceful work force in exchange for a growing
economic pie, nominal welfare reforms from the state, and
token participation in policymaking.(12)

Productionism and its benefits comprised a cornerstone of
corporatist ideology. Another cornerstone was the state's
role in promoting and protecting productionism and class
harmony. Emily Rosenberg has examined how America's corporate
and state elite altered their view of the state's relationship
to the capitalist sector--from a "promotional state" in the
period 1890 through World War I; to a "cooperative state"
during the 1920s; and finally, to a "regulatory state" during
the Great Depression and World War II.(13) By the 1940s, as
George Lipsitz has explained, state and capitalist elites
clearly "recognized the desirability of government action to
prevent economic instability, to help raise capital for
private enterprise, to secure new areas of investment, to
limit competition, to mediate between capital and labor, and
to lend legitimacy to the inequities and sacrifices demanded
by such a system."(14) Thus American elites advocated the use
of state power to balance the power of the major functional
groups and guarantee long-range stability.

Corporatist theory and practice did not always coincide.
Questions concerning the relative power or influence of functional groups, the real or imagined neutrality of the state
vis-a-vis those groups, and the stability or instability of
the corporatist structure as a whole remained problematic.
Corporatist ideology and institutions appeared to be universal
in form--that is, they did not seem to serve the interests of
any particular class. Corporatism held out the illusion of
capital class and labor elites sharing equally in the making
of policy; and the state serving as an impartial third party--
arbitrating disputes, coordinating power-sharing, and ensuring
fair play. But corporatism developed "within the parameters
of advanced capitalist society." The functional groups arose
out of the social relations of production, out of the capitalist division of labor. Corporatist structures were, therefore, class-based and reflected the class struggle. The capitalist class continued to dominate the political economy of
corporatist society. Capitalists and/or the state made concessions to the potentially dissident working class in order
to give it a stake in preserving the system. New Deal reforms
and participation in war boards, for example, gave organized
labor some benefits and a sense of achievement without undermining the leadership or vital interests of the capitalist
class.(15)

The capitalist and corporatist nature of American society
by 1940 did not mean the absolute rule of the capitalist class
or the state. On the contrary, the dialectical nature of capitalism and the relative weakness of corporatist structures in
the United States undermined consensus and harmony in American
society. Despite the cooptation of trade union leaders, for
example, rank and file workers engaged in a series of wildcat
strikes during World War II and a wave of industrywide and
general strikes in 1946. The state continued its efforts to
mediate the sometimes intense conflict of interest among different sectors of the capitalist class. Contests for power on

local, regional, and national levels continued in the postwar
era.(16)

State and capitalist class elites and the collaborating
leaders of organized labor did agree on the necessity of expanding American production. During the 1940s, this required
the rebuilding of old and the securing of new markets and
sources of raw materials abroad--including the Third World.
The development of markets and raw materials demanded, in
turn, the creation of the economic, political, and social conditions conducive for capital and technology export. The
prosperity and stability of America's own domestic socioeconomic and political structures postulated an expansionist foreign policy that entailed the internationalization of American
capitalism and corporatism. Domestic factors--the needs of
American capitalism as viewed by the nation's dominant class
and the state--thus shaped U.S. foreign relations. The existence of a global capitalist mode of production and the role of
the United States in that capitalist world-economy also sig-
nificantly contributed to national policies. Understanding
U.S.-Third World relations during the 1940s necessitates
examining the interaction of social forces on a national and
global plane.(17)

Immanuel Wallerstein and other scholars have described
the emergence and development--since the sixteenth century--of
a global economic structure. This capitalist world-economy
consists of a single division of labor and a multitude of political systems and cultures. As on a national level, global
capitalist relations of production comprise a class structure
that separates producers from the means of production. Two
basic classes emerge: a capitalist class that owns and/or
controls the productive forces and a propertyless, wage-earn-
ing class. A middle strata of small commodity producers and
skilled or professional workers also appears. Intersecting
and overlapping the world class structure is a territorial division of labor between core, periphery, and semiperiphery.(18)

Core states, such as the United States, employ highly
skilled, highly paid labor and sustain a large class of
technicians, professionals, and managers. The core special-
izes in high-profit, capital-intensive, diversified production. Agricultural production in a core state is usually more
capital intensive than much of the manufacturing activity in a
peripheral area. The urbanized and industrialized core, with
its advanced commercial and financial structure, appropriates
surplus from the whole world-economy.(19)

At the margins of the world-economy resides the periphery. The inverse of the core, the peripheral economy special-
izes in the production of primary commodities (raw materials
and agricultural goods) for sale on the world market. The
periphery uses low-wage and often coerced labor to produce
labor-intensive, low-profit, low-technology goods. Widespread
poverty, illiteracy, ill-health, and a highly skewed distribution of income and wealth characterize the underdeveloped
economies of the periphery.(20)

A semiperiphery stands between the core and periphery "in
terms of the kinds of products it exports and in terms of the
wage levels and profit margins it knows." Semiperipheral
countries contain a relatively equal mix of core and peripheral types of production. These nations export primary goods
to the core, while they manufacture goods for their own market

and the markets of weaker neighbors. They thus play "the role of peripheral partner to the core countries and core partner to some peripheral countries."   Core states may fall and peripheral areas may rise into the semiperiphery.   As both exploiter and exploited, the semiperiphery obscures the formation of a polarized world-economy. Within its own borders an intense class struggle develops between the contradictory interests of indigenous core producers and peripheral producers.(21)

Uneven and unequal development characterize political as well as economic structures in the capitalist world-economy. A nation's political system reflects the needs of the predominant economic sectors. Where core economic activities emerge and dominate, a strong state apparatus capable of manipulating markets develops.   Core states possess a high degree of political integration and ideological homogeneity. With a weak state and military structure, the periphery experiences the frequent "intervention of outsiders via war, subversion, and diplomacy." Thus the core perpetuates its dominance over the periphery.(22)

The ascent and decline of countries within the world-economy mirrors changes in technology and the environment and their socioeconomic consequences. "The key factor to note is that within a capitalist world-economy, all states cannot develop' simultaneously **by definition**, since the system functions by virtue of having unequal core and peripheral regions."(23)   The normal operation of the capitalist system sustains the basic core-periphery division.   Social, political, and economic inequalities are inherent in the capitalist mode of production. International inequality derives from the core's ownership and/or control of the world means of production and the periphery's relegation to selling raw materials, food, and labor power. The unequal exchange between rich and poor and a multitude of other imbalances are manifestations of this underlining problem.(24) Capitalist classes in individual nations and within the core as a whole have always recognized the necessity of controlling the means of production. Working together with the state, the capitalist class has produced foreign policies to serve its needs.   Through "colonialism, gun-boat diplomacy, interventionism, foreign investments, multinationals, and military and foreign aid," state and capitalist class elites have collaborated in maintaining command of the world means of production.(25) Through these mechanisms, the state fulfills its international function.   The extension of the core state's international function is linked to the role of the United States as a hegemonic power during the twentieth century.

According to Robert W. Cox, hegemony is an order among states "within a world economy with a dominant mode of production" and "a complex of international social relationships." In the mid-nineteenth century Britain supported a certain order within a capitalist world-economy. Pax Britannica attempted to maintain the international division of labor while containing class conflict.   The juxtaposition of material, ideological, and institutional forces made the United States a hegemonic power in the 1940s.(26) American production, trade, and finance reigned supreme. The U.S.'s goods dominated the world's markets, its multinational corporations gained control over a relatively large part of the world's productive forces, and its currency served as the universal medium of exchange.

The Great Depression and World War II convinced state and
capitalist class elites that America's economic, political,
social, and military security depended on an open and expanding liberal world system. They believed that internationalizing American capitalism and corporatism guaranteed a global
order consistent with their domination.(27)

Internationalizing American capitalism meant an internationalization of state functions. Extending the state's ju-
risdiction far beyond its territorial borders, according to
James Petras and Morris Morley, created an "imperial
state."(28) The imperial state, like the national state,
"does not function on the basis of some inner logic of its
own." Rather, it "responds to the interests and demands of
capitalists seeking to **move capital abroad** in order to pursue
accumulation activities on a global level." Through its
efforts to create and preserve the economic, social, political, and ideological conditions necessary for capitalist
expansion, the imperial state "embodies the present and future
collective interests" of the capitalist class.(29)

The capitalist class contains different elements--even
among those with international concerns. Some capitalists
focus on the welfare (profit) of their own individual firms.
More functionally oriented capitalists recognize industrywide
concerns, seek horizontal coordination among companies, and
request state help for the industry as a whole. American oil
corporations in the Middle East fall into this category. Finally, there are class conscious capitalists who understand
the immediate and long-range needs of the capitalist class as
a whole. These cosmopolitan system-makers directly or indi-
rectly contribute to state policy. As "in-and-outers," they
move back and forth between corporate boardrooms and government offices. Policy-formation organizations such as the
Council on Foreign Relations and the Committee for Economic
Development provide corporate officials, state policymakers,
and academic "experts" with an informal setting in which to
discuss policy options and strategy. While single enterprise
and industrywide capitalists define state intervention in
terms of profits and protecting property, cosmopolitan capitalists broaden the state's role to include creating and maintaining conditions for profitmaking and forcefully containing
threats and challenges to the entire capitalist class. Imperial state policymakers must have the flexibility to "mediate
the class interests of the ascendant groups within the ruling
class."(30)

Petras and Morley define the imperial state as "a complex
web of interrelated but functionally specific sets of agencies
[e.g., economic, coercive, ideological] coordinated at the top
levels of the executive branch" and "charged with promoting
and protecting the expansion of capital across state boundaries." Our examination of Third World economic development
will identify imperial state policymakers in the Department of
State and Department of Commerce and other government organs.
Executive branch policymakers possessed discretionary power in
making day-to-day tactical decisions. Power struggles within
the imperial state usually reflected differences over the
means rather than the ends of policy. Bureaucracies and
personalities often clashed over the specifics of development
policy toward the Third World. These confrontations sometimes
had a significant impact on a particular policy situation. In
rare instances, a series of tactical disputes had a cumulative

effect on strategy. But overall, imperial state policymakers
shared the same fundamental concerns and interests as the
dynamic cosmopolitan elements in the capitalist class. No
clashes arose over the need to maintain capitalism and its
concomitant social-political system.(31)

The goal of American foreign policy in the 1940s (indeed
throughout the twentieth century) was to internationalize the
American capitalist and corporatist system. The American
desire for hegemony took many forms. Robert Cox has explained
that hegemony "is expressed in universal norms, institutions
and mechanisms which lay down general rules of behavior for
states and for those forces of civil society that act across
national boundaries--rules which support the dominant mode of
production."(32) The imperial state sought to establish new
rules that would, in time, "influence and shape the behavior
of all other states on an ongoing basis."(33) As the capitalist class proclaims its interests to be the same as the
national interest, so does the hegemonic power equate what is
good for itself with what is good for the whole world-system.
By claiming its economic structure and social-political superstructure to be universally valid, the hegemonic power and its
imperial state attempt to convert their rules of the game into
universal truths and principles.(34)

American principles such as the free movement of goods
and capital across international borders, private enterprise
and markets, productionism, class harmony, and anticommunism
became the rules of the game during the 1940s. Through bilateral and multilateral negotiations and the establishment of
international institutions, imperial state policymakers sought
to achieve consensus among core states and acquiescence among
the nations of the periphery and semiperiphery to American hegemony. Pax Americana relied heavily on institutions to support U.S. domination. International organizations such as the
International Monetary Fund, the International Bank for Reconstruction and Development, and the International Trade Organization gave the appearance of diversity and pluralism, while
emphasizing the "universalism" of American policies.(35) By
utilizing these institutions, by manipulating Cold War rhetoric and anti-Soviet hostility, and by financing foreign capitalist reconstruction, America's imperial state overcame core
resistance to Pax Americana. Using its economic, ideological,
and coercive powers, the United States secured a wide measure
of consent among the core states. But the consent of a hegemonic world order is usually strongest in the core, where the
benefits are the greatest and where there is some sense of
shared interests. Consent weakens as one approaches the
periphery. It is here that challenges to hegemony may first
become manifest.(36)

As America's imperial state policymakers and capitalist
class elites formulated their global rules and set in place
their institutions, anticommunist propaganda, and other mechanisms for hegemony, they faced the potential opportunities and
dangers of peripheral underdevelopment. Policymakers conceived of economic development among poor countries primarily
as the by-product of policies that served the economies of the
capitalist core. Comparative advantage, free multilateral
trade, private enterprise, private capital, and technical assistance comprised the universal laws of Third World development. Policies based on these rules would bring some social
progress to the developing nations, but not at the expense of

world capitalist expansion.   As long   as the   global economic
pie grew,   absolute increases   in production would satiate the
Third World's ruling and   middle   classes--classes   willing to
collaborate with the core.   American officials understood that
their plans meant uneven and unequal development.   Few leaders
contemplated   a   total   alleviation   of   peripheral poverty or
closing   the   gap   between   rich   and   poor--either   within or
between nations.   Raising   the periphery   to the level of the
core required a   redistribution   of   international   wealth and
power that   obviously threatened the existing world-system and
class structure.   In addition,   not   all   Third   World nations
required   American   attention.   The imperial state designated
"countries possessing large reserves of strategic   raw materials and/or   substantial markets   for American   exports as more
critical   to   the   accumulation   process   than   countries with
limited markets and few, if any, strategic resources."(37)

America's postwar   programs for Third World development--
from Harry Truman's Point Four to John Kennedy's   Alliance for
Progress to   Ronald Reagan's   Caribbean Basin Initiative--were
little more than variations on a common theme.   Imperial state
officials sought   to bridge   the gap between rich and poor; to
coopt and integrate those classes in the periphery and semiperiphery that could guarantee their nations' continued participation in   the   capitalist   world-economy.   American leaders
argued that   participation in the world-system ameliorated the
Third World's internal deficiencies, which caused   poverty and
underdevelopment.   Variations in   American programs reflected
changing conditions   in the   world and   at home.   But changes
notwithstanding, these   programs naturally   sought to solidify
America's place as a   hegemonic core power in   the capitalist
world-economy, to   maximize the   benefits of   such a system to
other core states, and to minimize   the dangers   posed by poor
and potentially revolutionary peripheral nations.

American policymakers insisted that a particular nation's
internal conditions caused economic underdevelopment.   Yet the
solution to underdevelopment derived from participating freely
and openly in the capitalist world-economy.   Poverty caused by
internal deficiencies would be solved by the **external** capital,
goods, technology, and knowledge that were   the rewards   of an
integrated world-system.   This basic contradiction intersected
another one.   An   insufficient   internal   market characterized
most poor,   agrarian nations.   National or regional trade and
economic integration constituted one way to enlarge the internal   market   and   thus   stimulate demand.   But rhetoric aside,
American state officials and capitalist class   elites rejected
national and,   to a lesser extent, regional integration because
they threatened American economic   expansion into   the periphery.   It was far easier for the United States to penetrate and
dominate a divided market than a unified market.   The success
or failure   of American policies directed at Third World integration into the capitalist world-economy rested   on the ability of   the imperial   state and   capitalist class   to pierce a
Third World nation's social   structure and   create and sustain
lasting links with collaborator classes there.

U.S.-Third World   relations took several forms during the
1940s.   "Negotiated conflicts" developed between   American officials and those social classes in the periphery that accepted the international division of labor   and the   role of capitalism, but   who wanted to renegotiate the terms of trade, financing, and so on.   Collaborator classes included nascent in-

dustrialists, big business executives, import-exporters, and traditional large landowners. Although these groups had different relations with the imperial state and capitalist class, they tended to support opening markets, securing raw materials, and recruiting labor for multinational capital. They used their control over the indigenous state to perform these tasks and to bargain with the United States for economic and political benefits (e.g., loans, grants, technical aid, military assistance). "Irreconcilable conflicts" emerged between the United States and leaders of working class and peasant movements in the Third World. These groups tended to advocate substantial and fundamental reforms in the world-economy. Finally, intermediary conflicts developed between American leaders and middle classes in some Third World nations. These middle-sized bourgeois classes usually began by criticizing American policies and ended up negotiating with imperial state officials.(38)

During the 1940s American leaders confronted collaborator classes that wanted some degree of national economic and political integration for their nations. Third World leaders contended that unrestricted participation in the capitalist world-economy meant dependency and continued underdevelopment. At the same time, these officials wanted Western capital and technology. They were caught in the contradiction of trying to restrict Western capital, goods, technology, and skills, while attempting to attract them. American state policymakers knew that capitalists do not go abroad under restrictive conditions set by Third World rulers.

Third World development, according to U.S. officials, mandated a nation's total participation in the global trading and financial system and the use of American, or at least Western, capitalist models of development. These models encouraged the continued domination of collaborator classes and the growth of an indigenous middle class that would possess the purchasing power to acquire American goods and the "happiness that supposedly accompanied the satisfaction of consumer wants."(39) Bourgeois interests would seek social and political stability, place their faith in a productionist ideology, and reject all indigenous or foreign movements advocating a redistribution of wealth and power. Thus the United States hoped that its concept of economic development would short-circuit all social revolutions and deny power to nationalist, socialist, or autarkic forces.

These ideas constituted a part of American thinking on economic development. America's conception of economic development grew out of its needs as a capitalist, corporatist, and hegemonic core nation in a capitalist world-economy. The United States drew from evolving Western economic doctrines and its own historical legacy. The following section briefly examines these latter issues and clarifies how and why the American conception of economic development took the form that it did in the early 1940s.

DEVELOPMENT, ECONOMIC DOCTRINES, AND HISTORICAL LEGACY

A large and sometimes confusing literature exists concerning the definitions of such terms as development, growth, undeveloped, underdevelopment, and backwardness. Joseph Schumpeter, Bjorn Hettne, and other scholars have warned that "there is no all-purpose concept" of economic development, and that development should remain an "open-ended concept" to be defined "separately for every purpose."(40) This study seeks to determine the contemporary notions of development, and thus the economists, imperial state policymakers, and capitalist class elites of the 1940s will define development in their own terms.   Nevertheless, it is important to provide at least a general working definition.(41)

In its broadest and, perhaps, most comprehensive sense, economic development comprises a set of "complex processes of societal transformation."(42) As such it involves not merely the maximization of material production, but a raising of the level of sustenance and human dignity--an improvement in the quality of life.   This definition presents myriad problems, not the least of which are the cultural and ideological biases that go into defining "quality of life." The Appendix suggests 11 indicators of economic development, drawn from a variety of development studies.(43) These indicators point to the following components of a nation's economic development: productive capacity, economic diversity, health and educational care, and social welfare.   But there is much more to the concept of economic development.   All economic processes are intertwined with social and political institutions and vice versa.   Despite statements to the contrary, American policymakers either failed to grasp or ignored this insight. Working out of their own perceptions of American development and from the theories of prominent Western economists, U.S. leaders divorced economics from society as a whole and identified social and political, as well as economic issues, as purely technical ones.(44)

American policymakers' perception of economic development derived, in part, from the economic doctrines of the Western world.   Since the seventeenth century Western economists had defined development as a function of one or more of the following: production, human and natural resources, population growth, capital accumulation, the scale and specialization of production, efficiency, technology, innovation, foreign trade, and the internal market.(45) According to the vast majority of theorists, certain characteristics internal to a particular society caused that society's development or lack of development.   This conception of development held that a poor country was poor because it lacked capital, raw materials, skilled labor, technology, or a middle class, or possessed a "traditionalist orientation," and so on.   Such an argument established a dichotomy between "traditional" and "modern" societies and suggested that development was the process of "advancing" from the former to the latter stage.(46)

Central to this conception of economic development are the converging principles of international trade and specialization.   The theory of free trade holds that a country produce those goods or services for which it is best suited by virtue of its natural resources, labor, and so on.   This country purchases from other countries the goods in which those countries enjoy particular advantages of production. According to the principle of comparative advantage, each country should specialize in whatever product(s) it makes **relatively** most cheaply.   When a nation's degree of superior efficiency is greater for some goods than for others, that country benefits by importing the goods in which its efficiency is least superior and exporting the goods in which its efficiency is most superior. Similarly, as long as a country's degree of inferior efficiency is greater for some goods than for others, the country benefits by importing the goods in which its efficiency is most inferior and exporting the goods in which its efficiency is least inferior. Thus all productive energies are employed to the maximum advantage and benefit for all. In a setting of reasonable international equilibrium, the theories of free trade and comparative advantage promised to bring about a more efficient use of both domestic and global resources and a more rapid rate of progress in both rich and poor economies. Classical and neoclassical economists provided the basic components of this analysis.

Liberal economists from Adam Smith to John Stuart Mill to Alfred Marshall considered "the process of capital accumulation and the development associated with it to be a self-perpetuating and self-equilibrating mechanism which would continue to function adequately if it were not tampered with either by state intervention or restrictions on trade."(47) Smith, for example, viewed capital accumulation and the division of labor as the fundamental determinants of growth. Increasing profits--the backbone of capital formation--would stimulate development. He advocated free trade, private enterprise, and laissez-faire policies as ways to ensure domestic productivity and to raise world output.(48) Both Smith and David Ricardo recognized that technical knowledge, social capital, and entrepreneurial ability contributed to economic growth. The supply of arable land and population growth acted as limiting factors on development.(49) Ricardo, interested in the world division of labor and in the advantages derived from free trade, formulated the theory of comparative advantage. He naturally supported a policy of laissez-faire. Neoclassicalists, such as Marshall, treated economic growth as a "process which contains no special problems or phenomena of its own." They contended, however, that laissez-faire and free trade policies held the keys to capitalist progress. According to the neoclassicalists, development was a gradual and harmonious process in which all groups benefitted.(50)

Economists of the nineteenth century German school advanced the stage theory of development. Friedrich List, for example, singled out the introduction of manufacturing, with its higher productivity, and the subsequent movement from an agricultural to industrial stage as the dynamic element in the growth process. The accompanying social and cultural change ran from an agrarian society's indolence and traditional orientation to an industrial society's freedom, innovation, and future orientation.(51)

Joseph Schumpeter gave these concepts their modern form. In his Theory of Economic Development (1912), Schumpeter defined economic development as the process of creating new combinations of resources. Innovation, in the form of new goods, production methods, sources of raw materials, markets, and industrial organization, led to increases in entrepreneurial profits. This in turn encouraged investment and brought about greater production. Since Schumpeter examined the development process from within a capitalist society, he naturally found that capitalist "institutions, motivations, and rationality" formed the sociocultural framework that best facilitated innovation. He implied that the traditional patterns and values which persisted in underdeveloped countries hindered innovation. Poor, noncapitalist nations moved in a vicious circle of "low levels of entrepreneurial activity, of slow rates of growth output, and of stagnant institutions and values."(52)

With the 1930s depression, many economists "discovered" that Western Europe and the United States had reached a state of economic stagnation and maturity. Depression forced economists to modify the standard laissez-faire doctrine. Keynesians pushed for government intervention in the economy in the form of public investment programs and active monetary and fiscal policies.(53) Aside from this new emphasis on government action, Western economists persisted in talking about the basic requirements for economic progress in industrial states.(54) For most scholars, economic development continued to be a dynamic quantitative concept--that is, increasing production per capita and creating higher living standards.

During the 1930s a few Western scholars began to touch on the nature of development in the poor countries.(55) In 1931 Erich Zimmermann, an economic geographer, identified a global economic hierarchy: an "inner nucleus" of dominating, great industrial powers; an "outer rim, the periphery," of agricultural countries (also known as the "passive or dominated zone"); and "a twilight zone" of weak industrial nations whose influence fluctuated according to changing circumstances. Viewing this hierarchy as a danger to world peace and prosperity, Zimmermann urged the industrial powers to share their wealth and power with the mass of poor nations.(56) T. E. Gregory, a British economist, suggested that the West help to industrialize the poor regions. Industrializing the periphery, while causing some problems of readjustment in the West, would benefit the West through the expanded export of industrial and agricultural goods and capital.(57)

Colin Clark's Conditions of Economic Progress marked a breakthrough in development literature. The 1940 study found the world as a whole "a wretchedly poor place." Increasing productivity was the most important problem facing the vast majority of countries. Clark posited that global inequalities resulted from "some powerful secular force, probably related to the investment and savings tendencies in the countries concerned," and not from population or natural resources distribution. While not advancing a definite method for closing the gap between rich and poor, Clark suggested that shifting people from agriculture to manufacturing and commerce always resulted in a rise in national income levels.(58)

In 1943, Paul Rosenstein Rodan contrasted the autarkic Russian model of development with the model of foreign investment and free trade. He characterized the Soviet path to industrialization as faulty and wasteful because it reduced the international division of labor and supplied capital internally at the expense of an already low standard of living and consumption. Concentrating on heavy industry only added to the world surplus of capital goods. By moving poor regions onto the world capitalist highway, an international division of labor could be maintained and industrialization would proceed quickly and at a small sacrifice to consumption. "The aim of industrialization in internationally depressed areas," contended the author, "is to produce a structural equilibrium in the world economy by creating productive employment for the agrarian excess population."(59)

K. Mandelbaum's The Industrialization of Backward Areas (1945) constituted another breakthrough in development research and another contribution to the conventional analysis.

Advocating a policy of industrialization for poor and densely populated areas, Mandelbaum proposed that local governments play a "large and positive" role in the diversification of their economies. Achieving industrialization required poor nations to use the accumulated knowledge in the core countries. This would give "late-comers in industrialization the chance of relatively rapid development once they start on an intensive process of catching up."(60) In other words, the Third World would copy the history of the Western world "as an inevitable consequence of technological development."(61)

Thus, by the early 1940s, a nebulous economic development theory had permeated the West. Based on classical and neo-classical doctrines, and reinforced by studies on colonial regions and Eastern Europe, this theory identified the causes of underdevelopment as internal to a particular society. Development was the process of using capitalism, free trade, comparative advantage, laissez-faire policies, and technical assistance to "advance" from backward to "modern" economies.(62)

This analysis provided U.S. policymakers with some insights into underdevelopment and development. But critics contended that overall it was a static concept that obscured crucial historical relationships between the international socioeconomic and political structure, on one hand, and Third World underdevelopment, on the other.

Friedrich List attacked the universality of free trade, comparative advantage, and laissez-faire as early as the 1820s. List argued that ideology must adapt itself to different social frameworks. As a native of a developing German state, and as a visitor to, and observer of, the developing American political economy, List concluded that protectionism, state interventionism, economic planning, and balanced growth were the prerequisites for national integration. National integration, contended List, led to economic development.(63)

Marxists such as V. I. Lenin, Rosa Luxemburg, Maurice Dobb, and Paul Sweezy and non-Marxists such as J. A. Hobson and K. W. Rothschild examined the relationship between developed and underdeveloped countries in the global marketplace. These critics described how peripheral regions' low-priced land, scarce finances, cheap labor, and abundant and inexpensive raw materials attracted Western capitalists. They analyzed how core capitalist penetration dismantled "natural" economies of poor areas--destroying indigenous economic and social systems; establishing extractive mineral and agricultural industries; creating markets for Western manufactured goods; and prohibiting local industries and agriculture that competed with Western production. The rapid development of extractive industries and the construction of requisite transportation facilities produced great benefits for the Western imperialists and the small local collaborator classes, but not for the bulk of the indigenous population. In other words, capitalist intrusions into the Third World caused, or at least exacerbated, poverty there.(64)

According to K. W. Rothschild, the very free trade policies advocated by Western economists merely locked underdeveloped nations into poverty. A free trade policy allowed the great industrial nations to remain centers of heavy industry while relegating agrarian countries to opportunities in small-scale industries and agriculture. "Backward countries will remain backward just because they were backward before."

Rothschild concluded that poor nations could not create balanced economies in a world of free trade.(65)

Several Third World economists and politicians arrived at similar conclusions to those of the critics of Western doctrine. India's Dadahbai Naoroji (1825-1917), for example, developed the "drain theory," which explained how the British pumped wealth from India and left the country in poverty. Romesh Chunder Dutt (1848-1909) argued that the destruction of native industry and crafts by the British forced millions of Indians to seek refuge in agriculture, where, as increasing numbers subsisted on a fixed amount of land, income levels fell. An inequitable land tenure and revenue system exacerbated the situation. Both Naoroji and Dutt called for various forms of economic nationalism as the way to achieve Indian economic development.(66) In the 1920s and 1930s, Peru's Haya de la Torre attacked imperialist exploitation as the cause of backwardness. He urged Latin American countries to unite, fight imperialism, discard Western and Russian development paths, and build their own road to higher living standards. He advocated an "Indoamerican way" that would avoid the excesses of Western capitalism and include the nationalization of land and industries, the internationalization of the Panama Canal, and state economic planning.(67)

Of course, many Third World economists, political leaders, and businessmen accepted the conventional Western analysis with little or no qualifications. Thus in the Middle East a major economic and political trend viewed Arab poverty as caused by a combination of imperialism, stagnant indigenous social and economic institutions, lack of capital, illiteracy, and undeveloped resources. It saw the remedy for underdevelopment in Westernization and adherence to liberal capitalist doctrines.(68) American policymakers obviously favored these latter groups in the periphery. At best, policymakers tolerated--and, at worst, rejected--those in the periphery and core who questioned the validity of liberal capitalism. But it was not simply Western economic doctrines that cemented American imperial state and capitalist elites to the liberal capitalist concept. There also was the perceived experiences, actual policies, and felt needs of the United States.

Twentieth century American state and capitalist class leaders have tended to view their nation's economic development as occurring with a minimum of coercion and violence and a maximum of humanitarianism, equality, and democracy. Leaders have perceived that free trade and laissez-faire policies and comparative advantage contributed, in large measure, to America's successful development.(69) These forces presumably facilitated the transition of America from a rural agricultural and raw material producer and debtor economy to an industrial and urban consumer and capital goods producer and creditor economy. The same forces allowed for the most efficient use of America's substantial advantages in natural resources, commercial and entrepreneurial skills, and labor supply. In addition, these forces maximized American participation in the dynamic world economy of the nineteenth century. Within this framework the United States found new and growing sources of trade, technological innovation, capital, and labor.(70)

This idealized version of American economic development contains simplifications and distortions. Laissez-faire and free trade, while important parts of national mythology, have far from dominated national policies. The American republic

emerged in a mercantilist world--ready and eager to achieve
the mercantilist dream of a balanced and self-sufficient economy.   John Adams and other Founding Fathers viewed free trade
as a temporary measure for breaking into the mercantilist em-
pires of Europe while achieving economic integration at home.
While Thomas Jefferson preferred the ideals of free trade and
laissez-faire,   as president he pursued policies designed to
achieve an independent,   balanced   political economy.(71)

Throughout the nineteenth century, local and federal governments "intervened actively on a wide range of economic questions and in varied and complex interrelations with the activities of individuals and corporations."(72)   Even a cursory
reading of America's tariff history reveals the myth of free
trade.(73)

    American corporate and state leaders tended to generalize
their perception of the national development experience into a
universal model.   That model held that the United States began
as an agricultural and raw materials producer.   During this
stage the preconditions for economic progress (e.g., capital
accumulation, education,   civil order) were set.   Next came a
stage of accelerated growth stimulated by technological forces
and characterized by the rise of new industries and the expansion of agricultural production.   Finally, the United States
advanced to a stage of self-sustained economic growth.   All
along this path, basic liberal capitalist forces--especially
active participation in the world economy and laissez-faire
policies--gave crucial support to American progress.   This
perceived model of American economic development converged
with the actual historical needs of the American economy.

    Until the late nineteenth century, the United States
exchanged its agricultural and mineral resources for European
manufactured goods.   During its first century, America sought
foreign markets for its primary goods and foreign financial
resources for its development.   Commercialism, landed expansion, economic infrastructural development, massive immigration, and technological innovation led to the creation of a
national urban market and to industrialization.   The transformation from an agricultural and extractive export economy to a
consumer and capital goods export economy heightened the
importance of foreign markets.   By the 1890s, American state
and corporate elites had identified overproduction as the
cause of the nation's severe periodic depressions and had
acknowledged overseas expansion as the solution.   The need for
Third World markets, as well as European markets, intensified
as industrial capitalism shifted from a competitive consumer
stage to a monopoly stage.   With the appearance and growing
dominance of the large corporation in the early twentieth
century, American leaders sought not only foreign markets, but
overseas investment opportunities and secure sources of raw
materials.   This quest for raw materials and markets made
Third World areas essential for American economic expansion
and thus raised the issue of economic development.(74)

    America's concern with and concept of Third World econom-
ic development did not originate with Woodrow Wilson.   The administrations of Theodore Roosevelt and William Howard Taft
certainly extended American trade and investments into the
world's underdeveloped areas.   As secretary of war and as
president, Taft often noted how American capital could develop
Latin American and Asian transportation, public works, mines,
and agriculture.   In addition, American economic activity

would promote overall economic progress, democracy, and political stability in those regions. Wilson and his advisers,
nevertheless, became the most articulate spokesmen for these
views in the first quarter of the twentieth century. Wilson
sought to construct a "liberal capitalist world order" in
which international free trade and great power cooperation
would create the best environment for the economic development
of poor areas. American policymakers realized that such a
system of nondiscriminatory trade and cooperative capitalist
penetration of underdeveloped regions would greatly benefit an
America "bursting with expansive commercial energies and well
able to utilize effectively an Open Door to the markets and
raw materials of Africa and Asia."(75)

The idea of developing poor lands played a prominent role
in Wilson's approach to economic expansion abroad. America's
state and corporate elites believed that, just as "metropolitan industrial and finance capital" had developed markets for
manufactured goods in the American West, so would foreign investment create and expand markets overseas.(76) Secretary of
State William Jennings Bryan told the National Foreign Trade
Convention in May 1914 that American "enterprise, ability, and
genius" would build more and more markets abroad and thereby
make the United States "an increasing factor in the development" of the periphery. Government policies could "open the
doors of all weaker countries to an invasion of American
capital and American enterprise."(77)

The Wilsonian world view, as demonstrated by historian
Martin Sklar, held "large-scale corporate-industrial capitalism as the natural product of social evolution." Foreign investments and exports--a foundation of industrial and finance
capital--were, therefore, "indispensable to the nation's prosperity and social well-being." Moreover, foreign economic
expansion could carry "civilization, bourgeois liberal ideas
and institutions, and a better way of life to the agrarian
areas of the world."(78)

These sentiments were not simply rhetorical. Wilson and
other American officials believed that the Third World was not
only preindustrial, but really quasifeudal and almost precapi-
talist. The development of primary commodity production--
that is, the commercialization of agriculture--in agrarian
areas of the world thus would be a positive and progressive
step. Embracing a stage theory of development, Wilson and his
contemporaries saw the commercialization of agriculture as a
historically necessary stage prior to industrialization.
Bringing the agricultural sector into a money and market economy would stimulate demand in those societies. That demand
could be met by imported goods or, in certain specialized
areas, by local industry.

America's rejection of the League of Nations did not end
the quest for the Wilsonian world order, but pushed it in new
directions. Under the administrations of Warren Harding and
Calvin Coolidge--and especially under the leadership of Secretary of State Charles Evans Hughes and Secretary of Commerce
Herbert Hoover--the United States operated outside the League
framework to achieve global cooperation for political and economic goals. The United States actively pushed for an open
door in underdeveloped regions. Private American firms, with
state assistance, made some trade and investment advances in
parts of the Middle East, Africa, Southeast Asia, and Eastern
Europe.(79)

Throughout the 1920s American government and business discussions on Third World development remained within the context of providing the domestic economy with markets and raw materials. Economic development was synonymous with exploitation of the resources of poor lands. In the 1930s, Secretary of State Cordell Hull became a prominent advocate of economic expansion into peripheral areas. Hull's reciprocal trade concept implied that underdeveloped regions would function as raw material producers in the world division of labor. Free trade and specialization in primary goods production would bring prosperity and stability to these nations. Hull urged policies to facilitate the movement of capital from "financially stronger to financially weaker countries." This capital transfer was necessary to secure raw materials for the American economy and to stabilize Third World political and economic situations.(80) The comments of Hull and other policymakers on creating a postwar economic order reflected a growing state consensus on the need for world development.

CONCLUSION

Economic development theory was in its nascent stages before the Second World War. Advanced capitalist nations appeared to have a cursory interest in the vitality of poor, agrarian nations. Few Western economists prior to 1940 formulated theories or plans for the development of the periphery. Some scholars believed that economic growth was grinding to a halt in the core nations, and the 1930s depression seemed to confirm this assessment. In the underdeveloped nations, however, "where economic progress had not yet dug its own grave, conditions [were] propitious to start the cycle of progress and decay."(81) Poor agrarian nations, with their unexploited natural resources and potentially great markets, and assisted by modern technology, would quickly improve their economies.

American and other capitalist core leaders posited that societies evolved from a traditional underdeveloped state to a modern developed state. Capitalist core leaders contended that true development could only take place through the free play of market forces, the operation of comparative advantage, and the beneficial interaction between themselves and reform minded elites in the periphery. This interaction would bridge, but not close, the gap between rich and poor. Peripheral areas could profit from industrialization policies; but in most cases industrialization itself was superfluous. "Through foreign trade, specialization in the production of raw materials would serve economic and social progress as well as, or even better than, industrialization."(82)

American policymakers embraced these principles not merely because they manifested long cherished Western economic doctrines, but also because they reflected long-standing societal needs, national values, perceived national experiences, and consequent foreign policies. American state and corporate elites used this framework as the basis for wartime and postwar planning, even as economists articulated contrary theories and Third World nations pleaded their special needs.

NOTES

1.   Thomas J. McCormick, "Drift or Mastery?   A Cor-
poratist Synthesis for American Diplomatic History," Reviews
in American History 10 (December 1982): 320. For an introduc-
tion to the many works on the 1940s and the Cold War, see J.
L. Black, Origins, Evolution and Nature of the Cold War: An
Annotated Bibliographic Guide (Santa Barbara, Calif.:   ABC-
Clio, 1986); and Richard Dean Burns, ed., Guide to American
Foreign Relations since 1700 (Santa Barbara, Calif.:   ABC-
Clio, 1983). An example of the "Great Power fixation" applied
to U.S.-Third World relations is Robert A. Pollard's Economic
Security and the Origins of the Cold War, 1945-1950 (New York:
Columbia University Press, 1985), chap. 5.

2.   Robert W. Cox, "Social Forces, States and World
Orders: Beyond International Relations Theory," Millennium:
Journal of International Studies 10, no. 2 (1981): 134.

3.   V. Kubalkova and A. A. Cruickshank, Marxism and International Relations (Oxford: Clarendon Press, 1985), p. 64.

4.   Cox, "Social Forces," pp. 134, 137-39;   John G.
Gurley, Challengers to Capitalism: Marx, Lenin, Stalin, and
Mao, 2d ed. (New York: W. W. Norton, 1979), pp. 9-16.

5.   M. C. Howard and J. E. King, The Political Economy of
Marx (London: Longman, 1975), pp. 15-16, 27-29;   Douglas F.
Dowd, The Twisted Dream: Capitalist Development in the U.S.
Since 1776 (Cambridge, Mass.: Winthrop Publishers, 1974), pp.
33-38, 116; Gurley, Challengers, p. 41.

6.   Gurley, Challengers, pp. 41-42.

7.   Ralph Miliband, The State in Capitalist Society (New
York: Basic Books, 1969), p. 16.

8.   Antonio Gramsci, Selections from the Prison Note-
books, edited and translated by Q. Hoare and G. N. Smith (New
York: International Publishers, 1971), p. 261;   Edward S.
Greenberg, The American Political System: A Radical Approach
(Cambridge, Mass.:   Winthrop Publishers, 1977), p. 493;
Robert W. Cox, "Gramsci, Hegemony and International Relations:
An Essay in Method," Millennium: Journal of International
Studies 12 no.2 (1983): 164;   Ralph Miliband, Marxism and
Politics (Oxford: Oxford University Press, 1977), p. 67
(emphasis in original).

9.   James M. Cypher, "The Transnational Challenge to the
Corporate State," Journal of Economic Issues 13 (June 1979):
23;   Miliband, Marxism and Politics, p. 90; Ernest Mandel,
Late Capitalism, translated by J. DeBres (London: Verso,
1978), pp. 474-75. Also see Miliband, State in Capitalist
Society; and James O'Connor, The Fiscal Crisis of the State
(New York: St. Martin's Press, 1973).

10. Miliband, Marxism and Politics, p. 74; Leo Panitch,
"Trade Unions and the Capitalist State," New Left Review, no.
125 (January-February 1981): 27; Leo Panitch, "The Develop-

ment of Corporatism in Liberal Democracies," Comparative Political Studies 10 (April 1977): 79.

11.   Panitch, "Development of Corporatism," p. 61.

12.   McCormick, "Drift or Mastery?" pp. 323-27; Robert Cox, "Labor and Hegemony," International Organization 31 (Summer 1977): 407.

13.   McCormick, "Drift or Mastery?" pp. 326-27; Emily Rosenberg, Spreading the American Dream: American Economic and Cultural Expansion, 1890-1945 (New York: Hill and Wang, 1982).

14.   George Lipsitz, Class and Culture in Cold War America: "A Rainbow at Midnight" (South Hadley, Mass.:   J. F. Bergin Publishers, 1982), p. 5.

15.   Panitch, "Trade Unions," pp. 25-26;   Panitch, "Development of Corporatism," pp. 67-68, 79;   McCormick, "Drift or Mastery?" pp. 324-27;   Cox, "Gramsci," pp. 168-69.

16.   McCormick, "Drift or Mastery?" pp. 325, 327-28; Panitch, "Trade Unions," p. 29; Lipsitz, Class and Culture, pp. 14-86.

17.   Cox, "Social Forces," p. 141.

18.   Ibid.;   Immanuel Wallerstein, The Capitalist World-Economy (Cambridge, Mass.:   Cambridge University Press, 1979), pp. 5-6, 53, 15, 60, 158-59;   Christopher Chase-Dunn, "The Kernel of the Capitalist World-Economy: Three Approaches," in William R. Thompson, ed., Contemporary Approaches to World Systems Analysis (Beverly Hills, Calif.:   Sage, 1983), p. 73.

19.   Wallerstein, Capitalist World-Economy, pp. 18-19, 97, 162, 187, 279, 293;   Christopher Chase-Dunn, "The Development of Core Capitalism in the Antebellum United States: Tariff Politics and Class Struggle in an Upwardly Mobile Semi-periphery," in Albert Bergesen, ed., Studies of the Modern World-System (New York: Academic Press, 1980), p. 191.

20.   Wallerstein, Capitalist World-Economy, pp. 7, 97, 162, 185;   Chase-Dunn, "Development of Core Capitalism," p. 191.

21.   Wallerstein, Capitalist World-Economy, pp. 21-23, 68, 71, 92, 247;   Chase-Dunn, "Development of Core Capitalism," pp. 191-92.

22.   Immanuel Wallerstein, The Modern World-System I: Capitalist Agriculture and the Origins of the European World-Economy in the Sixteenth Century (New York: Academic Press, 1974), pp. 354-55;   Wallerstein, Capitalist World-Economy, pp. 21, 38, 274.

23.   Wallerstein, Capitalist World-Economy, p. 61 (emphasis in original).

24. See Samir Amin, Unequal Development (New York:
Monthly Review Press, 1976);   Arghiri Emmanuel, Unequal
Exchange (New York: Monthly Review Press, 1972);   Keith
Griffin, Internatioanl Inequality and National Poverty (New
York: Holmes & Meier Publishers, 1978); Richard C. Edwards,
Michael Reich, and Thomas E. Weisskopf, eds., The Capitalist
System: A Radical Analysis of American Society (Englewood
Cliffs, N.J.: Prentice-Hall, 1978); and David M. Smith, Where
the Grass Is Greener: Geographical Perspectives on Inequality
(London: Croom Helm, 1979).

25. Albert Bergesen, "From Utilitarianism to Globology:
The Shift from the Individual to the World as a Whole as the
Primordial Unit of Analysis," in Bergesen, ed., Studies of
Modern World-System, pp. 10-11.

26. Cox, "Gramsci," pp. 171-72;   Cox, "Social Forces,"
p. 140;   Nicole Bousquet, "From Hegemony to Competition:
Cycles of the Core?" in T. K. Hopkins and I. Wallerstein,
eds., Processes of the World-System, (Beverly Hills, Calif.:
Sage, 1980), p. 49.

27. Charles S. Maier, "The Politics of Productivity:
Foundations of American International Economic Policy After
World War II," International Organization 31 (Autumn 1977):
607-33; Fred L. Block, The Origins of International Economic
Disorder: A Study of United States International Monetary
Policy from World War II to the Present (Berkeley, Calif.:
University of California Press, 1977), pp. 1-69.

28. James Petras and Morris Morley, "The U.S. Imperial
State," in Petras, Class, State, and Power in the Third World:
With Case Studies on Class Conflict in Latin America (Mont-
clair, N.J.: Allanheld, Osmun & Publishers, 1981), p. 1.

29. Petras and Morley, "Imperial State," pp. 1-5
(emphasis in original).

30. Ibid., pp. 10-12;   G. William Domhoff, Who Rules
America Now? A View for the '80s (Englewood Cliffs, N.J.:
Prentice-Hall, 1983), pp. 56-156.

31. Petras and Morley, "Imperial State," pp. 10, 15-16;
Cox, "Social Forces," p. 146.

32. Cox, "Gramsci," p. 172.

33. Petras and Morley, "Imperial State," p. 1.

34. Bousquet, "From Hegemony to Competition," p. 50;
Cox, "Social Forces," p. 137.

35. Petras and Morley, "Imperial State," p. 1; Cox,
"Social Forces," p. 136-37, 143-45; Cox, "Gramsci," pp. 172-
73.

36. Cox, "Social Forces," pp. 140, 144; Alan Wolfe,
"The Irony of Anti-Communism: Ideology and Interest in Post-
War American Foreign Policy," in Ralph Miliband, John Saville
and Marcel Liebman, eds., Socialist Register 1984:   The Uses

of Anti-Communism (London: The Merlin Press, 1984), pp. 214-29.

37.   Petras and Morley, "Imperial State," pp. 5, 9.

38.   Ibid., pp. 8, 17-18.

39.   Frederick B. Pike, "Corporatism and Latin American-United States Relations," in Pike and T. Stritch, eds., The New Corporatism: Social-Political Structures in the Iberian World (Notre Dame: The University of Notre Dame Press, 1974), p. 148.

40.   Joseph Schumpeter, "Theoretical Problem of Economic Growth," The Tasks of Economic History, Supplement 7 (1947): 2;   Bjorne Hettne, Current Issues in Development Theory (1978), pp. 7-9. For a review of development definitions see Robert A. Flammang, "Economic Growth and Economic Development: Counterparts or Competitors?" Economic Development and Cultural Change 28 (October 1979): 47-61;   Lord Robbins, The Theory of Economic Development in the History of Economic Thought (New York: St. Martin's Press, 1968);   Michael Barratt Brown, What Economics Is About (London: Weidenfeld & Nicolson, 1970);   Simon Kuznets, Modern Economic Growth: Rate, Structure, and Spread (New Haven, Conn.: Yale University Press, 1966); Fritz Machlup, Essays in Economic Seman-tics (New York: New York University Press, 1975); H. W. Arndt, "Development Economics before 1945," in J. Bhagwati and R. S. Eckaus, eds., Development and Planning: Essays in Honour of Paul Rosenstein Rodan (London: George Allen & Unwin, 1972), p. 27; and Paul Streeten, "Development Dichoto-mies," in G. M. Meiev and D. Seers, eds., Pioneers in Develop-ment (New York: Oxford University Press, World Bank, 1984), pp. 337-61.

41.   For an interesting discussion of the ambiguity of "economic development," see F. Machlup, "Disputes, Paradoxes and Dilemmas Concerning Economic Development," in Machlup, Essays in Economic Semantics, pp. 269-301.

42.   Lisa Peattie, Thinking About Development (New York: Plenum Press, 1981), p. 32.

43.   United Nations, Research Institute for Social Development, Contents and Measurements of Socioeconomic Development (New York: Praeger, 1972); S. Kuznets, Modern Economic Growth (New Haven, Conn.: Yale University Press, 1966);   Carmelo Mesa-Lago, "A Continuum for Global Com-parison," in Mesa-Lago and Carl Beck, eds., Comparative Socialist Systems: Essays on Politics and Economics (Pitts-burgh: University of Pittsburgh Center for International Studies, 1975), pp. 92-120; Jacques Delacroix and Charles C. Ragin, "Structural Blockage: A Cross-National Study of Economic Dependency, State Efficacy, and Underdevelopment," American Journal of Sociology 86 (May 1981): 1311-47; Kurt Finsterbusch, "Recent Rank Ordering of Nations in Terms of Level and Rate of Development," Studies in Comparative International Development 8 (Spring 1973): 52-70;   Charles L. Taylor and Michael C. Hudson, World Handbook of Political and Social Indicators, 2d ed. (New Haven, Conn.:   Yale University

Press, 1972).

44. "Bourgeois theory," British economist Ben Fine explained, "takes the appearances of capitalism for granted and only studies the relationship between them. For bourgeois economic theory, the appearances that form the objects of analysis are the relations of production, distribution and exchange stripped of their social significance, as categories of capitalism." Ben Fine, Economic Theory and Ideology (London: Edward Arnold, 1980), pp. 8-9.

45. Richard T. Gill, Economic Development: Past and Present (Englewood Cliffs, N.J.: Prentice-Hall, 1973), pp. 3-26.

46. Bryan S. Turner, Marx and the End of Orientalism (London: George Allen & Unwin, 1978), pp. 10-11.

47. Frederick Clairmonte, Economic Liberalism and Underdevelopment: Studies in the Disintegration of an Idea (Bombay: Asia Publishing House, 1960), p. 38.

48. Taghi Kermani, Economic Development in Action: Theories, Problems, and Procedures as Applied in the Middle East (Cleveland: World Publishing, 1967), pp. 28, 31; Irma Adelman, Theories of Economic Growth and Development (Stanford: Stanford University Press, 1961), pp. 41-42.

49. J. M. Letiche, "Adam Smith and David Ricardo on Economic Growth," and J. Spengler, "John Stuart Mill on Economic Development," in Bert Hoselitz, ed., Theories of Economic Growth (New York: The Free Press, 1960), pp. 65, 84-85, 148.

50. Celso Furtado, Development and Underdevelopment (Berkeley: University of California Press, 1964), pp. 38-39; John Buttrick, "Toward a Theory of Economic Growth: The Neoclassicalist Contribution," in Hoselitz, Theories of Economic Growth, pp. 158-59, 178-79; Michael Barratt Brown, The Economics of Imperialism (Middlesex, England: Penguin Books, 1974), pp. 100-101, 35-36; Robert E. Baldwin, Economic Development and Growth (New York: John Wiley, 1966), pp. 26-29.

51. Bert Hoselitz, "Theories of Stages of Economic Growth," in Hoselitz, Theories of Economic Growth, pp. 195, 198-99, 201-202, 234, 238.

52. Kermani, Economic Development in Action, pp. 32-33; Adelman, Theories, pp. 107-8; Jere R. Behrman, "Development Economics," in Sidney Weintraub, ed., Modern Economic Thought (Philadelphia: University of Pennsylvania Press, 1977), p. 543; Erich Schneider, Joseph A. Schumpeter: Life and Work of a Great Social Scientist (Lincoln, Nebr.: University of Nebraska-Lincoln, 1975), pp. 1-11, 15.

53. Henry J. Burton, "Contemporary Theorizing on Economic Growth," in Hoselitz, Theories of Economic Growth, p. 240; Furtado, Development and Underdevelopment, pp. 52-56.

54. The extensive interwar literature on these topics included: Allyn A. Young, "Increasing Returns and Economic Progress, " The Economic Journal 38 (December 1928): 527-42; Robert Jarjolin, "Francois Simiand's Theory of Economic Progress," The Review of Economic Studies 5 (June 1938): 159-71; Emil Lederer, "The Problem of Development and Growth in the Economic System," Social Research 2 (February 1935): 20-38; and R. F. Harrod, "An Essay on Dynamic Theory," The Economic Journal 49 (March 1939): 14-33.

55. See, for example, J.W.F. Rowe, Markets and Men: A Study of Artificial Control Schemes in Some Primary Industries (New York: Macmillan, 1936); Royal Institute of International Affairs, The Problem of International Investment (London: Oxford University Press, 1937); I. Bowman, ed., Limits of Land Settlement (New York: Council on Foreign Relations, 1937); John S. Furnivall, Progress and Welfare in Southeast Asia: A Comparison of Colonial Policy Practice (New York: Institute of Pacific Relations, 1942); J. H. Boeke, The Structure of Netherlands Indian Economy (New York: Institute of Pacific Relations, 1942); Ida C. Greaves, Modern Production Among Backward Peoples (London: George Allen & Unwin, 1935).

56. Erich Zimmermann, "The Resource Hierarchy of Modern World Economy," Weltwirtschaftliches Archiv 33 (April 1931): 431-63.

57. T. E. Gregory, "Conclusions: An Economist's Comment," in G. E. Hubbard, Eastern Industrialization and Its Effect in the West (London: Oxford University Press, 1935), pp. 364-71.

58. Colin Clark, Conditions of Economic Progress (New York: Macmillan, 1940). For critiques of Clark's work see the reviews by E. Rothbard, Simon Kuznets, and Arthur Saly in, respectively, The Economic Journal 51 (April 1941): 120-24; The Manchester School of Economics and Social Sciences 12 (1941): 28-34; and Social Research 9 (September 1942): 420-21. Until the appearance of UN information, Clark's data were the basis for nearly every work on development economics in the 1940s. See Arndt, "Development Economics before 1945," p. 23; and Colin Clark, "Development Economics: The Early Years," in Meiev and Seers, eds., Pioneers, pp. 59-77.

59. P. N. Rosenstein Rodan, "Problems of Industrialization of Eastern and South-Eastern Europe," The Economic Journal 53 (June-September 1943): 203-210. Also see H. Frankel, "Industrialization of Agricultural Countries and the Possibilities of a New International Division of Labour," The Economic Journal 53 (June-September 1943): 188-91; and P. N. Rosentsein Rodan, "Natura Facit Saltum: Analysis of the Disequilibrium Growth Process," in Meiev and Seers, eds., Pioneers, pp. 207-21.

60. K. Mandelbaum, The Industrialization of Backward Areas (Oxford: Basil Blackwell, 1945), pp. iii-xx, 4, 16, 79.

61. Janet Abu-Lughod, "Some Social Aspects of Technological Development," in Mujid S. Kazimi and John Makhoul,
eds., Perspectives on Technological Development in the Arab
World (Association of Arab-American University Graduates,
1977), p. 40.

62. Clairmonte, Economic Liberalism, p. 193.

63. Ibid., pp. 32-33, 36-40;   Andre Gunder Frank,
Dependent Accumulation and Underdevelopment (New York:
Monthly Review Press, 1979), pp. 97-98.

64. J. A. Hobson, Imperialism: A Study (New York:
James Pott, 1902);   V. I. Lenin, Imperialism: The Highest
Stage of Capitalism (Peking: Foreign Language Press, 1975);
Rosa Luxemburg, The Accumulation of Capital, trans. Agnes
Swarzchild (1913; reprint ed., New Haven, Conn.:   Yale
University Press, 1951);   Nickolai Bukharin, Imperialism and
World Economy (New York: International Publishers, 1929);
Paul Sweezy, The Theory of Capitalist Development: Principles
of Marxian Political Economy (London: Dennis Dobson, 1942);
Maurice Dobb, Political Economy and Capitalism (London:
George Routledge & Sons, 1937).

65. K. W. Rothschild, "The Small Nation and World
Trade," The Economic Journal 54 (April 1944): 31-32.

66. V. B. Singh, From Naoroji to Nehru: Six Essays in
Indian Economic Thought (Delhi: Macmillan Co. of India,
1975), pp. 8-9;   Bhabatosh Datta, The Evolution of Economic
Thinking in India (Calcutta: Federation Hall Society, 1962),
pp. 3, 18; P. K. Gopalakrishnan, Economic Ideas of India (New
Delhi: People's Publishing House, 1959), pp. 143-54, 163,
171.

67. Albert O. Hirschman, A Bias for Hope: Essays on
Development and Latin America (New Haven, Conn.:   Yale
University Press, 1971), pp. 272-79.

68. Fauzi M. Najjar, "Nationalism and Socialism," in
Abdeen Jabara and Janice Terry, eds., The Arab World: From
Nationalism to Revolution, (Wilmette, Ill.:   The Medina
University Press International, 1971), pp. 3-5; Jean Paul
Charnay, Islamic Culture and Socio-Economic Change (Leiden:
E. J. Brill, 1971), p. 13; Albert Hourani, Arabic Thought in
the Liberal Age, 1789-1939 (London: Oxford University Press,
1962), pp. 339-40.

69. Dowd, Twisted Dream, p. 48;   Robert Packenham,
Liberal America and the Third World: Political Development
Ideas in Foreign Aid and Social Science (Princeton, N.J.:
Princeton University Press, 1973), pp. 11-60;   Francis X.
Sutton et al., The American Business Creed (Cambridge, Mass.:
Harvard University Press, 1956), pp. 36-52, 384-86;   James
Warren Prothro, The Dollar Decade: Business Ideas in the
1920s (Baton Rouge, La.:   Louisiana State University Press,
1954);   Beth McKillen, "The Foreign Political Economy of Four
Associations of Businessmen from 1912-1920," M.A. thesis,
Northwestern University, 1981.

70. Dowd, Twisted Dream, p. 47.

71. William Appleman Williams, The Contours of American History (Chicago: Quadrangle Books, 1966), pp. 123, 128-29, 164, 168-69, 221; Clairmonte, Economic Liberalism, pp. 27-29; Lloyd Gardner, Walter LaFeber, and Thomas McCormick, Creation of the American Empire, vol. 1: U.S. Diplomatic History to 1901 (Chicago: Rand McNally, 1976), pp. 21-22, 63-77.

72. Carter Goodrich, "Recent Contributions to Economic History: The United States, 1789-1860," Journal of Economic History 19 (March 1959): 25; Dowd, Twisted Dream, chapters 1-2; Clairmonte, Economic Liberalism, p. 25, note 53; Carter Goodrich, ed., The Government and the Economy, 1783-1861 (Indianapolis: Bobbs-Merrill, 1967).

73. Frank W. Taussig, The Tariff History of the United States, 7th ed. (New York: G. P. Putnam's Sons, 1923); and Sidney Ratner, The Tariff in American History (New York: D. Van Nostrand, 1972).

74. Gardner et al., Creation of the American Empire, pp. 20-22, 44, 266-72; Douglass C. North, The Economic Growth of the United States, 1790-1860 (Englewood Cliffs, N.J.: Prentice-Hall, 1961); Walter LaFeber, The New Empire: An Interpretation of American Expansion, 1860-1898 (Ithaca, N.Y.: Cornell University Press, 1963); Thomas J. McCormick, China Market: America's Quest for Informal Empire, 1893-1901 (Chicago: Quadrangle Press, 1967).

75. Speeches and memoranda by Taft, cited in William A. Williams, The Shaping of American Diplomacy, vol. 1, 1740-1914 (Chicago: Rand McNally, 1970), pp. 470-74; N. Gordon Levin, Jr., Woodrow Wilson and World Politics: America's Response to War and Revolution (New York: Oxford University Press, 1968), pp. 24, 237.

76. Martin J. Sklar, "Woodrow Wilson and the Political Economy of Modern United States Liberalism," in Ronald Radosh, ed., New History of Leviathan (New York: Dutton, 1972), p. 26.

77. Ibid., pp. 36-38; National Foreign Trade Convention, Official Proceedings, Washington, D.C., May 27-28, 1914 (New York: National Foreign Trade Council, 1914), pp. 208-209.

78. Sklar, "Woodrow Wilson and the Political Economy," pp. 58-59.

79. Joseph Brandes, Herbert Hoover and Economic Diplomacy: Department of Commerce Policy, 1921-1928 (Pittsburgh: University of Pittsburgh Press, 1962); Carl P. Parrini, Heir to Empire: United States Economic Diplomacy, 1916-1923 (Pittsburgh: University of Pittsburgh Press, 1969); Michael Hogan, Informal Entente: The Private Structure of Cooperation in Anglo-American Economic Diplomacy (Columbia, Mo.: University of Missouri Press, 1977).

80. Hull   speech,   1942,   cited   in Williams, Shaping of American Diplomacy, vol. 2,   1914-1968, pp.   158 note 1, 337; Lloyd Gardner, Economic Aspects of New Deal Diplomacy (Boston: Beacon Press, 1971), p. 190.

81. H. W. Singer, International Development: Growth and Change (New York: McGraw Hill, 1964), pp. 3, 5.   Singer labels the   pre-1945   period   as "D-pessimistic/U-optimistic"; pessimism concerning continued development in the developed countries, and optimism regarding the beginning of development in poor nations.

82. Adian Foster-Carter,   "Neo-Marxist Approaches to Development and Underdevelopment," and Krishan Kumar, "The Industrializing and the Post-Industrial Worlds," in Emanuel de Kadt and Gavin Williams, eds., Sociology and Development (London: Tavistock Publications, 1974), pp. 81-82, 331-32; Peter Gran, "Political Economy as a Paradigm for the Study of Islamic History," International Journal of Middle East Studies 11 (1980): 512-13; Gyorgy Cukor, Strategies for Industrializ-ation in Developing Countries (New York: St. Martin's Press, 1974), pp. 10-11.

1
Economic Development as a Postwar Goal

It is difficult to identify the exact course that the United States and the Allied nations traveled toward declaring world economic development as a postwar goal. Indeed, neither the coalition of United Nations nor individual states ever issued a proclamation or held a conference dealing exclusively with this subject. Yet, from the Atlantic Conference in 1941 to San Francisco in 1945, public and private officials and organizations discussed the necessity of promoting development in poor, agrarian areas.

Wartime discussions of world development consisted of two parts. First, policymakers considered the desirability of world development. Everyone recognized the advantage of some degree of development in the periphery. The crucial question became how such development would affect the core nations. The lessons of depression and war and the doctrines of free trade and comparative advantage led policymakers to conclude that the positive effects of controlled world development would far outweigh the negative effects. Within the framework of the capitalist world-economy, peripheral economic development might serve as the engine for growth in the core.

Policymakers shared a common view of the benefits of development to both poor and rich nations. Disagreement arose over how the advanced nations could aid the development of poor, agrarian countries. Answers to this question varied according to one's understanding of the nature of development and underdevelopment. Political and economic leaders in the periphery who believed that Western policies contributed to Third World underdevelopment contended that the core had an obligation to provide loans and grants as well as technical aid and exports to poor regions. American officials, on the other hand, viewed development as the sole responsibility of the Third World's private and public sectors. Those sectors had to openly and completely embrace the capitalist world-economy in order to benefit from direct foreign private investments, capital goods, and technical knowledge. Classes in both the core and periphery favored the establishment of an international development agency that might guarantee the advanced nations' investments from expropriation, while protecting the Third World from imperialism.

The U.S. government tentatively expressed a commitment to economic development in the Atlantic Charter. Although the

August 1941 document did not contain the word "development,"
it did call for international collaboration to secure economic
advancement, social security, freedom from want, and access to
the trade and raw materials of all nations.   As an Anglo-
American statement, the Charter foreshadowed the postwar economic objectives of those two core nations.   In particular,
the Charter reflected the American goals of nondiscrimination,
reduction of trade barriers, and equal access to world markets
and resources.   Article 7 of the Master Lend Lease Agreement
emphasized these same aims.   This free trade and open world
was crucial for the proper development of the Third World.
Secretary of State Cordell Hull and President Franklin D.
Roosevelt rarely went beyond these vague pronouncements for a
new world economic order when talking about the periphery.
Nevertheless, during World War II, the subject of developing
the Third World arose frequently within both the government
bureaucracy and the corporate and labor sectors of American
society.(1) Among these groups serious discussions focused on
the outlines of a postwar Third World development policy and
program.   These discussions revealed intriguing differences
over development tactics and strategy. Simultaneously, conflicts of substance and rhetoric between American policymakers
and Third World representatives emerged at various wartime
conferences.

CONSIDERING DEVELOPMENT: CAPITAL, LABOR, AND THE STATE

Global depression and world war forced America's elites
to consider the future of the nation and the world.   During
World War II a consensus emerged "on the magical foreign
solution for the achievement of domestic prosperity."   Corporate executives, imperial state policymakers, economists, and
trade union officials agreed that America's "welfare and
wealth" depended on expanding world trade and increasing global productivity.   High levels of productivity, full employment, and a high standard of living at home rested on the reconstruction of war-devastated economies, the revival of free
multilateral trade, and the development of poor areas.(2)
    Fortune magazine, a prominent voice of capitalist class
opinion, explained in the spring of 1942 that so long as there
were "appalling living standards [in] most of the world" the
"American frontier" would be open.   A 1944 poll revealed that
American business executives viewed the Third World--especial-
ly Latin America and Asia--as the area that would see the
largest increase in postwar overseas business expansion.   In
July 1942, The Magazine of Wall Street described how the
developed world was beginning to recognize and understand the
needs of "economically weaker regions."   Henry J. Kaiser, a
leading shipbuilder, told the National Association of Manufacturers in December 1942 that America would never achieve
significant prosperity "as long as there are hosts of people
living on the margins of poverty anywhere on earth."(3)
    Business officials concerned with economic development
agreed that foreign living standards could not be raised
through "international pump priming" or "gifts, charity, or
handouts."   Only "hard work" and direct foreign investments
and exports could increase the use of modern machinery, raise
labor productivity, and improve living conditions.   Direct
investments would help construct industrial plants and open

mines. American owned and operated plants would provide the
managerial and technical skills so lacking in "economically
retarded areas."   Business leaders approved the idea of having
local investors participate in American operations, thereby
eliminating charges of foreign exploitation and fending off
discriminatory legislation. Joint operations in the periphery
provided American capitalists with an opportunity to develop
links with indigenous collaborator classes.(4)

R. W. Gallagher, president of the Standard Oil Company of
New Jersey, joined his colleagues in arguing that the continuation of America's high standard of living rested on raising
living standards around the world.(5)   George Houston, a
member of the executive council of the Machinery and Allied
Products Institute, told a conference of the Institute in
November 1944 that the industrialization of poor regions would
create vast new opportunities for marketing American capital
goods and exporting American production and managerial techniques. Slow and gradual industrialization, argued Houston,
was best for underdeveloped countries. The United States had
to discourage grandiose and complicated development schemes,
while supporting small and simple projects. Industrializing
poor areas would serve the United States by bolstering global
trade and by alleviating possible postwar national employment
difficulties.(6)

Although the subject of world industrialization undoubt-
edly occupied many a Wall Street conversation during the war,
there was still a "big selling job" to be done. Many firms
and industries had prepared to distribute their goods in core
countries in the postwar period.   Relatively few, however,
planned on promoting and selling specialized machinery and
equipment or exporting technology and management to underdeveloped areas.   To remedy this situation, George Houston
called for the "joint activity" of capital goods producers in
the exporting of their products. Acting under the provisions
of the Webb-Pomerene Act, capital goods enterprises could join
in associations to sell their goods to Third World markets.
Few business leaders wrestled with the problem of financing
this export trade, although several mentioned the use of
credits from the Export-Import Bank and the proposed World
Bank.(7)

While recognizing its great benefit to both developed and
underdeveloped nations, corporate leaders did not consider
industrialization as a "panacea for all world ills."(8) World
industrialization required adjustments on the part of the
developed regions.   Business journals and speeches implied
that the core's control of Third World development could
reduce the threat of increased competition.   Some observers
contended that the United States should not fear creating
industrial rivals because "industrialization stimulates rather
than limits international trade" and because "economic self-
respect is the basis for international friendship." But this
economic development could not be founded on discriminatory
state controls.   _Fortune_ warned against allowing Third World
nations to "foist an economic feudalism," or to "carry state
control to the point of closing...markets to competition."(9)
An open door remained the key to postwar American foreign
prosperity--or at least so proclaimed elites in both the
capitalist class and labor movement.

During the 1940s the American Federation of Labor
hierarchy saw itself as the official representative of

organized labor on foreign policy issues.   AFL elites rarely
commented on Third World economic development per se, although
they expounded on improving working conditions and raising
living standards in poor areas. Labor leaders urged the U.S.
government to assist in achieving world development because
"world-wide economic health is essential to security" and
because "the low standards of backward areas" would handicap
American and world prosperity.   According to AFL officials,
the chief cause of oppressive labor conditions in Third World
regions was "economic underdevelopment."   To alleviate these
problems, labor elites advocated general economic, social, and
political development programs, support for the activities of
the International Labor Organization, and the conditioning of
"loans and other financial assistance to backward countries"
on "the adopting of minimum labor standards in these countries."(10)   Both labor and business were committed to a free
international trade system that would maximize world production.   The imperial state's analysis of and plans for development naturally paralleled the capital-labor consensus on Third
World advancement.
    Elite, quasipublic organizations such as the Council on
Foreign Relations (CFR) and the Committee for Economic Development (CED),   linked America's capitalist class to the imperial state. Founded on the corporatist belief in the mutual-
ity of interests between different classes in American society, the CFR and CED sought to devise governmental economic and
foreign policies throughout the 1940s. The academic and business research staffs of the CFR and CED worked closely with
state planning committees to pursue the "national interest."
    The Committee for Economic Development, created in Sep-
tember 1942, served as a "combination training, recruiting,
and legitimizing agency" for corporatists making their way
into or out of government service.   The Commerce Department's
director of the Bureau of Foreign and Domestic Commerce,
Carroll Wilson, received a paid leave of absence to serve as
the CED's executive secretary and assistant treasurer.   Undersecretary of Commerce Wayne C. Taylor divided his time between
official cabinet duties and unofficial work with the CED.
Will Clayton, head of the multinational firm of Anderson,
Clayton and Company, served as assistant secretary of commerce
(1942-44) and then as assistant secretary of state for economic affairs, while actively participating as CED trustee.(11)
    In a May 1943 letter to Paul Hoffman, CED chairman and
president of the Studebaker Corporation, Clayton urged the CED
to undertake a study on the relationship between domestic
production and employment, on the one hand, and expanded
foreign trade and investment, on the other. Hoffman agreed
with Clayton's request. In late 1943 Duke University Dean
Calvin B. Hoover headed the CED Research Committee's study
group on international trade and domestic employment.
Hoover's final report in November 1944 contended "that the
level of employment in the United States is not primarily
dependent on international trade."   The critical reaction to
Hoover's assessment was swift and predictable.   Chicago
investment banker John C. Fennelly responded that "full
employment is clearly possible without foreign trade in a
totalitarian economy," but not in the American economy. Paul
Hoffman explained that foreign trade on a large scale was
"indispensable to high employment **in the kind of economy with**

its high standards of living that Americans now enjoy."(12) Will Clayton concurred with his colleagues:

> If we are to achieve post-war, a gross national product of goods and services of 150 billion dollars, employing about 56 million workers, we can probably only do so by making substantial use of the entire productive facilities of the country.
> This will mean inevitably that we will produce a great deal more of some things than our domestic economy can absorb. Markets for these surpluses must be found abroad, if we are to avoid serious unemployment.(13)

While criticizing Hoover's logic on the need for foreign trade, Clayton and the other CED trustees agreed with the report's recommendations. Hoover stressed the need for the United States to cooperate in reviving international trade and in raising living standards around the world. He urged the CED to work with the state in reducing and eliminating artificial barriers to world trade, improving global efficiency, increasing production, and emphasizing the role of private, competitive enterprise.(14) In another report, the CED Research Committee supported the creation of international institutions to rationalize and stabilize currency exchange and to provide prompt and sound financing of reconstruction and development.(15)

CED officials and research staff recognized the need for the United States to play a hegemonic role in the world-economy. In November 1944, Will Clayton called on the United States to act as a responsible hegemonic power, as Britain had done after the Napoleonic Wars. "As the greatest military, economic, and financial power in the world, the United States faces colossal responsibilities and opportunities in an atmosphere of economic isolationism." The United States had to combat economic isolationism in the core and periphery. American capital and goods had to go abroad to meet the needs of war-devastated and underdeveloped economies or face a new round of international economic warfare. Clayton warned that "free enterprise will not survive another World War."(16) The Council on Foreign Relations, in which Clayton also participated, echoed many of these same sentiments.

Like the CED, the CFR was rooted in the "most internationally oriented sector of the United States capitalist class." In 1940, financed by a Rockefeller Foundation grant, the CFR inaugurated a series of exhaustive studies concentrating on the long-term problems of the war. The War and Peace Studies Project also planned for the peace. In December 1941, the State Department created its own Advisory Committee on Postwar Foreign Policy in the image of the CFR studies project. CFR study groups and State Department planning divisions closely collaborated during the war. From early 1940 to the fall of 1945, the CFR sent approximately 700 memoranda to the department--many of which became, with little or no revision, policy statements of the government.(17)

The CFR study groups often discussed the relationship between the United States and the Third World. As early as April 1941, a CFR study pointed to an integrated world econom-

ic order as America's primary postwar   goal.   CFR researchers
argued   that   America's   economic and political interests were
global   and,   therefore,   the   United   States   had   to   assume
hegemonic responsibilities.   William Diebold, a member of the
CFR research staff and a consultant   to the   State Department,
urged that   America's war aims include "the interests of other
peoples...not only those of Europe, but also of   Asia, Africa,
and Latin   America."   A June 1941 memorandum recommended that
the United States plan to establish an economic   structure for
Europe, East Asia, and the whole world.(18)

CFR planners suggested the establishment of international
institutions to act as mechanisms for   American hegemony.   To
carry out the provisions of the Atlantic Charter, for example,
a CFR study group proposed creating   an international economic
development   board.   With   research staffs in Washington and
London, the   board   would   survey   international resources in
order to   determine the   "needs and opportunities for socially
and economically desirable development projects."(19)

Two economists dominated the   CFR's   wartime   analysis of
Third World   economic development.   Alvin H. Hansen and Eugene
Staley produced numerous memoranda for the   CFR's Economic and
Financial Study   Group.   Their reports   provided the basis of
CFR debates and policy   recommendations to   the state bureauc-
racy.

Hansen,   a   professor   of   political   economy   at Harvard
University,   together   with   University   of   Chicago economist
Jacob Viner,   led the   Economic and Financial Group during the
war.   Hansen and   many other   economists and   corporate executives   feared   a   postwar   depression.   A liberal Keynesian,
Hansen advocated the adoption   of national   planning, progressive taxation,   and public welfare expenditures to avoid postwar collapse.   These   measures comprised   only one   part of a
broader program.   Hansen recognized the need to achieve international economic equilibrium   and   world   economic expansion.
He believed that this necessitated full employment and reduced
tariffs in   the   "industrially   mature   countries."   It also
demanded the industrialization and changing of economic structures in "the backward   countries."   Changing   structures in
Third   World   economies   meant "diversification of agriculture
and the spread of industrialization."(20)

Hansen believed that American and core   economic prosperity depended,   to a   significant extent, on the development of
the periphery.   Third World nations had "legitimate goals" in
seeking agricultural   diversification and basic transportation
and electric power projects.   They had a right to   "a moderate
degree of   industrialization consistent   with their resources,
especially the manufacture   of   light   consumers'   goods," the
processing of   indigenous raw materials, and the assembling of
"complicated industrial products manufactured abroad."   These
goals could "not automatically happen under the functioning of
a free world market," but required "international planning and
the continued guidance of international arrangements."   Hansen
explained that Third World development needed core technology,
skills, capital goods, capital, and supervision.   International institutions such as the World Bank could   help finance development projects   in the periphery.   Such projects should be
judged not on the basis of immediate profits, but on the long-
run benefit   to   world   capitalism.   Third World development
schemes that   increased international   productivity and standards of   living were   "thoroughly sound from the standpoint of

MURDOCK LEARNING RESOURCE CENTER

the whole world economy." Hansen acknowledged that the temporary use of exchange controls or tariffs could "serve as a
useful incubator in the process of growth and development."
But autarkic economic policies such as those practiced in the
Soviet Union were to be avoided at all costs. "What needs to
be accomplished is not to lower the level of consumption, but
to raise the level of output."(21) Alvin Hansen's interest in
Third World development derived from his assessment of America's domestic economic needs. His analysis of Third World development, while insightful and influential, was not exhaustive. Eugene Staley provided the most extensive review of
Third World development made by an American during World War
II.

Staley, a professor of international economics at the
Fletcher School of Law and Diplomacy and an economic adviser
to the Budget Bureau and the State Department (1942-44),
produced three studies on world development prior to 1945.(22)
Economic development, according to Staley, increased a
people's capacity to produce and consume. Development began
with the modernizing of agriculture and inevitably led to
industrialization. Staley viewed industrialization as a
natural progression from processing local raw materials to
manufacturing consumer goods. Rising living standards
naturally accompanied this sequence.(23)

Staley considered economic development as one of three
fundamental economic conditions for an enduring peace.(24)
The development of the Near and Far East, Africa, and Latin
America would improve global economic productivity and expand
international trade. Large-scale development projects in poor
areas would offer outlets for the core's idle capital, thus
solving the problems of insufficient investment rates. In
addition, massive development schemes would boost demand for
capital goods and thereby alleviate some of the demobilization
and readjustment problems in core countries. Staley concluded
that world development programs were the only alternatives to
"world-wide economic collapse" and the "liquidation of the
private enterprise system."(25)

Raising living standards elsewhere, argued Staley, would
not lower American standards. Efficient production increased
output, which led to increased consumption, and so on. Low
wages of foreign workers would rise as development brought
about an increase in labor productivity. The character of
trade between developed and developing nations might change,
but the volume of trade would increase, not decrease. Established industries in core nations would face a combination of
new markets and new competition. If the developed nations
could shift labor and capital into those production lines
where demand was rapidly rising, then these nations would
retain their lead and move on to higher living standards.(26)

Core nations could aid, inhibit, or be indifferent to the
development of peripheral regions; but the process itself was
inevitable. Staley warned that, if left to "natural forces,"
development would be accompanied by a series of violent
conflicts and by sudden economic upheavals in the core. To
avoid this, industrial nations had to participate in world
development. Hinting at America's growing domination in the
world-economy, Staley noted that the United States stood in a
strong position to either help or hinder Third World development. He recommended that the United States and other core
nations cooperate in stimulating and regulating their invest-

ments in poor nations   by providing   educational and technical aid and insuring free trade.(27)

Investing   private   or   public   capital in poor, agrarian countries was not "playing   Santa Claus."   Reasonable returns on investments   abroad were   to be expected.   The soundness of development investment depended on   its   effect   in increasing the   productive   capacity   of   the   borrowing   area and on the ability of debtor nations to earn foreign currencies.   Staley warned against investing in projects that enabled a country to substitute high-cost production   at   home   for   goods formerly imported.   Such import   substitution failed to raise the real income of the particular nation and harmed the trade prospects of core   nations.   Staley also cautioned against concentrating capital in heavy capital   goods industry,   as the   Soviets had done.   This strategy   postponed a rise in local living stand-ards.   Development policies,   urged Staley,   should adhere to the principle   of comparative   advantage; they should adapt to the particular resources and   circumstances of   the developing country.(28)

In each   of his studies, Staley advocated the creation of an international development authority.   This agency would aid member governments in   harmonizing their views on long-range development planning and financing, and in   coordinating world development   trade   policies.   By supervising the investment relationship,   the   agency   could   protect   both   investor and borrower.(29)

Staley's analysis and recommendations were the subject of much discussion in CFR meetings in late 1943 and mid-1944.(30) Critics   outside   the   CFR   attacked   Staley   for inadequately examining   international   loans   and   investments;   failing to explain how   the international   agency would encourage private firms to participate in   development   schemes;   minimizing the obstacles to   global economic   collaboration; and ignoring the political prerequisites and   consequences   of development.(31) CFR   officials   recognized   these weaknesses, but nevertheless viewed   Staley's   work   as   the   most   comprehensive wartime examination of Third World economic development.

The work   of Staley   and Hansen   and the views of CED and CFR officials   permeated   imperial   state   policymaking organs during World   War II.   Those agencies and departments readily accepted the need for capitalist expansion, free international trade, and   American hegemony.   They grasped the importance of Third   World   markets   and resources   for   postwar   American prosperity and stability.   Bureaucratic battles raged over who would oversee wartime and   postwar foreign   economic   policies. Those   conflicts   reflected   differences   between   New   Deal liberals such as Hansen, Staley, and   Henry A.   Wallace, and corporate liberals such as Clayton, Dean Acheson, Adolf Berle, and Nelson Rockefeller.

Vice President   Henry A.   Wallace had   close contact with Alvin Hansen,   Paul Hoffman,   and other economists and business executives associated with the CFR and   CED.   A committed New Deal   liberal   and   internationalist,   Wallace   believed   that America's   future   prosperity depended   on   the   growth   and vitality   of   the   global economy.   From   the 1930s onward, Wallace argued that America's   farms and   factories needed the world market.   Developing   the   economies of Asia and Latin America guaranteed   a   prosperous   America--"the   prosperity of the poorest   is of great significance to the most well-to-do." Wallace often noted that   in   the   postwar   period   the United

States and other core nations would have "to bring about rapid industrialization and improvement in nutrition in India, China, Siberia, and Latin America." Third World industrial and agricultural development would "open up an unlimited new frontier of opportunities for the investment of American funds and the work of American hands and brains."(32)

Wallace had a strong interest in developing Latin America. During the depression he appreciated the importance of Latin American markets for world trade. As secretary of agriculture during Roosevelt's first two terms, Wallace pushed for reciprocal trade treaties with Latin nations. He hoped to encourage there the cultivation and development of complementary products that could find markets in the United States. In April 1941, Wallace noted that the United States had "tremendous reserves of unused capital, technical understanding and trained labor eager to co-operate with our brothers to the south in the development of a hemisphere." Wallace favored the rapid industrialization of Latin America under U.S. guidance and with American capital and technical assistance. At various stops during a 1943 goodwill tour of the southern continent, the vice president emphasized hemispheric solidarity and the American interest in the proper and rapid development of the Americas.(33)

Wallace's commitment to Latin American and Third World economic development converged with his conviction that government regulation and planning contributed to economic equality and social security at home. If New Deal reforms--for example, the Social Security Administration, the Tennessee Valley Authority (TVA), the Rural Electrification Administration (REA)--could improve life at home, then similar state projects on an international level could achieve economic development and social reforms in the periphery. To this end, Wallace tried to manipulate the Board of Economic Warfare's primary goal of procuring and developing strategic raw materials for the war effort. Wallace and Milo Perkins--chairman and executive director of the BEW, respectively--planned "to combine the war emergency with model programs for economic development and improved labor and welfare standards abroad."(34)

During its brief life (1942-43), the BEW encouraged Third World nations to increase production of materials vital to the Allied war effort. Wallace and Perkins argued that Latin American and other Third World workers would produce more efficiently if they enjoyed improved working conditions, wages, health care, and nutrition. BEW officials tried to use procurement/production contracts to raise the standards of living of laborers in the periphery. In addition, the BEW sent out "small groups, which include engineers, to help nations like India set up industrial production with their own countries with a minimum investment of capital goods from this country." According to Wallace, everyone in the BEW "agreed that it was important to get industrialization spread over the so-called backward parts of the world." To facilitate such development, Wallace acknowledged that it was "appropriate" for the Third World to have high protective tariffs to "encourage infant industries." At the same time, Wallace and the BEW stressed the need for free trade policies, especially on the part of the United States and other core nations.(35)

Many imperial state policymakers felt that Wallace's application of New Deal social reforms and economic planning

to the Third World went too far. The attempt to expand BEW
operations into wartime foreign policy and postwar planning
outraged important groups within the imperial state bureaucracy. Secretary of State Cordell Hull and Secretary of Commerce
Jesse Jones viewed Wallace's BEW as an intruder in their
domains. Assistant Secretary of State Dean Acheson described
Wallace as an "impatient empire builder" and the conflict
between Wallace and Hull and Jones as "economic warfare at
home."(36)   Such bureaucratic infighting was common in the
Roosevelt administration.   FDR resisted centralizing power
under any individual, preferring instead a division of
authority that forced underlings to compete with each other.
In such a setting, Roosevelt retained control of decision-
making.   By mid-1943, the BEW controversy had become so
intense that it threatened wartime economic operations. In
July, FDR abolished the agency.(37)
     The BEW's death was not merely the result of a dispute
over power and perogatives. Wallace and his advisers viewed
themselves as the last of the New Deal liberals committed to
state-supported class harmony, economic democracy, and social
security. On the other side stood corporate liberals such as
Jones, Will Clayton, Dean Acheson, and Adolf Berle. This
latter group, which clearly came to dominate imperial state
policymaking from 1943 onward, advocated strong state-capitalist class coordination in achieving American hegemony.
Jesse Jones and his assistant, Will Clayton, agreed with
Wallace on the necessity for Third World economic development.
They disagreed over this should be achieved and under
whose direction.   Corporate liberals favored state actions
that would clear the way for private capitalist interests.
The key was to open up Third World economies for the beneficial spread of American corporations.
     Jones and Clayton opposed BEW contracts that raised wages
and improved working conditions in the periphery.   In discussing the possibility of passing on higher tin prices (in the
form of increased wages and/or food provisions) to Bolivian
workers, Jones insisted that the United States "avoid any
action that would make people think we were engaging in social
reforms of any kind." Jones and Clayton were appalled at BEW
officials' desire to use the agency as a starting point for
hemispheric TVAs and REAs.   Clayton--the head of the world's
largest cotton brokerage house--lamented that BEW officials
were using government "purchases abroad for social and economic ideas they wanted to spread." The board was nothing more
than a political expediency; a "sop to leftwingers."(38)
Clayton, Jones, and their colleagues in the State Department
emphasized the need for an open door in the Third World for
American corporations.   Henry Wallace believed in a neutral
state that represented some objectifiable "national interest."
He was tied, as historian Norman Markowitz has explained, to a
"mythical progressive capitalism."   Jones, Clayton, and
friends, on the other hand, recognized the class interest of
the imperial state; they accepted "American capitalism as it
really was and sought to impose it upon the world."(39)
     Parts of Henry Wallace's thinking about the United States
and the Third World did find a receptive audience among some
capitalist class elites. In the midst of bureaucratic and
political battles, Wallace and Nelson Rockefeller remained
friends. They shared a common interest in Latin American
affairs.   More importantly, they both believed in a new type

of American businessman--one who would combine the desire for profits with a commitment to social service.(40)

As head of the Office of Inter-American Affairs (OIAA), Rockefeller had the task of cleansing Latin America of Axis influences and creating hemispheric solidarity around U.S. policies. To achieve these ends, the OIAA initiated a major "cultural offensive" in Latin America--manipulating motion pictures, the press, and radio. Rockefeller did not stop with this propaganda effort. He devised technical assistance programs to improve living standards, increase productivity, and secure economic and political stability and goodwill in the region. Subsidiary agencies such as the Institute of Inter-American Affairs and the Inter-American Educational Foundation administered health and agricultural projects and assisted local primary and secondary schools. Rockefeller also appointed a U.S. Commission for Inter-American Develop- ment, all of whose members came from the CED's Inter-American Committee. Rockefeller and his CED colleagues placed Latin American development within their liberal capitalist and corporatist world view.(41)

Rockefeller believed that any societal problem could be solved with "sufficient determination and effort." The state, led by the executive branch, had to cooperate actively with the capitalist class in applying pragmatic, technical, and supposedly value-free considerations and policies to national problems.   Rockefeller perceived himself as an "indentifier and seller of solutions to problems deemed significant for the survival and well-being of the United States."(42) American economic prosperity and social stability, according to Henry Wallace, Cordell Hull, and others, demanded an open and ex- panding capitalist world-system. Developing the Third World, including Latin America, was inexorably linked to that system. Rockefeller identified technical assistance for agricultural expansion, health care, and education as one solution to the problem of the underdeveloped peripheral economies.(43)

Rockefeller's thinking on technical assistance revealed the underlying values and goals of America's capitalist class elites and imperial state policymakers toward the Third World. When devising his wartime assistance program, Rockefeller drew on the advice and experience of Rockefeller Foundation profes- sionals who had been active in Third World areas for several decades. He learned from staff doctors of the "vital impor- tance of health as a problem in the social and economic devel- opment of poorer nations."(44) Meeting peripheral world health needs, however, went beyond humanitarian concerns. Rockefeller understood that the Foundation's health and educa- tion programs in such peripheral areas as China were chiefly vehicles "to lead China to modernization, to develop a culture and economy that would make her more useful to Western na- tions."(45) Public health programs concentrated on curtailing "major epidemics and debilitating diseases." They "brought medical treatment and sanitation campaigns to plantations, mines, and factories" in individual nations and thus "aimed directly at improving the health of each country's work force." Educational programs focused on transforming cultures via creation of an educated elite that would spread "Western civilization" and capitalism throughout Third World societies. Rockefeller Foundation officials' humanitarian concern with the health and education of the periphery and Nelson Rockefeller's special fascination with Latin American development were intertwined with the interests of American capitalism.(46)

On the surface, Rockefeller's state-sponsored technical assistance programs resembled Henry Wallace's call for global public works projects. But Rockefeller, like other corporate liberals, emphasized the need for the imperial state to help create the economic infrastructure on which private capital could build. Economic development was to be a joint effort of the imperial state, private corporations, and collaborator classes in the Third World. During World War II Rockefeller's OIAA attempted to lay the foundation for future government-private sector cooperation in the development of peripheral economies. The activities of the Institute of Inter-American Affairs and other OIAA subsidiaries served as models for later government technical aid programs.(47)

Secretary of State Cordell Hull considered both the BEW and the OIAA as interlopers in State Department business. Yet, until 1943, only the BEW and OIAA had engaged in any systematic review of Third World economic development. State Department planners made only indirect references to world development during 1941 and 1942. In 1943 assistant secretaries Dean Acheson and Adolf A. Berle, both members of the department's Advisory Committee on Postwar Foreign Policy, began to consider the relationship between the United States and the Third World. Personal animosity toward each other notwithstanding, both men recognized the emerging hegemonic role of the United States in the capitalist world-economy. They acknowledged that the United States would have to be a capital exporting country in order to meet the needs of war-devastated and underdeveloped nations. Berle, a former member of Franklin D. Roosevelt's brains trust and professor of corporate law at Columbia University, predicted a substantial period after the war when the United States would "have to be the financial and economic pumping station, shock absorber, and general supply station" for most of the world. An "economic pumping station" would provide private capital investment and technical and managerial assistance to the core and periphery.(48)

Acheson, "a wealthy patrician who had spent the bulk of his adult life with Washington's leading corporate law firm" (Covington and Burling), became assistant secretary of state for economic affairs in February 1941. Sharing Cordell Hull's philosophy on trade, Acheson formulated and advocated policies designed to secure "an expanding and open world economy." A properly functioning capitalist world-economy required the dismantling of all preference systems and the end to economic nationalism. Acheson told Congress in 1943 of the need to have the United States, Great Britain, and other nations in the core and periphery negotiate "an arrangement which will have the effect of increasing the whole volume of production in the world, of consumption and employment and reducing the barriers of trade and doing away with discriminations."(49)

Berle and Acheson advocated maximizing world production in an open and private global market, rather than redistributing world resources and income via nationalist policies. Such development would guarantee prosperity and stability in the United States and throughout the capitalist world-economy. But neither Berle nor Acheson directly answered the question of who or what would pay for reconstruction and development. A September 1943 Advisory Committee report proposed an international investment agency to transfer funds from rich to poor regions.   Responding to a State Department memo on the sub-ject, President Roosevelt told Hull that "one of the most pressing problems in the field of foreign economic policy and operations is the handling and financing of reconstruction of war-torn areas and the correlation of such operations with a long-run economic development program."   Roosevelt wanted a special policy committee to recommend development programs and to coordinate activities of several government agencies in this field.(50)

During the   State Department's   reorganization in January 1944, Roosevelt approved the creation of a permanent inter-departmental committee to review foreign economic policy.   The new addition to the imperial state bureaucracy comprised rep-resentatives from the departments of State, Treasury, Com-merce, Agriculture, and Labor, the Tariff Commission, and the Foreign Economic Administration.   The Executive Committee on Economic Foreign Policy (ECEFP) convened on 18 April 1944. The Committee jumped into the development arena by defining "sound development" as the improvement of agricultural and mineral resources, transportation, power, and manufacturing industries. Economic expansion was to be in harmony with a nation's natural resources, geography, climate, and level of technology. Development aimed not at self-sufficiency, but rather at a "balanced development" that maximized "produc-tivity and [the] level of living by making economic use of those resources in which a country has a comparative advan-tage." The sound economic development of poor regions would provide the core with new capital and consumer goods markets. The economic development of the periphery, concluded the ECEFP, was a "worthy objective of United States policy."(51)

"GOOD FOR OUR POCKET-BOOK AND OUR SECURITY"

Few government officials questioned the need for postwar world development.(52) New Deal liberals, however, complained about the government's vague commitment to "help raise levels of living and productivity in the economically submerged coun-tries."   Harold D. Smith and Louis Bean of the Bureau of the Budget felt a need to "sharpen" the government's views on de-velopment.   In March 1943, Director of the Budget Smith wrote to President Roosevelt that the government needed to examine the effects that foreign development would have on the Ameri-can economy and the means by which the United States could assist in world development. The executive, contended Smith, must have the factual evidence to be able to say that helping other nations to raise their living standards would be "good for our own pocket-book and our own security."(53)

On the surface, the Bureau of the Budget might seem an unusual agency to call for a study on Third World development. But under Smith's direction, the bureau fulfilled its role as a "constant critic and improver of administration in the federal executive branch."   Smith, a master administrator, searched for ways to structure policymaking and make it both more efficient and more rational.   Henry A. Wallace observed that Smith "steps aggressively into all sorts of situations, views them from an all-over global standpoint, and tries to weld conflicting viewpoints into a single intelligent and energetic government policy." Smith applied this perspective

to the question of Third World development. He also shared
Wallace's plans for the BEW and supported Wallace and Perkins
in their battle against the bureaucracy.(54) Smith's request
for a comprehensive government study on Third World development must be seen in this larger context.

Acting on Smith's request, Roosevelt instructed Secretary
of State Cordell Hull to outline the beneficial and detrimental effects of past American efforts to raise foreign productivity and living standards. The president also wanted to
know about possible development programs, the probable effects
of foreign development on American and world trade, and the
minimum safeguards required to secure the maximum common
benefit and the minimum adverse effect on the United States
and the poor nations.(55)

FDR told Hull to "pool the ingenuity" of several state
agencies. Hull selected representatives from the U.S. Tariff
Commission, the Federal Trade Commission, and the BEW to
participate on the study committee. But the heart of Hull's
committee came from the State Department, Commerce Department,
and the OIAA. Assistant Secretary of State Dean Acheson
served as committee chairman. He was supported by Emilio
Collado, an economist and special assistant to Undersecretary
of State Sumner Welles. Collado had acted as Welles' hatchet
man in the battle against the BEW. OIAA Coordinator Nelson
Rockefeller and Assistant Secretary of Commerce Will Clayton
rounded out the committee membership.(56) The presence of
Acheson, Collado, Rockefeller, and Clayton on Hull's committee
and the death of the BEW in July 1943 guaranteed a report that
represented the analysis and recommendations of corporate
liberals and capitalist class elites.

Hull submitted the committee's final report to the president in late November 1943. In a cover letter, Hull reiterated his familiar free trade position, writing that investment
abroad depended "upon the United States pursuing a liberal
commercial policy."(57) The body of the report consisted of
four parts--corresponding to the four problems posed by
Roosevelt. Case histories of past international investments
revealed increased productivity in both lenders and borrowers.
Postwar global investment would contribute to the maintenance
of full employment at home by promoting and expanding capital
and consumer goods markets. Combined with the correct tariff
policies, investments would increase the quantity of inexpensive imports into the United States. Past experiences revealed a variety of investment dangers including protective tariffs, inexperienced investors, investments fixed in American
dollars, nationalist policies (expropriation and nationalization), and imperialism.(58)

Idle American capital could be profitably invested
abroad, expanding trade and absorbing otherwise unemployed
labor at home. But capital by itself was not sufficient to
solve problems stemming from inadequate managerial and technical knowledge in underdeveloped countries. These deficiencies hindered the potential opportunities for American capital
investment and export. Underdeveloped countries required
technical aid as well as capital.(59)

The Hull-Acheson committee recommended that the U.S. government monitor the activities of American investors and enterprises abroad. Loans extended over long periods of amorti-
zation with low interest rates should not unduly burden the
recipient's future foreign exchange position. Borrowing na-

tions would have to purchase in the United States some, but not all, materials or equipment for loan projects. In those instances where "broad policy dictates foreign investment," the government would assume the risk rather than private investors. The report emphasized that American capital be extended with the expectation of full repayment. Economically sound projects required proper managerial and technical assistance and included the improvement of public utilities, the development of natural resources, and the establishment of basic industries. Whatever the project, American investors had to establish lines of credit to be used as needed, rather than giving lump sums.(60)

The Hull-Acheson committee report summarized the liberal corporate thinking that had come to dominate imperial state agencies and capitalist class elites by late 1943. Echoing the findings of CFR and CED studies, the government report linked together domestic employment and production to the possible expanded trade, investment opportunities, and raw materials resulting from Third World development. Acheson and associates emphasized the role of private enterprise and private capital in the development of the periphery. They also stressed the state's role in maximizing the expansion of the private capitalist system--especially through the creation of free international trade. The report ignored New Deal liberals who warned of the inadequacies of a free market for poor peripheral societies and who urged state supported social and economic reforms. By 1944, Henry Wallace and his BEW allies had lost the battle with the State and Commerce departments over who would formulate and implement America's economic development policy for the Third World. In the winter of 1943-44, however, one of Wallace's "trusted aides" launched a departing salvo at Acheson, Clayton, and the others.

Louis Bean rose from an economist and researcher in Wallace's Department of Agriculture in the mid-1930s to special assistant to the director of the BEW in 1942. A year later, Bean joined the Bureau of the Budget as chief fiscal analyst with the task of studying postwar economic problems. His examination of peripheral economic growth and the world-economy led him to propose, in 1943, a United Nations conference on "the international use of long-term capital for the development of backward areas." In a 1944 report on Third World industrialization, Bean argued that the experience of Western core nations be "accelerated in industrially backward countries to accomplish in one decade what has usually taken several decades." Industrialization was the responsibility of the periphery, but international cooperation in capital and managerial assistance could hasten the process. The large gains accruing to poor, agrarian nations would be accompanied by an increased demand for core countries' industrial goods and services.(61) State Department planners carefully reviewed the report. Harry Hawkins, director of the Office of Economic Affairs, told Bean that international cooperation to stimulate economic development had its limitations, and that, ultimately, the free market, comparative advantage, and available resources determined a nation's economic development. Bean characterized Hawkins' comments as pleasant, but of little substance.(62)

When the Hull-Acheson committee submitted its final report, Bean carefully studied its analyses and recommendations. In early 1944 he presented a formal critique of the report and

an alternative examination of the president's four questions.
Bean criticized the State Department report for focusing on
bilateral development programs. Multilateral action and programs of national and regional development, according to Bean,
would multiply American investment and trade opportunities.
Bean cautioned against relying on the rule of "economically
sound" projects.   A development scheme might be unsound when
considered by itself, but could be more than appropriate and
desirable as "part of a larger development program including
complementary and supplementary enterprises."   Economically
sound projects might guarantee short-run profits, but not
long-run increases in global productivity and trade.(63)

     Labelling the report a sanitized study for mass consump-
tion, Bean espoused a bold political strategy to raise foreign
living standards. The U.S. government had to "consciously
promote the well-being of nations who appear to be prospective
friendly allies, and deny economic aid to others."   As Alvin
Hansen and Eugene Staley had pointed out, the free market by
itself could not develop the Third World. A successful global
development policy rested on increasing the federal government's control over foreign trade and investment.   Higher
world living standards required international cooperation and
planning, and this necessitated "discipline and the courage of
the disciplined group to take risks." Bean suggested that the
American people would risk increasing the state's powers "if
it were made clear that their security was primarily at stake,
and the economic benefits were made secondary." Bean's analysis was remarkably perceptive and prophetic.   A national
policy aimed at world development required a government that
had the "authority, power, and responsibility necessary to
carry it out." Such a state could act only if "the bulk of
our people honestly subscribe to the underlying principle."
Bean contended that the economic benefits that would accrue
from development abroad were insufficient to rally the American masses behind a powerful national government.   Only the
motive of political security was strong enough and could be
manipulated to accomplish this.(64)   Although overlooked in
1944, by the late 1940s imperial state policymakers had embraced Bean's recommendation--they manipulated a political
security threat (i.e., the danger of Soviet expansionism) to
unite the American public behind massive economic assistance
programs for Greece and Turkey (the Truman Doctrine), Europe
(the Marshall Plan), and the underdeveloped world in general
(Point Four Program).

     During World War II imperial state planners, together
with capitalist class policymaking organizations such as the
CFR and CED, formulated the outlines of an economic development policy for the Third World. Eugene Staley, Alvin Hansen,
Dean Acheson, Nelson Rockefeller, Henry Wallace, Louis Bean,
and others constructed a policy that emphasized America's
responsibilities as a hegemonic core power. They examined the
proper role of the periphery in the capitalist world-economy
and proposed the creation of programs and institutions based
on free multilateral trade, comparative advantage, and private
capital, markets, and property. Tactical differences arose
over how to achieve multilateralism and productionism and over
what sectors in American society would control development in
the periphery. The demise of the Board of Economic Warfare in
July 1943 and the Hull-Acheson report of November 1943 marked
the end of the tactical debate. Tactical debates and bureau-

cratic clashes notwithstanding, the guidelines for peripheral economic development were set. Motivated by economic and political self-interest, state and capitalist class elites cautiously committed the nation--state, capital, and labor--to freeing international trade, increasing productivity, and, persumably, raising standards of living in the periphery and semiperiphery. The American consensus on Third World economic development met varying degrees of acceptance and resistance from other states in the world-system.

THE WARTIME DEVELOPMENT DEBATE

When economic development issues arose at wartime international meetings, American imperial state policymakers received support from the former hegemonic core nation, Great Britain. British and American officials agreed that economic development could solve the problems of poverty, illiteracy, and disease in underdeveloped countries. Economic development and its presumed concomitant prosperity would stabilize potentially volatile areas. The British took a particularly strong interest in Third World development because they viewed it as crucial for their own reconstruction. In addition, British state officials considered foreign economic programs as a means to maintain indirect control over an empire that demanded political independence.(65)

The British approach to peripheral development derived, in large part, from Britain's role in the capitalist world-economy and from long experience with colonies. Through the 1920s, British state officials viewed a "natural" division of labor between the industrial metropolis and the agricultural/raw material periphery. Colonial development entailed increasing primary goods production through the construction of railways and ports and capital investment in mines and plantations. In 1926, the Committee on Industry and Trade speculated on the possible effect of peripheral industrialization on British trade. The Committee found that while the immediate effect of colonial industrialization would be to restrict Britain's export trade, in the long-run the periphery's demand for capital goods, expanded primary production, and increased purchasing power would actually expand British and world trade.(66)

With the onset of the Great Depression, British officials acknowledged the plight of primary good exporting economies in the periphery. In 1931, the MacMillan Committee on Finance and Industry announced the arrival of the "era of conscious and deliberate management" of colonial development. Only a handful of political leaders, however, advocated a transfer of capital from Britain to the colonies to assist in the latter's industrialization. Massive riots in the West Indies and West Africa in the late 1930s led a royal commission to propose the establishment of a welfare fund to finance educational, health, housing, land settlement, and employment projects in the colonies. In October 1939, the Colonial Office met to discuss the issue of colonial development. State officials and academic experts admitted that since Britain had ceased to export capital, the task of developing the colonies fell to international mechanisms. Margery Perham of Oxford University suggested that only the United States was in a position to subsidize the economic development of Britain's colonies. The question of American participation in colonial development remained a controversial subject within the British government for the duration of the war.(67)

War stimulated debate over, but few changes in, British colonial policy. In 1942, Perham lamented that the colonies' economic welfare still "swings helplessly up and down in the tide of world markets." As the war moved into its last stage, Colonel Oliver Stanley, secretary of state for the colonies, introduced a new colonial development and welfare act into the House of Commons. The secretary argued that Britain should finance colonial development because of the periphery's economic and strategic importance. Even a small addition to the purchasing power of colonial areas, contended Stanley, would create "vast new markets" for Britain.(68)

In a long memorandum on Britain's trade and balance payments, Richard Clarke analyzed the issues of Third World economic development, world markets, and Britain's postwar economy. An official in the Treasury's Overseas Finance Division, Clarke wrote in May 1945 that "the growth of world trade requires great economic development of backward countries." Peripheral economic development had to be "rapid and non-autarkic," entail increasing "agricultural efficiency," "the development of transport and electric power," and emphasize consumption. Clarke suggested that Britain use the sterling balances it owed (i.e., blocked sterling balances) to "the Colonial Empire, the Middle East, and India" and its political and administrative institutions in these areas to influence peripheral economic development. "We need not overtly use the sterling balances as a weapon; but the fact remains that if those countries want to be repaid in goods they will be very well advised to accept our advice on the general course of their development."(69)

Clarke recommended that his government formulate ten-year programs to meet the capital goods needs of Third World development projects. "This would give us a substantial export market and thus a long-term stability in our balance of payments." Britian would have to develop schemes for doubling the national income in each of its colonies over a 15-year period and achieving similar results in the Middle East and India. Funded sterling balances would pay for some of the development projects in the periphery. Clarke wondered how much capital the Third World nations would have to draw from the United States. Most British state officials recognized that Britain could not invest abroad except by paying off its debt. Clarke suggested that if Britain's balance of payments was in order, it might "be to our advantage to borrow from U.S.A. ourselves and re-lend as necessary;...and this might be a way round the difficulty that the Americans have a great deal of money to lend abroad but very little experience and knowledge of how to lend it." In any evident, Clarke concluded that so long as the United States provided untied loans for development purposes, Anglo-American cooperation would be worthwhile "both in order to express our view on the course of development which is desirable--again emphasising agricultural productivity--and to get our share of the exports involved."(70)

British state officials considered Third World economic development as crucial to their nation's economic recovery and future prosperity. Providing technology, equipment, and financial assistance to peripheral development offered the British a means of maintaining political influence in parts of the Third World.   Similarly, American imperial state policy-makers viewed economic development of the periphery as a con-dition for hegemony--as a way of achieving political stability in the world-system, creating vital new markets for American goods and capital, and exploiting Third World natural re-sources.   Economic development comprised another diplomatic tool of the core powers.   As such it was neither more nor less moral, humanitarian, sinister, or exploitative than any other instrument of foreign policy.   Although American and British officials differed over minor points of development policy, they agreed with Richard Clarke's analysis that "it is a ques-tion of guiding capital development and of persuading the leaders of these [Third World] countries of what is the best thing in the common interest."(71)   The common interest de-manded adherence to the principles of free trade, comparative advantage, private enterprise, private capital, and private markets.   Multilateralism depended on the non-autarkic econom-ic growth of the periphery.   Economic nationalism and autarky, however, retained strong support in both the core and periph-ery.

Early in the war several Third World nations raised objections to the American commitment to free trade.   India, for example, refused to sign a mutual aid agreement containing Article 7--which called for a reduction in tariff barriers. Indian leaders sought to retain control over and manipulate their postwar tariffs in order to protect infant industries. In 1943, the State Department's Harry Hawkins wrote that the United States would continue lend-lease arrangements with India through the British, rather than enter into "a separate agreement containing a watered down Article VII." A "diluted" Article 7 would allow India to follow a program of "exagger-ated self-sufficiency," and would set a bad precedent for con-templated pacts with other underdeveloped nations.(72) At various wartime conferences, poor nations criticized this argument and American plans for a postwar economic order.

The International Labor Organization's Philadelphia Convention in April 1944 emphasized international cooperation for world progress.   Surface amity did not cover deep con-flicts between rich and poor nations. A confrontation between British and British Dominion delegates reflected not only an intra-Commonwealth division, but a much deeper split between industrial and agrarian nations. Delegates from Australia and India suggested that the ILO immediately monitor the implemen-tation of core governments' promises to raise living standards in their colonies. The British strongly opposed this proposal and resented the statement by John Beasley, the Australian government representative, that Britain's policies toward colonial development were timid.(73) Australia, a country in the semiperiphery, had extensive plans for ascending within the world-economy.   Beasley criticized not the capitalist world-economy, but the short-sighted policies of core states like Great Britain.   He agreed with American and British planners that raising living standards in the core depended on domestic policy--increasing consumption, investment, and employment. Development in the periphery and semiperiphery, however, rested on national planning and a world market demand for their exports.   At the very least, explained Beasley, Third World economic development required international cooperation.(74)

More thorough critiques of the world-economy and core country policies came from the representatives of Third World labor movements. Vicente Lombardo Toledano, president of the Confederacion de Trabajadores de Mexico and head of the Confederacion de Trabajadores de America Latina, dismissed Beasley's suggestions for international collaboration as insufficient. A long-time Marxist and one of Mexico's most powerful labor leaders, Lombardo Toledano explained that Latin America had been subjected to the dictates of American and European needs for food and industrial raw materials. Latin America "is a continent of semi-colonial countries" dependent on the "big international monopolies." Multinational corporations exploited Latin America for capital investment, a source of raw materials, and a market for manufactured products. Lombardo urged the ILO to "take into account the special interest of the economically less developed countries." Latin America and the Third World had to control their economies. Lombardo suggested that peripheral countries create tripartite committees composed of government officials, workers, and employers. These committees would supervise foreign investments--insuring the distribution of capital to essential national projects, the payment of taxes and tariffs, the reinvestment of profits, and coordination with indigenous capital and the conservation of national resources. In the realm of trade, Lombardo recommended fair prices for the producers of both export and import goods, mandatory quotas of machinery and other capital goods that industrialized nations should export to underdeveloped nations, and stable exchange rates.(75)

Lombardo Toledano's recommendations were not merely rhetoric. Many colleagues from Latin America and Asia concurred with his demand for reforms in international and national economic relations. Ocampo Pastene, an adviser to the workers' delegation from Chile, requested that core nations--especially the United States--implement the Atlantic Charter and help diminish the inequality in the development of industry in the periphery. Cuba's labor delegate, Carlos Fernandez R., implored the core to revise international economic rules and to "establish conditions of true equality in the economic relations between great nations which control markets." An adviser to the Indian delegation reiterated Lombardo's plea that the ILO recognize the special needs of peripheral countries. The U.S. government delegation (including Assistant Secretary of State Adolf Berle), American Federation of Labor representatives, and the employers' delegation (including CED chairman Paul Hoffman) ignored these analyses and suggestions.(76) American officials opposed economic nationalist policies and any revision to the rules of the game--except those being designed in Washington. The ILO conference resolved none of the economic development problems raised by Third World labor and government officials. Conflicts evident in Philadelphia in April reappeared at Bretton Woods a few months later.

The July 1944 conference dealt with freely convertible currencies, stable exchange rates, and national economic policies. Forty-four nations agreed on the outline of a postwar monetary system that included an International Monetary Fund (IMF) and an International Bank for Reconstruction and Development (IBRD). The two institutions focused on international payments and investments, and not on trade, commodities, or relief. The IMF would help alleviate balance of pay-

ments difficulties, while the IBRD would provide and guarantee
loans to war-devastated and underdeveloped lands for economic
restoration and development.(77)

American and British economic experts wanted the IMF to
focus on currency convertibility and not on the special currency problems of poor nations. Several peripheral nations,
nevertheless, attempted to connect the issue of blocked
sterling balances to the fund. During the war nations within
Britain's sterling bloc had accumulated large balances in
British currency.   They hoped to transfer the balances into
goods and services that might facilitate national development.
Britain, however, blocked the exchange of sterling into other
national currencies because it lacked sufficient funds to
cover its debts.   India, Egypt, and Australia wanted the IMF
to liquidate at least part of their blocked sterling balances.
Mahmoud Saleh el Falaki, the Egyptian delegate, explained that
excluding the problem of indebtedness from the IMF "might
possibly weaken the whole mechanism of the Fund." Indian officials held that they could not be "asked to wait indefinitely until the United Kingdom reached a stage when sterling
would be freely convertible into other currencies."   Like
other underdeveloped countries, India was "pulsating with the
hope and aspirations of large scale industrial development to
raise the standard of living" of its people.(78)

Preoccupied with creating an effective payments system,
the United States and Britain opposed altering the IMF's
articles to satisfy the desires of the periphery. The issue
of blocked balances, argued American officials, could be best
solved between Britain and its creditors. To have the IMF
deal with sterling debts, stated one American economist, would
be to burden it with "tasks which it cannot successfully
undertake."(79)

Another controversy between developed and underdeveloped
nations arose over the functions of the proposed World Bank.
Before the conference American and British planners stressed
the reconstruction objectives of the IBRD. The bank would
supply capital to war-torn areas and facilitate a rapid and
smooth transition to a peace economy. In addition, the IBRD
would strengthen monetary and credit structures of various
countries. The IMF and World Bank would reduce the likeli-
hood, intensity, and duration of world depression. Only after
all this would the bank attack the problems of the periphery.(80)

Echoing the demands of other Third World nations, the
Mexican delegation suggested that the IBRD "encourage permanently the economic development of member countries." Assistant Secretary of State for Economic Affairs Dean Acheson
favored "equitable consideration" of the "competing claims for
loans of war-torn and undeveloped areas." He argued that the
ultimate criteria for loans should be "the need for and efficacy of the project." In practice this meant that projects
aimed at alleviating war-time destruction would appear more
worthy than projects aimed at battling long-term, endemic
underdevelopment. In the final draft of the bank charter,
reconstructing war-devastated economies and reconverting
productive facilities to peacetime operations took precedence
over developing poor areas' productivity and resources. The
bank charter also included stringent lending conditions and
focused on self-liquidating loans for specific projects rather
than broad programs.(81)

India, Egypt, and other Third World countries had hoped
to secure core recognition of their special problems at Bretton Woods. These nations' state officials felt that international conferences concentrated too much on the advanced industrialized nations and not enough on the underdeveloped
countries. Sir Shanmukham Chetty, an Indian delegate, agreed
with the core nations that balanced growth of international
trade constituted a legitimate postwar goal. Balanced growth
could not be restricted, however, to an equal volume of exports and imports. India and other agrarian nations attached
"great importance also to the balanced character and composi-
tion of international trade." Exchanging the periphery's primary goods for the core's manufactured goods did not constitute balanced trade. The agrarian states, contended Chetty,
had to industrialize and produce their own manufactured goods.
International organizations had to abandon their narrow outlook of approaching "all problems from the point of view of
the advanced countries of the West." Commenting on the Indians' attempt to get acknowledgment of the problems of underdeveloped countries, one American technical adviser observed
that "on the whole their purposes were not very well served."(82)

The underdeveloped countries continued their crusade
after the monetary conference. Latin American business and
state elites feared that U.S. commitments to reconstruct
Europe would relegate their national economies to oblivion
after the war. Latin officials sought assurances that American economic assistance would continued in the postwar period.
Some elite elements and working class leaders in Latin America
raised doubts about inter-American economic relations. They
pointed to how U.S. demands for strategic raw materials
created shortages and spiraling inflation throughout Latin
economies. Simultaneously, reciprocal trade agreements between the United States and Latin American countries brought
low tariffs and inadequate protection to nascent industrialization in the Southern Hemisphere. A growing number of
elites believed that if the United States refused to construct
a multilateral system "geared more directly to their own developmental needs, the only alternative was a recourse to economic nationalism." Latin leaders insisted on an inter-hemi-
spheric conference to deal with their economic problems.(83)

At the Inter-American Conference on Problems of War and
Peace held in Mexico City (Chapultepec) in February and March
1945, U.S. imperial state officials attempted to gloss over
the issue of economic development while securing Latin American commitments to a regional security system--that is, continued U.S. dominance over the hemisphere. Will Clayton, who
had replaced Acheson as assistant secretary of state for
economic affairs in late 1944, delivered the U.S. position on
economic matters. Clayton summarized the imperial state-
capitalist class consensus on Third World development. He
emphasized that Latin American economic development needs
would be met, in large part, by the reconstruction of European
productive capacity and markets and by the restoration of free
trade. He stressed the U.S. government's commitment to the
expansion of the world-economy through the removal of all discriminations in trade and the establishment of U.S.-designed
institutions such as the World Bank and the IMF. Clayton and
other state officials pushed through the conference the Economic Charter for the Americas. The Charter called for a pro-

ductionist strategy based on free trade, comparative advantage, and the use of private capital and private markets. It supported international organizations that would institutionalize U.S. hegemony, and it demanded an assault on economic nationalism in all its forms.(84)

Despite acquiescing to the Charter, Latin American government representatives left little doubt where they stood. Secretary of State Edward Stettinius acknowledged the "protracted" nature of discussions on economic issues at Chapultepec. He noted the "very considerable sentiment among the other American Republics in favor of many restrictive measures designed to protect their war-developed industries together with industries which they hope to see developed in the future." Government delegates from Mexico and Chile demanded hemispheric development and industrialization programs planned by the state and modeled after the Tennessee Valley Authority. The Cuban representative proposed that foreign (i.e., United States) capital investments in Latin America should be supervised and regulated by the state "under terms and conditions most favorable to the development of the countries benefited." Colombian delegates recognized the need to abolish trade barriers and to increase the volume of trade. But they insisted that such policies "be brought into harmony with the diversification of production in those American countries that are not sufficiently developed, and with their attainment of a higher degree of industrialization."(85)

The Economic Charter received strong criticism from working class organizations in Mexico. Lombardo Toledano denounced the Mexican government's position at Chapultepec as "subordinating the Latin American bloc to the arms of the United States State Department." The Mexican federation of labor published full page advertisements opposing the "archaic policy of free trade" and demanding that the United States provide capital goods for Latin America's "rapid economic development." U.S. officials dismissed Lombardo as a Communist and his criticism as Marxist rhetoric. But Lombardo's sentiments were shared by large numbers of Communist and non-Communist workers throughout Latin America. Even individual businesses favored local protectionism and questioned the Economic Charter. As historian David Green has pointed out, the United States did not convert Latin Americans to its ideology or programs at Chapultepec. "Latin American economic nationalism had not been downed, it had merely been temporarily frustrated."(86)

Frustrated or not, Third World countries sought to keep open international avenues for debating U.S. officials on the issue of economic development. Semiperipheral nations such as Australia found it relatively easy to press their development concerns directly on imperial state policymakers. In January 1945, for example, Australian Minister Frank McDougall sent Leo Pasvolsky--the secretary of state's special assistant in charge of postwar planning and the main liaison between the CFR and the State Department--a long memorandum on Third World development. The memo enumerated "reasons why the countries of Western civilization should...do everything in their power to assist progress in the underdeveloped countries." Third World development would result in greater world political and economic stability, larger markets for developed nations, and the improvement of life in the periphery. Core nations had to provide the underdeveloped areas with technical, capital, and

material assistance.   McDougall approved the funneling of
economic aid through international institutions like the IBRD
and the IMF.(87)   Pasvolsky and other American policymakers
had little quarrel with this assessment of core responsibilities for and benefits from Third World development.

Direct diplomatic contacts notwithstanding, the principal
mechanism for international discussion of Third World economic
development issues remained international conferences and, increasingly in late 1944 and early 1945, newly created international institutions.   At the Dumbarton Oaks and San Francisco
conferences, underdeveloped nations succeeded in molding an
economic and social council to coordinate the United Nations
Organization's socioeconomic activities.   The international
debate over economic development henceforth had a permanent
forum.(88)

CONCLUSION

Developing certain sectors of Third World economies had
been a part of U.S. public and private policy at least since
the late nineteenth century.   During the 1930s depression,
policymakers such as Secretary of State Cordell Hull, who were
committed to an expanding world market, stressed the importance of Third World areas for America's prosperity.   Even if
there had been no war, Third World economic development would
have become a major concern of American foreign policy.   More
than anything else, World War II provided the opportunity for
creating a new world order under U.S. guidance.   International
and national peace and prosperity demanded the continued
integration . of the Third World into the capitalist world-
system.   As the postwar international economic and political
structure took shape, core states gradually acknowledged the
need for world development.   The Atlantic Charter of 1941 did
not mention "development," but the United Nations Charter of
1945 gave "development" equal billing with "full employment,"
"higher standards of living," and "economic stability."(89)

During World War II, two concepts of economic development
dominated international discussions.   Ruling classes in poor,
agrarian nations emphasized industrialization as the key to
successful social welfare and agricultural programs.   To stimulate industrialization and to stabilize primary goods' prices
and halt the loss of foreign exchange reserves' purchasing
power, Third World elites pressed for protective tariffs,
import quotas, international commodity agreements, and local
government control over foreign investments and corporations.(90)

Core nations viewed economic development as the process
of integrating peripheral nations into the world system.
Adhering to the doctrines of comparative advantage and private
markets, American leaders held that increased efficiency and
productivity of agriculture and primary goods industries,
rather than industrialization, formed the basis for sound
development.   Advanced nations sought to capture the potentially vast markets for capital goods in the newly developing
regions.(91) Proposals for international development agencies
and the British regional approach to development constituted,
in part, attempts by core nations to control the development
process in the periphery.

Overall, the United States favored this type of Third World economic development. Imperial state and corporate elites recognized the advantages of such development to the American economy. Americans had great faith in their ability to extend economic and technological resources to under-developed regions and still maintain industrial leadership. American leaders sought to universalize their conviction that, in a market economy, benefits flow to all participants.(92) According to American state planners, a rational world economy based on economic liberalism would produce postwar peace and prosperity. Since reconstruction and development would be natural by-products of this system, there was no need for specific plans for development in poor regions. A consensus emerged among imperial state policymakers and capitalist class elites on the advantages of Third World development. A tactical debate raged between New Deal liberals such as Henry Wallace and corporate elites such as Will Clayton over the need for international New Deal institutions and programs for social and economic reform in the world-system. By 1944 the power of the corporate sector in the imperial state bureau-cracy had overwhelmed Wallace and his allies. The capitalist class-imperial state axis agreed on the ways to achieve development in the periphery--through free world trade, an international open door, and the free flow of technology, capital, and knowledge.

NOTES

1. U.S. Department of State, _Foreign Relations of the United States, 1941_, vol. 1, p. 368 (hereafter _FRUS_, followed by appropriate year and volume); Alfred Eckes, _A Search for Solvency: Bretton Woods and the International Monetary System, 1841-1971_ (Austin: University of Texas Press, 1975), pp. 38-50; Robert Asher, Walter M. Kotschnig, and William A. Brown, Jr., _The United Nations and Economic and Social Co-Operation_ (Washington, D.C.: The Brookings Institution, 1957), p. 35.

2. David W. Eakins, "Business Planners and America's Postwar Expansion," in David Horowitz, ed., _Corporations and the Cold War_ (New York: Monthly Review Press, 1969), p. 143.

3. "An American Proposal," _Fortune_ 25 (May 1942): 61; "_Fortune_ Management Poll," _Fortune_ 29 (May 1944): 28; V. L. Horoth, "New Trends for Trade after the War," _The Magazine for Wall Street_ 70 (25 July 1942): 373-74, 414; Editorial, "The British Empire and the United States," _Fortune_ 29 (January 1944): 94-95; Eugene Staley, _World Economic Development: Effects on Advanced Industrial Countries_ (Montreal: ILO Studies and Reports, Series B, No. 36, 1944), pp. 17-19. Also see Mortiz J. Bonn, "Constructive Imperialism in a New World," _Trusts and Estates_ 74 (February 1942): 129-31; _What Peace Will Bring_ (Farrel-Birmingham Company, 1941).

4. Brownless Haydon to Louis Bean, 19 May 1944, Subject File 1923-53, Industrialization, Louis Bean Papers, FDR Library, Hyde Park, New York; George E. Anderson, "International Pump Priming," _Banking_ 32 (August 1939): 20-21; Marcus Nadler, "Postwar International Economic Position of the

United States," Annals of American Academy 228 (July 1943):
97;   "Sees U.S. Postwar Foreign Aid Comprising Direct
Investments," The Commercial and Financial Chronicle, 21
October 1943, p. 1595;   James Petras and Morris Morley, "The
U.S. Imperial State," in Petras, Class, State, and Power in
the Third World: With Case Studies on Class Conflict in Latin
America (Montclair, N.J.:   Allanheld, Osmun & Publishers,
1981), p. 18.   Also see comments by executives of General
Motors Company in Fortune 30 (December 1944): 117;   the
article, "The China Trade," Fortune 23 (May 1941): 69-73, 117-
20; and the supplement to Fortune 25 (May 1942), The U.S. in a
New World: I. Relations with Britain, p. 16. For a different
opinion on investment in underdeveloped countries, see Eliot
Janeway, "U.S. Foreign Policy Must Make Friends Where the U.S.
Economy Will Need Them," Fortune 29 (March 1944): 79, 84, 88.

5. Gallagher defined America's high living standard as
free schools, a free press, three meals a day, automobiles,
refrigerators, electric irons, radios, vitamins, and calories.
Speech is enclosed in letter from A. G. Newmyer to Stephen
Early, Secretary to the President, 8 December 1943, Official
File 394, FDR Papers, FDR Library, Hyde Park, New York.

6. George H. Houston speech, "Postwar Exportation of
Capital Goods to Non-Industrialized Areas of the World,"
Subject File 1923-53, Industrialization, Bean Papers.

7. V. L. Horoth, "Increasing Tempo of World
Industrialization," The Magazine of Wall Street, 8 July 1944,
p. 336; Haydon to Bean, 19 May 1944, Bean Papers; Houston
speech, "Postwar Exportation," Bean Papers.

8. Horoth, "Increasing Tempo," p. 336.

9. "An American Proposal," Fortune 25 (May 1942): 63;
"The China Trade," Fortune 23 (May 1941): 120.

10. "After the War...What Then?," American Federationist
48 (March 1941): 9-11; "Labor in the Postwar World," American
Federationist 49 (December 1942): 14-16; "American Labor in
World Affairs," American Federationist 50 (July 1943): 9-12;
American Federation of Labor (hereafter AFL), Report of the
Executive Council, 62nd Annual Convention, 1942 (Washington,
D.C.: 1942), pp. 206-9; AFL, Report of Executive Council,
64th Annual Convention, 1944 (Washington, D.C.: 1944), pp.
157-60; "Safeguards Against Oppressive Labor Conditions in
Backward Countries," 4 February 1944, Folder: American Labor
Conference on International Affairs, General Files of the
Economist of the AFL, American Federation of Labor Papers,
State Historical Society of Wisconsin, Madison, Wisconsin.
For general background on the relationship between labor and
foreign relations see Ronald Radosh, American Labor and United
States Foreign Policy (New York: Random House, 1969); and
Jeffrey Harrod, Trade Union Foreign Policy: A Study of
British and American Trade Union Activities in Jamaica (Garden
City, New York: Doubleday, 1972).

11. Robert M. Collins, "American Corporatism: The
Committee for Economic Development, 1942-1964," The Historian
44 (February 1982): 153-55, 165, 172-73; Eakins, "Business

Planners," pp. 145-46.

12. Frederick J. Dobney, ed., Selected Papers of Will Clayton (Baltimore: The Johns Hopkins Press, 1971), pp. 71-73, 78-79; Committee for Economic Development (hereafter CED), Research Committee, International Trade, Foreign Investment and Domestic Employment (New York: CED, June 1945), pp. 10-11 (emphasis in original).

13. Dobney, ed., Selected Papers of Will Clayton, p. 98.

14. CED, International Trade, pp. 5-6, 13; Eakins, "Business Planners," pp. 151-52. Also see Calvin B. Hoover, "American Foreign Trade and Investment," in Arnold Zurcher and R. Page, eds., Postwar Goals and Economic Reconstruction (New York: Institute on Postwar Reconstruction, New York University, 1944), pp. 285-89, 292-94.

15. CED, Research Committee, The Bretton Woods Proposals (New York: CED, April 1945).

16. Dobney, ed., Selected Papers of Will Clayton, pp. 99-101.

17. Laurence H. Shoup and William Minter, Imperial Brain Trust: The Council on Foreign Relations and United States Foreign Policy (New York: Monthly Review Press, 1977), pp. 118-19, 148-61; Joseph C. Green to Cordell Hull, 14 April 1944, Subject File: Postwar Planning-General 1944-46, Cordell Hull Papers, Manuscript Division, Library of Congress, Washington, D.C.; Harley Notter, Postwar Foreign Policy Preparation, 1939-1945 (Washington, D.C.: U.S. Government Printing Office, 1949), pp. 19, 56, 80 note, 82-83, 131, 152.

18. William Diebold, Jr., "Economic War Aims: General Considerations; The Position as of 1 April 1941," Studies of American Interests in the War and the Peace (CFR, No. E-B32, Economic and Financial Group), pp. 13-15; W. Diebold and Eugene Staley, "The Economic Organization of Peace in the Far East," War and Peace Studies (CFR, No. E-B33, Economic and Financial Group, 20 June 1941); Eckes, Search for Solvency, p. 37.

19. "Tentative Draft of a Joint Economic Declaration by the Governments of the United States and the United Kingdom," War and Peace Studies (CFR, No. E-B45, Economic and Financial Group, 3 January 1942).

20. Alvin H. Hansen, "International Adjustment of Exchange Rates," War and Peace Studies (CFR, No. E-B64, 6 April 1943); Alvin Hansen, After the War--Full Employment (National Resources Planning Board, 1943), pp. 1-2, 21-23; Shoup and Minter, Imperial Brain Trust, pp. 120-21; Eakins, "Business Planners," pp. 149-50.

21. Alvin Hansen, "International Adjustment"; "International Development and Investment Bank," War and Peace Studies (CFR, 8 January 1944); "Underdeveloped Countries and Exchange Controls," War and Peace Studies (CFR, No. E-B72, 29 July 1944).

22. Eugene Staley, World Economy in Transition: Technology vs. Politics; Laissez-Faire vs. Planning; Power vs. Welfare (New York: Council on Foreign Relations, 1939);   E. Staley, "The Economic Origins of Peace," Preliminary Report and Monographs (New York: Commission to Study the Organization of the Peace, 1942);   E. Staley, World Economic Development.

23. Staley, World Economic Development, pp. 5-6.

24. The other conditions included free access to the world's markets and goods through peaceful exchange and economic stability.   Staley, "Economic Origins of Peace," p. 185. Also see J. B. Condliffe, Agenda for a Postwar World (New York: W. W. Norton, 1942), p. 171; R. B. Bryce, "International Aspects of an Investment Program," in S. Harris, ed., Postwar Economic Problems (New York: McGraw-Hill, 1943), p. 364;   P. N. Rosenstein Rodan, "The International Development of Economically Backward Areas," International Affairs 20 (April 1944): 157-59;   Commission to Study the Organization of the Peace, Fourth Report: Part II, The Economic Organization of Welfare (New York: Commission to Study the Organization of the Peace, November 1943), pp. 12-13.

25. Staley, World Economic Development, pp. 21-24; Staley, "Economic Origins of Peace," p. 192. For similar views see James B. Reston, Prelude to Victory (New York: Alfred A. Knopf, 1942), p. 193; Raymond Clapper, Watching the World (New York: McGraw-Hill, 1944), p. 320;   National Planning Association, International Development Loans (NPA, Planning Pamphlets No. 15, 1942), p. 37;   National Planning Association, "The Stakes of Bretton Woods," 23 April 1945, Special Subjects: Bretton Woods, Washington File, 1942-45, Unit IX, Bernard Baruch Papers, Seeley G. Mudd Manuscript Library, Princeton University, Princeton, N.J.;   Colin Clark, The Economics of 1960 (London: Macmillan, 1942), pp. 107-13.

26. Staley, World Economic Development, pp. 28-30, 21-23. For a different interpretation, see H. Frankel, "Industrialization of Agricultural Countries and the Possibilities for a New International Division of Labour," The Economic Journal 53 (June-September 1943): 188-96; K. Mandelbaum, The Industrialization of Backward Areas (Oxford: Basil Blackwell, 1945), pp. 16-18.

27. Staley, World Economic Development, pp. 25-26; Staley, World Economy in Transition, p. 285;   Staley, "Economic Origins of Peace," pp. 193-204. For more on technical aid, see Condliffe, Agenda, pp. 181-82;   Commission to Study the Organization of the Peace, Fourth Report, pp. 12-13; Herman Finer, The TVA Lessons for International Application (Montreal: ILO Studies, Series B, no. 37, 1944), pp. 216-30.

28. Staley, World Economic Development, pp. 5-6, 24-26. For similar views, see Economic Stability in the Postwar World: The Conditions of Prosperity After the Transition from War to Peace, Part II of the Report of the Delegation on Economic Depression (Geneva: League of Nations Publication, 1945.A.2), pp. 291-92, 302-3, 310-16;   Rosenstein Rodan,

"International Development," p. 161; National Planning Association, International Development Loans, p. 33; Bryce, "International Aspects," p. 365; Clark, Economics of 1960, p. 113; Mandelbaum, Industrialization, p. 19.

29. Staley, World Economic Development, pp. 84-91. Also see NPA, International Development Loans, pp. 34-36; Frankel, "Industrialization of Agricultural Countries," p. 196; Bryce, "International Aspects," p. 368; Finer, TVA Lessons; J.B. Condliffe and A. Stevenson, The Common Interest in International Economic Organization (Montreal: ILO Studies, Series B, no. 39, 1944).

30. "World Industrialization and International Trade," War and Peace Studies (CFR, No. E-B75, Economic and Financial Group, 18 November 1944).

31. See reviews by John Donaldson, Michael Heilperin, E. Beder, and Hans Neisser in, respectively, Annals of the American Academy 236 (November 1944): 199-200; The Political Science Review 39 (February 1945): 189-91; The Canadian Forum 24 (August 1944): 116-17; Social Research 11 (September 1944): 372-75.

32. Henry A. Wallace, Democracy Reborn, ed. Russell Lord (London: Hammond, Hammond & Co., 1944), p. 36; Henry A. Wallace, The Price of Vision: The Diary of Henry A. Wallace, 1942-46, ed. John M. Blum (Boston: Houghton Mifflin, 1973), p. 85; H. A. Wallace to Guy Irving Burch, 13 July 1942, Correspondence: Bun-Bur, Henry A. Wallace Papers as Vice President, FDR Library, Hyde Park, N.Y.; H. A. Wallace, Sixty Million Jobs (New York: Simon & Schuster, 1945), p. 132; Edward L. Schapsmeier and Frederick H. Schapsmeier, Prophet in Politics: Henry A. Wallace and the War Years, 1940-1965 (Ames: The Iowa State University Press, 1970), pp. 129, 24-98.

33. Wallace, Democracy Reborn, pp. 169, 214-17.

34. Schapsmeier and Schapsmeier, Prophet in Politics, pp. 38-41, 44-49; Wallace, Price of Vision, pp. 53-54; Norman D. Markowitz, The Rise and Fall of the People's Century: Henry A. Wallace and American Liberalism, 1941-1948 (New York: The Free Press, 1973), p. 69.

35. Board of Economic Warfare memorandum, "Postwar International Reconstruction," (n.d., probably written in April 1942), Entry 212, Box 117, Folder: Postwar Planning, Economic Program-Foreign Development Staff, Foreign Economic Administration, RG 169, U.S. National Archives, Washington, D.C.; Wallace, Price of Vision, pp. 53-54, 68-69 note 2, 57, 169.

36. Dean Acheson, Present at the Creation: My Years in the State Department (New York: W. W. Norton, 1969). p. 39.

37. Ibid., pp. 39-47; Wallace, Price of Vision, pp. 66, 219-29; Schapsmeier and Schapsmeier, Prophet in Politics, pp. 50-71; Markowitz, The Rise and Fall, pp. 66-73.

38. Jesse Jones, "Post-War Problems," Foreign Commerce Weekly, 16 October 1943, pp. 3-4; Wallace, Price of Vision, pp. 158-59, 68-69 note 2; Markowitz, The Rise and Fall, p. 70; Dobney, ed. Selected Papers of Will Clayton, pp. 62-67.

39. Markowitz, The Rise and Fall, p. 55.

40. Ibid., p. 52.

41. Emily S. Rosenberg, Spreading the American Dream: American Economic and Cultural Expansion, 1890-1945 (New York: Hill and Wang, 1982), pp. 206-9; Claude C. Erb, "Prelude to Point Four: The Institute of Inter-American Affairs," Diplomatic History 9 (Summer 1985): 249-54, 266;   Eakins, "Business Planners," p. 151 note.

42. James E. Underwood and William J. Daniels, Governor Rockefeller in New York: The Apex of Pragmatic Liberalism in the United States (Westport, Conn.: Greenwood Press, 1982), pp. 10-12.

43. Erb, "Prelude to Point Four," pp. 266-67.

44. Ibid., p. 252.

45. E. Richard Brown, "Rockefeller Medicine in China: Professionalism and Imperialism," in Robert F. Arnove, ed., Philanthropy and Cultural Imperialism: The Foundations at Home and Abroad (Bloomington: Indiana University Press, 1982), p. 138.

46. Ibid., pp. 138-40; E. Richard Brown, "Public Health Imperialism: Early Rockefeller Programs at Home and Abroad," American Journal of Public Health 66 (1976): 897-903.

47. Erb, "Prelude to Point Four," pp. 249-69.

48. "Brief Outline of Economic Problems of Peace," 17 December 1941, Records of Economic Committees: Committee on Postwar Foreign Economic Policy, Harley Notter Records 1939-1945, RG 59, U.S. National Archives, Washington, D.C.; Department of State (hereafter DOS), Bulletin (7 March 1942): 211; DOS, Bulletin (1 May 1943): 380; A. A. Berle, "The Uses of Victory," 19 September 1942, State Department, Subject File 1938-45, Postwar Plans, A. A. Berle Papers, FDR Library, Hyde Park, N.Y.; "Implications of a Program of Foreign Invest-ment," 10 May 1943, Economic Document E-151, Records of the Advisory Committee on Postwar Foreign Policy, Notter Records, RG 59;   Beatrice B. Berle and T. B. Jacobs, eds., Navigating the Rapids, 1918-1971: From the Papers of Adolf A. Berle (New York: Harcourt Brace Jovanovich, 1973), pp. xvii-xiv.

49. Philip H. Burch, Jr., Elites in American History: The New Deal to the Carter Administration (New York: Holmes & Meier Publishers, 1980), pp. 102-3, 82; Mark L. Chadwin, The Hawks of World War II (Chapel Hill: The University of North Carolina Press, 1968), pp. 58-59; Acheson, Present at the Creation, pp. 65-79; Lloyd C. Gardner, Economic Aspects of New Deal Diplomacy (Boston: Beacon Press, 1971), p. 281.

50. "Proposal for an International Investment Agency," 28 September 1943, Economic Document E-175a, Records of Advisory Committee, Notter Records, RG 59; Memorandum from Under Secretary to President, 21 February 1944 and memo from President to Secretary of State, 26 February 1944, PSF Subject: Post War, FDR Papers.

51. Notter, <u>Postwar Foreign Policy Preparation</u>, pp. 138-39, 218-19; ECEFP D-57/44, 23 September 1944, "Recommendations Regarding the Policy of the US Government with Respect to Economic Developments in the Other American Republics," 5.19B ECEFP Meetings 3.Documents, RG 353, U.S. National Archives, Washington, D.C.

52. Bernard Baruch warned against any American "attempt to raise world standards of living by lowering her own." Glenn Neville to B. Baruch, 2 July 1943, Unit IX, Washington File 1942-45, Special Subjects: Peace, B. Baruch Papers.

53. Memorandum, Director of Bureau of Budget to President, 12 March 1943, OF 5300 Living Standards Abroad, FDR Papers.

54. Acheson, <u>Present at the Creation</u>, p. 44; <u>Current Biography, 1943</u> (New York: H. W. Wilson, 1943), pp. 710-13; Paul H. Appleby, "Harold D. Smith--Public Administrator," <u>Public Administration Review</u> 7 (Spring 1947): 77-81; Markowitz, <u>The Rise and Fall</u>, pp. 66-67; Wallace, <u>Price of Vision</u>, p. 57 note 3.

55. FDR to Cordell Hull, 9 April 1943, OF 5300 Living Standards Abroad, FDR Papers. Also see Roosevelt's initial response to Smith's memo, FDR to Smith, 13 March 1943, OF 5300 Living Standards Abroad, FDR Papers.

56. FDR to Hull, 9 April 1943, OF 5300 Living Standards Abroad, FDR Papers; Wallace, <u>Price of Vision</u>, pp. 100 note 1, 136; Memorandum, Cordell Hull to FDR, 22 November 1943, OF 5300 Living Standards Abroad, FDR Papers. Oscar B. Ryder, chairman of the Tariff Commission, William H. English, Director of the Statistics and Economic Investigations of the FTC, and John F. Wharton, Chairman of the BEW's War Trade Staff, served on the Hull committee.

57. Hull to FDR, 22 November 1943, OF 5300 Living Standards Abroad, FDR Papers.

58. Digest of report in memorandum, S. I. Rosenman to FDR, 14 January 1944, OF 5300 Living Standards Abroad, FDR Papers. The full report can be found in Louis Bean memorandum to Director of Budget Bureau, 3 January 1944, Subject File 1923-53, State Department, Bean Papers, FDR Library.

59. Bean memorandum to Director of Budget Bureau, 3 January 1944, Subject File 1923-53, State Department, Bean Papers.

60. Memorandum, Rosenman to FDR, 14 January 1944, OF 5300 Living Standards Abroad, FDR Papers.

61. Current Biography, 1948, (New York: H. W. Wilson 1949), pp. 38-40;   Wallace, Price of Vision, pp. 11, 16, 101 note 1, 326; Markowitz, The Rise and Fall, pp. 104, 141, 335; Schapsmeier and Schapsmeier, Prophet in Politics, pp. 129, 184; Memorandum, Bean to Loeffler, 28 July 1943;   memo, Bean to Loeffler, 3 September 1943, International Full Employment, Subject File 1923-53, Bean Papers; Louis Bean, "International Industrialization and Per Capita Income," Studies in Income and Wealth, vol. 8 (New York: National Bureau of Economic Research, 1946); pp. 121-22, 141, 143.

62. H. Hawkins to Bean, 24 June 1944, Subject File 1923-53, State Department, Bean Papers.

63. "Memo in reply to President's letter of April 9 on Foreign Investment," Bean to Budget Director, 3 January 1944, Subject File 1923-53, State Department, Bean Papers.

64. Louis Bean memorandum, undated (probably early 1944), Subject File 1923-53, State Department, Bean Papers.

65. William Roger Louis, Imperialism at Bay: The United States and the Decolonization of the British Empire, 1941-1945 (New York: Oxford University Press, 1978), pp. 99-100, 402.

66. Ian M. Drummond, Imperial Economic Policy, 1917-1939: Studies in Expansion and Production (London: George Allen & Unwin, 1974), p. 33; A. J. Brown, Industrialization and Trade: The Changing World Pattern and the Position of Britain (London: Royal Institute of International Affairs, 1943), p. 36.

67. Partha Sarathi Gupta, Imperialism and the British Labour Movement, 1914-1964 (London: Macmillan Press, 1975), pp. 244-45; D. A. Low, Lion Rampant: Essays in the Study of British Imperialism (London: Frank Cass, 1973), p. 70; Nicholas Mansergh, ed., Documents and Speeches on British Commonwealth Affairs, 1931-1952, vol. 2, (London: Oxford University Press, 1953), p. 1074;   Margery Perham, Colonial Sequence, 1930 to 1949:   A Chronological Commentary Upon British Colonial Policy (London: Methuen, 1967), pp. 189, 192; Louis, Imperialism at Bay, pp. 104-105.

68. Perham, Colonial Sequence, pp. 228-29; Mansergh, Documents, pp. 1079-82.

69. Sir Richard Clarke, Anglo-American Economic Collaboration in War and Peace: 1942-1949, ed. Sir Alec Cairncross, (Oxford: Clarendon Press, 1982), pp. 98-99, 109-111.

70. Ibid., p. 111.

71. Ibid., pp. 112, 122-24, 98-99.

72. Asher et al., The United Nations, p. 35;   FRUS, 1942, 1: 749; FRUS, 1943, 4: 248-54.

73. Margaret Stewart, Britain and the ILO: The Story of Fifty Years (London: Her Majesty's Stationary Office, 1969), pp. 60-62. For background information on the ILO's reports on

the Third World, see ILO Studies and Reports, Series B (Social and Economic Conditions), Report no. 25, Social Aspects of Present and Future Economic Development in Brazil (1937); no. 26, Labour Conditions in Indo-China (1938); and no. 29, Problems of Industrialization in the East (1938). Also see Antony Alcock, History of the International Labour Organization (London: Macmillan, 1971), pp. 134, 139-40, 142-44.

74. International Labour Organization Conference, 26th Session, Record of Proceedings, Philadelphia, 1944 (Montreal: ILO, 1944), pp. 30-31. Henry Wallace believed that the Australians and New Zealanders were some of the most advanced thinkers on postwar employment issues. H. A. Wallace to FDR, 1 December 1944, Correspondence, FDR, Wallace Papers.

75. ILO Conference, pp. 72-75; Robert Paul Millon, Mexican Marxist: Vicente Lombardo Toledano (Chapel Hill: University of North Carolina Press, 1966), pp. 94, 96-97; Harvey A. Levenstein, Labor Organizations in the United States and Mexico: A History of Their Relations (Westport, Conn.: Greenwood Press, 1971), pp. 146-47.

76. ILO Conference, pp. 74-75, 88, 102, 104, 111-33, xv.

77. Eckes, Search for Solvency, pp. ix-x, 241.

78. E. Goldenweiser memorandum, "Issues at Bretton Woods," 29 July 1944, Subject File: International Negotiations--Bretton Woods folder, Emanuel Goldenweiser Papers, Manuscript Division, Library of Congress, Washington, D.C.; Department of State, Proceedings and Documents of United Nations Monetary and Financial Conference, vol. 1, (Washington, D.C.: U.S. Government Printing Office, 1948), pp. 127-28, 186-87, 426.

79. Eckes, Search for Solvency, pp. 91-93; Goldenweiser memo, "Issues at Bretton Woods."

80. Eckes, Search for Solvency, pp. 52-53, 154-59, 90-91.

81. DOS, Proceedings and Documents, vol. 1, pp. 485, 1016; Acheson, Present at the Creation, p. 84.

82. Goldenweiser memo, "Issues at Bretton Woods," and speech, "Bretton Woods Conference," 31 July 1944, in Subject File: International Negotiations--Bretton Woods folder, Goldenweiser Papers; DOS, Proceedings and Documents, vol. 2, pp. 1180-81.

83. David Green, The Containment of Latin America: A history of the myths and realities of the Good Neighbor Policy (Chicago: Quadrangle Books, 1971), pp. 170-71, 187; T. M. Campbell and G. C. Herring, eds., The Diaries of Edward R. Stettinius, Jr., 1943-1946 (New York: New Viewpoints, 1975), pp. 260-62.

84. Green, Containment of Latin America, pp. 174-76, 201, 207; Diaries of Stettinius, pp. 277-78; Dobney, Selected Papers of Will Clayton, pp. 111-121.

85. FRUS, 1945, 9: 148;   Green, Containment of Latin America, pp. 188-201, 207;   Samuel L. Baily, The United States and the Development of South America, 1945-1975 (New York: New Viewpoints, 1976), pp. 40-48;   Stephen G. Rabe, "The Elusive Conference: United States Economic Relations with Latin America, 1945-1952," Diplomatic History 2 (Summer 1978): 280-82.

86. FRUS, 1945, 9: 138;   Green, Containment of Latin America, pp. 198-99, 207.

87. F. McDougall to L. Pasvolsky, 28 January 1945, Department of State Decimal Files 800.50/1-2845, Record Group 59; Shoup and Minter, Imperial Brain Trust, p. 124.

88. Walter Sharp, The United Nations Economic and Social Council (New York: Columbia University Press, 1969), pp. 3-4; Documents of the UN Conference on International Organization, San Francisco, vol. 2, (New York: UN, 1945), pp. 450-51.   The concept of a special world body to deal with socioeconomic problems of poor nations originated in the 1930s. See Report of Special Committee to League of Nations, The Development of International Co-Operation in Economic and Social Affairs (Geneva: League of Nations Publication, A.23.1939); and L. K. Hyde, The United States and the United Nations: Promoting the Public Welfare--Examples of American Co-operation, 1945-55 (New York: Carnegie Endowment for International Peace, Manhattan Publishing, 1960), pp. 30-31.

89. Hyde, The United States and the United Nations, p. 87.

90. H. Mendershausen, "The Pattern of Overseas Economic Development in WW II: Its Significance for the Present," Economia Internazionale 4 (August 1951): 745-46; Asher et al., The United Nations, pp. 53-54.

91. Mendershausen, "Pattern of Overseas," pp. 745-46; Albert O. Hirschman, "Industrial Nations and Industrialization of Underdeveloped Countries," Economia Internazionale 4 (August 1951): 608.

92. Hirschman, "Industrial Nations," pp. 609-11; Albert O. Hirschman, "The Rise and Decline of Development Economics," in M. Gersovitz et al., eds., The Theory and Experience of Economic Development: Essays in Honor of Sir W. Arthur Lewis (London: George Allen & Unwin, 1982), pp. 373-74.

2
Reconstruction versus Development: 1946-1949

The Wilsonian vision of an American designed and dominated
world order appeared within reach in 1945. Standing atop the
global economic hierarchy, the United States controlled almost
two-thirds of all monetary gold, produced about 50 percent of
the world's gross domestic product, and possessed an industrial base untouched by wartime destruction. These conditions
supported the conviction held by the imperial state and
capitalist class that the United States could achieve global
integration and thus ensure prosperity and peace for other
core states and the periphery.(1)

Government planners understood the difficulty of internationalizing America's political economy. During the late
1940s imperial state policymakers developed three approaches
toward world economic integration. One approach stressed the
possibility of integrating contiguous areas like Western
Europe, Latin America, or the Middle East into regional
customs unions or free trade areas. Another plan envisioned
major industrial centers becoming poles of development around
which semiperipheral and peripheral areas would assemble.
Africa and the Middle East, for example, would be drawn to
Europe, Southeast Asia and China to Japan, and Latin America
and Canada to the United States. The last approach involved
the integration of all world markets--the advancement of
transnationalism and world capitalism. These plans were not
mutually exclusive and many policymakers believed in a natural
progression from regional, to polar, to global integration.
European and Asian reconstruction constituted an essential
element in all these schemes.(2)

American officials saw little need for special economic
programs to assist the poor, agrarian regions of the world.
Third World development would follow naturally from the
reconstruction of Europe and Japan and from the attainment of
free world trade and global specialization. At the same time,
the development of the underdeveloped countries would help
accelerate the recovery of war-torn areas by providing markets
and sources of raw materials.

American policymakers' view of economic development
clashed with the perceived needs and aspirations of various
classes in the Third World. Irreconcilable conflicts developed between the periphery's working classes and peasantry, on
the one hand, and America's imperial state and capitalist

class on the other.   The fundamental changes in national and international socioeconomic and political systems necessary to aid the Third World poor were incompatible with the operation of the capitalist world-economy.   Narrowing the gap between the rich and poor of the world-economy meant eliminating the cheap labor that helped perpetuate the global division of labor.   American state and capitalist class leaders recognized the incompatibility of their interests and those of the peasants and workers of the periphery.   U.S. development policies and programs aimed at winning the hearts and minds of the periphery's upper and middle classes; at bridging the interests between ruling classes.   Leaders of working class and peasant movements in the periphery gradually came to understand this situation.(3)

Traditional ruling classes and a nascent bourgeoisie in the periphery and semiperiphery shared the core's basic commitment to capitalism. At the same time they questioned the American argument that their development depended primarily upon core recovery and the revival of multilateralism.   They accused core nations of neglecting the special problems of poor countries. American leaders responded that Third World nations made unreasonable demands.   The periphery sought industrialization by some "quick and easy route"; wanted large loans with no strings attached; and avoided reforming archaic internal social and economic systems.(4)   These differences reflected a clash over tactics, not goals. Third World elites were committed to capitalism and capitalist development with some modifications. Thus the conflict between these groups and the United States was open to negotiation.

The "negotiable" conflict between the United States and the Third World found an important arena in the UN Economic and Social Council (ECOSOC). Discussions on the creation of regional economic commissions and an international trade organization, on the activities of the World Bank, and the formulation of a technical assistance program, all provided forums for development issues.   This chapter examines how American officials conceived of reconstruction and development as two sides of the same coin and how ruling classes in the Third World accepted the theory, but questioned the practice of American foreign economic policy.   Chapter three explores the crucial issues of development financing and technical assistance.

These chapters illustrate that both American leaders and the majority of rulers in the periphery and semiperiphery viewed Third World development as a function of internal deficiencies being remedied by external forces. For American imperial state and corporate elites the basic problems of poor, agrarian nations were similar to the problems faced by the United States and other industrialized capitalist nations in their premodern eras. Liberal economic policies and institutions could deal as effectively with the Third World as they had with advanced capitalist states.   The existing international system that rewarded core states could benefit the periphery.

Representatives of Third World collaborating classes challenged the proposition that their nations occupied the same position on the development continuum that had been held by the United States or Britain or Germany in an earlier era. At various international forums these officials contended that the problems of the Third World were different from those of

the core states. They suggested that certain modifications in
the existing world system could shape economic relations
between the core and periphery in such a way as to benefit
both sets of nations. They sought their fair share of capital
and technology in an international capitalist system that, by
definition, was unequal and unfair. The Third World was in
the dubious position of a slave depending on the kindness of
the master for freedom. During the 1940s, the voices of the
noncollaborating classes in the Third World who understood
these contradictions were often muted, usually ignored, and
always dismissed as Communists.

RECONSTRUCTION AND DEVELOPMENT: THE NEW WORLD ORDER

Speaking before a group of New York City bankers in May
1950, Francis H. Russell, the director of the State Department's Office of Public Affairs, described America's "over-all
design" for a new international order. Developed between 1945
and 1950, this hegemonic design consisted of three parts.
Reconstructing Europe took priority because "a healthy and
self-supporting Europe" underlaid global prosperity and peace.
Second, while developing the periphery would satisfy humanitarian and political motives, "the overriding and compelling
reason for drawing these nonproducing areas and peoples into
our design is that we cannot create a thriving and expanding
world economy without them." Finally, the attainment of
political stability, military security and peaceful resolution
of international disputes would create the confidence required
to stimulate world trade.(5) Although accurately describing
U.S. foreign policy, Russell's speech neither explained nor
analyzed how policymakers conceived of the interaction of the
three parts.
From the end of the Second World War until early 1947,
American policymakers viewed the reconstruction of war-devastated industrial areas and the development of underdeveloped
regions as functions of revived international trade, currency
convertibility, and the injection of private foreign capital.
Some immediate relief assistance was necessary, but trade and
private investment constituted the chief solution to destruction, dislocation, and underdevelopment. During this period
imperial state policymakers such as Will Clayton advocated
America's "liberal" capitalist scheme for integration.
Clayton--who dominated State Department thought on economic
matters from 1944 through 1947--and others considered free
trade and comparative advantage as the ways to ensure perfect
competition and the efficient play of market forces. The
objective of integration was the buying and selling of goods
and services in the marketplace. Independent private entrepreneurs comprised the subjects of integration and the arena
of activity was the world. Although this liberal corporate
framework emphasized private enterprise and free trade,
policymakers obviously envisioned an important role for the
state, including removing all obstacles to world capitalist
expansion--whether economic, political, or military; internal
or external. The state also had to eliminate protectionism,
trade restrictions and discriminations, and to ensure the
proper working of comparative advantage, specialization, and
the international division of labor.(6)

By early 1947, however, Clayton and other officials realized the difficulty of immediately achieving an expanded and
liberalized world trading system.   In his analysis of the
postwar international economy, Alfred Eckes concluded that the
convergence of three forces in 1947--political disorders,
European economic exhaustion, and the depletion of the British
loan--compelled the Truman administration to adjust its global
priorities. European rehabilitation and integration now took
precedent over the effort to reconstruct the world economy
along multilateral lines. In other words, the Marshall Plan
brought a "reorientation of American priorities," replacing
"universalism and convertibility" with "regionalism and
gradualism."(7)

Eckes' analysis explains how government officials came to
acknowledge world trade revival, not so much as the stimulus
for European recovery, but as the result of such recovery.
This, however, reveals only a tactical change, not a shift in
goals.   Global integration remained the ultimate objective--
although for obvious reasons American leaders omitted the
Soviet Union from the global context. International free
trade and currency convertibility were necessary, but not sufficient conditions for European recovery. Europe required
massive doses of economic aid from the United States. American leaders did not abandon their global plans--they merely
took a new road to achieve them.

Regionalism was not necessarily antithetical to global-
ism.   With regard to collective security, for example, regionalism became integrated into universalism.   American
policymakers sought regional collective security arrangements
under the supervision of the UN.(8) The United States opposed
political or economic regionalism when it took the form of
separate spheres of influence and conflicting blocs under
great power domination. Bad regional alignments such as the
British Ottawa Preference System, Japan's Co-Prosperity
Sphere, Nazi Germany's autarky in Central Europe, and the
Soviet state trading system, closed certain markets to the
United States. These systems did not contribute to international capitalist productivity and an expanding world marketplace. According to American policymakers, good regionalism
demanded interdependence between regions rather than self-
sufficiency in each area. A good regional organization would
increase productivity, specialization, income, and foreign
trade in the member countries and thus advance world economic
growth.(9) Will Clayton embraced this analysis and carefully
elaborated it among America's imperial state and corporate
elite.

Will Clayton described himself as a "liberal capitalist."
He shared a Wilsonian conviction that the United States "differed from all other nations in the purity and benevolence of
its motivations and goals." American exceptionalism made the
United States a rightful heir to the throne of hegemony; the
United States was uniquely suited to lead all nations to a
rational world order based on the American capitalist system.
Clayton's understanding of the world-economy derived from his
success as the founder and head of a multinational cotton exporting firm.   Anderson, Clayton and Company possessed cotton
oil mills and cotton gins throughout the world, including in
Latin America and the Middle East. By 1944, the company had
annual sales of $272 million. Clayton brought his cosmopoli-
tan understanding of the workings of the capitalist world-

economy to his service in the Export-Import Bank, the Commerce Department, the CFR and CED, and, finally, the State Department in 1944.(10)

Clayton favored the integration of the world-economy--the easy and free movement of money, goods, and services from one country to another. Confident in "functional relationships" among nations--relationships involving trade and finance-- Clayton sought an open and interdependent world economy. Closed regional blocs obviously hindered the attainment of this goal. The influencial Committee for Economic Development, on which Clayton served, noted that "every regional arrangement is, by its very nature, discriminatory against outsiders." In explaining the need for an American loan to Great Britain in 1946, Clayton warned that without the loan Britain would expand its Imperial Preference System, thus percipitating a fall in world trade, a curtailment in production and consumption, and a decline in living standards. "Under such a system, economic power, in time, becomes linked to political power, and economic blocs become political blocs, to disturb the peace of the world."(11)

Clayton's dislike for closed regional blocs and bilateral trade did not mean that he opposed all regional associations. While emphasizing free trade, the former cotton magnate understood that the particular problem of European reconstruction "would [not] magically go away." Once again Clayton's colleagues in the CED explained that where "insurmountable obstacles" to multilateral trade existed, "regional arrangements may sometimes achieve a higher degree of international specialization and increase productive efficiency by broadening the markets to which producers have ready access." Recognizing that Europe needed immediate aid for recovery and that the world's adoption of liberal trade policies rested on reconstruction, Clayton advocated UN assistance to war-devastated nations, a large loan to Britain, and the Marshall Plan for Europe. The latter would stimulate West European economic recovery and integration.(12)

European economic integration and eventual political unity, however, were not ends in themselves. Clayton held that the Marshall Plan prepared the way for the economic integration of Europe with other regions. The UN's Economic Commission for Europe, according to Clayton, complemented the proposed International Trade Organization. While the former dealt with urgent problems of regional reconstruction, the latter would deal with the "broad pattern of international trade relations" and the expansion of the world-economy. Emphasis on Europe's financial difficulties, asserted Clayton in September 1947, did not mean postponing America's trade program. As interdependent agencies, the International Trade Organization and the Economic Cooperation Administration were parts of a common policy, and neither could be totally successful without the other.(13)

While Clayton and other policymakers advocated special programs for European recovery and integration, they dismissed similar schemes for the development of the Third World. This policy reflected a conviction that European reconstruction and capitalist integration would lead to, and benefit from, peripheral development.

THE DOLLAR GAP

American planners attributed Europe's economic crisis, in part, to the loss of markets and intense competition from the United States. This trade disequilibrium manifested itself in the form of a dollar gap--that is, a lack of dollars in the world market. European, Asian, Middle Eastern, and African nations received insufficient amounts of dollars to purchase the American goods and services that they required for reconstruction and development. The dollar gap resulted from the United States' tendency to over-export and under-import, and the rest of the world's tendency to under-export and over-import. The ultimate solution, according American leaders, was the return of multilateral trade and the end of controls on currency exchange. Something had to be done in the short-run, however, to ameliorate the depressed economic conditions in Europe and the world. Failure to act would mean the possible triumph of nationalist (and perhaps socialist) economic policies around the world.(14)

Few American officials seriously considered, even as temporary measures, decreasing America's exports or having foreign nations restrict their imports of American goods. In the immediate postwar years, the United States served as the world's main source of consumer and capital goods. Export controls would obstruct the flow of international trade and hinder the reconstruction efforts of many countries, thus blocking world economic growth. At the same time, a reduction in American exports threatened important sectors of America's domestic production with unemployment and dislocation. When a recession hit the United States in 1948-49, the Council of Economic Advisers recommended that the government continue to supply dollars abroad in order to prevent a sharp curtailment in the purchase of American exports. Policymakers deemed the maintenance and expansion of U.S. exports as crucial for national and global economic well-being. The crux of the problem, therefore, rested on getting dollars to foreign countries so that they could buy American goods and services.(15)

Dollars could flow abroad via three major avenues. American imperial state and corporate leaders emphasized private enterprise participation in the reconstruction of Europe and Asia and in the development of the periphery. Private foreign investments and loans would allow the core and periphery to purchase supplies and services only the United States could provide. Private capital also could stimulate production that, in turn, could either earn dollars through exports or turn out dollar-saving commodities. Unstable economic and political conditions in Europe and Asia, however, discouraged private American investors. American direct private investments in Western Europe increased by $400 million from the end of 1945 to the close of 1949. Over the same period, American investments in Latin America and Canada grew by $1.8 billion and $1 billion, respectively. Government officials sought to stimulate private investments through guarantees, treaties, and liberal tax credits on income derived from abroad.(16)

A second avenue involved new, large-scale, public foreign aid programs. Like direct private investments, a government aid program would subsidize America's export trade and stimulate foreign productivity. The third approach, closely tied to the first and second, consisted of increasing American imports of foreign goods. American officials urged European countries to modernize old industries and to create new ones and thus produce goods that could be sold in the United States. In 1949, for example, policymakers recommended an acceleration in American imports from Third World countries-- especially the purchase of strategic raw materials. America's class-conscious capitalist class supported these efforts at defeating "protectionist nonsense" at home. If left un- checked, Fortune editors warned in mid-1946, protectionist lobbies could "wreck the kind of international order that business itself requires."(17)

A fiscally conservative and protectionist Congress endan- gered the imperial state bureaucracy's attempt to initiate and expand public aid programs and to increase American imports. In the late 1940s, Congress pushed for modifications in the reciprocal trade agreements act in order to protect the domes- tic economy. Corporate and labor leaders supported Hull's free trade concept in principle. In practice, however, com- petitive businesses sought to maintain their own tariffs, sub- sidies, and restrictive programs. Operating in fields charac- terized by low wages, low productivity, and limited capital investment, these enterprises fiercely competed for dominance in local or regional markets. Small- and medium-sized cotton producers in the South, for example, vehemently defended import quotas on foreign cotton. This position stood in sharp contrast to the free trade arguments being espoused by cotton magnate and imperial state policymaker Will Clayton.(18)

While supporting a three year extension of the reciprocal trade act in 1949, American Federation of Labor officials warned that unions did not favor each and every tariff reduction. Since some foreign competitors used sub-standard labor rules, import duties and tariffs protected production and employment in the United States. Even some large corpora- tions involved in international exchange demonstrated a certain ambivalence regarding import duties. For example, J. Howard Pew, head of Sun Oil Company, while a firm advocate of multilateralism, nevertheless viewed American tariffs as a "defense mechanism, rather than as a barrier to free trade." Throughout the 1940s, State Department officers tried to thwart congressional attacks on existing free trade measures while pushing free trade concepts on European and Third World nations. Congressional factions also obstructed administra- tion attempts to secure public foreign aid programs. Few assistance programs received congressional approval without being placed in an "anticommunist framework."(19)

As late as December 1949, State Department officers still disagreed over the relative merits of increasing American im- ports and extending foreign economic assistance programs. Economic officers held that expanded imports would solve the dollar gap, although they realized the domestic obstacles to substantial tariff reductions. The department's Policy Plan- ning Staff (PPS) advocated the immediate use of foreign eco- nomic assistance. Caught up in its own Cold War rhetoric, the PPS emphasized the threat of the Soviet Union and the need to use "unconventional economic measures" to hold the European political system together.(20) But even PPS officials recog- nized the link between European recovery and the development of poor, agrarian areas.

During the last half of 1949, imperial state policymakers began talking about the "near miracle" of Europe's industrial recovery. Western Europe had made important gains in produc-

tion and internal financial stability. But the "long-term
problems of economic adjustment" remained. PPS Director
George Kennan noted that "it is one thing to produce; it is
another to sell." European nations needed markets--"without
those markets they cannot secure the wherewithal for all their
essential imports."(21) Policymakers understood that a more
thorough integration of the Third World into the European and
world economy would help make European production more cost
competitive and supply markets for European exports.

Developing the underdeveloped nations would help close
the dollar gap and accelerate European reconstruction. With
modernized agricultural and extractive mineral sectors, poor
countries could serve as new sources of supply for Europe.
Europe thus could save its limited dollar reserves for normal
trade with the United States. Increased production in the
periphery would raise local living standards and thus provide
Europe with new markets. In addition, less developed countries could become major dollar earners if they produced goods
desired in the United States. The periphery, accumulating
dollars by selling certain agricultural and mineral commodities to the United States, could purchase American consumer
and capital goods or European exports. In the latter case,
dollars would travel circuitously from the United States, to
Third World nations, to Western Europe and Japan, and back to
the United States. The State Department's coordinator of foreign aid and assistance, Henry R. Labouisse, explained in mid-
1949 that "it makes no difference where they go, dollars just
need to get into circulation." American capital, asserted
George Kennan, had to go abroad.(22)

While American officials encouraged private investment in
the periphery, they sought to influence the enterprises and
projects into which that capital flowed. In keeping with the
needs of the European nations and the United States and with
the doctrines that emphasized agricultural and mineral development, American officers urged poor countries to concentrate
on the extraction and initial processing of raw materials for
export or on the manufacture of simple goods for local consumption. From 1945 through 1949, the value of private American direct investments in the manufacturing industries of the
underdeveloped European dependencies (including the British
West Indies, the Netherlands East Indies, and large areas of
Africa) increased by $7 million--a rise of about 58 percent.
United States investments in Latin American manufacturing
industries rose by $332 million--an increase of 77 per-cent--
during the same period. Investments in extractive industries-
-such as agriculture and petroleum production--increased by
$273 million or 122 percent in the European dependencies and
by $1,160 million or 109 percent in Latin America. In the
Middle East, American direct investment in manufacturing was
only $12 million compared to the $98 million invested in
petroleum in 1949.(23)

Policymakers linked the economic development of Third
World nations to European and international recovery and
integration. The imperial state believed that European
recovery required special economic assistance, but that Third
World development did not. When Latin American representatives asked about the possibility of a Marshall Plan for their
countries, Undersecretary of State for Economic Affairs Clayton replied that such aid "was not at all applicable to the
Latin American situation." Elaborating on arguments he first

presented at Chapultepec in 1945, Clayton explained that Western Europe needed emergency supplies of food and raw materials, while Latin America--and other peripheral areas--required capital goods for resource development and industrialization. The Marshall Plan would "put a firm economic foundation under Europe" and thus provide markets and capital for Latin American development.(24) American officials concluded that special aid programs for Europe and general efforts to revive world trade would contribute to Third World development; and world development would accelerate reconstruction and global integration.

In the Cold War atmosphere of the late 1940s, State Department officers portrayed economic development as a vehicle for halting the spread of communism. Members of the PPS, in particular, associated economic development of "backward" areas and reconstruction of Europe with the containment of the Soviet Union. At a June 1949 meeting, for example, PPS officers examined the question of European collaboration in African development. Africa offered Europe both markets and raw materials. George Kennan argued that the countries of Europe should regard "development of Africa as a common problem and merge their interests in it, raise a common European flag over those areas of Africa and proceed to their development." Focusing on a "common problem" could aid West European political integration and thus counter the unity of the Soviet bloc.(25)

Coordinator of Foreign Aid Labouisse supported Kennan's recommendations, but advanced strong and compelling economic reasons for European integration. Without European economic integration and Third World development, the United States would have to continue its "expansive ERP approach" to close the dollar gap. For Kennan, economic integration was a way of "buying ourselves successfully out of the box of communism and Russian expansion." ECA official Harlan Cleveland responded that the United States "from its own economic standpoint, is going to have to cover its own export surplus with gifts from somebody." Programs like the ERP served as effective short-run shock-absorbers for domestic recessions. Long-run American prosperity demanded world development and integration. Unlike Kennan, the majority of imperial state and capitalist class elites recognized the close connection between the economic and political effects of world development and reconstruction.(26)

America's capitalist class shared the imperial state consensus on the symbiotic relationship among European recovery, Third World development, and American prosperity. Corporate-dominated policy formation groups, such as the Council on Foreign Relations and the Committee for Economic Development, produced several reports on the importance of development in "all backward areas." In a variety of speeches and articles in the late 1940s, corporate leaders like Beardsley Ruml (chairman of the board of R. H. Macy and Company and a founder of the CED), William E. Knox (president of Westinghouse Electric International Company), and George H. Houston (president of a corporate consulting firm), among others, proclaimed the link between American export markets and world reconstruction and development.(27) A Fortune editorial in June 1947 summarized a basic capitalist class position regarding reconstruction, development, and American hegemony: "All over the world, American dollars, American

tools and machines, American engineers and supervisors have a
colossal task to perform in unison--not to exploit, but to
build up and nurture, and not out of altruism but with an eye
to the profits that come from markets made healthy."(28)
Recognizing the opportunities outlined by Fortune, several
capitalist class elites/imperial state officials established
their own firms to further Third World development and American capitalist expansion. In 1947 both Nelson Rockefeller and
Edward R. Stettinius created such corporations.(29)

Nelson Rockefeller's interest in Latin American development stemmed from his family's oil and financial operations in
the area, his 1939 tour of the continent, and his reign as
head of the Office of Inter-American Affairs (OIAA) and later
as assistant secretary of state for Latin American Affairs.
When James Byrnes replaced Edward R. Stettinius as secretary
of state in mid-1945, the department was reorganized and
Rockefeller was fired. Even without his imperial state bureaucratic position, Rockefeller remained committed to American economic and political hegemony in the postwar world. He
recognized the necessity of bridging the gap between the
periphery and core if that hegemonic system was to "function
satisfactorily, and if it was in any sense to be justified on
moral grounds."(30) Rockefeller prided himself on being a
"problem-solver," on "getting things done," and on setting an
example for others to follow. "Because he had such a proprie-
tary attitude toward his solutions he remained dissatisfied if
he could not achieve a position in which he would have the
authority and autonomy to implement those solutions."(31)
Rockefeller felt compelled to create his own structure, which
could assist Third World development and American capitalist
expansion.

Upon returning to New York in August 1945, Rockefeller
met with close advisers, including Beardsley Ruml. This
"brain trust on Latin America" conceived of a nonprofit
foundation--the American International Association for Economic and Social Development (AIA)--to promote "self-development"
in Latin America through technical assistance. Rockefeller
established AIA in July 1946. He explained to his father that
peoples in the Third World "must increasingly have reasons to
feel that their best interests and opportunity for the future
are identified with our country and our way of life."(32) On
9 January 1947 Nelson Rockefeller and his brothers created the
International Basic Economy Corporation (IBEC) as the profitmaking company that would implement AIA projects. Rockefeller
viewed IBEC's primary goal as demonstrating that private
capital could perform a "social" role abroad and at the same
time make a profit. While the imperial state could help
create conditions conducive for capital expansion overseas,
Rockefeller believed that the private sector had to take the
lead in developing the Third World. Victor Andrade, a
Bolivian businessman and bureaucrat who worked for IBEC in its
early years, observed that "Nelson Rockefeller risked large
sums of money in yet unexplored fields as well as his personal
prestige in the eyes of U.S. businessmen who viewed this new
kind of enterprise with skepticism."(33)

Initially capitalized at $2 million--the Rockefellers
boosted that figure to $4 million by August 1947--IBEC sought
to achieve economic development in Latin America by importing
U.S. techniques to increase food production, improve food
distribution, provide cheap services, and build new indus-

tries. During the late 1940s, Brazil and Venezuela became the focal points of IBEC operations because of their valuable natural resources, political significance, and earlier ties to Rockefeller through Standard Oil Company and the OIAA. In Brazil IBEC provided the technology and capital to produce high grade (hybrid corn) seeds, phosphates, and hogs, and to improve transportation. Rockefeller saw IBEC's activities as creating a "bridge" between core and periphery. More importantly, IBEC would demonstrate to other American capitalists and Third World officials that a private U.S. corporation, operating for profit and utilizing American "management, capital, and technical knowledge," could increase agricultural production, raise standards of living, build social housing, mobilize savings, and foster industrialization in the periphery.(34) The New York Times praised the Rockefeller effort to develop Latin America and called for more of this "new dollar diplomacy." In comments reminiscent of Henry Wallace's depiction of the underdeveloped world as America's new frontier, the Times observed: "Such ventures as this lie upon a new frontier that offers to many of this generation opportunities for adventure and advancement similar to those held out to an earlier generation by the American West."(35)

America's new economic frontier also attracted former secretary of state and former chairman of U.S. Steel Corporation, Edward R. Stettinius. Following the Yalta Conference in February 1945, Secretary of State Stettinius visited Monrovia, Liberia. There he was impressed with "the great contrast between profuse undeveloped natural resources and the needs of the people and the country for improved living standards, health and education." Stettinius believed that American capital and technology could develop Liberia's economy to the benefit of both nations. Two years later, Stettinius established Stettinius Associates, a New York based corporation capitalized at $1 million (of which Stettinius contributed $200,000) and staffed with engineers, businessmen, and lawyers who had worked with Stettinius during the war. In September 1947 Stettinius and the Liberian secretary of state announced plans for a "pioneer experiment" to develop Liberia's natural resources with private American capital and business know-how. Like Rockefeller, Stettinius "worked to set up a corporate-controlled system of economic aid to Liberia."(36)

The 1947 agreement between the Liberian government and Stettinius Associates--which had the blessing of the State Department--permitted the latter party to exploit certain Liberian agricultural and mineral resources. In return, the corporation would supervise construction of a modern transportation system, development of sewage facilities, and building of electric power plants. The parent corporation would receive 65 percent of the profits from natural resource development; the Liberian government would take 25 percent; and 10 percent would go to the Liberian Foundation, a nonprofit agency devoted to Liberian educational, health, and welfare programs. Enthused about the project, Stettinius approved studies of possible diamond mines, cocoa and coffee plantations, fisheries, and timber operations.(37)

Despite Stettinius' "idealism and boyish optimism," problems plagued the project. Subcontractors were slow to begin specific construction. The Export-Import Bank rejected the corporation's request for financing. Although Liberia's ruling class favored the deal and provided Stettinius with an

open door, internal political intrigue and an "unexpected
suspicion" of U.S. capitalists obstructed corporate activities. The former State Department secretary sought assistance from the imperial state. In February 1949 Stettinius
told imperial state officials that Liberia was crucial for
national security. He insisted that Liberia possessed vital
and scarce raw materials and that it was strategically located
"from the standpoint of U. S. protection of [the] Panama Canal
and Brazil." Stettinius even resorted to using the increasingly effective Russian bogyman argument. He warned that if
his company failed, "Communism, already at work in Africa,
would rejoice." Within a month, a severe heart attack forced
Stettinius to abandon the Liberian project.(38) Neither
Stettinius Associates nor Rockefeller's IBEC proved successful
in the late 1940s. Yet both corporations demonstrated the
capitalist class-imperial state consensus on the importance of
Third World development to the American economy. They also
reflected a growing "American corporate drive to expand the
concept of an Open Door by coupling profits and social
progress in the underdeveloped world."(39)

Organized labor in the United States also favored efforts
at securing multilateral trade and the integration of recon-
structed Europe and Asia with the developing Third World. The
American Federation of Labor Executive Council announced in
early 1950 that "there can be no effective integration of the
economy of democratic Europe unless its economic life becomes
more closely related with that of Africa, the Western hemisphere and the democratic countries and areas of Asia." Union
support for the government's development policy brought the
AFL and the Congress of Industrial Organizations into conflict
with labor unions in the periphery--especially in Latin America. At the Inter-American Conference at Chapultepec, Mexico
in early 1945, AFL and CIO officials supported Will Clayton's
call for increased private U.S. investments in Latin American
agricultural and extractive industries, a lowering of Latin
tariff barriers, and extensive U.S. industrial exports to the
continent. Latin American labor unions, led by Lombardo
Toledano and the leftist Confederation of Latin American
Workers (CTAL), attacked this policy because it undermined
local industrialization programs and aggravated dependence on
one-crop exports. AFL officials recognized their irreconcilable conflict with Lombardo and the CTAL. Acting through the
Free Trade Union Committee (FTUC), the AFL sought to destroy
CTAL and replace it with U.S.-style trade unions.(40)

Serafino Romualdi, the FTUC chief in Latin America,
criticized the Latin American labor movement for favoring
protective tariffs and controls over foreign capital. This
policy, contended Romualdi, reflected a fatal weakness in the
Latin labor movement--its focus on seeking political power and
changes in the socioeconomic structure, rather than concentrating on "bread and butter issues." By attaining a "saving
wage," argued Romualdi, the great mass of Latin American consumers could increase their purchasing power and lead the way
toward true economic development. In arguments identical to
those of Nelson Rockefeller and Will Clayton, AFL officials
contended that the problem in Latin America was not the distribution of wealth, but the production of wealth. "Illogi-
cal" protective tariffs led to the "dangerous" policy of "economic and industrial self-sufficiency." Romualdi explained
that to increase production, labor "must develop a new concept

of labor-industry relationships." Many Latin workers had mistakenly identified foreign capital as "an enemy" to "be harassed at every opportunity." Latin America had to reexamine the role of foreign capital, especially U.S. capital, and seek greater labor-capital cooperation. H. W. Fraser, a railway union leader, suggested that increased production in Latin America could be achieved "by an intelligent coordination of the three factors that produce wealth: state, capital, and labor." These three must be "harmonized" in Latin America, just as they apparently had been in the United States. AFL and CIO leaders thus believed that a corporatist framework among labor, capital, and the state, which supposedly had allowed for progress in the United States, could be exported to Latin America and the rest of the Third World and bring with it economic development.(41)

During the latter half of the 1940s, therefore, America's imperial state and capitalist class, with labor elite support, viewed peripheral development as vital for the expansion of world trade, the continued recovery of European economies, the promotion of political stability, the blocking of Communist expansion, and American economic prosperity. At the same time, policymakers regarded development as a natural outgrowth of a revived Europe and Asia, expanded world trade, and currency convertibility. This contradiction--the importance of economic development and a lack of specific programs to facilitate it--intensified the development debate that had begun during the war.

THE INTERNATIONAL DEBATE: ECONOMIC AND SOCIAL COUNCIL

The UN's Economic and Social Council (ECOSOC) emerged in the late 1940s as a principal arena for the reconstruction-development debate.(42) Initially, ECOSOC focused on reconstruction and full employment problems in the core. But even in its early days, ECOSOC's discussions drifted to the problems of the underdeveloped nations. The U.S. mission to the UN thought that the council and specialized agencies, such as the Food and Agriculture Organization, the International Labor Office, and the World Health Organization, were "well suited to attack the problems of developing underdeveloped areas." In the fall of 1946 ECOSOC directed its Economic and Employment Commission to establish a Subcommission on Economic Development. The subcommission concentrated on long-range development, giving particular attention to the poor, agrarian areas of the world.(43)

Composed of economic experts from India, Mexico, Brazil, China, the Soviet Union, Czechoslovakia, and the United States, the subcommission met several times during 1947. From the start, the U.S. representative, Beardsley Ruml, found himself on the defensive. Ruml complained that he spent much of his time trying to tone down the "half-baked" statements of the Indian and Soviet representatives--V. K. R. V. Rao and Alexander Morozov. The American mission to the UN had misgivings about the subcommission's emphasis on economic and political exploitation, particularly with regard to direct private investments in Third World countries. Despite American objections, the first subcommission report stressed the importance of political independence and freedom from foreign interference in the economic growth of a nation. The report contained other items that offended the United States.(44)

According to the report, economic development should promote higher living standards, full employment, and conditions of economic and social progress. The efficient and full use of human and natural resources, technology, and capital achieved development. Although warning that development and industrialization were not identical, the report noted that the latter process played a "decisive" role in the former. The report recommended the diversification of economic activities within poor states, greater financial and technical assistance to these areas, and Third World domestic reforms. Under special conditions--for example, protecting national security and stimulating certain sectors of the domestic economy--the subcommission approved the establishment of industries that might not be strictly economic according to comparative costs.(45)

State Department officials objected to the report on several grounds. First, the report exaggerated the danger of foreign investment. Reflecting the imperial state-capitalist class consensus, the department argued that international agencies should promote, rather than regulate, the flow of foreign private capital. This could be done by formulating and adopting a general investment code detailing the conduct and treatment of foreign investment. Second, under no circumstances should economic development aim at self-sufficiency. "Emphasis should be placed on economic interdependence and increased international interchange of goods and services rather than on economic independence."(46)

To avoid such errant reports in the future, the State Department recommended that the subcommission study the preconditions of, and obstacles to, economic development in Third World countries; the link between rationalized agriculture and industrialization; and the question of diversification versus specialization. Third World governments should be able to use subcommission studies to assess their own development plans. Finally, the department suggested that the subcommission be replaced with a full commission composed of government representatives. Imperial state bureaucrats believed that such a commission would be easier to control than the existing subcommission.(47)

American criticism had a negligible impact upon the subcommission and its second report, issued in June 1948. The majority of subcommission members again emphasized the importance of industrialization and attacked the operation of foreign capital in the periphery. U.S. representatives--Isador Lubin from the imperial state bureaucracy and Toni Sender of the AFL--objected to the report. Lubin, a former New Deal economist, insisted that the "dangers of direct investments were things of the past." Sender found the report lacking in concrete proposals.(48)

Publication of the report resparked the State Department's effort to dismantle the subcommission. Characterizing the body as "an admitted failure," department officers proposed the creation of a full commission on economic development, perhaps charging it with supervision of a UN technical aid program.(49) While trying to gain control of the runaway subcommission, the United States found itself and the UN being attacked from other quarters.

By the fall of 1948, peripheral nations had realized the extent of UN and American aid for European reconstruction. At the UN, delegates from Argentina, China, Egypt, India, Mexico, the Philippines, and other nations, criticized ECOSOC for failing to attack Third World problems.   In October, the Egyptian delegate described the periphery's need for capital and technology and for guarantees against the exploitative use of such aid. Two months later, a group of Third World nations pushed through the General Assembly a resolution recommending that ECOSOC give full and urgent consideration to all aspects of the underdeveloped world's development problems.(50)

On 25 February 1949, Assistant Secretary of State for Economic Affairs Willard Thorp responded to Third World criti- cisms. Thorp, an economist in Franklin Roosevelt's brains trust and later research director for Dun and Bradstreet, had served as Will Clayton's assistant for some time and shared Clayton's analysis of the capitalist world-economy. The as- sistant secretary told ECOSOC that Third World poverty derived from conditions within those nations. Development remained the sole responsibility of individual countries. Most devel- opment requirements--health care, education, financial sys- tems, order, and security--"were either wholly or mainly with- in the control of the individual nation and its people." Even the bulk of the capital necessary for development, asserted Thorp, "had to come from the people themselves." Neverthe- less, international action and cooperation would accelerate the process of development via the free flow of goods, knowl- edge, technology, and capital.   Thorp emphasized the impor- tance of the global flow of private investment and technology. He argued that poor countries must remove obstacles to private capital movement and create a favorable investment climate. Thorp concluded that development could be rapid, but that it would be measured in decades, not in years.(51)

The Lebanese delegate, Charles Malik, replied to Thorp's speech. He accused the United States of neglecting industri- alization as a vital element of development. Malik questioned the flow of American investments to poor nations and the relative distribution of World Bank funds for reconstruction and development purposes.   Even with reduced risks and guarantees, foreign capital's contribution to Third World development was uneven and unequal. Malik argued that private capital flowed into extractive industries, with their rela- tively high profits and minimum risks, rather than into indig- enous manufacturing or refining plants. It was time for the Marshall Plan idea to be extended "to a wider community em- bracing also the under-developed countries." Development schemes for the periphery abounded; now was the time to exe- cute those plans. Malik concluded that economic development could not be left to the "slow, dull, unplanned evolution of nature."(52)

Malik represented a country whose industrial sector and service economy (re-export trade, tourism, and banking) were developing under laissez-faire and open door policies. But Lebanon sought additional foreign capital and technology in order to enhance its chance for mobility within the world economic hierarchy.   Malik himself represented Lebanon's growing petty bourgeoisie.   The son of a physician, he graduated from the American University at Beirut (a BA in mathematics and physics) and Harvard University (MA and PhD in philosophy).   He worked for the Rockefeller Foundation's

health care unit in Cairo in the early 1930s and returned to
the American University as a professor in 1937.   His nation's
first minister to the United States, Malik espoused liberal
capitalist views on economics and politics.(53)

When Malik demanded industrialization and foreign capital
investment in the Third World, he did not seek autarky or
self-sufficiency for those nations.   Industrialization and
capital investment would increase the Third World's production
for export and its capacity to import capital and consumer
goods.   Such development would benefit all nations.   Malik
and Thorp disagreed not over fundamental questions of international economy or economic doctrines, but rather over the
best ways to achieve economic liberalism and capitalist expansion. Malik believed that in the short-run, public investment
programs had to supplement weak or nonexistent private capital
flows.   The United States disagreed.   American officials
pointed out that approximately 90 percent of U.S. private
capital investments abroad went to poor, agrarian nations.
(They neglected to mention that the bulk of those investments
concentrated in extractive raw material production.) The
United States reiterated its faith in private enterprise and
investments.   Third World economic and political reforms were
prerequisites for capital transfer.(54)

In the spring of 1949 the Subcommission on Economic
Development reemerged as a center of controversy. Throughout
the subcommission's third session, the Soviet economist,
Alexander Morozov, attacked the United States and other
capitalist core powers. Subcommission members dismissed most
of Morozov's comments as Cold War rhetoric. Nevertheless,
some of his observations struck a responsive chord among Third
World delegates.   India and Brazil joined the Soviet Union in
seeking protections against the "imperialist side-effects" of
direct foreign investment.   Drawing on his own country's
development experience, Morozov proposed that the periphery
concentrate · on heavy industrial development. The American
economist, Emilio Collado, called such advice nonsense and
insisted on "balanced" growth--that is, agricultural mechanization and slow and limited industrialization.   Collado, however, found little support for his position.(55)

In its third report (April 1949), the subcommission held
that industrialization, including the development of heavy
industry (within the framework of available resources and
materials), formed "the decisive phase in economic development."   Third World leaders had to emphasize domestic financing for industrial construction while seeking supplemental
foreign aid.   The report warned that foreign capital should
not come at the expense of a nation's economic and political
independence. Underdeveloped nations had to provide for local
participation in foreign operations--both in equity financing
and in management--and to require foreign firms to train local
workers. "Underdeveloped countries are justified in imposing
conditions which would make private foreign investments really
contribute to their economic development."   To remedy private
capital and World Bank neglect of the periphery, Rao of India
proposed the creation of a new international agency to fund
projects not normally accepted by orthodox banking institutions. Such development projects would require large-scale
investments over long periods of time. Rao acknowledged that
the bulk of these funds would have to come from the United
States.(56)

A footnote in the   report contained America's dissenting opinion penned by Emilio Collado. An imperial state bureaucrat, Collado had worked as an economic adviser in the State Department during World War II, participated in the 1943 Hull-Acheson committee on Third World economic development, and recently served as executive director of the IBRD. In addition, Collado had close ties to the corporate sector--functioning as a long-time assistant treasurer of the Standard Oil Company of New Jersey. It came as no surprise, therefore, that Collado refuted the subcommission's majority report by insisting that only "free private enterprise and institutions" could best organize an economy and achieve economic development. American private enterprise in particular could provide the capital and technology necessary for Third World development. Only when private financing was not feasible should the IBRD step in and assist peripheral nations.   Collado rejected Rao's proposal, contending that sufficient institutions already existed to deal with funding problems.(57)

Unable to control the Subcommission on Economic Development, the United States pressured the subcommission's parent body, the Economic and Employment Commission, to reject the April 1949 report. Mimicking the standard American line, the commission accused the subcommission of failing to properly analyze development issues and of failing to establish a balance between the responsibilities of capital importing and capital exporting countries.(58)

At a meeting of ECOSOC in late July 1949, Willard Thorp again argued that the underdeveloped nations must rely on their own resources for development, that such development takes decades to achieve, and that critics exaggerated the harmful effects of private foreign investment.   Tired of attacks against American aid policies, Thorp asserted that ECOSOC should not be discussing the United States' plan for world development, but rather what the UN and its agencies could do to alleviate world poverty.(59)

Third World nations considered American and UN efforts at facilitating development as inadequate. UN reports on financing development, terms of trade, technical aid, international capital movements, and full employment simultaneously exposed the extreme poverty of underdeveloped nations and sharpened the demands of poor countries.   Reports and studies whetted the appetite of Third World elites; they castigated the UN for failing to take appropriate action.   As George Hakim of Lebanon observed: "Inequality of development was, next to internal inequality of wealth, the most important social or economic problem of the age.   The United Nations could not afford, for its own sake and for that of the world, to disappoint the hopes that millions had fixed on it."(60) The UN attempted to meet this responsibility by establishing special regional economic commissions.

THE INTERNATIONAL DEBATE: REGIONAL COMMISSIONS

Article 68 of the UN Charter permitted ECOSOC to set up such commissions "as may be required for the performance of its functions." American policymakers initially opposed the establishment of regional economic bodies in ECOSOC. Regional commissions, feared State Department officers, might become autonomous and "supplant the parent council in importance and

prestige."   Regional groupings violated the department's traditional functional and global approach to world economic
problems. To a lesser extent, Americans worried that regional
organizations would threaten U.S. influence over UN economic
operations. Nevertheless, a regional economic commission for
Europe seemed a logical approach to the area's reconstruction
problems and was not inimical to global integration. The
United States favored Japanese and Chinese reconstruction and
acquiesced to strong local pressure for a proposed economic
commission for Asia. ECOSOC officially created the Economic
Commission for Europe and the Economic Commission for Asia and
the Far East in March 1947.(61)

In the fall of 1947, Middle East and Latin American
delegates proposed the establishment of economic commissions
for their respective regions, arguing that such organizations
would facilitate indigenous industrialization and economic
diversification. State Department officials countered that
the two areas lacked the reconstruction problems present in
Europe and Asia. Since economic development did not equal
reconstruction, the Economic Commission for Latin America
(ECLA) and Economic Commission for the Middle East (ECME)
lacked precedent. As firm advocates of the interrelationship
of reconstruction and development, imperial state bureaucrats
found themselves in an awkward position rationalizing this
last point. But rationalize it they did. Since development
and reconstruction constituted different problems, a wholly
new approach would have to be devised before formal organizations could be established. Policymakers also doubted the
efficacy of regional commissions in promoting development.
The UN and ECOSOC could best assist underdeveloped countries
by attacking development issues on a global and functional
level. The danger always existed that regional economic
bodies would become closed regional economic systems.(62)

Charles Malik once again challenged American arguments.
Creating bodies like ECLA and ECME would not necessarily result in regional autarky, claimed Malik. The Lebanese diplomat explained that countries belonging to the same region
naturally tended to establish closer economic ties with each
other. The alleged danger of regional autarky was far less
serious than the danger of Western domination over the Third
World. Malik believed that economic regionalism constituted
only a mild response to "economic penetration by extraregional
elements and forces."(63)

ECOSOC's ad hoc committee on ECLA noted that no line
could be drawn between reconstruction and development. Regional commissions could effectively deal with economic development without encroaching upon the domain of the functional
commissions, which operated on a global basis. Australian
officials, frequently the spokesmen for underdeveloped countries, pointed out that regional bodies had more "vitality"
than functional agencies and that they offered an opportunity
for more intensive consideration of an area's economic problems.(64)

Development and regional considerations aside, American
policymakers continued to object to ECLA and ECME. With regard to Latin America, officials believed that the proposed
ECLA would duplicate the work of the Pan American Union's
Inter-American Economic and Social Council. Since the United
States funded both the Pan American Union and ECOSOC, policymakers preferred that only one organization concern itself

with Latin American development. When the Pan American Union supported the establishment of ECLA, however, the United States dropped its objections. ECOSOC set up ECLA in early 1948.(65)

In the case of the Middle East, State Department officials felt that the region's economies competed with rather than complemented one another. An economic commission could do little more than settle water rights between countries. The existing Arab League's Economic Committee appeared to serve no particular function. Political problems, such as French and Soviet demands to be considered Middle East powers, also hindered the creation of an ECME. Finally, the unresolved question of Palestine made regional planning and coordination virtually impossible. Although State Department officials disliked the ECME idea, they tempered their public statements because of widespread Arab support for such a commission.(66)

In the winter of 1947-48, Egyptian and Lebanese representatives intensified their campaign for a regional commission. Albert Badre, an economic adviser for the Lebanese delegation, described the Middle East as an "intrinsically economically important" region. If developed, it would "be able to contribute materially to the development of other regions of the world."(67) An ad hoc committee on the ECME met in the spring and quickly became mired in the issue of great power membership. Britain, France, and the Soviet Union claimed membership in the ECME. American officials opposed Soviet participation, while Arab leaders resisted any European involvement. The French and British sought to prevent the commission from becoming an instrument of the Arab League and passing a "series of highly tendentious and embarrassing resolutions." The United States responded that "having an irresponsible ECME led by nations in the area is better than having ECME with Great Power leadership, but including the USSR."(68) The ad hoc committee recommended great power abstention.

The committee noted that an ECME could coordinate policies of local governments, collect and disseminate economic data, initiate development studies, and maintain and strengthen Middle East economic relations with other regions. American policymakers remained skeptical of an ECME, but acquiesced in the committee's recommendations because similar organizations existed for Europe, Asia, and Latin America. The Arab-Israeli war and conflicts among the Arab states ultimately blocked the creation of an ECME.(69) As the decade ended only ECLA stood as a regional commission designed to facilitate economic development. Paralleling the fight for regional development bodies, the Third World also tried to use the proposed International Trade Organization as a vehicle for economic development.

THE INTERNATIONAL DEBATE: INTERNATIONAL TRADE ORGANIZATION

When first proposed by the State Department in late 1945, the International Trade Organization (ITO) had little to do with underdeveloped nations. The ITO concept evolved from Cordell Hull's reciprocal trade policies and the traditional American view that international trade generated production and wealth for the United States and the world. In February

1946, the United States drafted an ECOSOC resolution calling for an international conference on trade and employment. The council passed the resolution and created a Preparatory Committee to set an agenda and draft a convention for an ITO. ECOSOC also requested that the committee consider the "special conditions" in poor, agrarian countries.(70)

State Department officers considered the promotion of industrial and economic development as functions of ECOSOC and its subcommissions, not of the ITO. In the draft ITO charter, however, department planners described one of the organ's purposes as encouraging and assisting in the general development of poor nations. They left the door open for a possible ITO commission on industrialization and economic development. The United States hoped that these vague promises, together with a specific section on commodity accords, would satisfy the ruling classes in the periphery.(71)

Even before the Preparatory Committee met, underdeveloped nations began objecting to America's proposed charter. Many peripheral and semiperipheral countries used restrictive measures to protect infant industries. When the committee convened in London in October 1946, India and Australia, supported by China, Brazil, Chile, and Lebanon, demanded the freedom to promote industrialization by employing import quotas. The United States rejected this proposal. India accused the United States and Britain of preparing a charter that served the interests of the core by keeping the "backward" nations in a position of economic dependence.(72)

The American delegation, fearing that this issue would destroy the entire ITO, made its "only important concession" of the conference. In return for assurances from the Australian delegation--the unofficial spokesman for the underdeveloped world--that it would drop its demand for import quotas, the United States drafted and introduced a procedure whereby the ITO could grant a country permission to make limited use of import restrictions. The imperial state conceded this "small" point in order to pave the way for free world trade and economic integration.(73)

Small concessions did not mollify the underdeveloped world. At the second meeting of the committee in Geneva (April-October 1947), and at the UN Conference on Trade and Employment at Havana (November 1947-March 1948), the underdeveloped bloc demanded a permanent ITO committee on economic development. The United States and other core nations opposed such a body because it would duplicate the work of existing international agencies and obscure the real duty of the ITO-- to maximize the movement of private capital and enterprise throughout the world. According to Mexico, Egypt, Pakistan, and other peripheral countries, core and underdeveloped nations shared responsibility for promoting development. American officials disagreed--no legal precedents compelled core nations to aid the Third World. The poor, agrarian nations countered that they had the right to restrict foreign investment, to regulate the activities of foreign enterprises, and to modify American provisions that encouraged the international flow of private capital. American representatives lamented that the Third World bloc did more to check the transfer of foreign capital than to stimulate it.(74)

Third World nations also demanded exceptions to the articles on tariff preferences and quantitative restrictions. Clair Wilcox of the Office of International Trade Policy, and

vice chairman of the American delegation to the various ITO
conferences, complained that the "backward" countries wanted
"an absolute free hand to impose quantitative restrictions
without prior consultation with the ITO." The United States
could not surrender this point, nor could it weaken its
position against tariff preferences. Will Clayton and Wilcox
defeated articles that would have obligated industrial
creditor nations to supply capital funds, equipment, and
technical aid to underdeveloped countries. They rejected
amendments depriving foreign investors of diplomatic protection. In the interest of attaining an international commitment to the most-favored-nation principle, however, the United
States compromised on economic development issues.(75)

On balance, the final ITO Charter allowed more interference with private investments than protection to investors.
Member countries, for example, could take any measure to
ensure that investments did not become the pretext for inter-
fering in those nations' internal political affairs. Governments also could set conditions for new investments made by
foreign nationals. The United States acceded to the creation
of regional preference systems for the purpose of economic
development. In addition, American negotiators reluctantly
agreed to a provision for "automatic" prior approval by the
ITO of the use of import quotas for the development of new
industries. Such quotas could be imposed for a limited time
and in two specific circumstances: industries established
during the war and industries using local raw materials for
which foreign markets were reduced or eliminated by the
actions of other governments.(76)

Imperial state leaders considered these sacrifices a
legitimate price for the free trade and private market world
they wanted. Policymakers with extensive corporate ties, such
as Will Clayton and Willard Thorp, downplayed the concessions,
describing them as special circumstances. Protection for
infant industries, for example, would be limited, temporary,
and under the control of the ITO. In explaining the concessions to the president of the International Telephone and
Telegraph Corporation, Clayton contended that America confronted a sick world in which binding commitments on trade and
capital protection had to allow exceptions to cover unusual
conditions. The ITO Charter recognized the exigency of certain restrictive and undesirable practices. Simultaneously,
argued Clayton, the charter "surrounds such practices with
controls and conditions which keep them within reasonable
bounds and it provides the discontinuation of these practices
as soon as the conditions which brought them about have
changed." Clayton told the U.S. Chamber of Commerce in June
1948 that the ITO could prevent the "return to the practices
of the international jungle--everyone for himself and the
devil catch the hindmost." Imperial state officials acknowledged that these concessions might adversely affect some
capitalist class enterprises in the short-run. But over the
long-run, these concessions protected the future interests of
the capitalist class as a whole.(77)

Divisions quickly emerged within the capitalist class and
the labor movement over the ITO issue in particular, and the
subject of Third World development in general. Overall,
competitive sector capitalists (comprising many small- and
medium-sized firms) saw a greater danger in accepting the ITO
than in rejecting it. The National Association of Manufac-

turers (NAM), the National Foreign Trade Council (NFTC), and the Chamber of Commerce of the United States attacked import quotas and preferential tariffs as detrimental to expanding world trade and criticized "industrialization at any cost" in the Third World. The NFTC and NAM also opposed the apparently unqualified American commitment to promote and facilitate the economic development of all ITO members. Such aid had to be based on the interests of the United States and the recipient country and managed not by governments, but by the private sector. Sound economic development was possible only if "promoted through capital funds and the technical and managerial know-how provided by private enterprise." Finally, the ITO Charter written in Havana offered no protection for private firms investing in Third World nations.(78)

America's monopoly capital sector and class-conscious capitalists appeared more divided over the ITO issue than did the competitive sector. From early in the postwar period, elite policymakers in the Council on Foreign Relations and the Committee for Economic Development had strongly favored "the policy of removing protective tariffs and other barriers to trade." After the conclusion of ITO negotiations in London, Fortune urged American business to support the proposed body. Acknowledging the charter's weaknesses--including its approval of quantitative restrictions in certain situations--Fortune editors nevertheless argued that the ITO at least made those restrictions "the exception rather than the general rule" while generalizing the most-favored-nation principle. A Fortune poll of 28,000 business executives in late 1947, however, revealed ambivalence within the corporate community over the ITO issue. Only 33 percent of those polled believed that the ITO would have a favorable effect on the American economy; another 33 percent had no opinion; and 34 percent felt the effect would be negligible or unfavorable.(79)

During 1948 and 1949 the ITO controversy split cosmopolitan capitalists. Beardsley Ruml told a meeting of magazine publishers in April 1948 that the "leaders of the underdeveloped countries are aroused and they are impatient." Despite their rhetoric regarding state trading and import quotas, Ruml contended that those leaders would soon reform their local economies to attract foreign capital and join the world marketplace. As a special adviser to the Puerto Rican government and a member of the board of directors of the Puerto Rican Industrial Development Company, Ruml frequently counseled that Caribbean government to alter its tax laws in order to attract U.S. private enterprise and capital. Ruml and William Batt, president of S.K.F. Industries and a member of the CED, viewed the Havana Charter as a product of international bargaining and compromise. The United States made necessary concessions to the periphery. With half of the world's population in turmoil, argued Batt, the United States must "direct and shape the economic and political emotion of these peoples." The ITO Charter offered America the opportunity to help direct and control Third World development while moving toward the goal of free world trade and economic integration.(80)

Not all corporate executives agreed with Ruml and Batt. Elvin H. Killheffer of E.I. duPont deNemours and Company and a delegate to the Havana Conference, claimed that the conference and the charter thoroughly indoctrinated poor nations "in the ideas of preferences, special discriminations, planned and

controlled economies." The periphery believed that the United
States possessed "limitless" power to aid in its development.
The weaknesses of the ITO, outlined by Killheffer and others,
soon led _Fortune_ to reverse its position on the organization.
In mid-1949, _Fortune_ editors characterized the ITO Charter as
"worthless...dull and ambivalent"; it "merely registers and
codifies the worldwide conflict between freer trade and
economic nationalism."(81)

The ambivalence with which corporate America approached
the ITO appeared in the CED's report on the reconstruction of
world trade. The June 1949 report echoed the liberal capitalist conviction that "a large and growing volume of international trade will foster the achievement of higher levels of
material well-being for ourselves and others." Unfortunately,
"the governments of many economically backward countries have
come to look on protectionism as a panacea which operates
almost automatically to promote rapid economic development and
higher living standards."   Although the committee vehemently
opposed direct state participation in international trade, it
recognized that "for the present we can neither ignore nor
reverse the trend toward statism."(82)

The CED suppported those charter provisions that limited
"invisible tariffs," controlled global cartels, checked the
use of intergovernmental commodity agreements, and provided
rules to govern state trading. The committee questioned, but
accepted quantitative import restrictions, protection for infant industries, and customs unions. It flatly rejected charter provisions dealing with international investment. Third
World development depended on a high volume of global private
investment, but the ITO Charter's language concerning investment provided no protection to U.S. investors against "arbitrary and discriminatory action by foreign governments." Of
the 28 members of the CED's Policy Committee, 23 approved the
ITO Charter, contingent on the elimination of the investment
clauses. The five dissenters found the charter an "imperfect
and defective agreement" and "a great victory of nationalism
and socialism over multilateral trade and private enterprise."(83)

Organized labor's position imitated the views of the
imperial state and corporate elite, but added its own bit of
self-interest.   The AFL hierarchy held that the ITO "must be
directed to expand world trade so as to raise the standards of
living to the highest possible level in each country rather
than to encourage standards of living to seek a common level."
In perfect corporatist logic, AFL elites argued that the ITO
had to facilitate ever-expanding world trade and production
rather than a redistribution of world resources and wealth.
The AFL proposed that the ITO raise all nations' labor
standards by prohibiting protective tariffs in the periphery,
while allowing the United States to selectively use such
restrictions. "A policy that restricts products made by cheap
labor under sub-standard working conditions from entering this
country will act as an efficient means to stimulate other
countries of the world to replace their effete methods of
production and to raise their standards of labor."(84)

Labor and monopoly ambivalence, combined with competitive
capital's out-right hostility, doomed the ITO in the United
States. Other pressing international and national commitments
preoccupied executive policymakers and the legislature.   Congress never ratified the ITO Charter.(85) The attempts of

underdeveloped countries to use the ITO as a vehicle for de-
velopment--via the provisions on trade, investment, and indus-
trialization--contributed to the organization's premature
death. America's capitalist class resisted "artificial" mechanisms for economic development in the periphery. Thus, despite strains and tensions, the capitalist class-imperial
state consensus on Third World development remained rigid; and
so did America's consequent policies and programs. The efforts of Third World ruling classes to modify America's perception of development capital and technical assistance met
with slightly different results, as the next chapter demonstrates.

NOTES

1. Alfred Eckes, Search for Solvency: Bretton Woods and
the International Monetary System, 1941-1971 (Austin: University of Texas Press, 1975), p. xi; Fritz Machlup, A History
of Thought on Economic Integration (New York: Columbia University Press, 1977), p. 14; M. Maximova, Economic Aspects of
Capitalist Integration, trans. Bryan Bean (Moscow: Progress
Publishers, 1973), pp. 98-100.

2. Maximova, Economic Aspects, pp. 127, 129-30; Gabriel
Kolko, The Politics of War (New York: Random House, 1968),
pp. 623-24; Fred L. Block, The Origins of International
Economic Disorder (Berkeley: University of California Press,
1977), p. 99. Assistant Secretary of State Adolf Berle was
committed to "continentalism"--that is, an integration of
Western Hemisphere countries with the U.S. at the center.
Berle believed that continentalism "could be adopted, with due
variations, by other continents or subcontinents." See
Beatrice Berle and T. Jacobs, eds., Navigating the Rapids:
From the Papers of Adolf A. Berle (New York: Harcourt Brace
Jovanovich, 1973), p. xxiv. Michael Barratt Brown, a British
political economist, has argued that by 1959 the world was
divided into five trade blocs. These corresponded to the
poles of development defined by Maximova. The blocs included
the American dollar area, the British Sterling bloc, West
Germany and the Common Market area, the Soviet communist bloc,
and the Japanese-Asian bloc. See Michael Barratt Brown, After
Imperialism (London: Heineman, 1970), pp. 356-57, 394 Table
28.

3. James Petras and Morris Morley, "The U.S. Imperial
State," in Petras, Class, State, and Power in the Third World
(Montclair, N.J.: Allanheld, Osmun & Publishers, 1981), p. 8.

4. Robert Packenham, Liberal America and the Third
World: Political Development Ideas in Foreign Aid and Social
Science (Princeton, N.J.: Princeton University Press, 1973),
pp. 112-13; Ignacy Sachs, The Discovery of the Third World
(Cambridge, Mass.: MIT Press, 1976), p. 136; Clair Wilcox, A
Charter for World Trade (New York: Macmillan, 1949), pp. 142-
43.

5. Francis H. Russell, "Design of the New World
Economy," Department of State (hereafter DOS), Bulletin, 22
May 1950: 806-8, 821. These same points had been summarized

by Assistant Secretary of State Will Clayton in August 1946 and by Walter Salant of the Council of Economic Advisers in December 1946. See Frederick J. Dobney, ed., Selected Papers of Will Clayton (Baltimore: The Johns Hopkins Press, 1971), pp. 168-69; and memorandum from Salant to Council of Economic Advisers, 12 December 1946, International Relations 1946-47 folder, Salant Papers, Harry S. Truman Library, Independence, Missouri.

6. For a theoretical analysis of liberal integration, see Maximova, Economic Aspects, pp. 97-102; Bela Balassa, The Theory of Economic Integration (Homewood, Ill.: Richard D. Irwin, 1961), pp. 1, 7; Machlup, History of Thought, pp. 1, 43-102; David Baldwin, Economic Development and American Foreign Policy, 1943-1962 (Chicago: The University of Chicago Press, 1966), pp. 53-57; David P. Calleo and Benjamin Rowland, America and the World Political Economy: Atlantic Dreams and National Realities (Bloomington: Indiana University Press, 1973), pp. 4, 39.

7. Eckes, Search for Solvency, pp. 217, 219. Political scientists have presented a similar argument regarding world political security. See, for example, Joseph S. Nye, Jr., ed., International Regionalism: Readings (Boston: Little Brown, 1968); and Ronald Y. Yalem, Regionalism and World Order (Washington, D.C.: Public Affairs Press, 1965), pp. 64-86.

8. Thomas M. Campbell, Masquerade Peace: America's UN Policy, 1944-1945 (Tallahassee: Florida State University Press, 1973); and J. Lloyd Mechan, The United States and Inter-American Security, 1889-1960 (Austin: University of Texas Press, 1961), pp. 268-77.

9. Lloyd Gardner, Architects of Illusion: Men and Ideas in American Foreign Policy, 1941-1949 (Chicago: Quadrangle Books, 1970), p. 113; ECEFP D-133/48, "Regional Preferences and Customs Unions," 18 October 1948, 5.19B ECEFP Meetings, 3.Documents, RG 353, U.S. National Archives, Washington, D.C.; Committee for Economic Development, The International Trade Organization and the Reconstruction of World Trade (New York: CED, June 1949), p. 19. Also see Machlup, History of Thought, pp. 79-80; and Maurice Parmelee, Geo-Economic Regionalism and World Federation (New York: Exposition Press, 1949).

10. Dobney, ed., Selected Papers of Will Clayton, pp. 6-9, 21-26, 36-43, 105-108; Gardner, Architects of Illusion, pp. 116-17. John Kenneth Galbraith described Clayton as a "brilliant, civilized and charming Texas businessman turned public official." He was "articulate, affable, assured and stubbornly his own man." J. K. Galbraith, A Life in Our Times: Memoirs (Boston: Houghton Mifflin, 1981), pp. 39, 168.

11. Dobney, ed., Selected Papers of Will Clayton, pp. 1-17, 154-55; CED, International Trade, p. 18. Clayton strongly opposed the Soviet economic bloc in Eastern Europe. Dobney, ed., Selected Papers of Will Clayton, pp. 156-58; Gardner, Architects of Illusion, pp. 113-38; Transcript, Nathan M. Becker Oral History Interview, 19 January 1973, p.

54 and   Transcript, Edward S. Mason Oral History Interview, 17
July 1973, pp. 6-7, 9, Harry Truman Library.   Becker   was an
adviser   to   the   assistant   secretary   of   state for economic
affairs in the late 1940s and   Mason was   a consultant   in the
Office of International Trade Policy.

12. Transcript, Becker   Oral   History,   pp.   54, 95-96;
Dobney, ed., Selected Papers of Will Clayton, pp.   104-5, 147-
61, 195-204, 219-22, 224-29;   CED, International Trade, p. 18.

13. Dobney,   ed.,   Selected   Papers of Will Clayton, pp.
195-97, 234-35.   Also see Michael J. Hogan, "American Marshall
Planners and   the Search for a European Neocapitalism," American Historical Review 90 (February 1985): 44-72.

14. The Economic   Cooperation   Administration (hereafter
ECA),   A   Report   on   Recovery   Progress and United States Aid
(Washington, D.C.:   ECA, February 1949),   pp.   12-13;   Charles
Kindleberger,   The   Dollar   Shortage (New York: John Wiley &
Sons and MIT Press,   1950), p.   5;   CED, International Trade,
pp. 15-18;   William   S. Borden, The Pacific Alliance: United
States Foreign Economic Policy   and   Japanese   Trade Recovery,
1947-1955 (Madison: University of Wisconsin Press, 1984), pp.
5-15.

15. ECA, Report, pp. 12-13;   Borden, Pacific Alliance,
pp.   5-15;   UNE   D-5/47,   ECEFP's   UN Economic Subcommittee,
"Recommendations of ECOSOC Regarding   International Action for
Facilitating   the   Better   Utilization of World Resources," 13
May 1947, 5.19E ECEFP   Subcommittee,   19.UNE   C.Documents, RG
353;   Robert Asher, Walter M. Kotschnig, and William A. Brown,
Jr., The United Nations   and Economic   and Social Co-Operation
(Washington,   D.C.:   Brookings   Institution,   1957), p. 242;
Memorandum,   "Report   of   Stabilization   Devices   Committee to
Council   of   Economic   Advisers,"   1   May   1949, International
Relations 1949 folder, Salant Papers.

16. Kindleberger, Dollar Shortage, p. 193;   Organization
of   European   Economic   Cooperation (hereafter OEEC), European
Recovery Programme: Second   Report   of   the   O.E.E.C. (Paris:
OEEC, February 1950), pp. 186, 209-10;   Memorandum, "Report of
Stabilization Devices Committee," 1   May 1949,   Salant Papers;
Samuel Pizer   and F.   Cutler, "Private U.S. Direct Investments
Abroad," Survey of Current   Business 31   (January   1951): 22;
Joseph   Zettler   and   F.   Cutler,   "U.S. Direct Investments in
Foreign Countries," Survey of   Current   Business 32 (December
1952): 8-9;   CED, International Trade, pp. 16-18;   Transcript,
Merwin Bohan, Oral History Interview, Truman   Library, 15 June
1974, pp.   62-64;   Charles Lipson, Standing Guard: Protecting
Foreign Capital   in   the   Nineteenth   and   Twentieth Centuries
(Berkeley: University of California Press, 1985).

17. ECA, A   Report   on   Recovery   Progress, pp. 12-13;
ECEFP's UN Economic Subcommittee, "Recommendations to ECOSOC,"
13 May   1947, 5.19E ECEFP Subcommittee, 19.UNE C.Documents, RG
353;   "The Choice for Business," Fortune 33   (June 1946): 3-4.
Also   see   William   E.   Knox,   "The Foreign Trade Myth," Vital
Speeches of the Day, 13 (15   December 1946): 155-57;   William
L. Batt,   "Fashions in   International Economy," Vital Speeches
of the Day, 13 (15 May 1947): 472-76.

18. Susan M. Hartman, Truman and the 80th Congress
(Columbia: University of Missouri Press, 1971), pp. 49-70;
George Lipsitz,   Class and Culture in Cold War America: "A
Rainbow at Midnight" (South Hadley, Mass.:   J.F. Bergin
Publishers, 1982), p. 6.

19. Testimony of Walter S. Mason, AFL, to Senate Finance
Committee, 22 February 1949, Box 38, Folder: International
Trade, Files of Director of Research, General Files, AFL
Papers, State Historical Society of Wisconsin, Madison, Wis.;
Mary Sennholz, ed., Faith and Freedom: The Journal of a Great
American, J. Howard Pew (Grove City, Pa.:   Grove City College,
1975), pp. 87-90;   Joyce Kolko and Gabriel Kolko, The Limits
of Power: The World and United States Foreign Policy, 1945-
54 (New York: Harper & Row, 1972), pp. 374-81.

20. Undersecretary's Meeting, "Two Approaches to the
Resolution of the US Balance of Payments Problems," 8 December
1949, Subject Files: Economic Policy, Records of the PPS,
1947-1953, RG 59, U.S. National Archives, Washington, D.C.;
ECEFP D-21/49 Rev 2, "Objectives and Nature of the Point IV
Program," 1 March 1949, 5.19B ECEFP Meetings, 3.Documents, RG
353.

21. George Kennan, "The International Situation," DOS,
Bulletin, 5 September 1949: 323-24;   ECA Administrator Paul
Hoffman statement to Joint Committee on Foreign Economic
Cooperation, 21 February 1950, in Raymond Dennett and R.
Turner, eds., Documents on American Foreign Relations, vol. 12
(1950) (Princeton, N.J.:   Princeton University Press, 1951),
pp. 74-76.

22. ECA, A Report on Recovery Progress, pp. 12-13;
OEEC, European Recovery Programme, pp. 186, 209-10;   OEEC,
Interim Report on the ERP, Report of the Overseas Territories
Committee, December 1948, pp. 48-49;   101st and 102nd
Meetings, 14 June 1949, Records of PPS, Meetings 1949, RG 59.

23. OEEC, Interim Report, pp. 48-49;   Pizer and Cutler,
"Private U.S. Direct Investments," p. 22 table 1; UN, Review
of Economic Conditions in Middle East, 1951-52, Supplement to
World Economic Report (New York: Department of Economic
Affairs, 1953, 1953.II.C.1), p. 105 table 56.

24. Dobney, ed., Selected Papers of Will Clayton, pp.
222-24;   OEEC, Interim Report, p. 57; Stephen Rabe, "The
Elusive Conference: United States Economic Relations with
Latin America, 1945-1952," Diplomatic History, 2 (Summer
1978): 286-88;   Samuel L. Baily, The United States and the
Development of South America, 1945-1975 (New York: New
Viewpoints, 1976), pp. 51-68.

25. Minutes of PPS Meetings, 4 December 1947, 8 April
1948, 26 April 1948, 12 May 1949, 3 June 1949, Records of PPS,
Minutes of Meetings, RG 59. For an introduction to the issue
of aid for China, see Grace M. Hawes, The Marshall Plan for
China: Economic Cooperation Administration, 1948-1949
(Cambridge, Mass.:   Schenkman Publishing, 1977).

26. PPS Meeting,   3 June   1949, Records of PPS, Minutes, RG 59.

27. Jacob Viner, The United States in a Multi-National Economy (New York: Council on Foreign Relations, 1945), pp. 11-12; Calvin B. Hoover, International Trade and Domestic Employment (New York: McGraw-Hill for CED, 1945), pp. 18, 31, 143, 135; Beardsley Ruml, "Thinking About the World and Its Economies," speech to National Association of Magazine Publishers, New York, 27 April 1948, Series II, Box V, folder 9, Beardsley Ruml Papers, Department of Special Collections, University of Chicago Library, Chicago, Ill.; Ruml speech to CED, 20 May 1948, Series II, Box V, folder 11, Ruml Papers; George Houston, "Industrializing Undeveloped Areas of the World," Dun's Review 57 (March 1949): 14-16, 46-53; "United States Opinion on Russia," Fortune 32 (September 1945): 238; William Knox, "Foreign Trade Myth," Vital Speeches of the Day 13 (15 December 1946): 155-57.

28. "To the Board of Directors of American Business," Fortune 35 (June 1947): 2-4.

29. Other firms set up to facilitate Third World development and profits included James M. Landis' Middle East Company, Robert R. Nathan's International Commercial Trading Company, and Lauchlin Currie's   International Development Company.   Landis was dean of the Harvard Law School and director of the American Economic Mission to the Middle East. Nathan, an economist, had been an administrator in the War Production Board and Office of War Mobilization and Recon-version.   Currie, a New Deal economist, served in the State Department and as deputy administrator of the Foreign Economic Administration.   "The U.S. Opportunity," Fortune 35 (June 1947): 83-85, 187;   "Fortune Shorts--Bureaucrats Meet Payroll," Fortune 33 (January 1946): 226.

30. William A. Williams, The Contours of American History (Chicago: Quadrangle Books, 1966), p. 460.

31. James E. Underwood and William J. Daniels, Governor Rockefeller in New York: The Apex of Pragmatic Liberalism in the United States (Westport, Conn.: Greenwood Press, 1982), p. 37.

32. Peter Collier and David Horowitz, The Rockefellers: An American Dynasty (New York: Holt, Rinehart and Winston, 1976), pp. 260-62.

33. New York Times, 10 January 1947, p. 1; Wayne G. Broehl, Jr., The International Basic Economy Corporation (Washington, D.C.: National Planning Association, Series on U.S. Business Performance Abroad, no. 13, 1968), pp. 4-11; Victor Andrade, My Missions for Revolutionary Bolivia, 1944-1962 (Pittsburgh: University of Pittsburgh Press, 1976), p. 124.

34. Broehl, The International, pp. 3-12; New York Times, 10 January 1947, p. 6; Collier and Horowitz, The Rockefellers, pp. 263-64.

35. New York Times, 11 January 1947, p. 18.

36. Thomas M. Campbell and George Herring, eds., The Diaries of Edward R. Stettinius, Jr., 1943-1946 (New York: New Viewpoints, 1975), p. 478; Rodney Carlisle, "The 'American Century' Implemented: Stettinius and the Liberian Flag of Convenience," Business History Review 54 (Summer 1980): 175-77; New York Times, 27 September 1947, p. 6.

37. Campbell and Herring, eds., Diaries, pp. 478-79; Carlisle, "The 'American Century,'" p. 177; New York Times, 27 September 1947, p. 6.

38. Campbell and Herring, eds., Diaries, pp. 479, 481; Carlisle, "The 'American Century,'" p. 178.

39. Carlisle, "The 'American Century,'" p. 191.

40. AFL Executive Council memorandum on Point Four, February 1950, Box 16, Folder: Point Four, Files of Director of Research, General Files, AFL Papers; AFL, Report of the Executive Council of the AFL, 68th Convention, 1949, (Washington, D.C.: AFL, 1949) pp. 58, 74; Ronald Radosh, American Labor and United States Foreign Policy (New York: Random House, 1969), pp. 357-71; Baily, The United States and the Development of South America, pp. 40-48.

41. Serafino Romualdi, "Labor and Democracy in Latin America," Foreign Affairs 25 (April 1947): 477-89; H. W. Fraser, "Organized Labor and the Economic Development of Latin America," 4 March 1948, Box 18, Folder: International Labor Relations, Files of Director of Research, General Files, AFL Papers; Florence C. Thorne, "Stable Production with Maximum Employment for Maximum Compensation," May 1947, Box 39, Folder: Economic and Social Council (UN), Files of Director of Research, General Files, AFL Papers.

42. For information on the formation of ECOSOC, see Louis K. Hyde, The United States and the United Nations: Promoting the Public Welfare (New York: Carnegie Endowment for International Peace, 1960), pp. 31-32, 36-39; Walter Sharp, The United Nations Economic and Social Council (New York: Columbia University Press, 1969), pp. 3-4; Campbell, Masquerade Peace, pp. 189-90, 204.

43. Asher et al., The United Nations, pp. 242, 446; Hyde, The United States, p. 89; Sharp, The United Nations, p. 73; Isador Lubin to W. A. Mackintosh, 2 July 1946, Correspondence re: ECOSOC (1946), V UN ECOSOC Papers, Isador Lubin Papers, FDR Library, Hyde Park, N.Y.; E. Penrose, "Coordination of Economic and Social Activities of International Agencies: With Special Reference to the Economic Development of Under-Developed Areas," 3 September 1946, folder: Development: Economic, Subject File, Records of the US Mission to the UN 1945-49, RG 84, U.S. National Archives, Washington, D.C.; UN, Yearbook of the United Nations, 1946-1947 (hereafter Yearbook followed by appropriate years) (Lake Success, N.Y.: UN, 1947), pp. 473-74.

44. UN, Yearbook, 1946-1947, p. 559;   Memorandum, William Fowler to B. Ruml, 3 December 1947, Subject File, "IO: ECOSOC: EMP: Subcommission on Economic Development, 1947-49," Records of the US Mission to the UN, RG 84;   ECOSOC, Official Records, 3d year, 7th session, Report on the Economic and Employment Commission, Supplement no. 1 (Lake Success, N.Y.: UN, 1947), pp. 7-10.

45. ECOSOC, Official Records, 3d year, 7th session, Report of Economic and Employment Commission, pp. 7-10; Asher et al. , The United Nations, p. 439.

46. Memorandum, Harold Spiegel to Paul Daniels, 6 January 1949, Department of State Decimal Files 501.BD/1-649, RG 59 (hereafter DOS followed by file number and RG 59); ECEFP D-48/48 Rev. 1, "Report of the Subcommission on Economic Development (E/CN.1/47)," 26 April 1948, 5.19B ECEFP Meetings 3.Documents, RG 353.

47. Memo, Spiegel to Daniels, 6 January 1949, DOS 501.BD/1-649, RG 59;   ECEFP D-48/48 Rev. 1, "Report of Sub-commission," 26 April 1948, 5.19B ECEFP Meetings 3.Documents, RG 353.

48. ECOSOC, Official Records, 4th year, 9th session, Report of the Second Session of the Sub-Commission on Economic Development, Supplement No. 11A, (New York: UN, 1948), E/CN.1/61, pp. 7-10;   Ernst Schwarz to Elmer Cope, 29 June 1948, Box 20, Folder 4, Microfilm edition, Elmer F. Cope Papers, Ohio Historical Society, Columbus, Ohio.

49. Memorandum of conversation, David Weintraub and William Fowler, 19 January 1949, and memorandum, Fowler to John Leddy, 21 January 1949, Subject File, folder: "Development: Economic," Records of the US Mission to the UN, RG 84; Willard Thorp to Isador Lubin, 4 February 1949, Subject File, "IO: ECOSOC: EMP: 1946-49," Records of US Mission to UN, RG 84.

50. Hyde, The United States, pp. 96-98;   UN, Yearbook, 1948-1949, (New York: UN, 1950), p. 433.

51. ECOSOC, Official Records, 4th year, 8th session, 7 February-18 March 1949, 251st Meeting, 25 February 1949 (Lake Success, N.Y.: UN, 1949), pp. 305-310. Also see memorandum of conversation, E. Phillips and William Fowler, 13 January 1949, Subject File, folder "Development: Economic," Records of US Mission to UN, RG 84.

52. ECOSOC, Official Records, 4th year, 8th session, 255th Meeting, 1 March 1949, pp. 348-55; Telegram, Warren Austin to Secretary of State, 2 March 1949, DOS 501.BD/3-249, RG 59.

53. George Hakim, "The Economic Basis of Lebanese Polity," and Charles Issawi, "Economic Development and Political Liberalism in Lebanon," in Leonard Binder, ed., Politics in Lebanon (New York: John Wiley & Sons, 1966), pp. 57-59, 73-74; Nicola A. Ziadeh, Syria and Lebanon (New York: Frederick A. Praeger, 1957), pp. 218-30, 240;   Current

Biography, 1948 (New York: H. W. Wilson, 1949), pp. 410-12.

54. ECOSOC, Official Records, 4th year, 8th session, 260th Meeting, 3 March 1949, p. 437; Pizer and Cutler, "Private U.S. Direct Investments," pp. 20-23.

55. ECOSOC, Subcommission on Economic Development, Summary Record of the 51st, 57th, 58th, 59th, 60th and 70th Meetings, 23, 28-30 March and 6 April 1949, E/CN.1/Sub3/SR 51, 57-60, 70.

56. ECOSOC, Official Records, 4th year, 9th session, Report of the 3rd Session of the Sub-Commission on Economic Development, Supplement No. 11B, (New York: UN, 1949), E/CN.1/65; Hyde, The United States, p. 128.

57. ECOSOC, Official Records, 4th year, 9th session, Report of the 3rd Session of Sub-Commission on Economic Development.

58. Report of the Economic and Employment Commission, E/1356 and E/CN.1/74.

59. ECOSOC, Official Records, 4th year, 9th session, 5 July-15 August 1949, (Geneva: UN, 1949), pp. 266, 268-70, 273-75, 433.

60. Ibid., pp. 393, 396; Hyde, The United States, pp. 128-29. Two UN reports on economic development appeared in 1949: Methods of Financing Economic Development in Under-Developed Countries (Lake Success, N.Y.: UN, Department of Economic Affairs, 1949); and Relative Prices of Exports and Imports of Underdeveloped Countries: A Study of postwar terms of trade between underdeveloped and industrialized countries (Lake Success, N.Y.: UN, Department of Economic Affairs, December 1949).

61. Sharp, The United Nations, pp. 17-19; Memorandum, D. Sandifer to Division of Financial Affairs, 13 September 1946, Subject File, "IO: ECOSOC: ECME," Records of US Mission to UN, RG 84; Memo, W. Fowler to J. Leddy, 21 January 1949, Subject File, folder "Development: Economic," Records of US Mission to UN, RG 84; David Wightman, Toward Economic Cooperation in Asia: The UN Economic Commission for Asia and the Far East (New Haven, Conn.: Yale University Press, 1963), pp. 14-19.

62. Memo, Sandifer to Financial Affairs, 13 September 1946; Memo of conversation, C. Malik and L. D. Stinebower, 3 June 1947, DOS 501.BD/6-347; J. Patterson to Secretary of State, 3 September 1947, DOS 501.BD/9-347, RG 59; ECOSOC, Official Records, 2nd year, 5th session, 19 July-16 August 1947, (Lake Success, N.Y.: UN, 1948), pp. 131, 135-36; ECEFP D-108/47, "Attitude of US Government Toward Possible Establishment of Regional Economic Commission by the UN for the Near and Middle East," 21 July 1947, 5.19B ECEFP Meetings, RG 353; George Marshall to London Embassy, 16 July 1947, DOS 501.BD/7-1647; Memo of conversation, John Jernegan and the Greek Ambassador, 18 January 1948, DOS 501.BD/1-2848, RG 59; Memo of conversation on the ECLA proposal, 21 July 1947, DOS

501.BD/7-2147; Memo of conversation, William Busser and Louis Halle, 28 July 1947, DOS 501.BD/7-2847, RG 59.

63. ECOSOC, Official Records, 2nd year, 5th session, p. 191.

64. UN, Yearbook, 1947-1948, p. 539; William Fowler to James Cooley, 13 January 1948, Subject File, folder "Development: Economic," Records of US Mission to UN, RG 84.

65. Memo of conversation, Busser and Halle, DOS 501.BD/7-2847; ECOSOC, Official Records, 3rd year, 6th session, Report of the Ad Hoc Committee on Proposed ECLA, Supplement No. 7 (New York: UN, January 1948); Hyde, The United States, p. 96; Sharp, The United Nations, pp. 17-18; UN, Yearbook, 1947-1948, p. 538.

66. ECEFP D-108/47, "Attitude of US Government Toward ECME," 21 July 1947, 5.19B ECEFP Meetings 3.Documents, RG 353. The discussion over the ECME neglected the wartime experiences of the Middle East Supply Center. See chapter 4 herein.

67. UN, Yearbook, 1947-1948, pp. 543-44; ECOSOC, Official Records, 3rd year, 6th session, pp. 109-13; Memo of conversation, W. Fowler, J. Jernegan, G. Merriam, 7 January 1948, DOS 501.BD-Middle East/1-748; Memo of conversation, Charles Malik, Merriam, H. Deimel, 26 January 1948, DOS 501.BD-Middle East/1-2648, RG 59.

68. UN, Yearbook, 1947-1948, pp. 544-45; Memo, H. Deimel to J. Satterthwaite, 10 February 1948, DOS 501.BD-Middle East/2-1048; Warren Austin to Secretary of State, 28 April 1948, DOS 501.BD-Middle East/4-2848, RG 59; Memo, L. Stinebower to H. Deimel, 3 June 1948, Subject File, "IO: ECOSOC: ECME," Records of US Mission to UN, RG 84; ECEFP D-86/48, "Report of the Ad Hoc Committee on the Proposed ECME," 28 June 1948, 5.19B ECEFP Meetings 3.Documents, RG 353. Soviet delegates argued that American membership in ECLA established a precedent for USSR membership in ECME. American officials countered that the United States had territorial possessions in the area, that it was a member of the Pan American Union, and that it joined ECLA in deference to the wishes of the Latin countries.

69. ECOSOC, Official Records, 4th year, 9th session, Report of the Ad Hoc Committee for the Middle East, Supplement No. 4, (Lake Success, N.Y.: UN, 1949), pp. 1, 6-12, 18-22; UN, Yearbook, 1947-1948, pp. 545, 523; ECEFP D-86/48, "Report on proposed ECME," 28 June 1948, 5.19B ECEFP Meetings, 3.Documents, RG 353; UN, Yearbook, 1948-1949, p. 523; Dean Acheson to Louis Hyde, 14 May 1949, DOS 501.BD/6-349; Dean Rusk to Willard Thorp, 29 June 1949, includes position paper on ECME, 13 June 1949, DOS 501.BD/6-2949, RG 59.

70. "Proposal for Expansion of World Trade and Employment," Department of State (hereafter DOS), Bulletin (9 December 1945): 913-19; DOS, Foreign Relations of the United States, 1946, vol. 1, pp. 1280 footnote, 1292 (hereafter, FRUS followed by appropriate year and volume); UN, Yearbook, 1948-1949, p. 1106. The State Department discussed the possibility

of creating a separate industrial office to aid underdeveloped
nations. See ECEFP D-138/45, "Technical Aid to Industrialization," 5 November 1945, 5.19B ECEFP Meetings, 3.Documents, RG
353.

71. "Proposed ITO Charter," DOS, <u>Bulletin</u> (29 September
1946): 585-89; ECEFP D-65/46, "Industrialization and Economic
Development," 17 July 1946 and ECEFP D-70/46, "Suggested Draft
of a Charter for an ITO of the UN," 25 July 1946, 5.19B ECEFP
Meetings, 3.Documents, RG 353.

72. <u>FRUS, 1946</u>, 1: 1349 note, 1361-64, 1359; ECEFP D-
95/46, "Preliminary Copy of Redraft of Charter for an ITO,"
December 1946, 5.19B ECEFP Meetings, 3.Documents, RG 353; UN,
<u>Report of the First Session of the Preparatory Committee of
the UN Conference on Trade and Employment</u> (London: UN,
October 1946), E/PC/T/33.

73. UN, <u>Report of the First Session of the Preparatory
Committee</u>.

74. <u>FRUS, 1948</u>, 1: 810, 812;   Richard N. Gardner,
<u>Sterling-Dollar Diplomacy: Anglo-American Collaboration in
the Reconstruction of Multilateral Trade</u> (Oxford: Clarendon
Press, 1956), pp. 365-66; Wilcox, <u>Charter for World Trade</u>;
ECEFP D-48/47, "Suggested US Position with Regard to Estab-
lishment of a Specific Commission on Economic Development by
Specific ITO Charter Provision," 18 March 1947, 5.19B ECEFP
Meetings, 3.Documents, RG 353.

75. <u>FRUS, 1947</u>, 1: 962-63;   Gardner, <u>Sterling-Dollar
Diplomacy</u>, pp. 366-67; UN, <u>Report of the Second Session of
the Preparatory Committee of the UN Conference on Trade and
Employment</u> (Geneva: UN, August 1947), E/PC/T/186, 1947.II.4.

76. <u>FRUS, 1948</u>, 1: 896-900;   DOS, <u>Participation of the
US Government in International Conferences: July 1, 1947-June
30, 1948</u> (Washington, D.C.: U.S. Government Printing Office,
1949), pp. 182-85; UN, <u>UN Conference on Trade and Employment:
Final Act and Related Documents</u>, (Havana: UN, March 1948),
E/Conf.2/78, 1948.II.D.4, pp. 8-13.

77. Dobney, ed., <u>Selected Papers of Will Clayton</u>, pp.
250-55; Willard Thorp, <u>Trade, Aid, or What?</u> (Baltimore: The
Johns Hopkins Press, 1954), p. 74; Wilcox, <u>Charter for World
Trade</u>; Dean Acheson, "Economic Policy and the ITO Charter,"
DOS, <u>Bulletin</u> (15 May 1949): 623-27.

78. Gardner, <u>Sterling-Dollar Diplomacy</u>, pp. 365, 372-76;
National Association of Manufacturers, <u>The Havana Charter for
an ITO: An Appraisal</u> (New York: NAM, Economic Policy
Division Series, no. 9, April 1949), pp. 3-7; National
Foreign Trade Council, <u>Position of the NFTC With Respect to
the Havana Charter for an ITO</u> (New York: NFTC, 1950), pp. 1-
4, 39-64; <u>Policy Declarations of the Chamber of Commerce of
the United States</u> (Washington, D.C.: July 1949), p. 100.

79. Hoover, <u>International Trade</u>, p. ix;   Edward S.
Mason, <u>Controlling World Trade: Cartels and Commodity
Agreements</u> (New York: McGraw-Hill for CED, 1945), pp. 239-40;

Karl Schriftgiesser, Business and Public Policy: The Role of the Committee for Economic Development, 1942-1967 (Englewood Cliffs, N.J.: Prentice-Hall, 1967), pp. 114-15; "Freer Trade vs Control," Fortune 35 (February 1947): 2-4; "The Executive Forecast," Fortune 37 (January 1948): 75.

80. B. Ruml, "Thinking about the World and its Economies," 27 April 1948, Series II, Box V, folder 9, Beardsley Ruml Papers, Department of Special Collections, University of Chicago Library, Chicago, Ill.;   B. Ruml to Treasurer of Puerto Rico, Sol Luis Descartes, 16 February 1949, Series I, Box I, folder 1c, and Luis Munoz Marin to Ruml, 29 April 1949, Series I, Box V, folder 1a, Ruml Papers; William Batt, speech to Academy of World Economics, Washington, D.C., 14 April 1949, 14.Addresses--Batt, William, "A Defense of the ITO Charter," The Chicago Council on Foreign Relations, Department of Special Collections, University of Illinois at Chicago, Chicago, Ill.

81. Elvin H. Killheffer, "International Trade Organization," Vital Speeches of the Day, 14 (1 June 1948): 489-93; "The ITO Charter," Fortune 40 (July 1949): 61-62.

82. CED, International Trade, pp. 1-2, 8-9, 12.

83. Ibid., pp. 22-32, 36-38. Members of the majority included Ruml, Philip D. Reed (chairman of the board of General Electric), Will Clayton, Henry Ford II (president of Ford Motor Company), George Harrison (chairman of the board of New York Life Insurance Company), and Amory Houghton (chairman of the board of Corning Glass Works).   The five dissenters included John D. Biggers (president of Libbey-Owens-Ford Glass Company), Henry L. Bristol (chairman of the board of Bristol-Myer Company), S. Sloan Colt (president of Bankers Trust Company), Fowler McCormick (chairman of the board of International Harvester), and J. Cameron Thomson (president of Northwest Bancorporation).

84. "Statement of the American Federation of Labor on the International Trade Organization," Box 18, Folder: International Trade Organization, Files of Director of Research, General Files, AFL Papers;   Testimony of Walter Mason, National Legislative Representative, AFL, on Extension of Reciprocal Trade Agreement Program before Senate Finance Committee, 22 February 1949, Box 38, Folder: International Trade, Files of Director of Research, General Files, AFL Papers.

85. William Diebold, Jr., The End of the ITO (Essays in International Finance, no. 16, October 1952, Princeton University), pp. 3, 5-6, 9-11, 15-18.

3
Reconstruction versus Development: Financial and Technical Aid

U.S. policymakers asserted that complete integration of Third World nations into the capitalist world-economy would provide the capital and technical assistance necessary for those countries' development. The private sector would be the best source of development capital, although policymakers recognized the need for public financing from such institutions as the World Bank and the Export-Import Bank. A precondition for the efficient and productive use of capital was technical assistance--that is, the transmission of learning, knowledge, techniques, and human resources from "modern" core nations to "traditional" peripheral nations. American policymakers viewed technical assistance as a relatively easy, inexpensive, and direct means of achieving economic development. U.S. officials considered technology and technical knowledge as objective, value-free forces. As with other aspects of development, collaborating classes in the Third World displayed a certain ambiguity toward American perceptions and policies regarding capital and technical aid.

FINANCING DEVELOPMENT

American imperial state and corporate leaders preferred private capital investments and loans for economic development. Policymakers hoped to facilitate and encourage private foreign investment and financing by negotiating treaties, eliminating inequitable taxes on income derived from foreign investments, securing investment guarantees, reducing national trade restrictions, and devising an international investment code.(1) Capitalist class elites in the CED, as well as class-conscious capitalists in the National Foreign Trade Council and the United States Chamber of Commerce, welcomed efforts to strengthen private enterprise and its operations abroad. They anticipated great benefits from the financing of Third World development.

Speaking at the National Foreign Trade Convention in November 1946, William K. Jackson--corporate lawyer (vice president and general counsel of United Fruit Company) and president of the United States Chamber of Commerce--declared that "we cannot indefinitely remain whole in a world that is broken." The economic development of "backward" regions would contain totalitarianism and would result in "incalculable rewards" for the United States.   By modernizing China, for example, "you fertilize a market of breath-taking size." Jackson asserted that the world needed "an invasion of American dollars, machinery, industrial efficiency, and technical talent." Jackson dismissed accusations of "economic imperialism."   "If what American business has done to improve conditions in the Caribbean is 'dollar diplomacy,' then I say, 'Let's have more of it--not dollar diplomacy but billion dollar diplomacy' with its great healing and productive benefits to all."(2)   But "billion dollar diplomacy" did not materialize in the late 1940s--at least not the way Jackson had envisioned it.

Prior to World War II, National City Bank of New York had created an international network superior to that of any other U.S. bank.   When the war ended, the bank's management hoped to quickly rebuild its foreign branch system in Europe and Asia and to expand elsewhere in the Third World.   But the Cold War in Europe, revolutionary unrest in Asia, and economic nationalism throughout much of the Third World dictated a policy of prudence.   Bank managers sought to avoid exchange controls and nationalization in the periphery.   Branch offices restricted themselves to financing trade and "servicing the foreign affiliates of the bank's corporate customers." Expansion into new Third World areas was postponed.(3)

Other American financial and industrial corporations shared National City Bank's concerns.   Corporate leaders blamed Third World governments for not creating the "environment conducive to an expanded flow of venture capital from the United States." Peripheral nations feared American economic and political domination--a characteristic of dollar diplomacy that Jackson conveniently overlooked--and wanted to control direct foreign investments.   To aid in economic diversification, Third World governments sought to impose protective tariffs and controls on currency exchange.   These policies, combined with political instability in many peripheral regions, led to relatively modest increases in private American foreign investments.   From 1945 through 1949, the value of private, U.S. direct investments in underdeveloped areas (Latin America, Asia, Africa, and the Middle East) increased from $3.9 to $6.7 billion.   The great bulk of the $2.8 billion gain in Third World areas (almost $2 billion) was in the capital intensive petroleum industry.   Private funds failed to support local agriculture, industry, transportation, and communication.   The burden of financing economic development, by default, fell to public national and international banking institutions.(4)

When American planners advanced their schemes for the International Monetary Fund (IMF) and the International Bank for Reconstruction and Development (IBRD) at Bretton Woods in 1944, they hoped that these institutions would stabilize and perpetuate a particular world order.   Both institutions rested on the goals of a liberal capitalist world-economy and American economic expansion.   At the same time they allowed for exceptions and detractions to deal with problem situations. Will Clayton assured Latin American countries at the Chapultepec Conference that "reasonable [exchange] controls may be unavoidable" and that "this is provided for in the Bretton Woods proposal." Clayton and other imperial state policymakers recognized the necessity of expressing American hegemony in universal terms. They were willing to make minor concessions that would secure the Third World's (and other core nations') acquiescence to American leadership. The IMF and IBRD became instruments in a larger hegemonic strategy. As they developed, the two financial institutions took on lives of their own. Yet they never deviated from the rules devised by a hegemonic America. The IMF and IBRD made financial assistance to the Third World "conditional upon reasonable evidence of intent to live up to the norms" of the capitalist world-economy.(5)

American officials wanted the International Monetary Fund to be a part of the "permanent machinery of international monetary relations rather than an emergency device to meet the special needs of the postwar years." Thus the IMF played an insigificant role in the postwar recovery of Europe and Asia. It played no role at all in the economic development of the periphery. The IMF refused to help debtor nations to solve their balance of payments problems and to provide credits to sustain the volume of poor nations' imports. The United States insisted that the IMF serve the purpose of exchange stability rather than development.(6)

Imperial state policymakers expected the IBRD to assume "primary responsibility" for reconstruction. The World Bank extended some short-term credits and long-term reconstruction loans to European nations, but spent most of its early years building a reputation for fiscal conservatism. John J. McCloy--Wall Street lawyer and trustee of the Rockefeller Foundation--became president of the bank in March 1947. During the previous year, McCloy had served on the Advisory Committee for Financing Foreign Trade--a group of industrial-ists and bankers appointed by President Harry Truman to consult with the National Advisory Council. McCloy worked under the direction of Winthrop W. Aldrich, chairman of the board of the Chase National Bank of New York. When he took over the IBRD, McCloy immediately strengthened the bank's image and secured investor confidence by filling high posi-tions with experienced private investment bankers. McCloy recognized that prudent and stringent loan requirements were inappropriate for war-torn areas where serious economic and physical dislocation made it difficult, if not impossible, to repay such loans. He began to alter the bank's lending proce-dures to deal with European conditions. But McCloy halted general purpose lending as soon as the Marshall Plan took charge of European reconstruction. The bank's new principal task became development lending.(7)

Between 1946 and 1953, the U.S. government extended some $41.3 billion for world reconstruction and development. The IBRD came in a poor second with $497 million for European re-construction and $1.253 billion for development. This poor showing resulted from the bank's operational policies and its conception of economic development. IBRD officials wanted their institution to be a sound business venture with its funds borrowed in the private market. Hence it made loans only where "reasonable" prospects of repayment existed. Eugene Black, the vice president of Chase National Bank who became IBRD president in 1949, urged that international capital transfers take the form of either loans for sound projects at close to commercial rates or outright grants. Soft or "fuzzy" loans had no place in international develop-ment finance.(8)

In considering loans, the IBRD judged specific projects in relation to the recipient's entire economy. Bank officials wanted to know whether prospective borrowers had an overall development plan, managers, skilled labor, and adequate local capital to complete the project. The IBRD did not finance the entire cost of any project; it provided loans in foreign exchange to finance that part of the cost of the scheme involving imported goods and services. Recipients of World Bank loans tended to purchase American exports. Between 1946 and 1953, 77 percent of the total IBRD loans ($1.495 billion) went to buy American goods and services. Very often, as a condition for bank financing, a country had to institute internal economic and financial reforms. In 1948, for example, the bank required Chile to repay defaulted bonds as the price for a long-term development loan. Bank policy sought to stimulate, directly or indirectly, private investment and private enterprise.(9)

The IBRD's reports and comments on individual loan proposals reflected the conventional wisdom on development. Bank executives emphasized tactics that focused on public overhead capital--railways, roads, power plants, ports, and communication facilities. An adequate economic infrastructure preceded all other development. The public sector had to plan and provide for these facilities, as well as create a satisfactory private investment climate. Agricultural, commercial, financial, industrial, and service development, however, comprised the realm of the private sector and market forces.(10)

What could the IBRD do to aid development? World Bank loans could help underdeveloped countries to meet the large foreign exchange requirements for infrastructural development. Bank "experts" would frame development policies and programs to mobilize private foreign and domestic capital and allocate that capital through market forces to its most productive uses. The bank sought to create conditions that encouraged a "steady and substantial stream" of foreign private investment. IBRD officials favored the private sector development of light industry in Third World nations and opposed public sector sponsored heavy industrial projects.(11)

The IBRD advanced relatively few funds to underdeveloped nations, believing that "money alone is no solution." According to bank executives, poor areas had a limited capacity for absorbing capital for productive purposes. Political instability, massive illiteracy, and poor health conditions hindered development. Technical assistance could remedy the education and health problems; such aid was a prerequisite for capital transfer. The extreme disparity between rich and poor within underdeveloped nations also obstructed capital investment. Moderate social reform--not radical reforms that would frighten away foreign capital--were also prerequisites for capital transfer. In the bank's first decade, loans went almost entirely to the financing of the foreign exchange costs of specific public utility projects.(12) The IBRD's relationship with the Middle East illustrates the bank's general policy toward the Third World.

By 1950, the IBRD had yet to grant any funds to Middle East countries. There had been loan offers to Egypt and Lebanon and a contemplated sterling credit for Iraq. The bank also toyed with the idea of forming a corporation responsible for planning and implementing all Middle East development projects. William Iliff, a loan officer, described the region as lacking a "fundamental climate" for proper development. Political, not economic or financial problems inhibited such a climate. The lack of capital, asserted Iliff, did not "brake the pace of development" as much as the area's inability to absorb capital. A shortage of skilled personnel to operate, manage, and administer projects constituted another obstacle to development. The Middle East and other poor regions, explained Iliff, were "most impoverished" in this "intermediate stratum of human competence."(13)

While the IBRD, with its cautious loan policy, failed to fund Middle East development, the U.S. Export-Import Bank (Eximbank) extended loans to several countries in the area. In operation since the mid-1930s, the Eximbank hoped to play a role similar to that of the IBRD in world development. Eximbank officials viewed the IBRD as a world banker, not as the world banker. IBRD executives, on the other hand, opposed Eximbank encroachment into development financing and held that the U.S. government should regard the World Bank as the main public source of loans for long-term investment. The two lending institutions battled each other into the 1950s-- stealing clients and concealing information on pending negotiations.(14)

The IBRD worked at a disadvantage since its charter required a 1 percent commission charge. This raised the IBRD's interest rate to 4.5 percent compared to the Eximbank's 3.5 percent. Between 1947 and 1951, the IBRD and Eximbank granted the same level of development loans--$525 million for the World Bank and $575 million for the Eximbank. The bulk of IBRD loans went for the development of basic utilities, while the Eximbank allocated funds for projects in manufacturing, mining, and agriculture. Eximbank credits usually financed the purchase of U.S. materials, equipment, and technical services. Although not restricted to American goods and services, over 77 percent of all IBRD loans also paid for these items.(15)

During the IBRD's formative period, American policy-makers pushed for increasing the Eximbank's lending authority. Eximbank board chair Leo T. Crowley, a conservative banker and ally of the corporate liberals, explained that financing joined "our need for foreign markets and the needs of foreign countries for our products." Congress raised the bank's lending authority from $700 million to $3.5 billion in July 1945. With its increased lending capacity and the slow development of the World Bank, the Eximbank emerged as a major international financial house. State Department officials continued to assist in formulating loan policy and negotiating credits with individual countries. The department sought to tie financial aid to the lowering of tariff barriers and the ending of exchange controls.(16)

The State Department's desire to have a say in foreign financing led to bureaucratic clashes. In making loans, the Eximbank considered the borrower's need for aid, its resources, its ability to use the funds effectively, and its capacity to repay. Bank executives examined possible private sources of capital, the impact of the loan on the American economy, and the recipient country's treatment of U.S. property, nationalization policies, and external debt record. Economic officers in the Departments of State and Treasury opposed loans based on considerations other than these criteria. Political officers favored "political" loans.(17)

In the spring of 1946, State Department economic officers and bank officials characterized the government's lending facilities as "sorely strained." Political officers, however, urged that Eximbank loans "be employed as an instrument of American foreign policy in the Near East." Loy Henderson, director of the Office of Near Eastern and African Affairs (NEA), proposed a $120 million line of credit to Middle East countries. "The expenditure of a few millions of dollars to help secure the stability of backward countries by raising the standard of living," argued Henderson, "would be a sound investment for the American taxpayer, who would thus be buying in the Near East the same form of anti-war insurance which he is purchasing in Europe and the Far East." NEA sought to use American capital, through the Eximbank, to push American policy in the region.(18)

Economic officers favored Middle East economic development. They supported moderate bank loans, but rejected the proposal for $120 million. The IBRD, according to these officials, was the proper agency for long-range Third World development; the Eximbank dealt with development loans only on an interim basis. Officers in the Office of Financial and Development Policy labelled NEA's suggestion a unilateral approach and out of line with the U.S. policy of seeking world development through international action. Financial officers proposed informing Middle East leaders of America's crucial role in creating and funding the World Bank. An IBRD loan thus equalled American government financial assistance.(19)

Despite the protests of economic officers in the State Department, the Eximbank became the principal banking institution extending credit to the Middle East and other underdeveloped regions. The IBRD's conservative lending policy made this necessary. By the end of 1949, the Eximbank had advanced $100 million in credit to Israel, $25 million to Saudi Arabia, and $71 million to Egypt. In addition, the bank was reviewing loan requests for Lebanon, Iraq, Syria, and Yemen.(20) But even the Eximbank's activities failed to meet the needs of many underdeveloped countries.

At the UN, Ecuador, Haiti, India, Lebanon, Syria, and others criticized the core nations for failing to provide essential development financing. Chile and Syria, noting the inability of developed nations to transfer capital either through private channels or through the IBRD and national banking institutions, demanded new funding methods. India proposed a new UN funding agency. Meanwhile, the United States favored a more liberal lending policy for both the IBRD and Eximbank. A memorandum from the Council of Economic Advisers in May 1949 conceded that the IBRD's lending policy might be "overcautious." In addition to pressing for a more generous World Bank, the council recommended that the U.S. government increase its foreign loans and grants by extending Eximbank guarantees on new private investments abroad, liberalizing tax credits on income from foreign investments, and negotiating treaties specifying the treatment of international capital.(21)

These policy proposals did not come to immediate fruition. As the decade ended, American policymakers continued to stress the role of private capital and enterprise in the advancement of the periphery. The U.S. government acknowledged a role for itself in aiding Third World development. Technical assistance theoretically paved the way for capital and capital equipment transfers to the underdeveloped world and provided a concrete example of America's concern for the development of poor nations.

TECHNICAL ASSISTANCE

America's concept of technical assistance assumed that, in a capitalist world-economy, knowledge and technology naturally flowed from the core to the periphery. This was part of a global "process of modernization, involving the spread of rationality and individualism, powered by transformation of the technical order."(22) For corporate liberals and imperial state policymakers, all the world's problems were becoming problems of basic and applied science--both the physical and social sciences. Solving underdevelopment simply involved the formulation and implementation of scientifically based policies. America's economic, industrial, and managerial "experts," as well as the corporate and state elite, failed to admit two related items. First, technology, science, and certainly economics were social processes permeated with the political and moral values of the societies in which they evolved. Second, the myriad difficulties facing Third World nations could not be "treated adequately purely as a question of basic or technological research in natural sciences or even in economic science." Such problems had to be considered within a social, cultural, and political economy context. The key slogan for U.S. policymakers when dealing with technical assistance, was "know-how," rather than "know-why." Policymakers avoided a public discussion of the crucial questions involving technology for what and technology for whom.(23)

One of the first moves toward technical aid for Third World development came in the UN General Assembly in late 1946. At the suggestion of the United States, the assembly incorporated the UN Relief and Rehabilitation Administration's advisory social welfare service into the UN. This service sent technical experts to advise governments on social welfare matters, establish and administer fellowships for study in the core, and organize seminars on social problems. In 1947, ECOSOC's Subcommission on Economic Development outlined future UN technical assistance programs. Direct technical aid would be provided only to and through governments which asked for it. Recipient countries would define the nature and scope of their problems. Technical aid could take the form of international teams of experts, training of indigenous personnel in core nations or within the periphery, and international conferences. By the fall of 1948 the UN had begun to act on these recommendations and had initiated limited technical aid projects.(24)

President Harry Truman's 1949 inaugural address shifted the focus on technical aid from the UN to the United States. Truman endorsed the work of the UN, praised the European Recovery Program, and outlined a North Atlantic defense pact. His "fourth point" called on the United States to "embark on a bold new program" of technical aid for the underdeveloped world. This fourth point suggested a program designed to achieve certain domestic and foreign economic and political objectives. Point Four marked the end of the almost exclusive public emphasis on postwar reconstruction in American foreign assistance policy. Rhetoric notwithstanding, Point Four was merely new wrapping for an old package; it was not a radical departure from previous American policy. Technical assistance always had been part of American foreign economic policy--as the operations of Nelson Rockefeller's OIAA and Henry Wallace's BEW demonstrated.(25)

Following the president's speech the imperial state bureaucracy slowly began to fill in the details of the Point Four program. Assistant Secretary of State for Economic Affairs Willard Thorp took charge of program development. Thorp created two committees to help formulate Point Four: an intradepartmental Technical Assistance Group and an interdepartmental Advisory Committee on Technical Assistance. In mid-February 1949, Thorp instructed his committees to examine the nature and objectives of Point Four, the relation of the program to UN activities, the flow of private investment into the periphery, and the criteria for selecting recipients of technical assistance. Over the course of the next six months, the imperial state bureaucracy debated issues, turned out reports, and made recommendations. Imperial state bureaucrats haltingly pieced together a program of technical assistance from their treasure-chest of cliches about private investment, private enterprise, comparative advantage, and free trade.(26)

Suggestions for the Point Four program came from outside the State Department. Walter S. Salant of the president's Council of Economic Advisers recommended that the government highlight the altruistic goals of Point Four. Public announcements could, for example, explain how the program would combat the "combination of desperate poverty and loss of hope for a better life" without resorting to the "old imperialism--exploitation for foreign profit." Other aspects of the program, cautioned Salant, should not "be put in a document for public release." The American public did not need to know whether recipients of technical aid were chosen on the basis of economic, political, or security considerations. Nor did the public need to know that Point Four should be designed to encourage the exportation of American capital to non-European areas in order to help Europe balance its international accounts after the ERP ended in 1952. Salant also stressed Point Four's potential contribution to maintaining domestic economic stability and productivity through the expansion of world trade. He recommended that planners design the program in such a way as to maximize domestic production, employment, and purchasing power--especially with respect to "geographical and economic sectors of the economy that would have to undergo severe readjustments if these goals were attained without substantial net foreign investment."(27)

The State Department's Commercial Policy Division viewed Point Four as a pretext for securing commercial treaties with underdeveloped nations. An underdeveloped country's willingness to commit itself to the principles of free trade and international specialization "might well be an important test in determining whether that country may prudently be considered a promising recipient of substantial American economic assistance." The division pushed for commercial treaties with all nations desiring Point Four aid.(28)

President Truman noted that the development of the Third World would "keep our own industrial plant in business for untold generations." Most imperial state policymakers believed that Point Four, by sharing knowledge and skills and encouraging capital investment, would improve Third World resources and eventually expand world production, exchange, and consumption. All this would reduce pressures for autarkic solutions to economic problems. By stimulating capital transfers to underdeveloped nations, technical aid would allow these nations to purchase American and European goods. With technical aid and capital goods, Third World countries would increase their own production of primary goods, and thus ease the drain of these items from the United States to Europe. Creating this balanced world economy required that Point Four shun enterprises that obstructed international specialization and the reduction of trade barriers. American policymakers planned to scrutinize Third World adherence to the doctrines of free trade and comparative advantage.(29)

Truman often asserted that Point Four had "nothing in common with either the old imperialism of the last century or the new imperialism of the Communists." In June 1949, the Advisory Committee on Technical Assistance acknowledged a well-worn truism of hegemony: Confessing a "self-interest **so broad as to be shared by most of the rest of the world** can do us no harm." The United States would proclaim what it always proclaimed, that it wanted prosperity and economic growth for itself and its neighbors. The committee linked economic and political development. Democracy could not survive and flourish in an environment of poverty, misery, and unrest. To counteract charges of imperialism, the Advisory Committee suggested that the government stress the voluntary nature of Point Four; that no country would endanger its sovereignty by accepting assistance. Other measures included encouraging investments by small- and medium-sized firms and helping poor nations to tap the profits of foreign enterprises by providing tax law and administrative technical aid. The United States should oppose laws mandating local participation in foreign enterprise, but should informally encourage American investors to do just this. The "era of gunboat diplomacy" was supposedly over. America's search for security and most-favored-nation treatment did not mean imperialism.(30)

The State Department's Technical Assistance Working Group recommended that the United States downplay the policy of encouraging strategic material development in the periphery. The United States had to avoid the appearance of using aid programs for the purpose of improving its raw material sources. But many officials believed that the imperial state "would be negligent if it did not exploit such possibilities." The Advisory Committee urged caution and suggested that technical assistance be dissociated from a strategic materials policy.(31)

Although disagreements continued over some aspects of the program, most imperial state planners concurred on Point Four's basic structure. Among other things, Point Four called for the "fostering" of international investment. State Department officers avoided linking technical aid to promises of investment. Underdeveloped countries suffered primarily because they lacked "the ability to organize and use their own resources" and, secondly, because they lacked capital. The two requirements for development were related, but not identical. Technical assistance could affect the direction and character of private and public loans. But Point Four never directly linked the processes of technical aid and capital transfer.(32)

Point Four sought to develop a country's natural, human, and capital resources.   The program emphasized agricultural production, since food, as Truman observed, was the "key to all productivity."   Technical information already "tested and proved in the United States" would be transferred to Third World nations.   In practice this often meant the transfer of techniques inappropriate for local peripheral conditions. Point Four ostensibly aimed at securing a broad participation of local labor in demonstration and training projects.   Yet most of the projects relied on capital intensive techniques-- especially in agriculture--which put large numbers of laborers out of work.   Above all, the technical aid program was to be a self-help program--a cooperative venture under which national development would flourish.   Government planners concluded that Point Four did not redefine U.S. policy objectives, but rather raised cooperation in economic development to a chief role among the instruments "for the accomplishment of existing objectives."(33)

In summary, the imperial state aimed Point Four at poor, agrarian areas; it hoped to use know-how to foster private investment.   As a long-range evolutionary program, Point Four presumably would serve humanitarian goals by improving life in the periphery; an economic purpose by stimulating domestic production, capital goods exports, raw material production, and general trade; and a political and Cold War function by building political democracy--or at least stability--and strengthening world peace. Possible projects included surveys of resources, agriculture, and industry and assistance in the implementation of development schemes. The United States and the recipient countries would share program costs. Technical aid would positively influence investor psychology, while helping to build Third World infrastructures.(34)   Point Four's emphasis on private foreign investments and the program's potential impact on economic development obviously interested capitalist class organizations.

The U.S. Chamber of Commerce created a special Point Four Committee that declared that the technical aid program should make full use of private initiative and capital, rather than government loans. Private enterprise would assist in the de- velopment and production of raw materials and agricultural goods, the processing of those materials, and the manufactur- ing of specialized goods. A "modest and carefully circum- scribed" government program, according to the chamber, would coordinate the activities of the public sector and private industry; cautiously expand technical aid in the fields of health, education, finance, and administration; encourage private capital and technology flows; and employ IBRD and Eximbank loans. The National Foreign Trade Council concurred, adding that public-private cooperation be restricted to proj- ects that, because of their magnitude or low return or politi- cal character, no longer attracted foreign capital.   Such projects might include irrigation and flood control, certain types of agricultural development, and construction of ports, railways, and roads.   The chamber and council suggested that the United States cooperate with those Third World nations that desired development, wanted American aid, and guaranteed fair treatment to American private capital and enterprise.(35)

The National Association of Manufacturers and the Chamber of Commerce disagreed over the importance of capital exports for American prosperity.   The chamber contended that the

United States could pick and choose its investment areas, refusing those regions where sufficient local capital existed or where a country maintained conditions unfavorable to investment. Foreign investment and world economic development, although beneficial, were not crucial for American growth. NAM saw aid to the Third World as "desirable and justified" in the interest "of our own national welfare and economic prosperity." Developing the Third World would provide the United States with valuable and needed markets, investment opportunities, and sources of raw materials.(36)

In general, capitalist class elites approved of a government-sponsored technical assistance program so long as it accompanied private capital expansion into the periphery. Editorials and articles in Fortune and Business Week insisted that Point Four stimulate private capital investments abroad. Both business journals, however, doubted whether the government program would have the desired effect. August Maffry, vice president of Irving Trust Company, Michael A. Heilperin, an economic consultant to the International Chamber of Commerce, and Joseph S. Lawrence, vice president of the Empire Trust Company in New York, contended that Point Four was worthwhile only if it led Third World governments to abandon restrictive economic policies and to provide a favorable climate for private foreign investors. Lawrence advocated shunting aside Point Four and forcing the peripheral nations to "toe the mark and comply with the conditions which in the past have made the international movement of capital possible and beneficial." Fortune warned against a government-sponsored global aid program that would replace private capital with public capital. The Wall Street Journal minced no words when it complained that once turned on, the spigot would continue to turn out assistance to peripheral peoples. Journal editors rejected "the premise that it is the duty of the United States to provide for economically backward peoples everywhere."(37)

Corporate liberals' conditional support for Point Four stood in sharp contrast to New Deal liberals' enthusiasm for technical assistance. The remnants of New Deal liberalism applauded Truman's bold new program. They hoped that Point Four would serve as the centerpiece for an expanded American development policy for the Third World. More importantly, Point Four reaffirmed their faith in American foreign policy. It gave American policy "a constructive and idealistic aspect" that hitherto had been obscured by the driving anti-Communist rhetoric of the Truman administration. Walter Salant, a veteran of the wartime Office of Price Administration--an agency characterized by the "flavor and fervor" of New Deal liberalism--pointed to the inadequacy of the name "Point Four" for a program "designed to strike a response in people's hearts and minds." Two former BEW officials now in private business, Milo Perkins and Morris S. Rosenthal, strongly endorsed the Point Four concept. They believed that the United States should supply as much technical assistance as possible to help spread the benefits of American capitalism and democracy to the Third World. At the same time, Perkins warned that economic development did not depend on technical assistance, but counted "primarily on private capital."(38)

Throughout the 1940s Nelson Rockefeller had tried to combine private capital investment with technical assistance to help develop Latin America. During World War II Rockefel-

ler's Office of Inter-American Affairs inaugurated a state-
sponsored technical assistance program for Latin America.
After the war, Rockefeller continued these activities as a
private citizen via the American International Association for
Economic and Social Development and the International Basic
Economy Corporation. Rockefeller welcomed Point Four as the
most significant development in American foreign policy in
decades. He testified before Congress on how technical assistance could stimulate peripheral development. Rockefeller's enthusiasm for the Point Four program derived, in part,
from his desire to return to government service. He hoped to
transform Point Four into a Marshall Plan for the Third World;
to create an institutional structure--much like the Economic
Cooperation Administration--that would incorporate all facets
of a foreign economic assistance program and which he could
administer.(39) Neither Congress nor the imperial state
bureaucracy wanted such a concentrated and centralized agency.

Capitalist class elites viewed economic development as
resting firmly on a foundation of private capital investment,
the private market, and free trade. Technical assistance was
a necessary, but not a sufficient ingredient for continued
economic growth. Henry R. Luce, founder of _Time_ and _Fortune_,
succinctly stated this position in early 1950. Luce explained
that "the popular idea of just giving them [i.e., Third World
peoples] our 'know-how' can have only very limited results in
itself; most of our 'know-how' works only in a business
economy." The only way to really "reform" the economies of
the Third World and to raise living standards was to integrate
them into the American marketplace and into the capitalist
world-economy.(40)

Organized labor once again followed the lead of the
imperial state and capitalist class elites. The AFL and the
CIO endorsed the basic provisions of Point Four, even though
the State Department totally ignored the possibility of labor
participation in the program. As early as 1945, CIO officials
had voiced an interest in rendering assistance to the "strug-
gling labor organizations of smaller or economically inferior
nations." In late 1948, AFL officials outlined a worker
training program for "backward economies" in which "experienced trade unionists" would go to underdeveloped countries.
Matthew Woll, chairman of the AFL's International Relations
Committee, and David Dubinsky, AFL representative to ECOSOC,
proposed that whenever a poor nation purchased American
machinery the AFL would assume responsibility for training
workers in the underdeveloped nation. The AFL's Free Trade
Union Committee actively sought to spread the gospel of
American-style trade unionism and American political economy
to the Third World. While supporting the Point Four program,
the AFL Executive Council urged that technical aid to poor
areas "include provisions for the transmission of bona fide
trade union, cooperative and farmers' 'know-how' which will
enable workers and peasants...to build effective democratic
unions and self help organizations." AFL officials did not
accept the entire Point Four package. Labor leaders questioned government protection for investors; they viewed such
guarantees as handouts to America's corporations.(41)

With the qualified support of capital and labor, the
imperial state bureaucracy finished draft legislation for a
technical aid program in late June 1949. Two bills went to
Congress--one dealing with foreign investment and the other

with technical aid. Business ambivalence concerning government investment guarantees led to the defeat of the investment
bill. In June 1950, Congress finally passed the technical
assistance bill as the Act for International Development.(42)
As some imperial state officials formulated the details of
Point Four and guided it through Congress, others attempted to
contain Third World development demands in the UN.

During February and March 1949, American delegates to the
UN diverted attention from Third World requests for studies on
financing economic development to the issue of technical aid.
On 4 March, ECOSOC adopted an American resolution asking the
secretary general to report on a comprehensive plan for an expanded technical assistance program for development through
the UN and its specialized agencies. This report, completed
in May, concluded that economic development required both
technical knowledge and finance. Domestic sources must supply
the principal initiative and the largest portion of capital
and labor for development. A successful program would aim at
balanced development and adapt to the needs and the resources
of the particular nation. Underdeveloped countries would have
to establish the internal conditions necessary for sound
development, conduct resource surveys, and prepare long-range
plans for industry, agriculture, finance, education, and
transportation. Technical aid programs required qualified
experts, supplies and equipment, and continuity--the need to
continue the program for many years, if not decades. First-
year estimates for the UN's technical aid program totalled
$5.94 million.(43)

The report on technical assistance--with its obvious
input by the United States and other core nations--sparked
another round of debates between rich and poor nations.
Lebanon's George Hakim identified financial aid, rather than
technical assistance, as the Third World's chief need. While
financial aid led to the provision of technical knowledge, the
possession of technical know-how did not necessarily bring
capital aid. Hakim contended that risks, returns on investment, convertibility of profits, and the general state of the
economy and capital accumulation in the industrial countries,
rather than technical aid, prepared the path for the international flow of capital.(44)

Poor, agrarian nations objected to both the form and
direction of the technical assistance programs advocated by
the United States and outlined in the Secretary General's
report. Middle East delegates, for example, noted that the
Third World possessed hundreds of surveys and development
schemes, but lacked the capital to implement those plans. Why
did capital have to follow technology? At the very least, argued these officials, technology and capital should flow simultaneously. Underdeveloped nations required more than
experts and technicians; they needed tools, equipment, and
materials.(45)

Few Third World countries, at least during the late
1940s, questioned American technical aid per se--that is, few
challenged the political and cultural "neutrality" of technical know-how. Some Third World officials realized that importing American technology and knowledge meant importing
concomitant American attitudes. But those who recognized this
problem also believed that a nation could "exclude `undesir-
able' aspects of modernization, especially with regard to
values, morals, manners, and behavior." As later experiences

would demonstrate, this was not an easy task. Capitalist development created its own value system.(46)

These concerns notwithstanding, Egyptian and Lebanese officials contended that technical aid had to contribute to the diversification of peripheral production. They criticized the Point Four program for neglecting industrialization. America's capitalist class and imperial state elites responded that the United States sought "sound" industrialization based on a nation's resources and its comparative advantage to produce certain goods. Arab officials countered that their countries desired the techniques and materials to develop manufacturing industries that, while not necessarily sound from the point of view of international specialization, were sound from the perspective of their own regional and national economies.(47)

Over Third World objections, ECOSOC adopted an American resolution that outlined an administrative structure and a set of principles for an expanded UN technical aid program. Assistance would be provided only upon request; industrial and agricultural projects would be selected on the basis of both economic and social goals and would be aimed at increasing productivity. The United States agreed to match cash contributions of other countries up to 60 percent of the total fund or to a specified maximum amount--whichever came first. Third World governments had to help finance and administer all projects. The General Assembly approved the ECOSOC resolution in November 1949 and soon thereafter established machinery to implement the program. Like Point Four, the UN Expanded Program on Technical Assistance began operations in late 1950. Both programs suffered from bureaucratic problems. The Soviet Union and many peripheral countries criticized the programs as neocolonialism and as mechanisms to ensure markets and investment opportunities for American goods, services, and capital. Underdeveloped nations continued to insist that they wanted and needed industrial plants, not industrial experts.(48)

RECONSTRUCTION VERSUS DEVELOPMENT: CONCLUSION

In 1945, state and corporate policymakers envisioned a postwar integrated world economy and political system dominated by the United States. Achieving the internationalization of American capitalism and corporatism required American assistance in the reconstruction of Europe and Japan and in the economic and political development of the Third World. American leaders believed that European recovery, multilateral trade, and currency convertibility comprised the keys to unlock the door of Pax Americana. Even when policymakers realized that Europe's economic difficulties, the Communist resistance to American plans, the anti-Western nationalism of newly independent peripheral states, and congressional protectionism and parsimony, all were more serious than previously thought, the goal remained the same--the tactics changed.

Officials increasingly warned of the Communist threat and began to support regional commercial and financial arrangements--particularly in the case of Europe--as the prerequisite for international free trade and currency exchange. The global approach was not discarded, however. The fight for the International Trade Organization and the European Recovery Program were parts of the same policy. Similarly, officials viewed the Economic Commission for Europe and the Economic

Commission for Asia and the Far East as regional arms of the UN's global operations. Most important, while imperial state policymakers handled the problems of Europe--and to a lesser extent Asia--on a regional basis, they continued to manage the development of the Third World on an international and functional level.

Selective development of the periphery comprised a crucial element in creating the American world order. Such development would help European recovery by supplying new markets and sources of raw materials and by easing the dollar gap crisis. The United States would directly benefit from the newly developed markets, investment opportunities, and raw materials in the Third World. American officials hoped that economic development, under the direction of private enterprise and the private marketplace, would bring political democracy to the periphery. Imperial state policymakers were convinced, however, that economic development would bring political stability to those regions--regardless of the particular form that stability might take. Ultimately political stability and the open door were more important to American hegemony than democracy.(49)

American leaders questioned the means, rather than the ends of economic development within the context of a capitalist world-economy. Imperial state discussions revolved around public versus private sector policies, multilateral versus bilateral schemes, global versus regional approaches, and technical versus capital assistance programs. Throughout the 1940s, the imperial state and capitalist class elites held that economic development in the periphery would progress as European and Japanese recovery advanced. Development, therefore, depended on special economic aid to the core powers of Europe and Asia and on the revival of free world trade. Public and private technical assistance combined with free trade, a revitalized capitalist core, currency convertibility, and favorable investment climates in the periphery would facilitate the transfer of private capital from developed industrial states to the underdeveloped world.(50)

Ruling classes in the Third World interpreted such policies as evidence of America's neglect of the periphery. They wanted a Marshall Plan for their countries. Often dismissing free trade and currency convertibility as insufficient policies, these nations sought to subordinate their commercial policy to economic development--to impose protective tariffs, import quotas, and controls on foreign enterprise. With visions of their own steel mills, manufacturing plants, and TVAs, Third World countries wanted capital and technology. They looked to the United States to lead the way--to shoulder the burden of financing such development. But these nations sought foreign capital and technology while simultaneously advocating state controls to foster industrialization. American and other core capitalists simply did not go abroad under those restrictions. Third World leaders slowly understood that the United States had modified the game perfected by their former colonial masters. If peripheral countries wanted to work within the capitalist world-economy, then they had to accept the inherent inequality and uneven development of that system; they had to accept the dependent development which that system allowed them.(51)

American officials attacked the poor nations' obsession with the rate of development and their desire for independent

development.   These nations were trying to force the rate of
change far beyond the capacity of their local economic and
social institutions.   Underdeveloped nations wanted too much,
too fast.   Rapid development caused inflation, economic
maladjustments, and political turmoil.   American policymakers
were probably more realistic than their counterparts in the
periphery. Knowing how the capitalist world-economy operated,
American officials never promised equity or fairness.   Instead, they noted that in a properly functioning capitalist
system, free trade, comparative advantage, and specialization
would bring growth to those sectors of peripheral economies
participating in the world system.   To a certain extent,
however, American officials were guilty of raising Third World
expectations. While stressing the need for slow and cautious
development policies in the periphery, many American corporate
and imperial state leaders described development as an easy
and painless process that naturally flowed from private
enterprise and free trade.(52)

Louis K. Hyde, a member of the American Mission to the UN
in the late 1940s, wrote that core nations began to realize in
1949 the limitations of liberal capitalism; that the social
and economic problems of the periphery "were beyond the reach
of orthodox trade and currency measures."   When the decade
ended, the United States and other core states began to recognize the inadequacies of the IMF, World Bank, the Eximbank,
and private enterprise and capital in achieving Third World
development. But American policymakers did not abandon their
faith in international free trade and world specialization--
nor could they.(53)

Political scientist David Baldwin has argued that the
lack of substantial world development in the 1940s and 1950s
did not derive from the nature of American policies per se,
but rather from the imperfect and incomplete implementation of
those policies. If free trade had actually been achieved,
then it could have led to the rapid development of the world's
poor regions. Underdeveloped nations, however, blindly attacked the only policy that could have saved them.   They
underestimated the contributions that free trade and comparative advantage could have made to raising living standards,
and they ignored the dangers of failing to adopt policies that
would promote international equilibrium. This variation of
the conventional wisdom, advanced by Baldwin and others and
held in principle by every American administration since World
War II, is problematic. It assumes, for example, that economic development is nothing more nor less than economic growth
(gross national product); it totally ignores the crucial issue
of basic human needs and the intricate problems of distribution; it reflects a superficial understanding of class relationships within the periphery and between the periphery and
the core. But in one important respect this analysis is
valid. American leaders correctly identified those policies
that would maximize American economic and political power in
the world.   They correctly advanced policies that would maximize world trade, increase the size of the global economic pie
(at least for a while), and lead to dependent development in
the periphery.(54)

Liberalizing trade could not by itself close or bridge
the gap between developed and underdeveloped nations because
free trade perpetuated and exacerbated world inequalities and
uneven development.   In a capitalist world economy "capital-

ist, semi-capitalist, and pre-capitalist relations of production [are] linked to each other by capitalist relations of exchange and dominated by the capitalist world market." Free trade and private capital transfers, advocated by the United States, aided the core nations by providing them with sources of raw materials, inexpensive labor, and markets for industrial goods. Trade and private capital stimulated primary goods production in the periphery--primary goods that had an inelastic demand in export markets. More important than this "unequal exchange," was the retarding and distorting effect that free trade--even imperfect free trade--had on peripheral economies. Advanced capitalist nations consciously and unconsciously forced Third World nations into primary production which distorted those nations' socioeconomic and political structures. Thus poor nations, as Michael Barratt Brown wrote, "suffered not simply from negative lack of development but from the positive distortions of **under**development."(55)

U.S. policymakers understood the inherent inequality and uneven character of an integrated world-economy based on free trade principles. They knew that the capitalist world-economy--and the American domestic economy--functioned on the basis of inequality and constant expansion. The inequalities--economic, social, political, cultural--were at the very heart of capitalism. America's capitalist class and imperial state embraced this system. They advocated policies that served to maintain and expand that system. Failure to support capitalism and its inequalities at home and abroad was suicidal. By constantly expanding the capitalist world-system and increasing production, systemic inequities presumably would be tolerated. American policy aimed at an absolute increase in world production and standards of living. By making the international economic pie bigger, the "needs" of poor, agrarian nations--specifically the needs of the indigenous ruling and middle classes willing to collaborate with the core--would be met and political stability assured. American capitalist class and imperial state leaders felt no obligation to aid the periphery. They believed it unnecessary to raise the Third World to an economic level equal to that of the core. The United States had no desire to tamper with an international order that it dominated. It felt no urge to redistribute the world's wealth and power (i.e., control over the means of production), just as its own ruling class abhorred the thought of redistributing its wealth and power among the citizenry at home. Substantial changes in, and fundamental challenges to, the capitalist world-economy threatened to result in such redistribution. Working within the capitalist world-economy and from a domestic capitalist and corporatist structure, American policymakers, at best, could engage in a form of global welfare capitalism. Such a program, advocated by Henry A. Wallace and other New Deal liberals, would involve global TVAs and public loans, grants, and technical assistance. The alternative was an emphasis on private enterprise development of the periphery. No other significant option existed if policymakers were to maintain and further world capitalism and American hegemony.

In the late 1940s the majority of America's capitalist class elites tended to oppose any attempt at international welfare capitalism. Corporate liberals such as Will Clayton and members of the Committee for Economic Development, accepted existing New Deal realities at home. They did not seek to elaborate or expand those same New Deal programs. Similarly, the CED and other capitalist class institutions doubted the efficacy of expanding the New Deal to the world. CED officials advocated a crucial role for the state in helping to strengthen private enterprise at home and abroad, but not in taking its place.(56) The imperial state produced policies within the parameters set by capitalist class elites. Some differences of opinion emerged and some tactical battles ensued, but consensus was the rule. American policy viewed economic development as the responsibility of the poor nations themselves. The only way to achieve development was for the periphery to openly and completely join the capitalist world-economy. Most Third World rulers accepted this wisdom. But they also contended that their nations required special, temporary treatment similar to that afforded Europe. According to peripheral leaders, the core nations had a responsibility to help alleviate balance of payments difficulties, to rectify the lack of capital, and to supply appropriate technology, among other things. Few officials in the Third World during the 1940s truly challenged the existing capitalist world-economy. The periphery's ruling elites sought reforms in, or temporary exemptions from, the dominant system--in order to alleviate the more blatant examples of indigenous poverty and thus consolidate their own positions at home.

As the 1940s ended, U.S. corporate and state policymakers continued to view Third World economic development as an integral part of American capitalist expansion abroad--a view held by their predecessors dating back to the late nineteenth century. The Great Depression, World War II, and the Cold War heightened the importance of such development, while simultaneously complicating its attainment. Extensive wartime destruction threatened Pax Americana and necessitated an active American role in the rebuilding of Europe and Japan. Policymakers hoped to fuse European reconstruction with Third World development in the overall goal of achieving the internationalization of American capitalism and corporatism. Although reconstruction and development were to occur simultaneously and were to feed upon one another, the juxtaposition of the two processes highlighted the growing gap between rich and poor nations. Moreover, the juxtaposition of European (and Japanese) recovery and Third World development revealed the American tendency to support the revival of capitalist core powers at the expense of the growing political and economic nationalism of the periphery.

These attitudes and policies were evident in all areas of American foreign relations, including American economic relations with the countries of the Arab East.

NOTES

1. NAC Document 2--1945, "Methods by Which the U.S. Extends Financial Assistance to Foreign Countries," 16.NAC, 5.19F Interdepartmental Committees Related to ECEFP, RG 353, U.S. National Archives, Washington, D.C.; ECEFP D-136/45, "Trade Expansion Proposals Involving Problems of Financing," 1 November 1945, 5.19B ECEFP Meetings, 3.Documents, RG 353; Walter Salant, "Foreign Investment and American Foreign Policy," 11 January 1949, Point Four folder, Salant Papers, Harry S. Truman Library, Independence, Mo.; ECEFP D-58/48

Rev. 1, "Statement of US Foreign Credit and Investment Policy," 11 August 1948, 5.19E ECEFP Subcommittee, 15.Petroleum Policy Committee, RG 353; Memo, W. Fowler to John Leddy, 21 January 1949, Subject File, folder "Development: Economic," Records of US Mission to UN, RG 84, U.S. National Archives, Washington, D.C.; 80th Congress, 1st session, House of Representatives, Doc. 365, Report of Activities of the National Advisory Council on International Monetary and Financial Problems (Washington, D.C.: U.S. Government Printing Office, 1947), pp. 16-21.

2. William K. Jackson speech, 13 November 1946, National Foreign Trade Council (hereafter NFTC), 33rd National Foreign Trade Convention, 1946 (New York: NFTC, 1946), pp. 380-84. For similar capitalist class views see ibid., pp. 31, 116, 119-20; NFTC, 34th National Foreign Trade Convention (New York: NFTC, 1947), p. xxiv; Adolf A. Berle to Joseph Alsop, 27 September 1946, Subject Files, 1946-71, U.S. Foreign Policy (General), 1946-52, A. Berle Papers, FDR Library, Hyde Park, N.Y.; National Association of Manufacturers (hereafter NAM), The Bold New Plan: A Program for Underdeveloped Areas (New York: NAM, Economic Policy Division Series no. 11, May 1949).

3. Harold van B. Cleveland, Thomas Huertas et al., Citibank, 1812-1970 (Cambridge, Mass.: Harvard University Press, 1985), pp. 218, 220.

4. UN, Yearbook of the United Nations, 1948-1949 (hereafter Yearbook followed by appropriate years) (Lake Success, N.Y.: UN, 1949), p. 455; Mira Wilkins, The Maturing of Multinational Enterprise: American Business Abroad from 1914 to 1970 (Cambridge, Mass.: Harvard University Press, 1974), pp. 298-301; NAM, Bold New Plan; U.S. Chamber of Commerce, Point Four Program (1949), pp. 13, 16, 20; S. Pizer and F. Cutler, "Private U.S. Direct Investments Abroad," Survey of Current Business 31 (January 1951): 20-23. Commenting on the nature of capital investment, Barratt Brown has noted: "Funds tend to go to safe rather than risky projects, to private rather than to public enterprise, to advanced rather than to poor economies, unless there are very special opportunities to be exploited, very considerable existing investments to be extended, or very important political purposes to be served." Michael Barratt Brown, After Imperialism (New York: Humanities Press, 1970), p. 229.

5. Frederick Dobney, ed., Selected Papers of Will Clayton, (Baltimore: Johns Hopkins Press, 1971), p. 116; Robert Cox, "Social Forces, States and World Orders: Beyond International Relations Theory," Millennium: Journal of International Studies, 10, no. 2 (1981): 136-37, 145; Robert Cox, "Gramsci, Hegemony and International Relations: An Essay in Method," Millennium: Journal of International Studies, 12, no. 2 (1983): 172.

6. Alfred Eckes, Search for Solvency: Bretton Woods and the International Monetary System, 1941-1971 (Austin: University of Texas Press, 1975), pp. 227-29, 211-12; "Meeting with McCloy," 8 March 1947, vol. 6, October 1946-March 1947, James V. Forrestal Diaries, Seeley G. Mudd Manuscript Library, Princeton University, Princeton, N.J.; Robert Asher, Walter

M. Kotschnig, and William A. Brown, Jr., The United Nations
and Economic and Social Co-Operation (Washington, D.C.:
Brookings Institution, 1957), p. 159; ECEFP D-48/48 Rev. 1,
"Report of the Subcommission on Economic Development," 26
April 1948, 5.19B ECEFP Meetings, 3.Documents, RG 353.

7. Eckes, Search for Solvency, pp. 219-20, 223;
Eleanora W. Schoenebaum, ed., Political Profiles: The Truman
Years (New York: Facts on File, 1978), pp. 343-46; Arthur M.
Johnson, Winthrop W. Aldrich: Lawyer, Banker, Diplomat
(Boston: Graduate School of Business Administration, Harvard
University, 1968), pp. 316, 319-20.

8. Eckes, Search for Solvency, pp. 223-25; IBRD, The
International Bank for Reconstruction and Development, 1946-
1953 (Baltimore: Johns Hopkins Press, 1954), pp. 42-56;
Louis Hyde, The United States and the United Nations: Promot-
ing the Public Welfare--Examples of American Co-Operation,
1945-1955, (New York: Carnegie Endowment for International
Peace, 1960), pp. 96-98; Edward Mason and Robert Asher, The
World Bank Since Bretton Woods (Washington, D.C.: The
Brookings Institution, 1973), p. 463.

9. IBRD, The International Bank, pp. 42-56; Hyde, The
United States, pp. 96-98; Mason and Asher, The World Bank, p.
463.

10. Mason and Asher, The World Bank, pp. 458-60.

11. Ibid., pp. 459, 465-66. For similar views expressed
by American officials see Walter Salant, "Foreign Investment
and American Foreign Policy," 11 January 1949, Point Four
folder, Salant Papers.

12. Mason and Asher, The World Bank, pp. 461-62.

13. Memo, Office of Financial and Economic Development
to Gordon Clapp, 6 September 1949, Miscellaneous Confidential
Correspondence ESM folder, Gordon Clapp Papers, Harry Truman
Library, Independence, Mo.; L. Douglas to Secretary of State,
4 March 1949, includes comments by E. Bayne of the IBRD staff,
DOS 890.50/3-449, RG 59, U.S. National Archives, Washington,
D.C.; William Iliff speech, Helen A. Kitchen, ed., Americans
and the Middle East: Partners in the Next Decade (Washington,
D.C.: Middle East Institute, 1950), pp. 43-45.

14. Mason and Asher, The World Bank, pp. 494-500.

15. Ibid.

16. Department of State, Foreign Relations of the United
States, 1946, vol. 1, pp. 1397-99, 1402-3 (hereafter FRUS
followed by appropriate year and volume); Memo, "Inclusion of
Financial Matters in Scope of ECEFP," 16 October 1945; "Relations between NAC and ECEFP," 17 October 1945; ECEFP to OFD,
19 October 1945; ECEFP to Robert Carr, 4 January 1946; ECEFP
to Willard Thorp, 6 January 1946; and memo of conversation,
State and Treasury officers, 26 February 1946, 5.19 Interdepartmental Committees Related to ECEFP, 16.NAC, RG 353.

17. <u>FRUS, 1946</u>, 1: 1412;   ECEFP D-58/48 Rev. 1, "Statement of US Foreign Credit and Investment Policy,"   11 August
1948, 5.19E ECEFP, RG 353;   Memo, Paul McGuire to Lewis Jones,
25 March 2946, DOS 890.51/3-2546, RG 59.

18. Memo, McGuire to Jones,   DOS 890.51/3-2546, RG 59;
<u>FRUS, 1946</u>, 7: 7-10.

19. <u>FRUS, 1946</u>, 7: 10-13.

20. Memo, Office of Financial and Economic Development
to G. Clapp, 6 September 1949, Misc. Confidential Correspondence, ESM folder, Clapp Papers.

21. UN, <u>Yearbook, 1948-1949</u>, p. 455;   Memo, Report of
Stabilization Committee to Council of Economic Advisers, 1 May
1949, International Relations 1949 folder, Salant Papers.

22. Lisa Peattie, <u>Thinking About Development</u> (New York:
Plenum Press, 1981), pp. 36-38.

23. Bichara Khader, "The Social Impact of the Transfer
of Technology to the Arab World," <u>Arab Studies Quarterly</u> 4
(Summer 1982): 226, 228-29, 232;   Ronald Charles Benge, <u>Cul-
tural Crisis and Libraries in the Third World</u> (Hamden, Conn.:
Linnet Books,   1979), pp.   35-36,   38-39,   42;   S. Dedijer,
"Social   Sciences   and   Social   Development,"   in Eugene
Rabinowitch and Victor Rabinowitch, eds., <u>Views of Science,
Technology and Development</u> (Oxford: Pergamon Press, 1975), p.
131.

24. Asher et al., <u>The United Nations</u>, pp. 437, 440;
Hyde, <u>The United States</u>, pp. 95-97; UN, <u>Yearbook, 1948-1949</u>,
p. 432;   ECOSOC, <u>Official Records</u>, 4th year, 9th session,
<u>Report of the Second Session of the Sub-Commission on Economic
Development</u>, Supplement No. 11A (New York: UN, 1948), pp. 1,
3-10, 14.

25. Department of State (hereafter DOS), <u>Bulletin</u>, (30
January 1949): 123; Harry Truman, <u>Memoirs</u>, vol. 2, <u>Years of
Trial and Hope</u>, (Garden City, N.Y.: Doubleday, 1956), pp.
226-39; William Brown and R. Opie, <u>American Foreign Assist-
ance</u> (Washington, D.C.: The Brookings Institution, 1953), p.
389; Francis Russell, Director of Public Affairs in State
Department, 1948-49, "Origins of Point Four," 16 December
1966, DOS F.W. 800.50TA/1-2849, RG 59.   For background on
Point Four see Thomas G. Paterson, "Foreign Aid Under Wraps:
The Point Four Program," <u>Wisconsin Magazine of History</u> 56
(Winter 1972-73): 119-26; and Claude C. Erb, "Prelude to Point
Four: The Institute of Inter-American Affairs," <u>Diplomatic
History</u> 9 (Summer 1985): 249-70.

26. <u>FRUS, 1949</u>, 1: 757-71;   Memo, William Fowler to W.
Thorp, 24 January 1949, Subject File, folder "Development:
Economic," Records of US Mission to UN, RG 84, U.S. National
Archives, Washington, D.C.;   State Department's Technical
Assistance Working Group (TAG), "Organization Arrangements for
the Development of the Technical Cooperation Program," TAG D-
11, 18 February 1949, DOS 800.50TA/2-1849, RG 59; "Scope of
the Program: Relation to International Flow of Capital," TAG

D3/1a, 11 February 1949, DOS 800.50TA/2-1849, RG 59; "Geographic Scope of Point IV Program," TAG D-2/4a, 28 February 1949, DOS 800.50TA/2-1849, RG 59; Dean Acheson, <u>Present at the Creation: My Years in the State Department</u> (New York: W. W. Norton, 1969), pp. 256-66.

27. Walter S. Salant, "Comments on 'Objectives and Nature of Point IV Program,'" ECEFP D-27/49, 18 February 1949, 5.19B ECEFP Meetings, 3.Documents, RG 353; Walter Salant, "Requirements of the Point Four Program," 13 May 1949, Point Four Folder, Salant Papers. Also see ECEFP D-21/49 Rev. 2, "Objectives and Nature of the Point 4 Program," 1 March 1949, 5.19B ECEFP Meetings, 3.Documents, RG 353; DOS, <u>Point Four: Cooperative Program for Aid in the Development of Economically Underdeveloped Areas</u> (Washington, D.C.: U.S. Government Printing Office, January 1950), pp. 1-36; <u>FRUS, 1949</u>, 1:774-83; and William S. Borden, <u>The Pacific Alliance: United States Foreign Economic Policy and Japanese Trade Recovery, 1947-1955</u> (Madison: University of Wisconsin Press, 1984), p. 28.

28. Herman Walker, TAG D-14/2, "Treaties of Friendship, Commerce and Navigation in Relation to 'Point Four,'" 4 April 1949, DOS 800.50TA/2-1849, RG 59.

29. Truman, <u>Memoirs</u>, vol. 2, p. 232; ECEFP D-21/49 Rev. 2, "Objectives," 1 March 1949, 5.19B ECEFP Meetings, 3.Documents, RG 353; Salant, "Requirements," 13 May 1949, Salant Papers; TAG D-10a, "Implications of a Technical Assistance Program for the Over-all Program to Expand International Trade," 14 March 1949, DOS 800.50TA/2-1849, RG 59.

30. Truman, <u>Memoirs</u>, vol. 2, p. 234; ACTA D-29, "Imperialism and Point 4," Advisory Committee on Technical Assistance, Economic Committees, Point Four, 5.35.4 Policy Papers (ACTA Documents), RG 353.

31. ACTA D-29, "Imperialism," RG 353; TAG D-10a, "Implications of Technical Assistance," 14 March 1949, DOS 800.50TA/2-1849, RG 59.

32. ACTA D-29, RG 59; TAG D-10a, DOS 800.50TA/2-1849, RG 59; TAG D-2/4a, "Geographic Scope of Point 4," 28 February 1949, DOS 800.50TA/2-1849; TAG D-3/1a, "Scope of the Program: Relation to International Flow of Capital," 11 February 1949, DOS 800.50TA/2-1849, RG 59.

33. Truman, <u>Memoirs</u>, vol. 2, pp. 233, 236; Richard J. Barnet and Ronald Muller, <u>Global Reach: The Power of the Multinational Corporations</u> (New York: Cornerstone Book, 1974), pp. 162-72; ECEFP D-21/49 Rev. 2, "Objectives," 1 March 1949, 5.19B ECEFP Meetings, 3.Documents, RG 353; <u>FRUS, 1949</u>, 1: 781-82.

34. DOS, <u>Point Four</u>, pp. 1-36, 47-75.

35. Brown and Opie, <u>American Foreign Assistance</u>, p. 391; U.S. Chamber of Commerce, <u>Point Four Program</u>, pp. 7-9, 19-20; NFTC, <u>36th National Foreign Trade Convention, 31 October-2 November 1949</u> (New York: NFTC, 1950), pp. xxiv-xxv, 140-179.

36. U.S. Chamber of Commerce, Point Four Program; NFTC, 36th National Foreign Trade Convention; NAM, Bold New Plan.

37. "Truman's Global Recovery Plan," Fortune 39 (March 1949): 75-76; Business Week, 26 November 1949, pp. 105-7; Joseph S. Lawrence, "Point Four--Constructive Therapy or Blood Transfusion?" The Annals of the American Academy of Political and Social Science 270 (July 1950): 16-21; Michael A. Heilperin, "Private Means of Implementing Point Four," The Annals of the American Academy of Political and Social Science 268 (March 1950): 54-65; "Point IV," Fortune 41 (February 1950): 89-96, 176-182; August Maffry, "Whither Point Four?," Vital Speeches of the Day, 16 (1 April 1950): 358-62; The Wall Street Jorunal, 29 September 1949, p. 6.

38. Alonzo L. Hamby, Beyond the New Deal: Harry S. Truman and American Liberalism (New York: Columbia University Press, 1973), pp. 355, 370-73; Salant, "Comments on Point IV," ECEFP D-27/49, 18 February 1949, RG 353; Barton J. Bernstein, "The Removal of War Production Board Controls on Business, 1944-1946," Business History Review 39 (Summer 1965): 243; Morris S. Rosenthal, "Point Four--Enough or Not at All," The Annals of the American Academy of Political and Social Science 270 (July 1950): 35-41; Milo Perkins, "Point Four and U.S. Foreign Policy," Vital Speeches of the Day, 16 (15 November 1949): 70-77.

39. Joe Alex Morris, Nelson Rockefeller: A Biography (New York: Harper & Brothers, 1960), pp. 271-72; Peter Collier and David Horowitz, The Rockefellers: An American Dynasty (New York: Holt, Rinehart and Winston, 1976), p. 266.

40. Henry R. Luce, "The Reformation of the World's Economies," Fortune 41 (February 1950): 60-61.

41. John P. Windmuller, American Labor and the International Labor Movement, 1940 to 1953 (Ithaca, N.Y.: Institute of International Industrial and Labor Relations, Cornell University, 1954), p. xii; Jeffrey Harrod, Trade Union Foreign Policy: A Study of British and American Trade Union Activities in Jamaica (Garden City, N.Y.: Doubleday, 1972), pp. 116-17, 119-20; AFL, Report of the Executive Council of the American Federation of Labor, 68th Convention, October 1949 (Washington, D.C.: AFL, 1949), p. 58; Matthew Woll and David Dubinsky, "Proposals Submitted by Consultants Representing AFL," Box 39, folder: ECOSOC, Files of Director of Research, General Files, AFL Papers, State Historical Society of Wisconsin, Madison, Wis.; AFL Executive Council, memo on Point Four, February 1950, Box 16, folder: Point Four, Files of Director of Research, General Files, AFL Papers; Hamby, Beyond New Deal, p. 372.

42. Brown and Opie, American Foreign Assistance, pp. 391-94; Charles Lipson, Standing Guard: Protecting Foreign Capital in the Nineteenth and Twentieth Centuries (Berkeley: University of California Press, 1985); FRUS, 1949 1: 787; FRUS, 1950 1: 846.

43. Hyde, The United States, p. 108; Brown and Opie, American Foreign Assistance, pp. 400-401; UN, Secretary General, Technical Assistance for Economic Development (Lake Success, N.Y.: UN, May 1949), pp. 6-8, 13-17, 20-35, 53-73.

44. Hyde, The United States, p. 108; ECOSOC, Official Records: 4th year, 9th session, p. 392.

45. Norman Burns, NEA economic officer, speech in Kitchen, ed., Americans and the Middle East, pp. 4-5; ECOSOC, Official Records: 4th year, 9th session, p. 395.

46. Benge, Cultural Crisis, p. 42.

47. Kitchen, ed., Americans and the Middle East, pp. 50-54; UN, Yearbook, 1948-1949, pp. 449-56.

48. Hyde, The United States, pp. 109-10, 115-21; Brown and Opie, American Foreign Assistance, pp. 400-401; Asher et al., The United Nations, pp. 449-53; UN, Technical Assistance; Walter Sharp, The United Nations Economic and Social Council (New York: Columbia University Press, 1969), pp. 82-85.

49. Robert A. Packenham, Liberal America and the Third World: Political Development Ideas in Foreign Aid and Social Science (Princeton, N.J.: Princeton University Press, 1973), pp. 46-48.

50. Ibid.; Hyde, The United States, pp. 201, 209.

51. Hyde, The United States, pp. 92-93, 209; Packenham, Liberal America and the Third World, p. 48.

52. Hyde, The United States, p. 210.

53. Ibid., pp. 129-30; Asher et al., The United Nations, p. 158.

54. David Baldwin, Economic Development and American Foreign Policy, 1943-1962 (Chicago: University of Chicago Press, 1966). For detailed analyses and critiques of the liberal capitalist framework see the works cited in note 55. Also see Frederick Clairmonte, Economic Liberalism and Underdevelopment: Studies in the Disintegration of an Idea (Bombay: Asia Publishing House, 1960); A. Emmanuel, Unequal Exchange: A Study of the Imperialism of Trade (New York: Monthly Review Press, 1972); and Andre Gunder Frank, Capitalism and Underdevelopment in Latin America (New York: Monthly Review Press, 1971). One of the difficulties in analyzing the relative merits of free trade, private enterprise, and comparative advantage, is that bourgeois scholars have conferred, as Michael Harrington mentioned in a similar context, "a kind of eternity, a natural law objectivity" upon them. Scholars such as Alfred Eckes, David Baldwin, and John Braeman (see Braeman, "The New Left and American Foreign Policy During the Age of Normalcy: A Re-Examination," Business History Review 57 [Spring 1983]: 73-104) consider it foolish to tamper with the "facts" of free trade, the "natural law" of comparative advantage, and so on. But as many political economists have

shown, free trade and its cohorts are neither natural nor
rational laws and, therefore, can be subject to investigation
and criticism.

55. Ernest Mandel, Late Capitalism (London: Verso,
1978), pp. 341-76; Gunnar Myrdal, An International Economy:
Problems and Prospects (New York: Harper & Row, 1956), pp. 1-
3, 9-11, 288-89, 291-92; Gunnar Myrdal, Development and Under-
Development: A Note on the Mechanism of National and International Economic Inequality (Cairo: National Bank of Egypt,
1956), pp. 8-12, 27-32, 47-51; Michael Barratt Brown, The
Economics of Imperialism (Middlesex: Penguin, 1974), pp. 229-
55; M. Barratt Brown, After Imperialism (London: Heinemann,
1970), pp. ix-xvii, quote on p. x; R. B. Sutcliffe, Industry
and Underdevelopment (London: Addison-Wesley Publishing,
1971), pp. 327-28, 337-46; Maurice Dobb, Economic Growth and
Underdevelopment (New York: International Publishers, 1963),
pp. 5, 17-25, 45-51; Celso Furtado, Development and Underdevelopment (Berkeley: University of California Press, 1971),
pp. 129-40; Andre Gunnar Frank, Dependent Accumulation and
Underdevelopment (New York: Monthly Review Press, 1979), pp.
1-12, 172-98.

56. Kim McQuaid, Big Business and Presidental Power:
From FDR to Reagan (New York: William Morris, 1982), p. 119.

4
America's Development Policy and the Arab East: 1942-1949

The assumptions, logic, and contradictions that characterized America's general Third World economic development policy also framed U.S. policy toward Arab East development. Prior to World War II, American leaders advocated an open door in the Middle East. But the government took little interest in the region's living standards or general economic growth.(1) The presence of thousands of American military and civilian personnel in the region during the war, however, gave the United States a new perspective on the Arab East. Economic, political, and military officers stationed throughout the Middle East voiced an interest in the region's future development and its relations with the United States. America's unprecedented wartime penetration of daily Middle East life, combined with traditional interests (missionary and educational work, commerce, and especially oil production) and with general wartime goals (internationalizing American capitalism and corporatism) made the Middle East a vital area for the United States.(2)

In April 1945, the interdepartmental Executive Committee on Economic Foreign Policy (ECEFP) approved a State Department policy paper on the Middle East. The April paper, originally drafted in the Office of Near Eastern and African Affairs and the Office of International Trade Policy, ended a two-year discussion on American economic policy in the Middle East. Carried on by the middle and lower echelons of the State Department and by field personnel, the discussion touched issues such as America's general interests in the area, cooperation with Britain and the Soviet Union, trade and exchange problems, financial and technical aid, and economic development. The ECEFP report revealed the imperial state's desire for postwar American hegemony and, simultaneously, exposed the difficulties that the United States would face in creating and guiding a new international order.(3)

1945 ECEFP REPORT AND MIDDLE EAST DEVELOPMENT

Imperial state policymakers identified trade, oil, and strategic-political concerns as America's principal objectives in the Middle East. As in other areas of the world, American officials sought an open door and "dependable and friendly customers" in the Middle East. Policymakers also hoped to expand existing American oil facilities and to secure new concessions. Increased Arab oil production, while important for the war effort, was even more vital for postwar reconstruction. American policy sought to "substitute Middle East oil for Western Hemisphere, and particularly United States oil in European markets." Both increased trade and oil production would contribute to general economic development by providing needed capital and materials. At the same time, economic development would facilitate and strengthen commerce and the oil industry.(4)

Government officials viewed the Middle East as a breeding ground for world war--especially between Great Britain and the Soviet Union. William S. Culbertson, head of a special economic mission to the Middle East in 1944, warned that if the United States allowed regional forces to evolve naturally, it would have to "scramble around" to protect its interests. On the other hand, it could "go into that region and take an intelligent and constructive part in the solution of its various problems." This latter policy involved cooperating with the Arab states and other concerned powers to remove "economic instability and economic discontent." A policy of economic development would raise living standards, alleviate disease and illiteracy, and remove "the discontent which may cause the Near Eastern peoples to turn toward the Soviet Union." A development policy also would increase trade and investment opportunities for the United States, as well as extend "our ideas of political liberty and economic development in this area as elsewhere."(5)

The April 1945 report summarized America's goals in the Middle East as preserving peace, promoting the welfare of the peoples, and protecting and advancing U.S. commercial, raw material, and strategic interests in the region. In lieu of maintaining a large military force in the Middle East, the United States would pursue "an actively implemented economic policy." Such a policy depended, to some extent, on the government's ability to maintain peaceful cooperation among the great powers and to reduce international trade barriers. Similarly, Congress' willingness to appropriate funds for technical and financial aid and the readiness of private banks and businesses to participate in development financing and trade expansion would all determine the success of America's economic policy in the Middle East. With the proper domestic and international support, imperial state policymakers believed that the Arab nations' desires "to stand on their own feet" would parallel an American policy that fostered "the economic advancement of the Middle East peoples" and facilitated their "freedom from external interference and exploitation."(6)

By the end of 1945, a consensus within the imperial state bureaucracy held that a program of economic development would be an effective instrument of American foreign policy in the Arab East. Some officials argued that this policy required great power coordination in order to lessen the conflicts that naturally arose from competing ideological, political, and economic interests. Rhetoric notwithstanding, American policymakers never held great hopes for international cooperation in the Middle East. State Department officials admitted that long-run accommodation with the USSR was impossible as long as America's primary goal consisted of maintaining and extending its economic system and political ideals in the Arab

East.   Russia had an effective weapon in the Arab countries'
"political and economic frustrations which the western capitalist world has both created and been unable to alleviate."
Alexander C. Kirk, minister to Egypt, explained that the British wanted to make the Arab states "dependent in perpetuity
both economically and politically upon the Empire." Washington officials hoped to increase absolute British economic
strength--that is, "assist it to maintain itself as a great
power"--while decreasing its relative strength in the Arab
East.(7)

     Assistant Secretary of State Adolf Berle understood
America's dilemma. If the United States refused to underwrite
the British and French colonial system in the region, then the
Soviets would expand. With the Russians in control of Middle
East oil, European recovery would be dependent on them. The
Soviets would exclude every vestige of American economic
interest in the region. Berle observed that Britain had long
followed a similar obstructionist policy.   "The immediate
question," reflected Berle, "is whether the 'keep off' sign is
written in Russian or English." The former corporate attorney
quickly added that although the British often violated in
practice free trade and the open door, they did respect those
principles. Soviet policy was, at best, obscure.   Therefore,
while the United States could deal with Britain's evolutionary
changes in the Arab East, it could not contend with Soviet
revolutionary alterations.(8)

     The ECEFP report portrayed the Middle East as a battle-
ground between private enterprise, democratic Britain, and
autarkic, authoritarian Russia. While the British wished to
maintain their oil holdings and imperial communication lines,
the Soviets· sought to secure their Middle East frontiers and
to prevent a coalition of regional capitalist nations against
them.   The ECEFP paper suggested that America coordinate its
policies with those of the other large powers, but the report
really advocated independent U.S. action. America had to lead
the way in strengthening the Arab East through economic devel-
opment--technical aid, private and public credit, and the
removal of trade restrictions.   Critics of this unilateral
approach pointed out that the United States had other international responsibilities and could not achieve Arab development
by itself.(9)

     "Mutual coordination" aside, the ECEFP report specified
financial, commercial, technical, and regional means to
improve Middle East economies and living standards. All the
recommendations hinged, to one degree or another, on the
revival and expansion of multilateral trade.   Increasing
global trade relied, in turn, on the reduction of trade
barriers, the elimination of discriminatory measures, and "a
constructive American economic policy facilitating a substantial increase in American imports."(10)

     Financing development depended upon creating favorable
conditions for private American capital and solving Arab
exchange and repayment problems. Maximizing the Middle East's
economic benefits from the American exploitation of oil
resources would facilitate capital transfers to the region,
while safeguarding U.S. concessions.   American financial
assistance to the Arab countries rested on three pillars.
Private loans took precedence over public loans. Washington
officials doubted whether Congress was "prepared as yet to
approve commitments of large sums of United States government

funds in the Middle East." All loans and investments had to
be based on sound business practices and considerations.
Finally, development financing ultimately depended on multilateralism. "Dollar credits in themselves, even if used to
purchase American capital goods and thus to increase the productivity capacity of the Middle East," argued the ECEFP report, "will not necessarily provide either a permanent increase in the Middle East's capacity to absorb American exports or the means of repayment of dollar credits." Financial
aid to the Middle East and Third World required a solution to
the dollar gap and the world trade disequilibrium.(11)

     Some bureaucrats warned that blocked sterling balances
and the dollar gap would obstruct American loans to the Middle
East. Others feared that without "tangible" evidence of America's commitment to development, the Arabs would look toward
the USSR "for a cure of their economic and social ills and as
the mainspring of power in the Near East." In the late summer
of 1945, Undersecretary of State Dean Acheson and the Division
of Near Eastern Affairs proposed that Congress create an annual fund of $100 million for promoting American political and
strategic interests in the Middle East. Specifically, the
fund would cover those situations where "repayment with
interest, in dollars, cannot be guaranteed because currency
exchange and trade did not happen to run in the right direction." Although sympathetic to the idea, Secretary of State
James Byrnes vetoed the proposal because of congressional
resistance to extensive foreign aid programs.(12) By the end
of 1945, therefore, the State Department had decided that
private and public financial aid for Arab development would be
made on a commercial basis--on the nature of the projects and
the ability of the country to repay the loan. A successful
program would depend on vigorous world trading in general and
on increased trade between the United States and the Middle
East in particular. Increased Middle East exports to the
United States would guarantee the proper flow of dollars into
Arab nations. The issues of trade and dollar exchange were
intricately tied to Anglo-American relations in the Middle
East and, most importantly, to the Middle East Supply Centre
(MESC).

     The British created the MESC in April 1941 to develop and
administer "a program of centralized overseas trade control
and economic mobilization." With its headquarters in Cairo,
the center reduced the use of allied shipping for civilian
goods imported into the region, thus freeing space for
military supplies, while minimizing civilian hardships caused
by reduced imports. The United States joined the MESC in
1942. In 1943, the government created the American Economic
Mission to the Middle East (AEMME), in part, to ensure that
wartime economic controls would not adversely affect American
entrepreneurs after the war. James Landis, AEMME director,
observed that as MESC controls tightened, the percentage of
American commercial exports to the Middle East fell when
compared to British exports. Arguing that MESC controls
discriminated against American trade, Landis, William Culbertson, and others urged the United States to liquidate those
controls no longer necessary for the war effort and increase
American export-import trade with the Arab East.(13)

     Increasing American trade depended on correcting the
dollar exchange problem. Sterling area foreign exchange
controls required that all dollars and other hard currencies

be surrendered to a central authority in London. This "dollar pool" then allocated dollars to member nations in accordance with the relative urgency of their military and civilian needs.   American policymakers realized that the scarcity of dollars forced Britain to encourage the use of sterling instead of dollars and the use of sterling area products instead of American goods.   Without dollars, Middle East countries could not purchase American capital goods, thus hindering American trade and Middle East development.   If Britain advanced sufficient dollars to the sterling bloc nations, it would endanger its own recovery and obstruct general European reconstruction and the revival of multilateralism. Washington officers observed that promoting American exports to sterling nations in the Middle East, without promoting imports from those nations, would make it impossible for the British to pay their debts to, and purchase goods from, the United States.   Landis and Culbertson, both strong proponents of free trade and private enterprise, nevertheless urged the sterling countries to insist that Britain make available their dollar earnings.(14)

The ECEFP report emphasized that Middle East development depended on that region's increased trade with the United States.   This trade, in turn, rested on a solution to the area's foreign exchange difficulties.   Only   revived international trade and expanded American imports from the Middle East could resolve the exchange problem.(15)   This reasoning allowed American leaders to ignore the positive benefits that might accrue from liberal loan and general economic development projects in the Arab East. Such programs would mean nothing without increased world trade. The end of 1945 saw no firm American answer to the question of trade and dollar exchange.   Once again, policymakers resorted to technical assistance as the easy way to aid Third World economic development.

When President Roosevelt's special representative in the Middle East proposed a technical assistance program for the region in late 1943, Assistant Secretary of State Dean Acheson accused Patrick J. Hurley of indulging in "messianic globaloney." But in April 1945 the ECEFP recommended that the United States participate in local Arab development by "responding in full measure to requests for technical and advisory assistance." The ECEFP urged that laws providing for the payment of American advisers in the Philippines and Latin America be revised to include technical experts in the Middle East and the rest of the world.   Meanwhile, the State Department had approved the extension of a cultural relations program to the Near East and Africa. Policymakers viewed the program as a means of exchanging health, welfare, and educational information with the Arab peoples.(16)   The ECEFP report tied together technical aid, trade, and financing into a broad economic policy for the Middle East.   Implementation of this broad policy raised questions concerning a regional approach to Middle East development.

British officials originated the regional concept. Faced with growing Arab nationalism, Britain needed a new basis of power in the area.   The Foreign Office suggested that the governing principle of British postwar policy in the Middle East be regional economic development. Sir Edward Grigg, who became the British minister resident in the Middle East in late 1944, argued that Britain would "stand or fall in the

Middle East by her influence upon the promotion of social justice and betterment." Grigg's predecessor, Richard Casey, predicted an "economic collapse in the area" if the British did not guide the Arabs' "incoherent" desire for closer association into "healthy and fruitful channels." Of course, such a policy would prevent the Arab movement from "degenerating" into a "form of acute nationalism hostile to our influence." Casey, Grigg, and other British officials viewed the MESC as a legitimate instrument to achieve Arab economic development and to maintain British influence in the region.(17)

At bilateral meetings in 1944, American and British officers discussed possible postwar uses for the MESC. British representatives contended that the center furnished a "great opportunity to help develop economic cooperation, coordination and unity among the Middle Eastern countries." American officers, while sympathetic to the concept of an indigenous economic organization, opposed the continuation of the MESC into the postwar period. James Landis explained that the center tied the United States to "a British pattern of trade which by force of circumstances cannot expand as rapidly as ours." American diplomats and consuls in the Middle East believed that the MESC relegated the United States to a junior partner position in the region. Continuation of the center would be a "fatal blunder." On the other hand, an advisory economic body with equal British and American participation might provide valuable technical services, help restore order and security to the region, and preserve American influence and prestige.(18)

The ECEFP recommended that the United States encourage creation of a regional institution "initiated, supported, and operated by the local Middle East governments" for development purposes. The United States would provide technical and advisory assistance. Some State Department officers presumed that a regional agency would accelerate Middle East economic integration, thus paving the way for eventual global integration. Others feared that wide adoption of the regional approach would "encourage autonomous regionalism with possible intensification of nationalistic sentiments [and] preferential arrangements." Officers in the field complained that the economic problems of Arab countries varied and were not susceptible to regional solutions.(19)

In principle the United States supported the idea of an autonomous Middle East economic organization. In practice, however, America's concern with ending obstacles to free trade, abolishing the MESC, asserting an equal role to that of Britain in the area, and integrating Middle East countries into the world-economy outweighed its detached support for a regional development body. The question of an Arab East development organization never received serious attention within the American imperial state bureaucracy. A bureaucratic struggle over who would formulate and implement U.S. economic policy in the Middle East further obscured planning for regional specialization and market integration.(20)

As head of the AEMME, which centralized American economic authority and administration in the region, James Landis advocated a regional approach to U.S. policy in the Arab East. In a long memorandum to Washington in August 1944, Landis conceded that not all Middle East economic problems required regional handling. But the majority of issues, ranging from inflation to the Pan-Arab movement, were regional matters.

Landis argued that the Near East Division in Washington could
not adequately synchronize Middle East affairs because "the
feel of the situation--a feel that is derivable only from
close and constant contact with affairs--is absent."(21)

The State Department's separation of economic and political issues complicated policy coordination from Washington.
Officers handled economic policy along functional lines,
giving it geographic coordination only at relatively low
bureaucratic levels. Political policy, on the other hand,
received geographic consideration at high levels. Landis,
among others, urged the fusing of economic and political
policy and the implementing of a regional approach in order to
alleviate the department's administrative and policy confu-
sions.   But the ECEFP report only suggested the staffing of
diplomatic posts with sufficient personnel trained to evaluate
"agriculture, industry, and trade, and to facilitate technical
and advisory assistance, and to give constructive aid to
traders engaged in commerce between these countries and the
United States." In May 1945, NEA assumed primary responsibility for the coordination of all economic issues affecting the
Middle East.(22)

Noncareer State Department officials and members of
outside agencies continued to call for an American regional
economic office in the Middle East.   In-and-outers such as
Landis, Culbertson, and Colonel Harold Hoskins--who became
American economic adviser in the Middle East after the demise
of the AEMME in 1945--had no particular stake in the existing
foreign policy apparatus. Foreign Service Officers in the
field and in Washington jealously guarded their dwindling
prerogatives against scores of new and old agencies encroaching into foreign affairs. The battle against the Board of
Economic Warfare--discussed earlier--constituted just one of
numerous campaigns State Department personnel waged against
interlopers during World War II. In the Middle East, old-line
diplomatic officers such as Alexander Kirk resisted attempts
by Landis to coordinate policy. Landis often complained about
his never ceasing difficulties with the State Department
bureaucracy. As the United States entered the postwar era,
Kirk and his colleagues successfully blocked the creation of a
regional unit--both inside and outside the State Department--
to deal with Middle East economic issues.(23)

U.S. economic development policy, summarized in the April
1945 ECEFP position paper, adhered to the imperial state's
liberal capitalist framework. The report emphasized creating
the proper conditions for development--free international
trade, currency convertibility, private financing, the open
door, and some degree of international cooperation. American
officials viewed Middle East development as both an aim and
instrument of foreign policy in that region. Raising the
area's living standards and productive capacity would bring
economic and political stability to the region, thus lessening
the chances of great power confrontation over the area. Many
officials expected development to bring the Arab East into its
proper role in the world-economy--as a supplier of oil and
marketplace for Europe and Asia and a buyer of American goods,
services, and capital.

A regional economic organization appeared as one way to
develop the Middle East and integrate the local states into
the world-economy.   Following the British lead, several
American planners sought a regional body that would direct

Arab development along the path of free enterprise, free trade, and comparative advantage. Other officials worried that regional economic unity would entail restrictive trade policies. The MESC, which achieved a degree of regional economic integration during the war, was unacceptable in peacetime because it required trade and exchange controls. In addition, some American officers argued that economic development problems were worldwide and required global and functional analysis and planning.

In principle, a regional economic organization for the Middle East sounded desirable. In practice, however, imperial state policymakers' concern with removing wartime controls and with formulating a global and functional approach to development issues led those officials to undermine the planning and creation of such an organization. Career State Department officers objected to proposals for a regional approach to the conduct of U.S. economic policy. These individuals feared the penetration of extradepartmental actors into the foreign affairs arena. The State Department opposed the regional approach because it obstructed the quest for the "Holy Grail" of free and private international trade and because it threatened the future operation of the department and the Foreign Service.

DEVELOPMENT AND THE "PENTAGON TALKS"

During the war, corporate and imperial state leaders had realized the strong reciprocal links between European recovery and Middle East development--especially Middle East oil development. The imperial state bureaucracy understood the postwar Arab East's strategic and economic importance for the United States. Nevertheless, by the end of 1946, the Truman administration had become preoccupied with other regions.(24)

Assistant Secretary Will Clayton's economic divisions directed most of their energy and resources toward Europe and Asia. Secretary of State George Marshall and his successor, Dean Acheson, insisted that the economic development of areas like the Arab East fell under the responsibility of the UN. Officers in the NEA readily admitted that Middle East development was not on the "front burner." Loy Henderson, director of NEA, dismissed the importance of a "revolution of rising expectations" among the Arab masses. Yet America's interest in securing and exploiting Middle East oil resources and in maintaining peace in the region required visible, tangible proof of an American commitment to the area. Having ruled out an American military presence in the region, State Department officials focused on extending financial and technical assistance. But as one department officer noted, the United States received so many requests for aid in the late 1940s that "it was not searching for new areas to spend money." Any assistance for the Arab East would have to fit into the larger program of European and Asian reconstruction. The imperial state bureaucracy's middle and lower echelons tried to come to grips with these problems during the Anglo-American "Pentagon Talks" in the fall of 1947.(25)

On 20 March 1947--just one month after the British officially informed the State Department that they would soon suspend economic and military aid to Greece and Turkey-- Foreign Secretary Ernest Bevin sent a memorandum to Secretary of State Marshall. Although overshadowed by the earlier note, which initiated the Truman Doctrine, the 20 March memorandum was no less significant. Bevin told Marshall that the British government attached great importance to "the social and economic development of the Middle East." Describing the situation there as "not healthy," Bevin contended that the region's economic development would "contribute considerably to the internal stability and security of the area and reduce the danger of revolutionary developments and of Communist penetration."   Development programs required massive "outside assistance," much more than the British alone could provide. This was a fertile field, proposed Bevin, for Anglo-American coordination and cooperation.(26)

This request for American help represented Britain's last chance at reviving its policy of economic partnership with the Arab states.   Devised during the war, this policy sought "to present Britain in the role of a benevolent and welcome senior partner in developing the Middle East" in order to prevent that region's "degeneration into acute nationalism hostile to British influence." When Bevin became foreign secretary in 1945, he established a Middle East Office in Cairo and a Middle East Secretariat in London. These new bodies were to replace the recently dismantled MESC and to implement the new partnership.   Bevin's hopes for the office and for Arab economic development went unrealized. Britain's own economic dislocations made it difficult to meet Arab development needs. Arab suspicion of British organs and specific antagonism over the Palestine issue further hindered Anglo-Arab relations. Forced to seek American assistance in Greece and Turkey by early 1947, Britain also requested U.S. aid in the economic development of the Arab East.(27)

In late September 1947, Dennis A. Greenhill of the British Middle East Secretariat described the Middle East's race against the spread of Communism and an exploding population.   Since Britain's own economic crisis rendered it unable to supply much more than advice, "only the United States Government can give practical help to the Middle East." American policymakers, of course, sought to keep the Middle East open to Western economic, political, and cultural interests. Given heavy national commitments elsewhere and Britain's established position in the Middle East, the State Department advocated that Britain "continue to maintain primary responsibility for military security in the region." At Bevin's request, British and American representatives met in Washington in October and November 1947 to discuss these political and military issues.   But at Britain's insistence, the agenda for the "Pentagon Talks" also included consideration of Middle East development questions.(28)

U.S. officials supported assistance for Arab economic development.   They focused on agricultural expansion and limited industrialization as the keys to such development. The Arab states had to reform land tenure laws and develop appropriate commercial and financial institutions for agricultural advancement.   State Department experts recommended that manufacturing and transport facilities develop according to local requirements and resources; that the Arabs concentrate on semimanufactured goods and extractive industries and leave heavy industrial production to the advanced capitalist countries. Although the Middle East dollar-sterling crisis was a component of global reconstruction, policymakers suggested that, where possible, the United States increase imports from the area, extend Eximbank loans, and encourage private capital export. For their part, the Arab states could reduce foreign exchange controls, acquire more direct command over their dollar earnings, encourage private capital investment, and make use of IBRD funds. The U.S. government would provide technical aid to the Arabs and instruct American oil companies to insure that oil royalties were used in ways most beneficial to the indigenous populations.(29)

At the conclusion of the talks, American and British representatives agreed that their countries solve Middle East economic and social problems along lines compatible with Western concepts and ideals. Ultimate responsibility for resolving these problems, however, rested with the Arab countries themselves. Supporting "sound schemes," the United States and Britain agreed to review all development projects in light of their respective commitments and plans for economic reconstruction and development elsewhere. In other words, Middle East economic development would become a component of European and Asian reconstruction. The United States and Britain favored establishing the widest possible cultural and technical links with "those groups who may be most influential in promoting the sound economic and cultural development of their countries."(30)

President Truman endorsed the principles and recommenda- tions of the "Pentagon Talks," as did the British cabinet. Secretary Marshall and Foreign Secretary Bevin carefully characterized the talks as an exchange of similar views rather than a formal agreement or even an understanding between the two governments. This recognition of the "harmony" of Ameri- can and British interests in Middle East economic development was important as the United States attempted to incorporate that region--primarily through its oil production--into European recovery.(31)

ERP, THE MIDDLE EAST, AND OIL

In testimony before the House Committee on Foreign Affairs in January 1948, administration officials argued that the European Recovery Program depended largely on Middle East oil. Secretary of Defense James Forrestal, for example, maintained that "the recovery of Europe as well as the business of the world" required "the development of Middle Eastern oil resources to their maximum extent." President Truman, State Department officers, and other imperial state leaders considered Middle East economic development as "the other side of the medal of Western European recovery." If Middle East markets did not develop by the termination of the ERP in 1952, warned American officials, then friction would occur between West and East European nations over trade outlets. Middle East integration into Western Europe--as a supplier of oil and as a purchaser of manufactured goods--was absolutely essential. The State Department instructed its missions in the Middle East to explain to the local govern- ments that the ERP was "a world recovery program" with "concrete benefits" for the Arabs.(32)

Middle East nations doubted the spinoff effects of the ERP. Egyptian officials insisted that ERP countries, when buying goods from the Arab East, use Marshall Plan dollars in

order to transfer scarce currency into the region. State
Department planners gradually realized that instead of
increasing the dollar flow into the Arab East, Britain's
obligations to the ERP hindered that nation's dollar support
to Arab states. In 1949, American leaders concluded that
increased ERP allocations would not fill the Middle East
dollar gap. Paul H. Nitze, deputy to the assistant secretary
for economic affairs, asserted that new programs would have to
be initiated to meet the dollar requirements of the Arab
East.(33)

In addition to the dollar gap problem, the Arab-Jewish
conflict over Palestine threatened the link between the ERP
and Middle East economic development. The State Department
opposed the UN General Assembly resolution calling for the
partition of Palestine. To successfully establish a Jewish
state in Palestine, the United States would have to extend
massive economic and military aid to the Zionists. Any such
assistance would result in deep Arab hostility toward the
United States and thereby pose a "serious threat to the
success of the Marshall Plan." In April 1948, Undersecretary
of State Robert Lovett warned that a war over Palestine would
jeopardize ERP success because large-scale European oil
requirements from the Middle East would not be met. When
heavy fighting broke out, some American officials feared oil
sanctions or cancellations of American concessions. Both
British and American leaders ruled out economic pressures
against the Arabs as a means of stopping the war. They
worried that such measures would wreck the ERP.(34)

Clark Clifford's arguments offset State Department
pessimism. President Truman's special counsel asserted that
the Arabs must have "oil royalties or go broke." Saudi
Arabia, for example, received 90 percent of its revenues from
American oil royalties. The Arab states had to have dollars.
According to Clifford, the Arabs' "social and economic structure would be irreparably harmed by adopting a Soviet orientation, and it would be suicide for their ruling classes to come
within the Soviet sphere of influence." Self-preservation,
contended Clifford, "will compel the Arabs to sell their oil
to the United States." Clifford's analysis was basically
correct, although serious problems did arise from American
recognition of Israel. While Saudi oil production continued
to increase during the late 1940s, Iraqi production decreased
in 1948 and only slightly advanced in 1949.(35)

The closing of the Haifa refinery explains the decline in
Iraqi oil production. The British-owned refinery received
crude oil from Iraqi fields via a pipeline of the Iraq
Petroleum Company. Arab labor unrest in mid-April 1948 forced
a shutdown of the refinery. The Iraqi government cut the
pipeline after the onset of full-scale war with Israel.
British officials calculated that the idle refinery would
cause a drain on Britain's dollar reserves amounting to $50
million a year. In June 1948, the British asked UN Mediator
Count Folke Bernadotte about the possibility of getting an
Israeli-Arab agreement to establish Haifa as an international
port under UN auspices. Israel rejected the proposal. American policymakers agreed with Israel that Haifa was an integral
part of the Jewish state. Nevertheless, Secretary of State
Marshall, among others, believed that Haifa offered a "unique
opportunity for practical cooperation between Arabs and Jews,
since one side controls the crude oil and the other the

refining capacity, while both sides need the final product."
All attempts to solve the Haifa refinery problem failed.(36)

Oil, of course, linked Middle East economic development
with European recovery. U.S. oil companies, the most aggres-
sive American investors abroad during the late 1940s, invested
the bulk of their capital in the Middle East. Even before the
formulation of the Marshall Plan, American oil firms had
recognized Western Europe as the logical market for Middle
East production. The Oil and Gas Journal, the principal trade
publication of the American oil industry, viewed Middle East
oil development as the key to meeting the needs of Europe and
Asia and, at the same time, providing Arab governments with
the "revenues with which to end the impoverishment of many
centuries." Adhering to State Department suggestions that
they conduct their operations in "such a manner as to foster
the economic advancement and to raise the standard of living"
of the local peoples, U.S. oil firms planned to train thousands of nationals in the "arts and skills of the petroleum
industry." Middle East oil production gradually rose from 7.5
percent of the world total in 1945, to 10.1 percent in 1947.
During the first seven months of 1946, 62 percent of France's
total crude oil imports came from the Middle East. The United
States, however, continued to dominate the refined oil market,
supplying 63 percent of France's processed petroleum products.(37)

With the announcement of the Marshall Plan in mid-1947,
American firms accelerated their planning and operations in
the Middle East. Officials from the American Petroleum
Institute, Socony Vacuum Oil Company, and Standard Oil Company
of New Jersey (the largest American corporation in the 1940s),
among others, proclaimed that the speed and vigor with which
Middle East oil could be developed was the most important
element in bringing "national health" back to Europe. In late
1948, executives of the Arabian American Oil Company (Aramco)
boasted about their "junior Marshall Plan" in the Middle East.
Aramco president William F. Moore explained that in an effort
to meet Europe's oil needs, the expanded oil industry operations in the Middle East were, in effect, financing a regional
development program. Investments in the area totalled $1.5
billion by the early 1950s. While the Marshall Plan added $16
to the per capita income of the 16 ERP nations, Middle East
oil development increased per capita income in ten countries
by $6 to $9. American oil firms contended that private oil
development would raise Arab living standards, aid in European
recovery, protect American oil supplies, and not cost the
American taxpayer anything. Industry officials opposed
Marshall Plans for the Third World. If the imperial state
would just help to create favorable conditions for private
investment, argued these executives, then world development
would naturally follow, as it had apparently done in the
Middle East.(38)

The influx of American and other foreign capital into the
Middle East definitely expanded the area's oil production.
The Middle East provided 12.2 percent of the world's total
production in 1948, and 15.1 percent in 1949. By the end of
1948, Middle East oil comprised 47 percent of the ERP nations'
crude oil imports. With Middle East oil, the Eastern Hemisphere quickly approached energy self-sufficiency. But while
Middle East crude increasingly met Europe's requirements, the
United States continued to supply that area with higher valued

refined oil products.   Between April and mid-November 1948,
Saudi Arabia and Iraq supplied Europe with crude oil valued at
$51.6 million; the United States provided only $2.5 million of
crude.   During the same period, the two Arab states sent
Europe $54 million worth of refined petroleum goods, while the
United States furnished Europe with $107.3 million of proc-
essed products.   In 1948, the United States supplied Europe
with 17 percent of its total quantity of imported oil, but 33
percent of the total value of imported oil.(39)

The difference in prices between crude and refined oil
demonstrates part of the inequity inherent in extracting and
selling raw materials relative to producing and selling manufactured or processed goods.   The price differential also un-
derlines the conflict between large international oil firms
and smaller domestic companies.   In October 1949 the Independent Petroleum Association of America denounced the use of
American tax dollars to finance the giant United States companies' oil production in the Middle East and refinery facilities in Europe that were capturing American export markets.
By 1949 lower tanker rates and pipelines had made Middle East
oil competitive in Europe with Texas crude. Small domestic
producers felt threatened by European refineries which processed Middle East oil.   "We are creating a Frankenstein mon-
ster," warned the president of the Plymouth Oil Company, "that
will seriously cripple the effectiveness of the domestic oil
industry." Large international oil companies with investments
in Middle East oil and in refineries in the Middle East and
Europe dismissed these criticisms.   Imperial state officials
continued to support Middle East oil development because of
its crucial importance for European reconstruction, Middle
East economic development, and the revival of multilateralism.(40)

The American policy to integrate Middle East oil into the
European economies succeeded.   In 1950 Middle East oil supplied 69 percent of Europe's total oil imports.   East Asia
simultaneously imported 66 percent of its oil from the Middle
East.   Total Middle East production rose from 35,558,000
metric tons in 1946 to 88,613,000 in 1950. In 1946 the Middle
East produced 9.4 percent of the world's total output, while
in 1950 it produced 16.9 percent. Expanded production resulted in increased oil royalties. Direct payments to Middle
East oil producers grew from $55.6 million in 1946 to $193.3
million in 1950. Whether these enlarged revenues contributed
to economic advancement is problematic and is examined in
chapter five's case study of Saudi Arabia.(41)

Oil dominated American economic interests in the Middle
East.   In 1949 U.S. direct net investments in Arab oil comprised 86 percent ($98 million) of America's total Middle East
investment ($114 million).   The dollar gap and the instability
created by the Palestine controversy hampered imperial state
and corporate efforts at diversifying American investment and
commercial interests in the region.   While pushing for Arab
East oil development, State Department officers recommended a
long-range policy of "positive economic assistance" to the
countries of the area.   When an uneasy peace settled on the
region in 1949, the department offered the proposed Point Four
program to the Arab states. Truman and other imperial state
leaders hoped to use technical aid, in conjunction with IBRD
funding, to develop Middle East economies and markets.(42)

Max Thornburg best summarized the rationale behind the State Department's plan for technical aid to the Arab East. A former executive of the Standard Oil Company of California and head of the State Department's Office of Petroleum Adviser, Thornburg lived in the Middle East during most of the 1940s. Thornburg contended that although Middle East development opportunities abounded, the region did not need "great capital expenditures" as much as it required "brains and determination among the peoples themselves." Development, explained Thornburg, necessitated better practices, better use of land and water, and all-weather roads and transport. The Middle East had to develop agriculture and light industry and to avoid the establishment of heavy industry. Such a development scheme required "only the collaboration of the governments and the private individuals of the countries involved rather than heavy expenditures of capital from abroad." According to Thornburg, America's most significant contribution to Middle East economic development would be technical knowledge in the fields of agriculture, commerce, and finance.(43)

Arab governments emphasized the limitations of the technical assistance approach to economic development. Point Four funds, for example, would not pay for the administration and equipment requirements that development projects entailed. "Knowledge of resources itself," contended George Hakim, counselor to the Lebanese legation in Washington, "is not economic development." Hakim argued that private foreign investment in Arab oil was "not directed towards the general development of the Middle Eastern countries, but towards the export of crude oil to the European market." Private capital sought high profits and tended to exploit workers and consumers in underdeveloped countries in order to maximize those profits.(44)

The criticism of Middle East officials notwithstanding, America's economic assistance policy continued to revolve around stimulating private enterprise and investment, integrating Arab economies into European economies via the ERP, and providing technical assistance through programs like Point Four. United States leaders initially hope to cooperate with the British in the Arab East, but Britain's own economic crisis made such collaboration unrealistic. Britain's blocked sterling balances, for example, inhibited Arab states from purchasing needed American capital and consumer goods. The Arab-Israeli war disrupted local economies and hampered foreign efforts at developing those nations. Imperial state policymakers refused to consider financial aid for the Middle East while the Palestine issue remained unresolved. Yet, at the same time, several imperial state officials hoped to use economic development as a possible approach to Arab-Israeli cooperation.

REGIONAL DEVELOPMENT: PALESTINE

Palestine's potential for national and regional economic development was the key to Zionist stategies. During World War II Zionist officials took every opportunity to praise the advances made by Jewish settlers in Palestine, describe the huge absorptive capacity of the country, and explain how Palestinian development could contribute to the economic growth of the entire Arab East. In a letter to President Roosevelt in June 1943, Zionist leader Chaim Weizmann outlined how Palestine's "modern, resourceful, and energetic" industry might become the center of a large export trade in the Near East. Also in 1943 Jewish Agency representatives explained to unsympathetic State Department officers how a Jewish Palestine would provide abundant opportunities for the "undeveloped" Arabs by creating markets and employment. Foreign Service Officers in Palestine responded that Jewish Palestine's high living standards made it difficult, if not impossible, to assimilate itself into a true regional Arab economy. A political settlement to the issue of a Jewish state was a prerequisite to regional development, not vice versa. Imperial state bureaucrats observed that American interests in Arabian oil and in future trade opportunities in the region far outweighed any potential commercial and financial benefits resulting from relations with a Jewish state. During World War II the United States officially considered Palestine a British problem and dismissed talk of economic development until settlement of the country's political future.(45)

In the postwar period proponents of a Jewish state in Palestine continued to emphasize two points. First, Palestine, with the proper development, could absorp hundreds of thousands of Jewish refugees without adversely affecting the living standards of the area. Second, the mere presence of an advanced agricultural, industrial, and commercial nation--as Jewish Palestine was to become--would set an example for all countries to follow and, therefore, would contribute to the region's economic development. Jewish Agency officials and private American economists and engineers such as Robert Nathan, Walter C. Lowdermilk, and James B. Hays made these arguments in hearings before the Anglo-American Committee of Inquiry and the UN Special Committee on Palestine (UNSCOP). Both these committees examined the problem of Palestine's future as an Arab and/or Jewish state.(46)

In September 1947 UNSCOP recommended that Palestine be partitioned into two independent states, one Jewish and the other Arab. This plan allowed for large-scale Jewish immigration and the establishment of a Jewish-Arab economic union. The economic union would consist of a customs union between the two states, a joint currency system, a single foreign exchange rate, common use of railways, highways, ports, airports, and postal, telephone, and telegraph services, and joint economic development. Zionist leaders interpreted the economic union as a means of having the Jewish state subsidize the economically weaker Arab state. Instead of an economic union, Jewish Agency officials advocated that each state achieve economic sovereignty, with the corresponding freedom to pursue its own development. The Zionist attempt to replace economic union with economic separatism failed. The economic union provision remained in the final partition plan approved by the UN General Assembly on 29 November 1947.(47)

During the various international hearings on Palestine, the Jewish Agency and its supporters emphasized the positive role that Jews had played and would continue to play in the economic advancement of the Palestinian Arabs. Yet when UNSCOP proposed an economic union that would have linked the economies of Jewish and Arab states, Jewish officials resisted the plan. Zionists fought for a sovereign nation and anything that violated that sovereignty, such as an economic union imposed from the outside, was unacceptable. Rhetoric aside, the Zionist goal of integrating hundreds of thousands of

Jewish refugees into the Palestinian economy would be complicated if the Jewish nation had financial and economic obligations to a sister Arab state. While Jewish leaders continued
to believe that Jewish development would directly benefit the
surrounding Arab peoples, they sought to achieve this goal on
their own terms, on their own volition, and in their own good
time.

Events in Palestine quickly by-passed the Arab-Jewish
union question. Arab leaders rejected the partition plan. In
1948 violent confrontations between Arab and Zionist forces
intensified.   The Truman administration, which initially
favored partition, changed its position as it became clear
that partition could not be peacefully implemented.   When
Britain formally ended its mandate in May 1948, the resulting
Arab-Israeli war created new obstacles to Middle East economic
development--including the problem of Arab refugees.(48)

In its early stages, the Arab exodus from Palestine was a
spontaneous reaction to the tension and fear that characterized the country in the months following the UN partition
resolution. By June 1948, approximately 70 percent of the
Arab population of Palestine had left the country. At the end
of 1950, only 167,000 Palestinian Arabs resided in Israel,
compared with the approximately 750,000 who had lived in the
area prior to 1948. By July 1948, the mass exodus became a
disaster as epidemic and starvation threatened those in
refugee camps. Israel refused to repatriate the refugees and
the Arab states refused to resettle them. Immediate relief
assistance came from various international agencies such as
the International Children's Emergency Fund, the Red Cross,
and the World Health Organization; and from private American
organizations like the Near East Foundation, Aramco, and
Bechtel (an American construction company operating in the
Arab East).   In late 1948 the United States approved $16
million for Palestinian relief aid.   Meanwhile, the UN
established a body to coordinate international relief activities and administer $29.5 million in direct relief aid. The
UN also created a Conciliation Commission for Palestine (CCP)
to mediate a political settlement, facilitate refugee repatriation and resettlement, and assist in Middle East socioeconomic development.(49)

At CCP meetings in Beirut and Lausanne in the spring and
summer of 1949, the refugee issue obstructed truce discussions. UN officials concluded that a comprehensive answer to
the refugee problem existed only within "the framework of the
economic and social rehabilitation of all the countries in the
Near East."   On 23 August the CCP established an Economic
Survey Mission to examine the Middle East situation and to
recommend a program for solving the refugee issue and developing the region.   American officials, who had already correlated economic development and refugee problems, strongly
supported this move. Both Secretary of State Dean Acheson and
Assistant Secretary for Near Eastern and African Affairs
George McGhee agreed that this economic approach would improve
the prospect of a general Palestine accord.(50)

Gordon R. Clapp, then chairman of the board of the Tennessee Valley Authority, became chief of the mission. Together with deputy chairmen from Britain, France, and Turkey and a
technical staff, Clapp proceeded to Beirut in mid-September
1949.   The Clapp Mission filed an interim report in November
and a final report in December.   Both reports focused on

developing a comprehensive works program in which refugees would become self-supporting and at the same time create works of lasting benefit to the countries concerned. Short-term and small-scale public works programs and pilot demonstration projects would provide individual governments with vital experience, improve the productivity of refugee areas, and lead the way to larger development schemes. Selected projects had to be labor intensive and thus employ hundreds of refugees, begin operations soon, stimulate spin-off projects, and contribute to "a more complete economic development." Large numbers of refugees could be employed to improve the Arab East's two great resources and needs--land and water--through terracing, afforestation, road, irrigation, and water conservation projects. The Clapp Mission recommended an 18 month combined direct relief and works program at a cost of $54.9 million.(51)

American officials "heartily endorsed" the report. They found it sensible and perceptive and agreed with its emphasis on "small projects which would train people in multiple skills." Initially, State Department officials believed that the recommendations "provided hope of ameliorating the lot of the Palestinian refugees and pointed the way to more long-range economic improvements of the area." But Secretary Acheson soon began to doubt the efficacy of the Clapp Mission recommendations in light of Arab and Israeli intransigence on resettlement and repatriation, respectively. Acheson, who had earlier put great faith in the economic approach, now contended that Middle East economic development was impossible without a regional political settlement.(52)

Despite American, Arab, and Israeli misgivings, the General Assembly adopted the Clapp Mission proposals in December 1949. The Assembly established the UN Relief and Works Agency for Palestine Refugees in the Near East to implement the direct relief and works programs and to consult with local governments on future programs. The agency's major goal was to employ refugees on demonstration projects in Arab countries on such a scale as to permit termination of direct relief in 1950. But the agency failed to meet the deadline for ending relief. Arab leaders hampered the program. They realized that the program would lead inevitably to the resettlement of the refugees in their countries, thereby undermining both their own domestic policies and the right of the refugees to return to their homes and land in Palestine. Some agency projects benefited local governments, but makeshift schemes did not economically (or socially) integrate the refugees into the indigenous societies. The Clapp Mission recommendations notwithstanding, U.S. officials continued to link American economic aid to the Arabs with a settlement of the refugee problem and with a general Palestine peace treaty.(53)

CONCLUSION

America's postwar policy toward Middle East economic development roughly followed the 1945 ECEFP paper recommendations. Imperial state policymakers assumed that Middle East development would raise living standards and bring political and economic stability to the region. Economic growth, designed and implemented under the direction of American capitalist principles, would prevent Soviet or British or any other outside power's control of the area.   Policymakers also realized that economic development would create trade, invest-ment and general business opportunities for American private enterprise and capital in the Arab East.   In the immediate postwar years, U.S. leaders presumed that Middle East develop-ment, like Third World economic development in general, would naturally flow from the revival of multilateral trade, inter-national currency stabilization, and European reconstruction.

The Pentagon Talks in the fall of 1947 produced Anglo-American agreement that Middle East economic development required active local participation, resolution of the blocked sterling and dollar gap crises, reduction of trade barriers, establishment of favorable conditions for foreign investment, and assistance from Western technical experts.   But Britain was financially unable to support Arab East development schemes, while the United States had already committed itself to extending massive aid for European reconstruction.   Ameri-can officials believed that Middle East economic development could be tied directly to European recovery.

The key to this integration was the development of Middle East oil. European and Asian reconstruction depended on a secure source of energy.   The Middle East would become that source.   Oil development, contended American policymakers, would secure for the local countries capital necessary to finance general economic development.   As Middle East oil revived European economies, those nations would manufacture consumer goods and capital goods needed in the peripheral states of the Arab East.   Imperial state leaders concluded that integrating the Middle East into Europe made special public economic assistance programs for Arab development unnecessary. The integration of Arab oil into European and Asian economies succeeded.   But several problems blocked the anticipated movement toward Arab development.   Chapter five examines this issue.   Suffice it to say that obstacles to development included the dollar gap, blocked sterling bal-ances, the lack of forward and backward economic linkages in the capital intensive oil industry, international and regional conflicts, and the Palestine dilemma. This latter issue di-verted time, energy, and resources--both in the Arab East and in the United States--away from the long-range concern of eco-nomic progress to the immediate problem of war and refugees.

Imperial state officials insisted that regional economic development depended on a political settlement in Palestine. In other areas of the Third World where conflict and political instability were evident, American officials held that econom-ic recovery and development depended on "effective solutions for fundamental political and military conflicts which are stifling production and trade."(54)   Nevertheless, imperial state policymakers attempted to use regional economic develop-ment as a stimulus for Middle East cooperation and as a means of facilitating a political solution to the Arab-Israeli dispute. When this effort failed, officials returned to the standard explanation that Middle East economic development re-quired European and Asian recovery.   Special economic assist-ance to the Arab East was of dubious value; certainly it was impossible under the conditions of war between Arabs and Jews.

American officials continued to suspect regional develop-ment plans for the Arab East. Suggestions for regional TVAs were obviously impossible because of the lack of cooperation among the states of the Arab East.(55) But other reasons led to America's rejection of regional economic development. While seeking to integrate the Middle East economies, especially Middle East oil, into the European economy and the larger world-economy, American planners ignored the economic integration of the Middle East itself. Imperial state policymakers feared that the talk of regional economic cooperation among "have-not" nations contributed to the rhetoric of anti-imperialist, anti-Western, and anti-capitalist governments. When underdeveloped countries banded together to deal with the West, they usually sought "to get handouts or loans, to bargain for goods or over prices, or simply to exert political weight."   Functional economic integration, according to American leaders, was impossible in the Middle East--despite discussion of Middle East economic homogeneity.(56)

Throughout the 1940s, therefore, imperial state officials dismissed regional development as a viable means for achieving economic growth in the Middle East. Consequently, imperial state and capitalist class elites were left with individual country-by-country development schemes to fulfill America's hegemonic goals.

NOTES

1. John A. DeNovo, <u>American Interests and Policies in the Middle East, 1900-1939</u> (Minneapolis: University of Minnesota Press, 1963), pp. 167-209;   Benjamin Shwadran, <u>The Middle East, Oil and the Great Powers</u> (New York: Praeger, 1955), pp. 204-80; Leland Harrison to Roger Derby, 20 January 1927, DOS 890g.51/10, RG 59, U.S. National Archives, Washington, D.C.

2. Frederick Winant to Dean Acheson, 10 December 1942, DOS 800.24/614, RG 59;   FDR to Rev. Endicott Peabody, 23 December 1943, OF 700 Palestine, FDR Papers, FDR Library, Hyde Park, N.Y.;   Department of State, <u>Foreign Relations of the United States, 1943</u>, vol. 4, pp. 330-36 (hereafter <u>FRUS</u> followed by year and volume);   Memo of meeting regarding cultural affairs, 9 June 1943, DOS 111.Advisory Committee/1-644, RG 59;   "New Trade Waters Chartered," <u>Business Week</u>, 4 December 1943, p. 47; <u>FRUS, 1944</u>, 5: 1-2;   James Landis to Wallace Murray, 30 August 1944, Annex A of report, DOS 800.24/8-3044, RG 59; <u>FRUS, 1944</u>, 3: 1-30;   Eduard Mark, "Allied Relations in Iran, 1941-1947: The Origins of a Cold War Crisis," <u>Wisconsin Magazine of History</u> 59 (Autumn 1975); John DeNovo, "The Culbertson Economic Mission and Anglo-American Tensions in the Middle East, 1944-45," <u>Journal of American History</u> 63 (March 1977): 913-36;   John DeNovo, "American Relations with the Middle East during World War II: Another Watershed?" paper, July 1971.

3. Minutes of 20 April 1945 meeting of ECEFP, 5.19B ECEFP Meetings, 4.Minutes ECEFP M-18/45, and ECEFP Documents D-64/45 and D-71/45, ECEFP Meetings, 3.Documents, RG 353, U.S. National Archives, Washington, D.C.; <u>FRUS, 1945</u>, 8: 34 note 5;   Memorandum, Loy Henderson, 3 May 1945, DOS 890.50/5-345, RG 59.

4. L. L. Short to Dean Acheson, 28 July 1944, DOS 800.24/7-2844, RG 59; L. Henderson to Cordell Hull, 20 September 1944, DOS 890G.50/9-2044, RG 59; Paul Ireland to Gordon Merriam, 24 November 1944, DOS FW 890.50/9-1244, RG 59; F. Winant, "Proposed US Economic Policy in the Middle East," 12 September 1944, Subject File: Special Mission to Middle East, Box 131, William S. Culbertson Papers, Manuscript Division, Library of Congress, Washington, D.C.; Phillip J. Baram, The Department of State in the Middle East, 1919-1945 (Philadelphia: University of Pennsylvania Press, 1978), pp. 224-31; F. Winant, "Recommended US Economic Policy in Middle East," 8 March 1945, DOS 800.24/3-745, RG 59; "Report of the Mission and Supplementary Reports," 15 November 1944, pp. 9, 18-20, DOS 033.1151R/11-1544 Culbertson Mission, RG 59; E-252, "US Petroleum Policy in the Middle East," 13 January 1944, Division of Economic Studies, Records of Advisory Committee on Postwar Foreign Policy, Notter File, RG 59; W. Culbertson to C. Hull, 6 October 1944, unbounded correspondence 1944, Box 25, Culbertson Papers; Culbertson, "Principles of Economic Policy," Department of State (hereafter DOS), Bulletin (25 February 1945): 299-301.

5. Memo, W. Culbertson to D. Acheson, "Should the US Assume Additional Responsibility in the Middle East?" 6 February 1945, unbound correspondence 1945, Box 26, Culbertson Papers; Policy Committee Document PC-8, "Report to the Policy Committee Regarding US Interests in...and the Near East," and Annexes to PC-8, 1 November 1944, Records of Policy and Planning Committees, Notter File, RG 59; FRUS, 1945, 8: 34-35, 45-46; Policy Committee, Annex J to PC-8, 4 November 1944, "The Near and Middle East Beyond the Immediate Periphery of Russia," Notter File, RG 59; P. Ireland to G. Merriam, 24 November 1944, DOS FW 890.50/9-1244, RG 59; F. Winant, "Recommended US Economic Policy in Middle East," DOS 800.24/3-745, RG 59; Short to Acheson, DOS 800.24/7-2844, RG 59; A. A. Berle, Memo A-B/1, "Principal Problems in Europe," 26 September 1944, Policy Committee, Notter File, RG 59; G. Merriam, "American Economic Policy in the Middle East," 15 January 1945, Annex II to the Coordinating Committee Report, 2 May 1945, DOS 800.50 Middle East/5-245, RG 59.

6. FRUS, 1945, 8: 34-38; Minutes of 20 April 1945 meeting of ECEFP, 5.19B ECEFP Meetings, 4.Minutes, and Documents D-64/45 and D-71/45, 5.19B Meetings, 3.Documents, RG 353.

7. FRUS, 1945, 8: 36-37; Memo, Ireland to Merriam, DOS FW 890.50/9-1244, and Merriam, "American Economic Policy in the Middle East," DOS 800.50 Middle East/5-245, RG 59; Alexander Kirk to Secretary of State, 25 April 1944, DOS 890.50/3, RG 59; Culbertson Mission Report, DOS 033.1151R/11-1544 Culbertson Mission, RG 59; DeNovo, "Culbertson Economic Mission," pp. 923-26.

8. B. Berle and T. Jacobs, eds., Navigating the Rapids, 1918-1971: From the Papers of Adolf A. Berle (New York: Harcourt Brace Jovanovich, 1973), pp. 539-42; James Moose to Secretary of State, 10 December 1945, DOS 800.50 Middle East/12-1045, RG 59.

9. FRUS, 1945, 8: 37-38; Financial Affairs Division,
"Proposals for a Near East Regional Economic Organization,"
n.d. [probably May 1945], ECEFP Policy Decisions D-71/45 and
"A Comparison of ECEFP D-71/45 and the FN Paper" n.d. [proba-
bly May 1945], ECEFP Policy Decisions, RG 353.

10. FRUS, 1945, 8: 35-39.

11. G. M. Richardson Dougall, "The Petroleum Division,"
October 1944, Records of Economic Committees, Notter File, RG
59;   Raymond F. Mikesell, report on Middle East Financial
Conference, enclosed in James Landis to Secretary, 18 May
1944, DOS 800.50/1468, RG 59; FRUS, 1945, 8: 36, 38-39; Paul
McGuire to L. Henderson, 15 January 1945, DOS 890G.50/9-2044,
RG 59.

12. Financial Affairs Division, "Proposals for a Near
East Regional Economic Organization," ECEFP Policy Decisions,
D-71/45, RG 353; Memo, Phelps, 11 May 1945, 5.19J ECEFP
Subject File, 3.Finance: Reconstruction Financing, RG 353;
FRUS, 1945, 8: 43-48.

13. Martin W. Wilmington, The Middle East Supply Centre,
ed. Laurence Evans, (Albany: State University New York Press,
1971), pp. 1-4, 77-80, 163-64; Memo of conversation, London,
14 April 1944, DOS 740.0011 Stettinius Mission/137, RG 59;
Landis to Murray, 21 September 1944, DOS FW 890.50/9-1244,
Landis to Murray, "The US Trade Position in the Middle East,"
Annex G to 12 September 1944 memo, DOS 800.24/9-1244, and
Landis to Murray, 13 September 1944, DOS 800.24/9-1344, RG 59.

14. ECEFP D-142/45, 7 November 1945, "The Sterling Area
Exchange Problem," 5.19B ECEFP Meetings, 3.Documents, RG 353;
Arthur Paul speech to Export Advisory Group, 19 September
1944, folder: Import-Export Advisory Committee, 1944-46,
Arthur Paul Papers, Harry Truman Library, Independence, Mo.;
Culbertson Mission Report, pp. 4-9, 17-18, DOS 033.1151R/11-
1544 Culbertson Mission, RG 59; Supplementary Report B,
"Economic Problems Common to the Area," p. 23, DOS
033.1151R/11-1544 Culbertson Mission, RG 59; ECEFP D-94/44,
"Policy with Respect to Future Area Programming," 15 December
1944, 5.19B ECEFP Meetings, 3.Documents, RG 353; James Landis
to Department and FEA, 26 December 1944, DOS 890G.5151/12-
2644, RG 59; Merriam, "US Economic Policy," 15 January 1945,
Annex II to Coordinating Committee Report, 2 May 1945, DOS
800.50 Middle East/5-245, RG 59; F. Winant, "Trade Controls
Today in the Middle East," DOS, Bulletin (21 January 1945):
80-82; Winant, "Recommended US Economic Policy," DOS
800.24/3-745, RG 59.

15. FRUS, 1945, 8: 36, 39, 41; ECEFP D-120/45, 7 September 1945, "Sterling Exchange and Blocked Balances," 5.19B
ECEFP Meetings, 3.Documents, RG 353. Some officers felt that
the United States was ignoring the potential markets of the
Arab East; others did not see much future for American-Arab
trade. See Colonel Harold Hoskins to Secretary of State, 28
June 1945, DOS 800.50 Middle East/6-2845; Memo, B. Calder to
L. Henderson, 14 July 1945, DOS 890.50/7-1445; Memo, Coppock
to C. Wilcox, 10 October 1945, DOS 890.50/10-1045, RG 59.

16. General Patrick Hurley to President, 21 December 1943, and memo, Acheson to E. Stettinius, 28 January 1944, Assistant Secretary Correspondence 1941-45 folder, Dean Acheson Papers, Harry Truman Library, Independence, Mo.; Memo, W. Murray to B. Long, 14 August 1944, DOS 890.01A/8-1444 and Merriam paper, 15 January 1945, DOS 800.50 Middle East/5-245, RG 59; F. Winant, "Proposed US Economic Policy," 12 September 1944, Subject File: Special Mission to Middle East, Box 131, Culbertson Papers; FRUS, 1945, 8: 36, 38; Memo, "The Postwar Program of the Department of State in Cultural Relations," pp. 31-35, folder: Cultural Relations to 1942, Box 190 Breckinridge Long Papers, Manuscript Division, Library of Congress, Washington, D.C.; Sumner Welles to R. C. Thomson, 22 February 1943, DOS 811.42700/2-2243 and memo of meeting concerning cultural relations, 9 June 1943, DOS 111.Advisory Committee/1-644, RG 59; Dorothy Franck, "Cultural and Scientific Competition in the Near East," The Record 2 (1 April 1946): 1-9; Memo, C. Thomson to Shaw and Frank, 10 May 1943, DOS 811.42700/5-1043, RG 59.

17. William Roger Louis, Imperialism at Bay: The United States and the Decolonization of the British Empire, 1941-1945 (New York: Oxford University Press, 1978), pp. 50-52; C. Van H. Engert to L. Henderson, 7 December 1945, DOS 890.00/12-745; Richard Casey, "Future Economic Policy," in NEA memo, "The Future of the MESC," 16 March 1944, DOS 740.0011 Stettinius Mission/3-1944 Mission of Undersecretary Stettinius, RG 59.

18. Memo of conversation 18 April 1944, DOS 740.0011 Stettinius Mission/139; Report to C. Hull on conversations in London, 22 May 1944, DOS 740.0011 EW Stettinius Mission/112.5, RG 59; MESC--Washington, Meeting no. 64, 10 July 1944, folder: MESC Committee Meeting Minutes III, British Empire and Middle East Branch, Subject File of Director, 1943-44, Entry 445, FEA, RG 169; L. Pinkerton to Secretary, 22 September 1944, DOS 800.24/9-2244, RG 59; Guy Hunter, "Economic Problems: The MESC," in George Kirk, The Middle East in the War (London: Oxford University Press, 1952), pp. 190-93; J. Landis to W. Murray, Annex B, "The Significance of the MESC," 30 August 1944, DOS 800.24/8-3044; Landis to Hull, 27 September 1944, DOS 800.24/9-2844; W. Eddy to Secretary, 12 September 1944, DOS 800.24/9-1244; Dreyfus to Hull, 3 July 1943, DOS 800.24/1016, RG 59.

19. FRUS, 1945, 8: 36; Financial Affairs Division, "Near Eastern Regional Economic Organization," May 1945, ECEFP Policy Decisions, D-71/45, Folder: American Economic Policy in the Middle East, RG 353; W. Rountree report in S. P. Tuck to Secretary, 11 September 1945, DOS 800.50 Middle East/9-1145; P. Ireland, "Hoskins' Proposals," 10 October 1945, DOS 890.50/10-1045; J. Moose to Secretary, 15 August and 28 August 1945, W. Murray to Secretary, 4 September 1945, L. Pinkerton to Secretary, 20 and 22 August 1945, DOS 800.50 Middle East/8-1545, 8-2845, 9-445, 8-2045, 8-2245, RG 59; Wilfred Benson, "Regional Collaboration for the Development of Impoverished Areas," War and Peace Studies (CFR, 3 May 1943, no. P-B63, Political Group), pp. 2-4.

20. For examples of Americans who planned for Arab East regional development see Ernst Bergmann, "Suggestions for a Development Plan of the Middle East," 18 November 1943, Subject File, 1923-53, Middle East, Louis Bean Papers, FDR Library, Hyde Park, N.Y.; F. Julius Fohs, "General Introduction to Studies on Development and Land Settlement Potentialities of Some Countries of the Middle East," 2 March 1943, Document 587, Records of Advisory Committee on Postwar Foreign Policy, Notter File, RG 59.

21. Landis to Murray, Annex A, 30 August 1944, DOS 800.24/8-3044, RG 59; Landis, "Anglo-American Cooperation in the Middle East," Vital Speeches of the Day 11 (1 May 1945).

22. Landis to Murray, DOS 800.24/8-3044, RG 59; Memo, "Re Proposed Reorganization," A. Berle to Secretary, 27 December 1943, State Department Subject File: Hull, Memorandum to--August-December 1943, Adolf Berle Papers, FDR Library, Hyde Park, N.Y.; Series of letters from Livingston Merchant to Henry Labouisse, 12 and 16 December 1944, 6 and 17 January 1945, Correspondence and Related Material 1944-53, Folder: Labouisee, Henry R., 1944, Livingston Merchant Papers, Seeley G. Mudd Manuscript Library, Princeton University, Princeton, N.J.; Culbertson Mission Report, DOS 033.1151R/11-1544 Culbertson Mission, RG 59; Culbertson, "Information Memorandum Concerning the Recommendation of the `Corporation,'" 11 December 1944, unbound correspondence 1945, Box 26, Culbertson Papers; FRUS, 1945, 8: 35; F. Winant, "Transfer from LA to NEA of Responsibility for Policy and Coordination of Economic Affairs in Middle East," 4 May 1945, DOS 800.50/5-445, RG 59.

23. Culbertson, "Information," 11 December 1944, Box 26, Culbertson Papers; Memo, Radius to Taft, 28 August 1945, DOS 800.50 Middle East/8-2845; Department to Cairo legation, 16 March 1945, DOS 883.50/3-1445; Hoskins to Secretary, 31 July 1945, DOS 124.836/7-3145; J. Moose to Secretary, 25 August 1945, DOS 800.50 Middle East/8-2545; W. Murray to Secretary, 4 September 1945, DOS 800.50 Middle East/9-445; L. Pinkerton to Secretary, 22 and 31 August 1945, DOS 800.50 Middle East/8-2245 and 8-3145; S. Tuck to Secretary, 3 September 1945, DOS 800.50 Middle East/9-345; Arthur Paul (FEA) to Will Clayton, 12 October 1945, DOS 890.50/10-1245; Memo, L. Henderson to Russell, 10 December 1945, DOS 800.50 Middle East/12-1045, RG 59; John O. Iatrides, Ambassador MacVeagh Reports: Greece, 1933-1947 (Princeton, N.J.: Princeton University Press, 1980), pp. 391-92. For a detailed account of the bureaucratic battle over a regional office in the Middle East, see Nathan Godfried, "Economic Development and Regionalism: United States Foreign Relations in the Middle East, 1942-1945," Journal of Contemporary History 22 (July 1987): 481-500.

24. FRUS, 1945, 8: 13-15, 45-46; FRUS, 1946, 7: 1-4, 7, 16-17; Transcript, Joseph C. Satterthwaite, Oral History Interview, Harry Truman Library, Independence, Mo., 13 November 1972, pp. 4, 10, 12-13.

25. FRUS, 1945, 8: 44, 47-48, 15; FRUS, 1946, 7: 1-4, 7, 16-17; Transcript, Harry N. Howard, Oral History Interview, Harry S. Truman Library, Independence, Mo., 5 June 1973;

Memo, L. Henderson to Luthringer, 4 June 1946, DOS 890.51/6-446, RG 59; Transcript, Satterthwaite Interview, pp. 11-12, 17-18, 27; Transcript, Loy Henderson, Oral History Interview, H. S. Truman Library, 14 June and 5 July 1973, pp. 37, 56, 60-61, 66, 166-68, 197; Memo of conversation, Henderson, British Minister J. Balfour, 6 August 1946, DOS 890.50/8-646, RG 59.

26. FRUS, 1947, 5: 504-5; William Roger Louis, The British Empire in the Middle East, 1945-1951: Arab Nationalism, the United States, and Postwar Imperialism (New York: Oxford University Press, 1984), pp. 109-12.

27. FRUS, 1947, 5: 511-13; Mohammad Iqbal Ansar, The Arab League, 1945-1955 (Aligarh: Institute of Islamic Studies, Aligarh Muslim University, 1968), pp. 10-15.

28. FRUS, 1947, 5: 506-10, 513-20, 488-96.

29. Ibid., pp. 544-52.

30. Ibid., pp. 614-17.

31. Ibid., p. 625; FRUS, 1948, 5: 76.

32. United States Foreign Policy for a Postwar Recovery Program, Hearings before the Committee on Foreign Affairs, House of Representatives, 80th Congress, 1st and 2nd session, (Washington, D.C.: U.S. Government Printing Office, 1948), pp. 234, 242, 545; FRUS, 1948, 5: 47, 84, 1352; FRUS, 1949, 6: 52, 898.

33. FRUS, 1949, 5: 765; Memo of conversation, "US Policy of Economic Assistance for Middle East," 7 May 1948, Folder: Economic Development, US Mission to UN, RG 84; Memo, H. Deimel to G. McGhee, 12 August 1949, DOS 800.50TA/8-1249, RG 59.

34. FRUS, 1948, 5: 550-51, 553, 597, 622-23, 805, 938, 1181, 1217.

35. Memo, C. Clifford to Truman, 8 March 1948, folder, Palestine: US Policy with regard to Palestine, Clark M. Clifford Papers, Harry Truman Library, Independence, Mo.; FRUS, 1948, 5: 692-95; Stephen H. Longrigg, Oil in the Middle East: Its Discovery and Development (London: Oxford University Press, 1968), p. 478, Appendix II. For a thorough discussion of American imperial state and corporate views concerning whether Aramco risked losing its oil concession in Saudi Arabia, see Louis, British Empire in Middle East, pp. 193-203.

36. FRUS, 1949, 6: 80-82, 137-40, 143, 145, 682, 1224, 162-63; FRUS, 1948, 5: 1122-23, 1157-58, 1168, 1176-77, 1132-33.

37. Mira Wilkins, The Maturing of Multinational Enterprise: American Business Abroad from 1914 to 1970 (Cambridge, Mass.: Harvard University Press, 1974), pp. 314-15, 321, 301 table XII; FRUS, 1946, 7: 18-22, 26; John A. Loftus, "Oil in United States Foreign Policy," The Oil and Gas Journal 45 (17

August 1946): 74-75; Memo of conversation, State Department and Socony-Vacuum Oil Company, 6 March 1946, DOS 890.00/3-646, RG 59; "Saudi Arabia and Kuwait Expansion Features Middle East Development," Oil and Gas Journal 45 (28 December 1946): 171, 175; C. O. Wilson, "The Middle East--Its Present and Future," Oil and Gas Journal 44 (29 December 1945): 185; "The Middle East," Oil and Gas Journal 45 (18 January 1947): 35; "Middle East Provides Most of French Crude," Oil and Gas Journal 45 (15 March 1947): 57; Longrigg, Oil in the Middle East, p. 478.

38. "A.P.I. Sessions," Oil and Gas Journal 46 (22 November 1947): 35; "Development of Middle East Called Necessary to Fulfill Marshall Plan," Oil and Gas Journal 47 (22 July 1948): 51; "Spread of Middle East Oil Development Called Key to European Recovery," Oil and Gas Journal 47 (7 October 1948): 129; "Middle East 'Junior Marshall Plan' Costs Taxpayers Nothing," Oil and Gas Journal 47 (18 November 1948): 54; "Financing Foreign Oil," Oil and Gas Journal 48 (3 February 1949): 37. Imperial state and capitalist class elites firmly believed that oil development contributed to Arab economic development. See Raymond F. Mikesell and Hollis Chenery, Arabian Oil: America's Stake in the Middle East (Chapel Hill: University of North Carolina Press, 1949); F. Julius Fohs, "Deposits and Development," Problems of the Middle East (New York: Proceedings of a New York University Conference, 1947), pp. 88-91; FRUS, 1946, 7: 18-22; Memo, G. Mattison to L. Henderson, 28 August 1947, Subject File: Memoranda of Conversations (folder 2), Clayton-Thorp Papers, Harry Truman Library, Independence, Mo.

39. "Foreign Oil Policy Revolves around ECA," Oil and Gas Journal 47 (30 December 1948): 177, 181; Longrigg, Oil in the Middle East, p. 478; Wilson, "Middle East," p. 184; C. O. Wilson, "International Petroleum Outlook in Relation to Operations in the US," Oil and Gas Journal 45 (8 June 1946): 68-69; Lester L. Thompson, "Rival Middle East Companies Show Way to International Cooperation," Oil and Gas Journal 45 (7 September 1946): 69; "ECA and Oil," Oil and Gas Journal 48 (4 August 1949): 21.

40. Dahl Duff, "Lower Tanker Rates Increase World Competition of Middle East Oil," Oil and Gas Journal 48 (11 August 1949): 52, 142; Charles J. Dugan, "Imports, Foreign Oil Aid Draw Fire of Independents in Annual Meeting," Oil and Gas Journal 48 (6 October 1949): 150; Fohs, "Deposits and Development," pp. 88-91; David H. Finnie, Desert Enterprise: The Middle East Oil Industry in its Local Environment (Cambridge, Mass.: Harvard University Press, 1958), pp. 58-60.

41. UN, Department of Economic Affairs, Review of Economic Conditions in the Middle East, 1951-52, Supplement to World Economic Report (New York: UN, March 1953, 1953.II.C.1), pp. 58-59; UN, Department of Economic and Social Affairs, Economic Development in the Middle East, 1945 to 1954 (New York: UN, 1955, 1955.II.C.2), p. 3.

42. UN, Review of Economic Conditions, p. 103; Memo of conversation, "US Policy of Economic Assistance for Middle East," 7 May 1948, Folder: Development: Economic, US Mission

to UN, RG 84, U.S. National Archives, Washington, D.C.; John Gillis to W. Culbertson, 21 June 1945, unbound correspondence 1945, Culbertson Papers; William Swingle, vice president of NFTC, to Seldon Chapin, 4 February 1946, DOS 800.50 Middle East/2-446, RG 59; NFTC, 32nd National Foreign Trade Convention, 1945 (New York: NFTC, 1945), p. 217; J. Landis, "Middle East Challenge," Fortune 32 (September 1945): 161-64, 176; FRUS, 1949, 6: 52, 65, 67-68, 77-78, 173-74, 178, 693, 792, 836; Memo of conversation, Dennis Greenhill, Melenbaum and Gorlitz, 8 November 1949, DOS 890.50/11-849, RG 59.

43. Cairo Embassy to Department, 18 June 1949, 500 Economic Matters 1949, Cairo Post Records, Entry 59A543, RG 84; William Diamond, "Economic Review: Activities of the International Bank in the Middle East," Middle East Journal 3 (October 1949): 455; Gordon Clapp, "Technical and Economic Partnership," in Helen Kitchen, ed., Americans and the Middle East: Partners in the Next Decade (Washington, D.C.: Middle East Institute, 1950), pp. 25-29; Report of Director of Education, H. B. Allen, Annual Reports, 1943-46, Near East Foundation, New York; FRUS, 1949, 6: 1430-40; W. C. Lowdermilk to J. Satterthwaite, 21 March 1949, includes memo on "Exporting American Know-How in Rural Reconstruction Projects on the Land," DOS 800.50 TA/3-2149, RG 59; Max W. Thornburg, "Turkey: Aid for What?," Fortune 36 (October 1947): 106-7, 171.

44. George Hakim, "Point Four and the Middle East: A Middle East View," Middle East Journal 4 (April 1950): 183-95; Advisory Committee on Technical Assistance, "Replies from the field to circular on Point 4," ACTA D-8/3, pp. 24-38, 26 July 1949, Folder: "5.35.2 Point Four Explanation Book," Economic Committees, RG 353; Said Hemadeh, "Economic Factors Underlying Social Problems in the Arab Countries," lecture at UN Social Welfare Seminar for Arab States, August-September 1949, Correspondence "K-Q," ESM folder, Gordon R. Clapp Papers, Harry Truman Library, Independence, Mo.

45. Dr. Chaim Weizmann to FDR, 29 June 1943, OF 700-Palestine, FDR Papers; Memo of conversation, E. Kaplan, M. Boukstein, L. Henderson, G. Merriam, 13 July 1945, DOS 867N.50/7-1345, RG 59; Ernst Bergmann, "Suggestions for a Development Plan of the Middle East," 18 November 1943, Subject File, 1923-53, Middle East, Bean Papers; FRUS, 1943, 4: 758-60; L. Pinkerton to Secretary, 20 December 1945, DOS 800.50 Middle East/12-2045, RG 59; FRUS, 1944, 5: 616-21, 648; Iraqi Minister to FDR, 10 March 1945, PSF Diplomatic Iraq, FDR Papers. For examples of articles on the absorptive capacity of Palestine, see Abraham Revusky, "The Absorptive Capacity of Palestine," Palestine Can Take Millions (London: The Jewish Agency for Palestine, 1944); Rita Hinden, "Palestine and Colonial Development," The Political Quarterly 13 (January 1942): 91-99; E. Schmorak, Palestine's Industrial Future (Jerusalem: Rubin Mass Publisher, 1946); Alfred E. Kahn, "Palestine: A Problem in Economic Evaluation," The American Economic Review 34 (September 1944): 538-60.

46. For background on the Anglo-American Committee of Inquiry and UNSCOP, see John Snetsinger, Truman, the Jewish Vote, and the Creation of Israel (Stanford: Hoover Institu-

tion Press, 1974), pp. 21-24, 49-50, 56-57; Richard Crossman, *Palestine Mission, A Personal Record* (New York: Harper & Brothers, 1947), pp. 35-36; Jewish Agency for Palestine, *The Jewish Case Before the Anglo-American Committee of Inquiry on Palestine: Statements and Memoranda* (Jerusalem: The Jewish Agency, 1947); Jewish Agency for Palestine, *The Jewish Plan for Palestine: Memoranda and Statements by the Jewish Agency for Palestine to the United Nations Special Committee on Palestine* (Jerusalem: The Jewish Agency, 1947).

47. Snetsinger, *Truman, the Jewish Vote*, pp. 56-57; Howard M. Sachar, *A History of Israel: From the Rise of Zionism to Our Time* (New York: Alfred A. Knopf, 1976), pp. 283-85, 292; UN, *Yearbook, 1947-1948*, (Lake Success, N.Y.: Department of Public Information, UN, 1949), pp. 251-52; *FRUS, 1947*, 5: 1211, 1225, 1241-42, 1251.

48. For a review of the events during the period between November 1947 and May 1948, see Sachar, *History of Israel*, pp. 295-314; and Snetsinger, *Truman, the Jewish Vote*, pp. 73-102.

49. Don Peretz, *Israel and the Palestine Arabs* (Washington, D.C.: The Middle East Institute, 1958), pp. 4, 6, 8-11, 69; Rony E. Gabbay, *A Political Study of the Arab-Jewish Conflict: The Arab Refugee Problem, A Case Study* (Geneva: Librarie E. Droz, Etudes D'Historie Economique, Politique Et Sociale, XXIX, 1959), pp. 54, 65-68, 108-18, 122-25, 268-73, 284-85, 290-93, 295, 299-303; Michael Assaf, "The Arab Refugee Problem and the State of Israel," in Sophie Udin, ed., *The Palestine Year Book and the Israeli Annual, 5709* (New York: Zionist Organization of America, 1949), pp. 232-47; Mizra Khan, "The Arab Refugees: A Study in Frustration," in Walter Z. Laqueur, ed., *The Middle East in Transition: Studies in Contemporary History*, (London: Routledge & Kegan Paul, 1958), pp. 237-42; Edward H. Buehrig, *The UN and the Palestinian Refugees: A Study in Non-Territorial Administration* (Bloomington: Indiana University Press, 1971), p. 15; *FRUS, 1948*, 5: 1151, 1295, 1311-12, 1315, 1324-26, 1330, 1333, 1364-65, 1405-6, 1427-28, 1444, 1454-59, 1479-80, 1486-87, 1498-99, 1532, 1554-55, 1635, 1648; *FRUS, 1949*, 6: 935, 945-48, 1020-21, 1034-35, 1065-68, 1204, 1216, 1262, 1363; UN General Assembly, 4th session, 1949, *Interim Report of ESM*, 8 November 1949, Doc.A/1106, p. 17.

50. Peretz, *Israel and the Palestine Arabs*, pp. 11, 34-40, 58-63; Gabbay, *A Political Study*, pp. 238-63; Khan, "Arab Refugees," p. 243; *FRUS, 1948*, 5: 1696-97; *FRUS, 1949*, 6: 805, 1232, 935-39, 1219-21, 1329, 1317-18; UN General Assembly, *Interim Report of ESM*, p. 17; Buehrig, *The UN and the Palestinian Refugees*, p. 33.

51. Peretz, *Israel and the Palestine Arabs*, pp. 12, 61-63; UN General Assembly, *Interim Report of ESM*, pp. 17-19, 25-28; Buehrig, *The UN and the Palestinian Refugees*, pp. 33-37; Hertha Kraus, "Work Programs in International Aid: Employment of Arab Refugees, 1949-52," in H. Teaf and P. Franck, eds., *Hands across Frontiers: Case Studies in Technical Co-operation* (Ithaca, N.Y.: Cornell University Press, 1955), p. 522; *FRUS, 1949*, 6: 1477, 1505-6; Memo, G. Clapp to members of ESM, 17 November 1949, Memoranda and Drafts of ESM Report

folder, Gordon Clapp Papers;   UN, General Assembly, <u>Final Report of the UN Economic Survey Mission</u>, 28 December 1949.

52.   Transcript, Harry Howard Interview,   pp. 86-88, 95, 98-99;   <u>FRUS, 1949</u>, 6: 1506, 173, 177-78, 67-68, 1463-64; Peretz, <u>Israel and the Palestine Arabs</u>, pp. 240, 245.

53.   <u>FRUS, 1949</u>, 6: 1529-30, 1557, 1564;   Peretz, <u>Israel and the Palestine Arabs</u>, pp. 69, 13; Louis Hyde, <u>The United States and the United Nations</u>, (New York: Carnegie Endowment for International Peace, Manhattan Publishing, 1960), p. 71.

54.   W. Butterworth to Acting Secretary, 27 October 1948, DOS 890.50/10-2748, RG 59.

55.   For information on the concept of TVAs in the Middle East, see Feliks Bochenski and W. Diamond, "TVAs in the Middle East," <u>Middle East Journal</u> 4 (January 1950): 52-55;   Hans Heymann, "Toward Economic Regionalism and Its Political Potentialities," Heymann to Norman Armour, 18 March 1948, DOS 890.50/3-1848, RG 59. For details on economic disintegration in the Middle East, see Alfred Musrey, <u>An Arab Common Market: A Study in Inter-Arab Trade Relations, 1920-1967</u> (New York: Praeger, 1969), pp. 40, 57, 70-73.

56.   C. J. Shohan, "Economic Regionalism in the Far East," 23 August 1949, DOS 890.50/8-2349, RG 59. State Department officials paid lip-service to organizations like the League of Arab States, which sought regional economic development. In private, however, these policymakers noted that the Arab League's Economic Committee had "not been used to much effect for want of a basic economic justification." "Attitude of US Government Toward Possible Regional Economic Commission for Middle East," ECEFP D-108/47, 21 July 1947, 5.19B ECEFP Meetings, 3.Documents, RG 353; Robert MacDonald, <u>The League of Arab States: A Study in the Dynamics of Regional Organization</u> (Princeton, N.J.:   Princeton University Press, 1965), pp. 9-11, 40-41, 192, 196.

5
Arab East Development and the United States, 1942-1949: Case Studies

The centerpiece of America's economic policy in the Arab East was economic development. Corporate officials, especially those in the oil industry, placed development high on their agenda. Middle East development figured prominently Britain's postwar plans as well. Among the economic and political elites of the Arab East, the desire for development--and its anticipated socioeconomic and political rewards--intensified during the 1940s. Arab rulers came to view development as a way to attain nationalist goals while maintaining their own wealth and power.

By the 1940s, Arab East intellectuals and political leaders viewed development from several perspectives. One approach embraced liberal capitalist economic doctrines and questioned Islam's value and effectiveness in achieving economic growth. Some adherents of this perspective identified imperialism as the cause of underdevelopment, while others saw a combination of causes--including imperialism, stagnant socioeconomic institutions, lack of capital, illiteracy, and undeveloped resources. Regardless of the source of underdevelopment, these Westernists agreed that the Arab East had to adopt the techniques and systems of the industrialized nations in the West. Disagreements arose over how to achieve Westernization--some urged an immediate and complete separation from Islamic tradition, others suggested a more gradual break. Westernists included Charles Issawi of Egypt, Charles Malik of Lebanon (and most of Lebanon's Christian bourgeoisie), Iraq's Prime Minister Nuri-es-Said, and the Wafd party of Egypt.(1)

Conservative Islamists rejected the Westernist argument and asserted that Islam best facilitated and stimulated capital accumulation and economic progress. The movement to revitalize Islam was a conscious choice made by some Arab elites; a choice made in opposition to foreign intervention. Theorists such as a M. Hamidullah and Sayyed Abulala Maudoodi contended that the Islamic economy was closely tied to Islamic politics, culture, and moral code. Islam provided a "unique blue-print for the structure and growth of society." It combined the virtues of private enterprise with an equitable distribution of wealth, while avoiding the evils associated with capitalism and socialism.(2)

The advocates of an Islamic economy spoke and wrote in generalities; they offered few specific programs for economic

development.   Nevertheless, they contributed to the general
development discussion by recognizing that economic development entailed transformations throughout society and by urging
reforms in political, moral, and social spheres.   Although
their answer was not new, it was comprehensive. Westernists
also realized the need for extensive reform.   But like American leaders, the Arab modernists failed to see the cultural
and psychological aftershocks of introducing alien systems
among their peoples.
     The Arab East's conceptions of economic development
reflected regional socioeconomic divisions.   Westernist
concepts were strongest among the area's political and
economic elites and bourgeoisie, while poor urban and rural
workers leaned toward conservative Islamic concepts. Caught
between peasants and workers on one side, and an expansive
bourgeoisie on the other, an intermediary class evolved "an
assimilative, utopian, eclectic mentality."   From this petty
bourgeoisie rose theorists who devised an Islamic reform or
traditionalist reform concept of development.   Having its
roots in the Nahda movement of the nineteenth century--which
sought to "assimilate the great achievements of modern
European civilization, while reviving the classical Arab
culture"--the Islamic reform movement advocated a return to
traditional moral and political codes, while accepting
European technology and economic organization.   This group
"developed an ideology based on the notion of 'nonexploiting
capitalism,' the communal harmony of Islam and the possibility
of social development without class conflict."   This "third
way" between Western capitalism and classical Islam characterized the programs of petty-bourgeois-led parties such as the
Muslim Brotherhood, Young Egypt, and the Ba'th.(3)
     All three strains of Arab East development thought were
"dependent"--that is, they derived from Western capitalist
and, to a lesser extent, socialist doctrines, or reacted
against such ideologies.   In the case of the conservative
Islamists, much of their theoretical analysis came from the
Indian subcontinent rather than from the Arab East. Those
groups possessing the most power in the Arab East--the
modernists and reformers--anticipated and sought American
financial and technical aid for development.   These groups
displayed ambivalence toward American arguments that European
economic recovery would provide the Middle East with markets
and sources of capital and consumer goods. Arab leaders
criticized the United States for linking a Palestine settlement to development assistance. American officials blamed the
dislocation of World War II, the primary importance of
reviving world trade and reconstructing the economies of
Europe and Japan, and the economic, social, and political
fractures caused by the Arab-Israeli war for hindering the
flow of American aid and capital to the majority of Arab
states.   These same concerns and difficulties, however, did
not obstruct private or public American aid to Saudi Arabia
and Palestine/Israel.
     The desire to maintain and extend oil concessions in
Saudi Arabia led imperial state and capitalist class elites to
participate in the planning and implementation of Saudi economic development. Meanwhile, American Zionist organizations
and private American businessmen played a vital role in the
economic progress of Jewish Palestine and Israel.

The following section presents case studies of American economic development policies toward and relations with Egypt, Saudi Arabia, and Israel.   These countries have been chosen because they represent nations at different stages of socioeconomic development (see the Appendix).   Israel was clearly the most developed nation in the Arab East and Saudi Arabia the least; Egypt appeared in the middle of the economic development continuum.   The following studies demonstrate that U.S. attitudes toward economic development in these countries were not based on the particular country's relative stage of socioeconomic development, but rather on the economic and political opportunities and benefits that each country offered the United States and on the importance of each in the overall scheme of Pax Americana.

EGYPT

Egypt's intermediate position on the economic development continuum made it both an attractive and a threatening country for foreign economic penetration.   During World War II, American interest in Egypt's economic development focused on trade. Egypt's desire to rid itself of British imperialism coincided with America's goal of increasing its share of trade and investment in Egypt.   Career Foreign Service Officers and political in-and-outers in Cairo and Washington became obsessed with creating an American economic presence in Egypt and throughout the Middle East.   Although locked in a bureaucratic struggle over who would implement policy in the region, both groups urged their superiors to respond favorably and immediately to informal Egyptian requests for American capital, technology, and advisers.

Alexander Kirk, the American minister to Egypt during the early part of the war, personified the career FSO position on policy in the Middle East.   A quintessential upper-class diplomat, Kirk had entered the diplomatic service in 1915 after studying at elite preparatory schools and Yale University, traveling in Europe, and receiving a law degree from Harvard Law School.   His father's "soap millions" (the elder Kirk had made a fortune in soap manufacturing) helped to subsidize Kirk's income at various diplomatic posts.   During World War II, Kirk served as the American minister to both Egypt and Saudi Arabia (1941-1943) and later as ambassador to Greece and Italy.   Kirk, a devoted adherent to the open door and American hegemony, distrusted the British and took every opportunity to expand American influence in the Arab East at their expense.   After numerous encounters with Kirk, Harold MacMillan, the British Minister Resident at Allied Headquarters in Northwest Africa, wrote that the American diplomat was "a millionaire, a dilettante--and an intellectual snob." MacMillian acknowledged that Kirk was clever and generous and that he had a mind, "but does not apply it to any creative purpose.   He is an excellent diplomat."(4)

In 1942 Kirk glowingly described existing U.S. economic interests in Egypt and hinted at greater investment and commercial opportunities.   He urged officials in Washington to make overtures toward Egypt.   At Kirk's request, Raymond F. Mikesell, the Treasury Department representative in Cairo, studied the feasibility of establishing an American bank in Egypt.   Both men agreed that such a bank would be "an important means of extending American commercial and industrial interests" in Egypt and throughout the region.(5)

Like Kirk and Mikesell, James Landis favorably viewed America's future economic relations with Egypt. The director of the American Economic Mission in the Middle East explained to State Department officers that Nile River development required some "mechanism like the TVA" and that the United States was an obvious choice for aiding in the creation of such an authority. Establishing an American bank in Egypt and an American-Egyptian Chamber of Commerce also would promote and expedite trade and investment between the two nations. Landis, a former head of the Securities and Exchange Commission and a New Deal liberal, saw a role for the United States in the rehabilitation of Egypt's industrial plant, utilities, and railways; expansion of municipal services; and creation of new industries based on available raw materials.(6)

Several obstacles tempered imperial state officials' enthusiasm concerning expanded American-Egyptian economic relations. Egypt's inability to attain dollars, in particular, inhibited trade with the United States. Kirk and Landis believed that the British consciously manipulated exchange controls to the disadvantage of the United States. Landis urged Egypt to leave the sterling area or be "dragged down to the inevitable lower standards that will characterize the sterling countries." American purchasing of Egyptian goods would help transfer dollars to Egypt. But a congressional report explained that Egypt's chief export, cotton, could not compete with domestic American supplies and synthetic substitutes. American exports to Egypt would be limited, noted the report, until a "method of securing more dollar exchange either through Britain or by direct loans from the United States can be worked out." The problem swirled in a vicious circle.(7)

A potential obstacle involved the industrialization process. The United States worried about **how** Egypt and other peripheral nations industrialized. As Landis commented in a December 1944 speech, the United States would not aid Egypt if it followed a path of "mercantilism, uneconomic and political subsidies, narrow nationalism, [or] group preferences." Congressional reports characterized pending Egyptian legislation to increase indigenous managerial and financial control of foreign companies operating in Egypt as discouraging American capital investment. One commercial adviser recommended tying American economic aid to Egyptian assurances that "such assistance would not result in strengthening Egyptian nationalism, with all its resultant restrictions and controls." British officials also cautioned that industrialization was not an "economic panacea." A Middle East Supply Centre report recommended that Egyptian industry confine itself to "a series of simple operations within the capacity of the Egyptian worker." American and British policymakers agreed that Egypt would have to take its proper place as a primary producer in the world-economy if it hoped to secure foreign financial and technical assistance.(8)

In 1944 Landis became involved in a private scheme to foster commercial links between the United States and Egypt and the entire Arab East. Dan T. Moore, who had served on Landis' staff both in Washington and Cairo, "dreamed up a `Middle East Company' to tap Landis' expertise as a middleman between American manufacturers and Middle Eastern countries."

Similar in concept to the Rockefeller effort in Latin American (IBEC) and Stettinius' company in Liberia, the Middle East Company was to aid in Middle East development by facilitating export-import trade with the United States. Landis was excited about the plan, which would have stationed him permanently in Cairo, overseeing trade trends in the region. But the problem of blocked sterling balances and other obstructions to free trade and the open door weakened the company's prospects. Already exhausted with British machinations and quickly tiring of "dickering" with American businessmen, Landis returned to Harvard University in 1945. He retained his position as chairman of the board and remained a figurehead for the company for some time.(9)

Landis' departure from Egypt did not end American pressure on Britain to end its trade controls there. As World War II ended, the United States continued to encourage private American trade and investment in Egypt. Meanwhile, Egyptian political and business elites sought to promote economic development by creating conditions within which private enterprise could prosper. Thus the Egyptian government acted to stimulate the private sector and have it lead the way to development.(10)

In 1945, the Egyptian government combined various projects in agriculture, industry, commerce, and public service into a 50.5 million Egyptian pound Five Year Plan. Officials hoped to finance the scheme by internal loans, cotton exports, and the sale of war surplus. Administrative incompetence and increased spending for defense hindered the plan and other efforts at economic development. The conflict with Israel forced an increase in Egyptian military spending from 8.8 percent of government expenditures in 1944-45 to 21 percent in 1949-50. During the same period, funding for education, health, and social services increased from 16 to 18 percent. The scarcity of dollars and the inability of sterling area countries to satisfy Egyptian import needs forced the nation to maximize its receipts of hard currencies and reduce, whenever and wherever possible, its imports from dollar areas. This inability to purchase capital goods on the world market obstructed national efforts at industrialization and the modernization of agriculture.(11)

In an attempt to develop domestic industries, the Egyptian government used protective tariffs, subsidies, rebates on state railroads, and preferences in government contracts. Legislation in 1947 limited foreign participation in the financing and managing of new companies to 49 percent. By the end of the 1940s, Egyptian nationals still held less than 50 percent of the total capital of joint stock companies registered in the country. In general, government policies only partially succeeded in developing the industrial sector. What the government gave in protective legislation, it took away with bureaucratic red tape, inconsistent policies, high taxes, and failure to promote standardization.(12)

Egypt's bourgeois leaders believed that national development could be achieved "best with the cooperation of foreign capital and technicians." In April 1947, Mahmoud Hassan, the Egyptian ambassador to the United States, explained that his country sought American investment, materials, and services in order to expand its industrial base. Egypt welcomed a $5.6 million Eximbank credit for the purchase of American chemical goods. Such loans, however, were rare. Imperial state

officials offered to increase imports of Egyptian long staple
cotton in order to alleviate Egypt's dollar shortage.   But
representatives of the American Cotton Shippers Association
and the Cotton Textile Institute succeeded in maintaining
measures to protect domestic cotton production.(13)

The National Bank of Egypt criticized the United States
for "not fully practising the principles of commercial nondiscrimination which she is preaching to others."   Bank
officials viewed America's "arbitrary quota" as the chief
cause of Egypt's dollar shortage. Although anger over the
American policy in Palestine affected bilateral trade, the
principal cause of the decline was Egypt's lack of dollars.
Without dollars, Egypt relinquished those goods which it
desperately needed and that the United States could supply--
such as wheat, lubricating oils, sheet iron and steel, internal combustion engines, tractors, and textile machinery.(14)

In mid-1947 Britain agreed to the immediate release and
total convertibility of part of the blocked balances owed to
Egypt.   With some freely convertible currency in hand, Egypt
left the sterling area. Several weeks later, gold and dollar
losses forced Britain to renege on its commitment to full
convertibility. Egypt found itself outside the sterling area
with all its reserves in British currency. In desperation,
Egypt relaxed and subsequently removed trade regulations
against all countries accepting sterling.(15)

Lacking the dollars to purchase American goods and unable
to attain the items it needed from the war-wrecked British
economy, Egypt turned to short-term barter and bilateral
agreements. In March 1948 Egypt and the Soviet Union signed a
pact exchanging cotton for wheat and corn. This act violated
America's policy of fostering in Egypt "conditions conducive
to expanding world trade."   The State Department reminded
Egyptian leaders "of our view that barter and bilateral agreements, particularly if long-term and if developed into a network, divert trade into uneconomic channels and reduce the
volume and benefits of world trade."   This warning notwithstanding, Egypt expanded bilateral trade and instituted new
import controls.   With the increasing value of cotton on the
world market during 1949 and 1950, Egypt sold cotton against
dollars while purchasing as much as possible with sterling
assets. All these efforts failed, however, to supply the
nation with sufficient development materials.(16)

Egyptian requests for capital aid from the United States
fell on deaf ears. American policymakers directed Egypt to
international agencies such as the World Bank. The instability created by the Arab-Jewish conflict over Palestine served
to reinforce America's policy of avoiding large public financial aid programs for Egypt and the entire Arab East.   Imperial state officials insisted that a Palestine settlement was
a prerequisite for American aid to the region.(17)

The appointment of Stanton Griffis as American ambassador
to Egypt in July 1948 appeared to mark a renewed American
interest in Egypt's economic development. A New York investment banker, Griffis brimmed with "an interest in industrial
development." Warned by embassy staff to moderate his comments on the development issue, Griffis nevertheless told
Egyptian leaders that he recognized their country's aspiration
and potential for industrial progress and the "helpful role
America might play" in achieving that goal.   In the fall of
1948 the American ambassador proposed that the United States

provide technical, financial, and material assistance for Egypt's ambitious Aswan hydroelectric and industrial project. Griffis also recommended that the United States increase dollar markets for Egyptian cotton by removing or expanding quotas, increasing off-shore purchases of Egyptian cotton under the Marshall Plan, and marketing Egyptian cotton in Japan for dollars. In exchange for this development aid, Egypt would negotiate a settlement with Israel. The State Department quickly vetoed this idea. Aside from the appearance of an outright bribe, Washington worried that such a precedent would have hundreds of poor, agrarian countries clamoring for similar aid.(18)

Another event in 1948 ignited Egyptian interest in American economic aid. Implementation of the Marshall Plan led some Egyptian officials to speculate on American designs for the economic advancement of the Third World. In the spring and fall of 1948 rumors abounded in the Egyptian press concerning an impending Marshall Plan for the underdeveloped periphery. One press report quoted a figure of $3 billion as the initial sum of a Middle East Recovery Program. In early 1949 the Egyptian prime minister raised the question of a Marshall Plan for Egypt. He suggested that America encourage ERP nations to purchase Egyptian cotton with dollars. The prime minister hoped that the United States sincerely wanted to help poor nations. "It would be better to do nothing at all than to raise their hopes only to dash them to the ground." By the fall of 1949 "many Egyptians regarded the question [of a Middle East Marshall Plan] as too hypothetical." Egyptian financiers and public officials focused instead on the ERP, applauding it as "an unprecedented act of international solidarity." National Bank officers hoped that Egypt "would benefit, indirectly, through the economic recovery of Europe and that the effect of this plan will be to reduce the world stringency of dollars."(19)

Egyptian nationalists suspected private American investments. They stressed the lesson of British imperialism and asked whether foreign capital could be used without sacrificing national economic and political independence. Egypt's delegate to the Arab League, Zaki Hashem, explained that foreign investors concentrated "on developing primary production for export and on services meant to facilitate that purpose." Foreign capital did not, therefore, develop a balanced economy, but rather "accentuated its lopsided development and accelerated the rate of depletion of natural resources." Such logic led Egyptian nationalists to pass legislation limiting the percentage of foreign capital in new domestic industries and requiring that foreign mining operations meet all domestic demands for their product and export only the surplus. State Department officers asserted that these "narrow and nationalistic economic measures" retarded Egyptian development. In May 1949 the State Department outlined a policy in which the United States would lend assistance "where appropriate" in the form of technology and "moderate" Eximbank loans for sound short-term and self-liquidating projects. Egypt, in turn, would have to amend its company and mining laws and take other "reasonable measures which will attract private investments and commercial activity."(20)

Egyptian industrialists heeded the State Department's warnings and sought the repeal of "nationalistic" measures in order to secure American capital and technical aid. Desiring loans and investments on a cooperative basis, the industrial bourgeoisie warmly received Eximbank credits to help pay for American machinery, the opening of a Ford Motor Company assembly plant, and the construction of an American-sponsored rayon plant. These elements of Egypt's ruling class also concurred with American thinking that technical aid and "favorable" local economic conditions would result in the flow of private foreign capital into Egypt. At the same time, these groups argued that the United States, Britain, and international financial institutions controlled by the core often misunderstood the peculiar problems of peripheral areas. National Bank executives attacked the IBRD for lumping together the development needs of nations like Argentina and Chile with the needs of nations such as Egypt and India. While eager to receive funds for irrigation systems, Egyptian leaders wondered why the World Bank dismissed their plans for industrial development. IBRD and State Department officers responded that Egypt had the experience and technicians for irrigation projects, but not for steel construction. Accepting this criticism, Egyptian leaders looked to the proposed Point Four program for aid in bolstering national managerial and technical skills.(21)

American planners sought to use Point Four to help Egypt balance its payments and trade and develop an economy complementary to that of Europe and the United States. When Egyptian officials inquired about "the size of Egypt's slice" of Point Four, the American embassy told them to submit a survey of national development projects that would require technical assistance. While the purpose and mechanics of Point Four confused some Egyptians, industrial leaders again accepted the American view that technical aid would stimulate private capital investment. For the industrial bourgeoisie private capital was far more flexible than governmental loans, although there was a need for both types of financing. According to both imperial state policymakers and Egypt's bourgeoisie, the greatest enemy of economic development was not private foreign capital, but "misguided popular" attempts to control such capital. Whether accepting Point Four as a stimulus for private foreign investment or hoping that it was a prelude to massive "Marshallite" aid, the Egyptian government signed a Point Four agreement in May 1950.(22)

American government aid to Egypt from 1945 to 1950 amounted to only $19.9 million in credits and grants. This was far short of what Egypt wanted and did not approach the aid given to Europe or Japan or even the net aid extended or promised to Saudi Arabia or Israel. While waving the flag of free trade, the United States placed import quotas on Egyptian cotton and hindered Egypt's acquisition of dollars. Like all Arab states, Egypt resented the American position on Palestine and aid to Israel. Finally, Egyptian leaders, while willing to work within the capitalist world-economy, questioned the American obsession with private capital flows to peripheral nations. "The talk about overseas investments of American capital," commented the National Bank of Egypt, "is old and the difficulties it encounters in countries with planned or controlled economy are enormous, so there only remains for Americans `to try to stimulate.'" American efforts to aid the development of poor nations, complained Egyptian financiers, "are meagre and are not of the kind to solve world problems,

since most of them do not contain any definite programme of
action."(23)

Egypt's unsatisfactory experience with the United States
over the issue of economic development illustrated the contradictions faced by many Arab states within the periphery--
including Iraq, Lebanon, Syria, and Jordan.   Egypt's industrial and financial bourgeoisie sought foreign capital and
technology to pursue a Western model of capital-intensive
development.   Western capital and technical aid--whether
through private or public channels--and Western models of
development intensified Egyptian dependency on the West.
Rhetoric notwithstanding, significant segments of Egypt's
bourgeoisie advocated policies that hindered national economic
diversification, integration, and, hence, independence.(24)
The issues of capital and technical aid and development models
emerged in entirely different form in the case of American
economic relations with Saudi Arabia and Israel.

SAUDI ARABIA

In May 1939 the first tanker docked at Ras Tanura to load
oil from the newly producing Dhahran fields.   Oil company
officials anticipated expanded drilling, transport, and
refinery operations. King Ibn Saud hoped to use his new oil
royalties to solidify his power and slowly "modernize" his
country. But war disrupted the world's oil markets, endan-
gered tanker transport to and from the Persian Gulf, and
inhibited American investment in distant oil projects. Saudi
oil production fluctuated during the war--15,000 barrels per
day in 1940; 12,000 in 1943; 21,000 in 1944; and 59,000 in
1945.   The fear of depleted oil reserves in the United States
and wartime demands for oil inevitably made development of the
Arabian fields an important wartime goal.(25)   Saudi oil
development was vital for the conduct of the war in Europe and
Asia and for the course of postwar reconstruction in those
areas.   King Ibn Saud and his advisers wanted expanded production to underwrite national economic growth and political
stability.

The U.S. interest in Saudi Arabian oil has been the subject of several studies.(26)   The following analysis focuses
on how American imperial state and corporate policymakers
decided to use economic development as a means to maintain and
extend American oil concessions in Saudi Arabia.   American
interest in Saudi Arabia, however, transcended the politics
and economics of oil.   Private and public sector leaders
perceived Saudi Arabia as another showcase of America's technology and way of life, a demonstration of what the United
States could do for the underdeveloped countries of the Arab
East. But Saudi Arabia made a poor model for other peripheral
nations to emulate.   The Saudi-American relationship was
unique.   Saudi and American officials agreed on fundamental
issues of economic development and assistance. A harmony of
interests among American and Saudi ruling elites was so strong
that the negotiated conflict between periphery and core--
evident in most American contacts with the Third World--was
almost missing in American-Saudi Arabian relations during the
1940s. In many ways, Saudi Arabia was the supreme achievement
of American development policy in the 1940s--a country

experiencing political stability and economic growth, but little economic development.

War meant financial disaster for Saudi Arabia. Oil production slowed and royalties decreased. The pilgrimage to Mecca--King Ibn Saud's principal source of revenue prior to the war--came to a virtual halt. Government revenues fell precipitiously, as did the income of the merchants of Mecca and Jidda. The king sought and received assistance from the United States and Great Britain. American and British subsidies helped to keep King Ibn Saud in power, his people alive, and his kingdom quiet throughout the war. The two core powers acted to protect the petroleum resources of Saudi Arabia and to enhance their own images among the Arabs of the Middle East. Assistance to Saudi Arabia was closely tied to King Ibn Saud's apparent wish for national development.(27)

United States officials saw what they wanted to see in the king of Arabia. Almost everyone who came into contact with Ibn Saud identified him as a progressive and farsighted monarch--one who desired the economic advancement of his country. Max Thornburg, the State Department's petroleum adviser, once explained that while the king remained obedient to the Koran, he sought to "adapt the circumstances of modern life to meet the sensibilities of his people." Patrick Hurley, President Roosevelt's special representative in the Middle East during the war, described Ibn Saud as a "man of vision and executive ability ready to lead his people in keeping with the progress of the world." Karl Twitchell, an American engineer with long experience in Arabia, wrote that the king was "hospitable to western science and western ideas that promise to increase the prosperity of his country."(28)

According to American observers, Ibn Saud's faith and confidence in the United States equalled his desire for economic progress. Impressed with the work of Americans like Twitchell and oil company officials, the king sought further American technical and financial assistance. Hurley reported in 1943 that the Saudi monarch wanted aid in creating irrigation projects, a network of roads, a public health system, and "other essentials for the welfare of the people and the support of an independent nation."(29) On one side stood a man dedicated to his nation's progress and eager to accept American aid and leadership. On the other side stood a core nation seeking to expand its oil holdings and to secure Arab goodwill for the war effort. It was an ideal match.

One obstacle blocking the ideal match was the British effort to retain some influence in Saudi Arabia. Once again Alexander Kirk eloquently stated the American position. According to Kirk, Saudi Arabia had become a battleground between British and American hegemony. "Needless to say a stable world order can be achieved only under the American system." The benefits of the American system were self-evident--at least to Kirk. An internationalized American capitalist and corporatist system would "help backward countries to help themselves in order that they may lay the foundation for real self dependence."(30) Real independence in Saudi Arabia, according to Kirk and his colleagues, was only possible under the Saudi monarchy and American guidance.

Ibn Saud and his American admirers shared a commitment to the status quo in Saudi Arabia--to the preservation of the ruling family. During the 1940s a small proportion of Saudi government revenues went into genuine economic development programs. Funds secured from American oil operations and from American government subsidies usually flowed into security-related schemes (e.g., communications, subsidies for bedouins) and--especially in the late 1940s and 1950s--the importation of foodstuffs and consumer and luxury goods. Ibn Saud's conception of economic development revolved around maximizing his family's control of Arabia.(31)

The imperial state bureaucracy linked together Arabian oil, economic development, and Ibn Saud's continued rule. The Office of Petroleum Adviser noted that without an expanded oil development program, "Saudi Arabia must reconcile itself to remaining indefinitely in its present backward state." James Landis contended that the United States would have to retain the king's friendship and strengthen the Saudi government's ability to maintain law and order. Wartime subsidies would temporarily hold Ibn Saud's goodwill. But only a program of economic development would promote government stability "so that the death of the king will not destroy the kingdom that he created." Expanded oil industry operations would increase revenues to the government, which could then be used for development schemes. The Arabian American Oil Company (Aramco) had to ensure that its operations directly benefitted the lives of local workers. Extending American air service to selected cities would improve contacts and establish new trade links with Saudi Arabia. Improving living conditions in cities such as Jidda was vital so that "good American talent can be induced to go there." America had to supply advisers and experts, argued Landis, in order to reform the inefficient Saudi administrative and financial systems.(32)

Landis assumed that American government financial assist-ance would be forthcoming in the postwar years. Wary of increased government activity in economic affairs, however, imperial state bureaucrats such as Paul McGuire insisted that the State Department and Aramco reach an agreement as to the respective roles of private and public capital in Saudi Arabia. Placing faith in the private enterprise system, the State Department economic officer found nothing wrong with entrusting the national interest to a private firm like Aramco. But McGuire also realized that Ibn Saud would not postpone national development until his operating budget was balanced and all his debts paid. McGuire recommended the establishment of a "development program financed with United States government funds advanced against future royalties contingent upon the establishment of an American advisory system."(33)

A State Department memorandum on long-range financial aid to Saudi Arabia combined the suggestions of Landis and McGuire. The report, which came across Roosevelt's desk in late 1944, pointed out that Arabian oil was strategically and economically important to the war effort and to postwar recon-struction. A stable Arabian government, founded on a strong economy, would be the best protection for the American oil concessions. U.S. financial and technical support for Saudi economic development, contended McGuire, would "demonstrate the difference between the American and British approaches to the problems of backward nations, and emphasize the greater capacity of America for providing continuous and constructive material assistance." Roosevelt approved the policy for the United States.(34) Even before 1944, however, the United

States had begun extending aid for Arabia's agricultural and financial development.

In May 1942, responding to Ibn Saud's request for a survey of local water resources and agricultural possibilities, the United States sent an agricultural mission to Saudi Arabia. Led by Karl Twitchell, the mission examined the reclamation project at al Kharj. Al Kharj, approximately 50 miles south of Riyadh, was the site of a small experimental farm. By 1942 Aramco technicians had already written geological and topographical reports for the project. The oil firm also provided pumps and tractors and laid out some of the irrigation system. The mission recommended the use of American irrigation techniques, fertilizers, and agricultural equipment to expand cultivation from 2,500 to 25,000 acres. Al Kharj struck the imagination of the Americans and it became the focus of private and public America's wartime and postwar efforts to develop Saudi agriculture.(35)

Initially restricted to an advisory role, Aramco gradually decided that it should either abandon the al Kharj project or take sufficient authority and supply adequate personnel to do the job right. With the approval of the king and finance minister, Aramco became Arabia's "Reclamation Bureau" from 1942 through 1944. The company surveyed and built canals, secured and supervised the installation of pumps and other equipment, and generally applied American farming experience to the al Kharj project.(36)

In late 1944 the State Department sent a new agricultural mission to Saudi Arabia to direct and supervise the construction of irrigation canals and introduce new methods of planting crops. Using techniques developed in the American southwest, these advisers irrigated and cultivated the Arabian desert along American lines. When the mission terminated in June 1946, al Kharj was still a "kitchen garden for the royal palaces." The experiment had negligible effects on farming in other areas of the country and on general food production for the populace. The Dutch minister to Saudi Arabia observed that the Americans wanted "large open spaces for their machinery and any small farmers that happened to be in their way were asked to settle elsewhere." As early as August 1944, James Landis had questioned the efficacy of the project, contending that it was poorly conceived and executed. But the project continued despite its weaknesses because it demonstrated America's commitment to Ibn Saud and his development schemes.(37)

Providing financial aid for Saudi Arabia had more concrete results and evoked more controversy than the issue of agricultural assistance. Despite some misgivings about government financing, State Department officers concurred that the United States should extend development capital to Saudi Arabia. "The precedent for such development programs is well established," explained Paul McGuire, "and they have been approved by the American people both on humanitarian grounds and as a stimulus to American exports." In late 1944 the department submitted to the president an aid program for Saudi Arabia. The Near East Division (NEA) recommended that Congress appropriate $27 to $56 million to meet Arabia's budgetary and exchange deficits for five years pending development of adequate oil royalties and resumption of the pilgrimage. Some economic officers objected to this short-term aid, lamenting that such "subsidies" were "destined to failure in the Congress." While doubts remained concerning subsidies to meet Arabia's immediate deficits, a departmental consensus formed on NEA's proposal to have the Eximbank extend "development loans to finance long range projects for the improvement of economic conditions and living standards in Saudi Arabia."(38)

As predicted, the department's combined short-term financial aid program and Eximbank loan failed in Congress. Officials changed their strategy when reports from the field indicated that British capital might finance the development projects and public services earmarked for American support. The State Department pushed for an enlarged development loan without waiting for action on the blocked budgetary assistance program. Even after congressional approval, however, bureau-cratic red tape delayed the Eximbank from drafting a loan agreement until late December 1945. The new loan totalled $25 million--$5 million for "public works and other useful development projects approved by the Bank" and $20 million to finance the acquisition of American goods and services. With appropriate planning by the Saudi government, the State Department hoped that the new development loan would meet both the immediate budgetary and the long-range development needs of Ibn Saud.(39) Policymakers recognized, of course, the need for private American capital in Saudi Arabia.

Oil royalties to the Saudi government increased national revenues. But, as already noted in the case of the al Kharj project, the oil company's participation in local development went beyond the realm of oil. During the war, the company advanced $10 million to the Saudi government. Company representatives advised the royal house on how to reduce expenditures, while lobbying the American government for lend-lease aid and loans. The construction of wells, pipelines, pumping stations, refineries, and transportation facilities required the hiring and training of hundreds of workers. Aramco provided housing, water, sanitary facilities, and educational instruction for its Arab employees. At the Dhahran field station, the firm maintained a hospital for Arab workers. Company doctors, working with local authorities, tried to eliminate malaria from the surrounding towns. In May 1940 the company's first school for Arabs opened in a village outside Dhahran. By the end of 1941 enrollment had grown from 19 to 150 students, and Aramco had constructed two additional school houses. Instructors began to teach Arabic writing and grammar as a prerequisite to basic English.(40)

Aramco appeared to be contributing to Saudi socioeconomic development--at least in the firm's little domain along the Persian Gulf. But appearances could be deceiving. Aramco, with the support of the conservative monarchy, outlawed all strikes in the oil fields. In early 1943, when Indian workers tried to organize their Arab brethren to strike for improved housing and extended vacation privileges, Aramco and the Saudi government prohibited all labor meetings and deported the Indian "agitators." More than a year later, reports reached Saudi officials of Aramco discrimination against Arab workers. American officials in Jidda dismissed the reports as anti-American propaganda. The Saudi monarchy decided not to inves-tigate the complaints.(41) Although information on these incidents is incomplete, they nevertheless raise questions and doubts about the idyllic relationship between Aramco and the Saudi Arabs.

From the onset of operations Aramco realized that success depended on contributing to Saudi development. This was evident in the firm's training, housing, and health care programs; its participation in the al Kharj project; and its general economic aid to Ibn Saud. Aramco's desire to increase oil production and profits meant extending greater royalties to the government and engaging in larger nonoil related activities.(42)

But policies undertaken because of enlightened self-interest had unanticipated and unenlightened effects. Aramco's invasion of Saudi Arabia brought about the desert Arab's first meeting with large numbers of Westerners. Until Aramco began drilling for oil, contact between Westerners and bedouin had been sporadic. Westerners living in Arabia congregated around the ruling classes. The influx of American oil workers changed things. As missionaries of the American way of life, American technicians and engineers had a firm conviction--perhaps arrogance--about the superiority of their technology and their economic and political ideology. The Dutch minister to Arabia observed that American workers were never at a loss to boast how their technology would conquer the Arabian desert. Americans believed that production was the key to economic security and to a high living standard. They were certain, wrote Aramco chronicler Wallace Stegner, that a bedouin "who had never in his life needed more than a camel, a woman, and a smooth piece of sand, would be a happier man for having learned to also like oranges, castor oil, and a Ford pickup."(43)

Americans showed how a new way of life could be brought into the desert, if one had the money. The Saudi Arab observed the Americans' technical and scientific skills, mechanized culture, and high standard of living, while noting that these Westerners gave no sign of a belief in God. It was difficult for the Arabs to reconcile the discrepancy between material wealth and spiritual indifference. The Americans did little to explain the dichotomy and Ibn Saud did his best to contain the discussion. Americans could not visit villages or bedouin tribes without official Saudi government supervision. Arabs were not allowed into American camps if their work did not require them to go there. Government controls notwithstanding, Aramco and its rendition of the American way of life gradually invaded the Arab consciousness.(44)

The transformation begun by Aramco was well advanced among the ruling class by the end of 1945. The king was committed to solidifying his rule through national development. In the aftermath of war, Ibn Saud and his advisers planned to use oil production and royalties as the basis for development. Saudi development schemes--a mixture of the practical and the ostentatious--met religious needs, domestic political requirements, and personal desires. While seeking to destroy Arabia's "backward tendencies" with Western economics and technology, Ibn Saud did not want to "upset the basic religious and social patterns of his countrymen." The king felt obliged, therefore, to improve the facilities for pilgrims coming to the holy places of Islam. At the same time, Ibn Saud and the royal family used oil and pilgrim revenues--which they considered the personal income of the sovereign--to their advantage. The al Kharj experiment provided fruits and vegetables for the royal palace. Ibn Saud ordered the construction of an uneconomical railway from

Dammam to Riyadh because the rulers of Egypt and Iran had similar railroads leading to their capitals.(45)

American officials supported Ibn Saud's development plans because of oil. Throughout the 1940s American policymakers feared that the absence of "some concrete and immediate sign of improvement" in the economic condition of the local population would lead to Arab dissatisfaction "with King Ibn Saud's administration, and the resulting unrest may seriously jeopardize the safety of the American oil concession." Imperial state and corporate interest in oil demanded that the United States provide for Saudi Arabia's imports and advance funds against future oil royalties for economic development projects. In addition, Saudi Arabia--with its relative political stability, oil revenues, and desire for American assistance--presented a perfect opportunity for carrying out a "constructive developmental policy in the Near East."(46)

Dispatches from Foreign Service officers in Saudi Arabia in 1946 and 1947 reported that expanded oil production intensified Arabia's links with the world-economy. Americans observed that the country was becoming a "land of opportunity and a new frontier for enterprise." Apparent progress led the Saudi government to seek additional American loans. When the State Department suggested that Saudi Arabia contact the IBRD, the king replied that his nation would not be "internationalized." In 1946 Saudi and Eximbank representatives worked out a flat $10 million loan for the purchase of American cereals, textiles, agricultural equipment, and automotive materials. Early in 1947 Ibn Saud requested a new $50 million loan to construct railroads and harbors. J. Rives Childs, America's diplomatic representative in Arabia, viewed the proposed loan as a powerful lever to force Ibn Saud to accept outside supervision of Saudi finances. The State Department, however, rejected the loan in May 1947, explaining that it competed with, rather than encouraged, private investment capital.(47)

By early 1948 department officials argued that, with his growing oil income, Ibn Saud should "put his financial house in order and obtain loans on their economic merits and not on the basis of politics." But when Judd Polk, the Treasury Department representative in the region, visited Saudi Arabia in the spring, he reported that converting oil revenues into "lasting productive gains" was a "sobering" problem; that it was difficult to find "promising lines of economic development in so barren a land." Saudi officials had to confront the problem of diversifying their economy before oil reserves ran out. It appeared that Ibn Saud and his advisers had little notion what constituted "promising lines of economic development." Nevertheless they found little difficulty in spending the available oil royalties and more. In March 1948 Ibn Saud requested $20 million from the Eximbank for public utility and airport expansion and the importation of foodstuffs and noncapital goods. Although the NEA approved and the Eximbank authorized a $15 million loan, the Saudi government failed to use the funds and allowed the credit to lapse--a protest against American policies toward Israel.(48) The Arab-Israeli conflict did not, however, put a permanent damper on American-Saudi relations. By early 1949 officials of the two nations were once again discussing ways to achieve Saudi development.

America's "large and rapidly growing economic interest" in Arabia led imperial state policymakers to raise the status of the U.S. legation in Jidda to an embassy. Ambassador Childs told Ibn Saud that the United States sought to aid in Saudi development because it would ensure the country's independence, inhibit the spread of Communist doctrine, and provide vital oil for European recovery. Americans proudly pointed to the agricultural mission at al Kharj, the United States Air Force training mission, and the vocational programs of Aramco as models of technical assistance. In a letter to the king, President Truman suggested that Saudi Arabia demonstrated the perfect operation of the Point Four concept-- public American technical aid working with private American capital. Throughout 1949 State Department economic officers examined possible Point Four projects, including advisers to help reform the nation's "hit and miss financial and economic practices." Meanwhile, the Eximbank approved credits for the construction of various development projects. From the end of World War II through the first half of 1950, public U.S. loans and credits to Saudi Arabia totalled $38.2 million. Substan- tial private American investment and assistance complemented this governmental aid.(49)

Aramco continued to be the principal private American enterprise in Saudi Arabia during the late 1940s. As the firm expanded its drilling and refining operations, it also increased its participation in Saudi development. Childs praised the company for taking a "far-sighted view" and accepting its "social responsibilities to Moslem Saudi Arabia." Aramco, for its own self-interest, advocated the creation of a single national currency with a fixed foreign exchange rate in terms of the dollar and gold and adequate controls over the internal money supply and disposition of foreign exchange. These reforms were couched in terms of Arabia's "progressive development." Aramco urged the U.S. government to send a financial mission to Riyadh. On its own, Aramco continued to employ, house, educate, and provide health care for sections of the population. All this aimed at deriving profits and "intangible dividends of goodwill."(50)

During the late 1940s Aramco employed between 10,000 and 12,000 Arabs--approximately 60 percent its entire work force. But these employees constituted a negligible percentage of the Saudi work force. In December 1949, only 0.17 percent of Saudi Arabia's six million people worked for the oil company. Aramco sought to raise the general educational and health care levels of its workers and their families. Enrollment in technical and vocational training programs increased from 171 Arabs in 1947 to 3,556 at the end of 1949. In 1946 and 1947 the company and the Near East College Association jointly organized and supervised a Saudi educational program. Aramco's staff of 26 doctors (12 Americans), 97 nurses, and 278 hospital attendants continued to serve the medical needs of employees and their local communities.(51)

Aramco's assistance to construction and industrial development was institutionalized in 1946 with the establish- ment of an Arab Industrial Development Division (AIDD). Headed by an Aramco engineer, William Eltiste, AIDD's staff designed and planned public utilities and community and indi- vidual enterprises. In 1950 the agency took control of the al Kharj farm project. Local taxes, payments to indigenous labor, total purchases, royalties, transport charges, training programs, AIDD, and other activities constituted, according to Aramco officials, a "Marshall Plan for the Near East."(52)

Bechtel International Corporation, the San Francisco-based engineering and construction company, also contributed to Arabia's physical development. Bechtel's operations included airport, harbor, road, and electrical power plant construction. Between 1947 and mid-1949, Bechtel built the Riyadh power plant, cleared roads to Mecca and Medina, and constructed the Jidda airport and harbor additions, among other jobs. In the summer of 1949, Bechtel built and equipped a modern coffee house in Jidda, which introduced the ice cream soda into Arabia. During the late 1940s the company employed about 636 Arabs and 90 Americans per project. Like Aramco, Bechtel inaugurated an ambitious on-the-job training program for local labor.(53)

Aramco and Bechtel officials believed that their companies' activities in Saudi Arabia did more to advance Saudi development than any public aid program. Aramco considered itself "the chief support of Arabia's expanding economy." This was true. But the questions raised by Judd Polk remained unanswered: Were the projects conducted by Aramco and Bechtel for the Saudi government contributing to the country's economic and social development? Were they laying the groundwork for substantial development when oil reserves became depleted? In at least two respects Americans may have led Saudi Arabia down the wrong path. America's preoccupation with capital intensive technology resulted in the mechanization of Saudi agriculture. Capital intensive projects had no firm basis in the Saudi economy and would not last beyond the expenditure of the last oil dollar. More importantly, oil production itself established no linkages with the rest of the Saudi economy. As Fred Halliday and other political economists have noted, oil has "no 'backward linkages' in that it employs a tiny labour force, and acquires its capital and technology from abroad"; nor "does it establish 'forward linkages,' in that most of its product is exported." Reaping the benefits of Arabian oil necessitated patronizing the Saudi royal house. American imperial state and capitalist class elites realized the weaknesses of Saudi finances, the problem of inflation, and even the danger of drilling too many wells around Riyadh. At times they tried to share these concerns with Saudi leaders, but they never pressed these issues. The imperial state was committed to the stability and prosperity of the Saudi ruling family--at least as long as the oil flowed. The interests of the conservative rulers of Saudi Arabia thus coincided with the interests of America's imperial state and capitalist class elites. All groups attempted to ensure the continued viability of the existing regime. Polk raised crucial issues--pertinent in the 1940s and after--unfortunately, few leaders considered them.(54)

For American policymakers there were, of course, more immediate and pressing problems. Saudi oil was crucial for European recovery and, therefore, private and public leaders supported Saudi oil development and any projects that would facilitate better relations between the United States and the royal house. The question of overall Saudi and Arab East development and the role of the United States in such development had to be considered in relation to the economic reconstruction of Europe and Japan. But a second consideration forced itself upon American policymakers. The future of Palestine/Israel became a major dilemma for imperial state officials. Unlike Saudi Arabia, where private and public

American interests meshed, Palestine/Israel presented a problem for most government officials and an opportunity and cause
for certain private sectors of American society.

PALESTINE/ISRAEL

During the 1940s Jewish Palestine, and later Israel, was
the most economically developed area in the Arab East. Although the British mandate of Palestine was technically one
country, in reality it possessed two separate social, cultural, and economic communities. Prior to World War II, 30.8
percent of Jewish Palestine's national income originated in
industrial activities and 9.4 percent in agriculture. The
corresponding figures for the Arab sector were 15.4 and 24.2
percent. Almost 24 percent of the Jewish income came from
finance, real estate, education, and health, compared to 11
percent for the Arabs. The 1936 per capita income of Arabs
and Jews was, respectively, 17 and 44 Palestinian pounds.
Significant differences also appeared between the two communities' industry and agriculture. Most of the fellaheen owned
subsistence farms, produced cereal crops, aimed at self-sufficiency, and were heavily in debt. Jewish farmers worked on
individual, collective, or cooperative farms; produced citrus
crops, dairy products, and poultry; and sold their produce to
urban consumers. In 1943-1944 Jewish farmers sold about 75
percent of their total output on the market compared with Arab
farmers' 35 percent. The 1936 average income of an Arab
farmer was 24 Palestian pounds; his Jewish counterpart earned
52 Palestinian pounds. Jewish-owned enterprises dominated
Palestine's manufacturing sector. In 1945, over 80 percent of
all Palestinians employed in manufacturing worked in Jewish
firms. Arab manufacturers, with their small handicraft shops
and lack of machinery, produced goods for very small local
markets, while Jewish firms aimed at a national market.(55)
During the war State Department officers believed that
the Arab-Jewish struggle over Palestine threatened American
plans to stabilize the Arab East, to pump Arab oil into
Europe, and to integrate the region into the capitalist world-
economy.(56) They viewed the controversy as a no-win situation. While the imperial state bureaucracy avoided the question of Palestine's development, many private American businesses and organizations participated in Jewish Palestine's
wartime development and postwar planning.
The Palestine Economic Corporation (PEC), founded in New
York in 1926, was the largest private American business
enterprise in Palestine during the 1940s. PEC president
Julius Simon explained that his firm's primary goal was "not
to produce the largest possible profits, but to assist in a
sound development of the country." Simon added that stimulating Palestine's industry, commerce, banking, and agriculture
would "prove beneficial to the United States by opening up an
important export market for American products." The PEC
operated through subsidiaries and direct investment in basic
industrial firms. As of 1945 the PEC's four major subsidiaries in Palestine promoted cooperative practices; advanced
short- and intermediate-term loans for the purchase of farm
equipment; built factories for rental to small manufacturers;
extended long-term construction loans for low-cost standard-
ized housing; and conserved and expanded water resources. The

PEC also invested in electrical and mining companies and hotels. By the end of 1945, PEC assests in Palestine amounted to $3.5 million. While profits concerned PEC directors, so did the desire to develop a Jewish state in Palestine. The PEC was a quasi-Zionist business whose chief officers--for example, Simon and chairman of the board Robert Szold--were prominent members of the American Zionist movement.(57)

Two other private American firms had interests in Palestinian development. In 1942 the AMPAL-American Palestine Trading Corporation began assisting, through financial and commercial means, the development of Palestine's agricultural and industrial resources. Between 1942 and 1946, AMPAL loaned $800,000 to the Jewish National Fund to purchase land for housing and irrigation and $600,000 to the Histadrut Institutions (the Central Federation of Jewish Labor). To encourage American-Palestinian trade, AMPAL united its commercial activities with those of the PEC. Like the PEC, AMPAL was a privately capitalized American corporation interested in developing Palestine for both private gain and Zionist goals. The American Economic Committee for Palestine provided technical aid to the country. Since 1932 the committee's 200 technical and business members had offered their specialized knowledge and experience to Palestine's manufacturers, farmers, bankers, and merchants. The committee also supplied information and assistance to Americans who wished to establish trade with, or invest capital in, Jewish Palestine.(58)

Combining equal doses of business acumen and Zionism, the PEC, AMPAL, and the Economic Committee viewed Palestine's development as both a means and an end. Organizations such as the Zionist Organization of America (ZOA), Hadassah, and the Jewish National Fund, however, saw economic development as merely one way--albeit an important one--to attain the Jewish state. The ZOA funded a Palestine Economic Bureau that interested American industry in Palestinian development. Hadassah, the Women's Zionist Organization, sponsored health and educational programs and construction projects throughout the country. The Jewish National Fund purchased land in Palestine for the Jewish people. Between 1900 and 1944, American Jews donated almost $22 million for the national land purchasing program in Palestine. Over the course of four decades, American Jews sent some $90 million to Palestine for socioeconomic, scientific, and educational advancement. American private investment in Palestine totalled $39 million in 1939 and approached $50 million by 1945.(59)

During the war, U.S. citizens supervised two economic investigations of Palestine. In December 1943 M. H. Blinken, president of the American Palestine Institute (API)--a self-proclaimed "non-partisan research organization"--proposed a comprehensive economic survey of Palestine. Blinken selected Robert R. Nathan to head the API team. Nathan, a New Deal economist, had served as director of the National Income Division in the Commerce Department and as chairman of the War Production Board's Central Planning Division. He shared with Henry Wallace a commitment to active state participation in the economy. Wallace "had the highest regard for" Nathan, describing him as "the best of the young economists around Washington." Blinken chose Nathan for the latter's expertise in national income and resources and in economic planning.(60)

While his staff examined available background material on the Middle East, Nathan sought a visa to visit Palestine. The

British High Commissioner of Palestine rejected the request, arguing that the survey could stir up trouble among Arab and Jewish extremists and that inflated wartime conditions had distorted Palestine's economy.   State Department officers, hoping to avoid American entanglement in the Palestine morass, concurred with the British position.   Even pleas to Nathan's personal friend, Undersecretary of State Edward R. Stettinius, failed to alter the department's stand.   In mid-1944, Nathan requested and received help from Harry Hopkins, special assistant to the president.   Hopkins wrote to the Earl of Halifax, the British ambassador in Washington, describing Nathan as a personal friend and a "thoroughly reliable person," and asking that the British reconsider the visa application.   After a meeting with Nathan, Halifax agreed to review the matter.   British officials in London eventually overruled the High Commissioner and gave Nathan a visa.(61)

The API mission surveyed Palestine between December 1944 and March 1945.   The final report appeared in 1946, but in October 1945, Nathan sent Secretary of State James F. Byrnes a summary memorandum.   Nathan found Palestine to be the "most rapidly expanding economic center of the Middle East."   Jewish development had raised the Arab population's living standards to levels higher than those prevailing in neighboring countries.   The API mission contended that Palestine could absorb up to 1,125,000 Jews during the next decade; and that this immigration could be "economically healthy and self-sustaining" and compatible with a rise in both Jewish and Arab living standards.   Intensive use of the land, rather than land supply was crucial in determining the number of immigrants the country could absorb.   The API's development plan included land reform, cheap credit, irrigation systems, and educational programs for Arab farmers; integrating Palestinian citrus and other fruits and vegetables into the European market; expanding Jewish-based manufacturing firms in order to supply local, regional, and eventually world markets; and government fiscal policies to mobilize resources for commercial expansion, development, and the general welfare.   Nathan estimated that Palestine would need $1.9 billion for development purposes over the next ten years.   A large part of this capital could come from Germany in the form of reparations, with the World Bank, the Eximbank, and private lenders supplying additional funds.(62)

As the API completed its work, another group of Americans formulated plans for a Jordan Valley Authority (JVA).   Walter Clay Lowdermilk, a leading American soil expert and assistant chief of the United States Soil Conservation Service, toured the Middle East in 1938-39.   His mission, sponsored by the Department of Agriculture, examined land use in the region. Among the area's "poverty-stricken and wasted lands," Lowdermilk praised the Jewish farmers of Palestine for doing the "finest reclamation work of modern times."   Lowdermilk's book, Palestine: Land of Promise (1944), described how "Palestine with its unique possibilities of reclamation" could solve the Jewish refugee problem and raise Arab living standards.   Palestine required a great reclamation project that would develop the region's water and power resources while providing room and work for millions of Jewish immigrants.   Patterned after the Tennessee Valley Authority, the JVA would provide water and power, control floods, reforest land, extract minerals from the Dead Sea, and begin the reclamation of the Negev.(63)

In 1942 Lowdermilk sent a draft of his JVA plan to Dr. E. Neumann, a leading American Zionist. At Neumann's prompting, Zionist leaders visited TVA headquarters, inspected dams and power stations, and interviewed TVA engineers. Colonel Theodore B. Parker, chief engineer of the TVA, outlined the necessary engineering studies and recommended personnel for a JVA survey mission. With the support of the Jewish Agency and the American Palestine Foundation Fund, a Commission on Palestine Surveys was created with James B. Hays, a former TVA project manager, as chief engineer. The commission began its work during the winter of 1942-1943, but did not submit a final report until January 1946. The proposed JVA project would provide irrigation for at least 606,000 acres, compared to the 100,000 then under irrigation, and furnish more than 660 million kilowatt hours of hydroelectric energy per year. At a cost of approximately $250 million, Lowdermilk found the plan comparable to American reclamation operations. John Savage, the consulting engineer, explained that the JVA's major features would be considered "ordinary" in the United States. But the Arab East was not the United States. The survey attested to the JVA's technical feasibility, but left unanswered the political question. State Department officials, British leaders, and Arab rulers attacked the plan as technically unsound and politically impractical. The controversy over the JVA and over the economic future of Palestine continued into the postwar period.(64)

In order to create an independent Jewish state in Palestine and to absorb hundreds of thousands of refugees, the Jewish Agency, and later the Israeli government, advocated a large and positive role for the state in economic planning and development. Quasigovernmental agencies during the mandate period purchased land, built agricultural settlements, and provided most of the Jewish sector's economic and social needs. War and a deluge of immigrants determined the fate of Israel's economy between 1948 and 1950 and demanded a planned economic development program. Development schemes for Palestine and Israel rested on regional political security and sufficient quantities of capital. Jewish leaders considered the United States as "the only major potential supplier of capital" in the postwar period. Although most of the investment trusts in Palestine--for example, the PEC and AMPAL--obtained their funds from a "Palestine-minded public," future development would have to draw upon the financial and technical resources of the U.S. government.(65) The imperial state, however, refused to consider economic aid for Jewish Palestine/Israel until the middle of 1948.

One of the first requests for American capital assistance came from Robert Nathan. In late 1945 Nathan resigned his post as deputy director of the Office of War Mobilization and Recovery to protest the Truman administration's conservative fiscal policies. He founded the consulting firm of Nathan Associates to assist economic development in the periphery. In early 1946 Nathan met with Undersecretary of State Dean Acheson and asked for help in securing a congressional authorization of $250 million from the Eximbank. This capital would finance construction of a Jordan Valley hydroelectric project. Acheson worried that unilateral American development aid might be miscontrued as the direct result of Jewish pressure. In addition, the project site covered an area under British mandate. Acheson, Assistant Secretary of State for

Economic Affairs Will Clayton, and Treasury Secretary Fred Vinson believed that the best way to handle this request would be to make it part of a larger appropriation for development projects throughout the Arab East. Domestic and international complications might be avoided if Congress increased the Eximbank's lending authority to cover TVAs for the Jordan Valley, the Tigris-Euphrates Valley, and the Nile Valley. The Near East Division disapproved of the scheme. Loy Henderson, chief of NEA, argued that any legislation aiding Jewish Palestine would hinder Arab-American relations because such aid would recognize the Jewish Agency as an "appropriate borrower." Arabs regarded the agency as a Zionist vehicle for dominating Palestine. Henderson contended that the Eximbank did not need outside agencies to decide what organizations were acceptable borrowers. An interdepartmental committee, however, dismissed Henderson's objections and proposed that the president ask the IBRD and the Eximbank for funds to develop the Arab East countries, including Palestine. In late July 1946 Truman announced that he would recommend to the Congress the granting of loans to Palestine and other Middle East states "for sound development projects if for any reason such projects cannot adequately be financed through the International Bank."(66)

Jewish Agency officials pressed the United States to untie economic assistance for Jewish Palestine from general Arab East aid. Lacking the status to directly approach the IBRD, Jewish leaders, in May 1947, asked the State Department for help in securing a possible Eximbank loan of $75 to $100 million. Henderson and Acheson vetoed any financial discussions while the UN Special Committee on Palestine worked on its report. A month later, the Palestine Economic Corporation asked for an Eximbank credit of $5 million in order to purchase American textile and agricultural equipment and raw materials for use in Palestine. The Palestine Foundation Fund, a nonprofit corporation, agreed to guarantee the proposed line of credit. Henderson attacked the plan as a Zionist scheme to secure a government loan. NEA deemed it "undesirable" for the Eximbank or any other government lending agency to extend loans to groups in Palestine "until the future of that country becomes more clear." The Eximbank obeyed Henderson's dictate and declined to consider the loan. In this instance, Henderson did not object to having the bank take orders from outsiders.(67)

With the General Assembly's approval of the UNSCOP partition plan in November 1947, the Jewish Agency renewed its efforts to initiate financial discussions with the United States. But once again the State Department rejected such overtures. NEA official Gordon Merriam found the Jewish Agency's latest request for a $500 million loan impractical. Merriam argued that American aid to Jewish refugees should continue through international channels, that resettlement and development programs could not be implemented in an atmosphere of political hostility, and that the Eximbank was capable of conducting its own affairs without external influences. Finally, Merriam raised the specter of Communism. The Jewish Agency, observed Merriam, was dominated by left-wing labor parties whose leaders were of Russian or Eastern European origin. "There is grave danger that the United States, by private and governmental financial assistance to Jewish Palestine, would in fact be financing a community and a government which would sooner or later come under Soviet Russian domination."(68)

In the first half of 1948, as the State Department waited for the Palestinian political situation to stabilize, it rejected all proposals for economic aid to the Jewish state. Philip C. Jessup of the American mission to the UN warned that with the Jews' superior organizing ability, efficiency, and human and financial resources, and in the absence of an over-all economic aid program for the Arab East, Israeli economic development would likely outstrip that of the surrounding Arab countries. This could lead "to expansionist pressures in Israel and jealousy and resentment among the Arabs." Jessup proposed a comprehensive development scheme for the entire region. State Department officials remained skeptical of any economic solution to the Palestine issue. Career officers in NEA, led by Henderson, believed that American economic and political interests in the Arab East were best secured by supporting the Arab nations' ruling classes and not by creating a Jewish state in Palestine.(69)

In late May 1948, Chaim Weizmann, president of the Provisional Government of Israel, met with President Truman and inquired about arms aid and an Eximbank loan. Truman and his advisers rejected the arms request, but allowed Israel to apply for a $100 million loan. Foreign Minister Moshe Shertok described the loan as based on "sound schemes of investment and economic development." But the State Department continued to opposed any and all loans to Israel. Political officers argued that the United States could not give capital to Israel without granting similar aid to the Arab states. Economic officers maintained that the loan was not justified on strict-ly banking grounds--although the Eximbank thought otherwise. In August, acting Secretary of State Robert Lovett explained that the loan would hinder efforts at peace mediation in the Middle East and that the "resumption of hostilities would render promises to repay almost meaningless." Secretary of State George Marshall commented that the United States would sympathetically review Israel's application for an economic development loan following a Middle East settlement.(70)

Meanwhile, President Truman hinted to Israeli officials that such loans would be granted. Since his meeting with Weizmann in late May, Truman had assured various Jewish leaders that a loan would be forthcoming. In mid-August, the president suggested to State Department officers that the United States not flatly turn down the Israeli request. "Of course," explained Truman, "I don't want any loans made that are not proper for the Bank to make but this situation has all sorts of implications." Truman's allusion to "all sorts of implications," referred to the approaching presidential election and the importance of the Jewish vote in crucial areas. The State Department reluctantly altered its position on the Israeli loan. In late August, Undersecretary Lovett informed Israel that the Eximbank would consider loans for specific projects--especially for schemes in which Israel could promise the repayment and service of loans on sound banking principles.(71)

Truman assured Weizmann in late November that the bank was actively reviewing long-term loans to Israel. The presi-dent also indicated his desire to extend economic aid to all the countries of the Middle East. Israeli officials apparent-ly endorsed this policy. At a meeting with Lovett in December, Eliahu Epstein, the Israeli representative to the United States, relayed his government's firm belief that "Israel could not exist as a flourishing oasis in a Near Eastern desert in which political, social, and economic conditions were deteriorating." American aid to the Arabs, explained Epstein, would prevent Soviet intervention and would provide long run benefits for the Arab states, Israel, and the United States.(72)

At the end of 1948 Eximbank officials approved the Israeli loan, noting that since the "United States was going to support Israel in every reasonable way, [the bank] would take one project out of the $100 million program and carry it through to its conclusion." The loan conformed to the bank's statutory responsibility of obtaining reasonable assurance of repayment. On 19 January 1949 the Eximbank formally announced the authorization of a credit of $35 million to Israel to finance the purchase of American equipment, materials, and services in connection with agricultural development projects. A further credit of $65 million would finance programs in communications, transportation, manufacturing, housing, and public works.(73)

The Eximbank loan was the first step in Israel's plan to secure larger American developmental assistance. In February 1949 Israeli and State Department officers met to coordinate Israeli requests for American technical advisers in finance, commerce, social welfare, and public service.(74) Both countries hoped to use the Point Four program, but the Arab-Israeli conflict jeopardized American-Israeli cooperation in the realm of technical assistance and economic development.

In May 1949 the State Department pressured Israel to repatriate substantial numbers of Arab refugees and to compromise with its neighbors on territorial boundaries. Department officers recommended withholding American technical and economic aid to Israel and removing contributions to the United Jewish Appeal from tax exemption status. When Israel continued to veto proposals on the refugee and boundary issues in the summer, Truman went along with the department and ordered a delay in allocations under the Eximbank loan. Department officers explained that the temporary halt, while not a loan cancellation, was necessary in order to properly review recent events in the Middle East. Assistant Secretary of State George McGhee described this as an "act of prudence and in line with procedure normally followed in evaluating conditions for foreign financial assistance." Due to a bureaucratic slip, however, Israel learned that the State Department, and not the bank, initiated the loan suspension. The Israeli ambassador angrily assured McGhee that political and economic pressure tactics would not work. The Israeli government remained intransigent on the refugee issue, and the United States abandoned loan manipulations as a means of forcing Israeli concessions. Loan payments resumed in late October. Israel subsequently submitted proposals for 39 industrial projects at a cost of $11 million. The Eximbank approved the financing of 28 projects at $6.1 million.(75)

Thus, by the end of 1949, the U.S. government actively supplied economic aid to Israel. The initial loan of $100 million "formed the basis of Israel's development program." Private American organizations such as the PEC and various Zionist organizations continued their support for the new Jewish state. A National Security Council report in October

1949 warned that Israel's extensive development program would make it dependent for the near future on large scale external financing through foreign capital investment, loans, and voluntary contributions. The NSC feared that even with American loans, Israel would be unable to achieve the development necessary to integrate an unlimited number of immigrants into the local economy. Unrestricted immigration might gradually force Israel to develop submarginal areas and to expand industrialization within the country. The Israeli government might ultimately be tempted to seek additional territory. To forestall such an event, the NSC suggested a massive economic development program for the entire Middle East through regional cooperation.(76)   Unfortunately, neither the NSC nor anyone else knew how to foster regional cooperation for economic development.

CONCLUSION

During the 1940s the states of the Arab East, regardless of their relative stage of development, sought American aid in breaking restrictive political and economic ties with Europe and advancing their socioeconomic welfare. Local elites hoped to accomplish these goals while solidifying their own wealth and power. Egypt, Iraq, Syria, and Lebanon had accumulated large sums of capital--primarily in the form of debts owed by Britain and France--during the war. Wartime restrictions and controls stimulated local industry and some infrastructural development. Yet internal and external political and economic problems plagued Arab development in the postwar period. Domestic instability, governmental inefficiency and corruption, blocked foreign balances, regional war, intense nationalism and xenophobia, and international monetary and trade policies all hindered development.(77)

The United States supported Arab attempts at development planning and offered technical assistance. Imperial state leaders pushed for ending British and French trade and currency controls in order to allow American capital and consumer goods into the area. Policymakers emphasized the need to create conditions conducive to private American enterprise and capital. State Department officers encouraged a certain amount of indigenous economic planning so long as it reduced inefficient administration, focused on expanding primary goods production and extractive industries, and allowed moderate social reforms. Deviation from these policies meant violating free trade and comparative advantage, and this threatened America's goal of an integrated capitalist world-economy.

While favoring Arab economic development in principle, the United States gave little concrete support for such development. Policymakers contended that Arab economic growth would be a natural off-shoot of European reconstruction and the revival of multilateral trade. Officials in Egypt, Iraq, and Lebanon accepted this argument to a certain extent. But many criticized America's inertia in supplying capital and technical aid to the region. As one of the more developed states in the region--and the most willing to accept America's capitalist ideology and hegemony--Lebanon became an unofficial spokesman for its poor brethren. During the 1940s Lebanese officials, particularly at the UN, pointed to America's ineffective attempts at stimulating economic development solely through free trade and private enterprise. Lebanon and the other Arab East nations solicited and warmly received American assistance, although they complained that it came too slowly and in too small packages. Egypt, Iraq, Syria, Lebanon, and Jordan also realized the discrepancy between the American public and private aid they received and that given to Saudi Arabia and Israel.(78)

American capital, goods, and services flowed into Saudi Arabia and Palestine during the 1940s. Oil's importance to the war effort and especially to postwar reconstruction demanded active American participation in Saudi economic development. In the case of most Arab states, imperial state bureaucrats meticulously reviewed those nations' plans for local development and then usually deferred action. Policymakers did their best, however, to comply with Arabia's requests for aid. American involvement in Arabian development led a few imperial state and capitalist class elites to realize the dangers of bringing the Western capitalist notion of "modernization" to underdeveloped societies. But this realization altered neither the flow nor nature of aid. More than any other Arab state, Saudi Arabia fit into America's conception of world development. Private and public financial and technical aid effectively integrated the Saudi economy (i.e., oil) into the world-economy.

The explosive situation in Palestine made imperial state officials reluctant to discuss future development there. Since the question of economic development constituted a crucial element in the Zionist program, U.S. policymakers avoided it. Only after the creation of Israel, and with the strong leadership of the president, did the imperial state bureaucracy agree to discuss economic assistance for Israel. State Department officials continued to believe that Israel hindered American hegemonic goals in the Arab East. At least through the 1940s, these officers continued to obstruct economic assistance by using Eximbank loans as a lever to produce Israeli political concessions.

While the imperial state reluctantly considered financial and technical aid to Palestine/Israel, American Jews, through private missions, businesses, and Zionist organs, contributed heavily to the economic progress of the country. It is ironic that in the one country where the imperial state stood relatively silent, large amounts and diversified types of private capital did flow to aid in the economic development of an underdeveloped nation. Even before the influx of public American economic and military aid, Israel was closely linked economically to the United States. As the 1940s came to a close, American participation in the economic development of Saudi Arabia and Israel, for entirely different reasons, far exceeded its involvement in the development of any other state in the Arab East. Moreover, Saudi Arabia and, to a lesser extent, Israel, did reap benefits from the reconstruction of Europe and Asia and from integration in the capitalist world-economy. Indeed, both nations eventually ascended into the semiperiphery--each securing its own particular type of economic growth and internal political stability. But the experiences of these nations provided poor models for the other underdeveloped nations of the periphery.

NOTES

1. Fauzi M. Najjar, "Nationalism and Socialism," in Abdeen Jabara and Janice Terry, eds., The Arab World: From Nationalism to Revolution (Wilmette, Ill.: The Medina University Press International, 1971), pp. 3-5; Jean-Paul Charnay, Islamic Culture and Socio-Economic Change (Leiden: E. J. Brill, 1971), p. 13; Albert Hourani, Arabic Thought in the Liberal Age, 1789-1939 (London: Oxford University Press, 1962), pp. 339-40; Z. Y. Hershlag, Introduction to the Modern Economic History of the Middle East (Leiden: E. J. Brill, 1964), p. 230.

2. Najjar, "Nationalism and Socialism," p. 4; Abdallah Laroui, The Crisis of the Arab Intellectual: Traditionalism or Historicism? (Berkeley: University of California Press, 1976), pp. 42-43; M. Hamidullah, "Islam's Solution of the Basic Economic Problems," Islamic Culture 10 (April 1936): 214-17, 222, 227, 230-33; S. A. Maudoodi, Economic Problems of Man and Its Islamic Solution (Lahore: 1955), pp. vii-viii, 440-41, 14-17, 26-29, 66-69; Khalifa Abdul Hakim, Islam and Communism (Lahore: Institute of Islamic Culture, 1962), pp. 199-205.

3. Najjar, "Nationalism and Socialism," p. 4; Laroui, The Crisis, pp. vii, 116, 159-165; Bryan Turner, Marx and the End of Orientalism (London: George Allen & Unwin, 1978), pp. 75-78; Ishak Musa Husaini, The Moslem Brethren: The Greatest of Modern Islamic Movements (Beirut: Khayat's College Book Cooperative, 1956); James P. Jankowski, Egypt's Young Rebels--"Young Egypt": 1933-1952 (Stanford, Calif.: Hoover Institution Press, 1975); Kamel S. Abu Jaber, The Arab Ba'th Socialist Party: History, Ideology, and Organization (Syracuse, N.Y.: Syracuse Unversity Press, 1966).

4. Department of State (hereafter DOS), Biographical Register of the Department of State, 1945 (Washington, D.C.: U.S. Government Printing Office) and Current Birography, 1945 (New York: H. W. Wilson, 1946), pp. 323-25; Harold MacMillan, War Diaries: Politics and War in the Mediterranean, January 1943-May 1945 (New York: St. Martin's Press, 1984), p. 683. A quantitative analysis of the Foreign Service is Nathan Godfried, "A Profile of the United States Foreign Service, 1910-1940: Professionalization Without Democratization," M.A. Thesis, University of Wisconsin-Madison, 1975.

5. Alexander Kirk to Secretary, 29 January 1942, DOS 883.50/35, RG 59, U.S. National Archives, Washington, D.C.; James Landis to F. Winant, 25 September 1943, DOS 883.61A/15, RG 59; Phillip Baram, The Department of State in the Middle East, 1919-1945 (Philadelphia: University of Pennsylvania Press, 1978), p. 190; A. Kirk to Harry Hopkins, 15 January 1944, enclosed is R. Mikesell's "Report on the Desirability of Establishing an American Bank in Egypt," Egypt folder, Special Assistant to President, 1941-45, Group 24, Harry Hopkins Papers, FDR Library, Hyde Park, N.Y.

6. Memo, J. Landis to P. Alling, 26 September 1944, DOS 883.607/9-2644; Landis to D. Acheson, 30 August 1944, Annex C, "Specific Objectives of American Policy in Egypt," DOS 800.24/8-3044, RG 59.

7. Mikesell report, Hopkins Papers; S. P. Tuck to Secretary, 27 December 1944, includes J. Landis address, "U.S.-Egyptian Economic Relations," 22 December 1944, DOS 883.50/12-2744; Landis to Acheson, 30 August 1944, DOS 800.24/8-3044; Cairo legation to Department and FEA, 26 December 1944, DOS 890G.5151/12-2644; Tuck to Secretary, 11 September 1945, memo by Joel Hudson, DOS 800.50 Middle East/9-1145, RG 59; House of Representatives, 79th Congress, 2d session, Postwar Economic Policy and Planning, Report 1527, pt. 2, "Statistical Analysis of Economic Conditions of Selected Countries of Europe and the Middle East," 7 February 1946 (Washington, D.C.: U.S. Government Printing Office, 1946), pp. 51-52.

8. Landis speech, 22 December 1944, DOS 883.50/12-2744; Hudson memo, DOS 800.50 Middle East/9-1145, RG 59; House of Representatives, Postwar Economic Policy, pp. 51-52; MESC Intelligence and Information Section, "Preliminary Survey of Egypt," January 1945, British Empire and Middle East Branch, Entry 450, Bureau of Areas, FEA, RG 169, U.S. National Archives, Washington, D.C.; Joseph E. Jacobs to Secretary, 29 April 1944, includes report by British Chamber of Commerce, DOS883.50/42, RG 59.

9. Donald A. Ritchie, James M. Landis: Dean of the Regulators (Cambridge, Mass.: Harvard University Press, 1980), pp. 133-34; New York Times, 5 February 1946, p. 3; 22 March 1946, p. 12; 25 March 1946, p. 28.

10. Baram, Department of State in Middle East, pp. 187-91; Tuck to Secretary, 6 July 1944 and Department to Cairo legation, 12 July 1944, DOS 883.6463/7-644; Memo of conversation, State Department, FEA and Westinghhouse Electric, 11 November 1944, DOS 883.6463/11-1144, RG 59; Patrick O'Brien, The Revolution in Egypt's Economic System: From Private Enterprise to Socialism, 1952-1963 (London: Oxford University Press, 1966), pp. 46-54; Egyptian Government, Ministry of Social Affairs, Social Welfare in Egypt (1950), p. 135; Anthony M. Galatoli, Egypt in Midpassage (Cairo: Urwand & Sons Press, 1950), pp. 151-60.

11. UN, Department of Economic Affairs, Economic Development in Selected Countries: Programmes and Agencies (Lake Success, N.Y.: UN, October 1947, 1948.IIB.1), pp. 190-91; The Royal Institute of International Affairs, The Middle East: A Political and Economic Survey (London: Royal Institute, 1950), p. 187; A. N. Cumberbatch, Overseas Economic Surveys, Egypt: Economic and Commercial Conditions (London: His Majesty's Stationery Office, 1952), pp. 23-24; Charles Issawi, Egypt at Mid-Century: An Economic Survey (London: Oxford University Press, 1954), pp. 94, 208, 221-23; O'Brien, Revolution in Egypt, p. 54; UN, Department of Economic and Social Affairs, Economic Developments in Middle East, 1945 to 1954 (New York: UN, 1955), pp. 29, 46, 48; Egyptian Government, Ministry of Social Affairs, Social Welfare in Egypt, pp. 135-36; Samir Radwan, Capital Formation in Egyptian Industry

and Agriculture, 1882-1967 (London: Ithaca Press, Middle East Centre, St. Antony's College, 1974), p. 136.

12. UN, Economic Developments in Middle East, 1945-54, pp. 40-41, 52;   O'Brien, Revolution in Egypt, p. 56;   Radwan, Capital Formation,   p. 200;   Issawi, Egypt at Mid-Century, pp. 206-8;   Raymond Flower, Napoleon to Nasser: The Story of Modern Egypt (London: Tom Stacey, 1972), p. 163;   Robert L. Tignor, State, Private Enterprise, and Economic Change in Egypt, 1918-1952 (Princeton, N.J.:   Princeton University Press, 1984), pp. 175-214.

13. Mahmoud Hassan speech, 11 April 1947, OF 283, Harry Truman Papers, Harry Truman Library, Independence, Mo.; Galatoli, Egypt in Midpassage, pp. 150-51, 156;   DOS, Foreign Relations of the United States, 1947, vol. 5, pp. 618, 544-46, 548-50, 784 (hereafter FRUS followed by year and volume); U.S., House of Representatives, Hearings Before the Subcommittee of the Committee on Agriculture, 78th Congress, 2d session, December 1944, pp. 211-20, 271-76, 331-34; U.S., Tariff Commission, The Import Quota on Long Staple Cotton, supplemental report to President, 14 July 1948, report 161, 2d series (Washington, D.C.:   1948), pp. 4-6, 19-20.

14. National Bank of Egypt, Economic Bulletin 1, no. 3 (October 1948):   144;   Cumberbatch, Egypt, p. 32;   UN, Department of Economic Affairs, Review of Economic Conditions in Middle East, 1949-50 (New York: UN, 1951), p. 73.

15. Royal Institute of International Affaris, Great Britain and Egypt, 1914-1951 (London: Royal Institute, 1952), pp. 160-61;   Bent Hansen and Karim Nashashib, Foreign Trade Regimes and Economic Development: Egypt (New York: National Bureau of Economic Research, 1975), pp. 28-29;   UN, Economic Developments in Middle East, 1945-54, p. 45.

16. FRUS, 1948, 5: 86;   FRUS, 1949, 6:   210-11;   Royal Institute, Britain and Egypt, pp. 29-32;   National Bank of Egypt, Economic Bulletin 2, no. 2 (1949): 57;   Issawi, Egypt at Mid-Century, pp. 208-9, 206 note 1;   Radwan, Capital Formation, p. 200;   UN, Economic Developments in Middle East, 1945-54, pp. 41-42.

17. FRUS, 1947, 5: 625;   FRUS, 1948, 5: 76, 47, 84, 550-53, 1696-97;   FRUS, 1949, 6: 52, 898, 805, 1232;   Memo of conversation, "US Policy of Economic Assistance for Middle East," 7 May 1948, Folder: Economic Development, US Mission to UN, RG 84, U.S. National Archives, Washington, D.C.

18. Memo, G. Evans to S. Griffis, (probably September 1948);   "Daily Review of Arabic Press," US Embassy Cairo, 12 September and 17 October 1948, General File, June-October 1948, Stanton Griffis Papers, Harry Truman Library, Independence, Mo.;   Memo of conversation, S. Griffis, J. Satterthwaite, H. Deimel, 30 November 1948, DOS 883.50/11-3048, RG 59.

19. "Review of Arabic Press," US Embassy Cairo, 17 October 1948, Griffis Papers;   S. Tuck to Secretary, 6 and 9 March 1948 and 1 April 1948, DOS 890.50/3-648, 3-948, 4-148, RG 59;

National Bank of Egypt, Economic Bulletin 1, no. 3 (October 1948): 144;   Cairo Embassy to Department, 5 and 21 February 1949, and Jefferson Patterson to Secretary,   12   March 1949, Folder 500 Economic Matters, 1949, Entry 59A543, Cairo Post Records, RG 84;   World Town Hall Seminar, Cairo--Summary #8 by Chester S. Williams, 3 August 1949, Microfilm Reel 18, Box 27, Folder 2, Elmer F. Cope Papers, Ohio Historical Society, Columbus, Ohio.

20. Zaki Hashem,   "Financing A   Planned Process of Economic Development in Underdeveloped Countries," L'Egypte Contemporaine 42 (January 1951); FRUS, 1949, 6: 210-14.

21. Dorothea Franck and Peter Franck, "The Middle East Economy in 1948," Middle East Journal 3 (April 1949): 207-8; National Bank of Egypt, Economic Bulletin 1, no. 3 (October 1948); Memo, J. Patterson to H. Howard, 24 March 1949 and 3 May 1949, Duncan to Patterson, 1 April 1949, and Patterson to Department, 30 April 1949, Folder 500 Economic Matters, Cairo Post Records, RG 84.

22. Richard Nolte, "Point IV in Egypt: An Egyptian View," American Universities Field Staff Reports, Northeast Africa Series 1, no. 1 (September 1953): 1-8; J. Patterson to Secretary, 12 March and 1 July 1949,   Department to Cairo Embassy, 26 July 1949, and memo, "Some Aspects of Point 4 for Egypt," 23 November 1949, Folder 500 Economic Matters 1949, Cairo Post Records, RG 84; Patterson to Secretary, 19 March and 15 August 1949, DOS 800.50 TA/3-1949, 8-1549, RG 59;   S. Lacknay Bey, "Point IV: Its Role in Fostering Private Investment," L'Egypte Contemporaine 42 (January 1951): 23-32.

23. UN, Review of Economic Conditions in Middle East, 1949-50, p. 76;   "United States Aid to Middle East, 1940-1951," Middle Eastern Affairs 4 (February 1953): 59-60; National Bank of Egypt, Economic Bulletin 2, no. 3 (October 1949): 111.

24. Tignor, State, Private Enterprise, p. 23.   Although Tignor argues against the notion of Egypt's dependent development, his data actually confirm the existence of such a relationship.

25. David Howarth, The Desert King: A Life of Ibn Saud (London: Collins, 1964), p. 198;   D. Van der Meulen, The Wells of Ibn Saud (New York: Praeger, 1957), p. 143; U.S. Senate, 82d Congress, Staff Report of Federal Trade Commission, International Petroleum Cartel (Washington, D.C.: 1952), p. 113.

26. See Irvine Anderson, Aramco, the United States and Saudi Arabia: A Study of the Dynamics of Foreign Oil Policy, 1933-1950 (Princeton, N.J.:   Princeton University Press, 1981); Aaron D. Miller, Search for Security: Saudi Arabian Oil and American Foreign Policy, 1939-1949 (Chapel Hill: University of North Carolina Press, 1980); and Michael B. Stoff, Oil, War, and American Security: The Search for a National Oil Policy, 1941-1947 (New Haven, Conn.:   Yale University Press, 1980).

27. Karl Twitchell, Saudi Arabia: With an Account of the Development of Its Natural Resources (Princeton, N.J.: Princeton University Press, 1958), pp. 21, 25-28, 51-57; Western Arabia and the Red Sea (Great Britain: Naval Intelligence Division, 1946), pp. 515-20; Howarth, Desert King, pp. 199-200.

28. Memo, Office of Petroleum Adviser to E. Collado, 5 July 1943, DOS 890F.51/52, RG 59; P. Hurley to FDR, 9 June 1943, PSF Diplomatic, Saudi Arabia, FDR Papers, FDR Library, Hyde Park, N.Y.; K. Twitchell, "American Ideas for Arabia," Asia 42 (November 1941): 631. Twitchell--the "father of economic development" in the Arabian peninsula--had been a technical adviser to Ibn Saud since the early 1930s. He participated in the oil negotiations between Standard Oil of California and Ibn Saud. See Richard Sanger, The Arabian Peninsula (Ithaca, N.Y.: Cornell University Press, 1954), pp. 244, 100-101; Twitchell, Arabia, pp. 243-45, 249-50.

29. Hurley to FDR, 9 June 1943, PSF Diplomatic, Saudi Arabia, FDR Papers.

30. FRUS, 1944, 5: 690.

31. Tim Niblock, "Social Structure and the Development of the Saudi Arabian Political System," in Niblock, ed., State, Society, and Economy in Saudi Arabia (London: Croom Helm, 1982), pp. 75-78, 88-96.

32. Memo of conversation in State Department, 17 July 1943, DOS 890F.515/24; Memo, Office of Petroleum Adviser to Collado, 5 July 1943, DOS 890F.51/52; J. Landis to D. Acheson, "Specific Objectives of American Policy in Saudi Arabia," 30 August 1944, DOS 800.24/8-3044, RG 59; Van der Meulen, Wells of Ibn Saud, pp. 185-89.

33. Memo, P. McGuire, "Some Observations on the Saudi Arabian Problem," 3 November 1944, DOS 890F.51/11-344; McGuire, "Conclusions on the Saudi Problem," 7 November 1944, DOS 890F.51/11-744, RG 59.

34. Memo, W. Murray to Secretary, 1 December 1944, DOS 890F.51/12-144; Secretary of Navy to Secretary of State, 18 December 1944, DOS 890F.51/12-1944; Murray to Secretary, 20 December 1944, DOS 890F.51/12-2044; William Eddy to Secretary, 12 July 1945, DOS 800.50 Middle East/7-1245; W. Murray, "Report on Arabian Problem," and minutes of 65th meeting of Policy Committee, 28 June 1944, copies in instructions to American mission at Jidda, 8 July 1944, DOS 890F.51/7-1244; Notes for conference with Secretary, 5 July 1944, DOS 890F.6363/7-544; Eddy to Secretary, 2 November 1944, DOS 890F.24/11-244; McGuire memoranda, 3 and 7 November 1944, DOS 890F.51/11-344, 11-744; J. Landis to D. Acheson and L. Crowley, 3 June 1944, DOS 890F.515/113, RG 59.

35. Howarth, Desert King, pp. 199-200; Twitchell, Saudia Arabia, pp. 30, 45-50; Twitchell, "American Ideas," p. 631; Van der Meulen, Wells of Ibn Saud, pp. 205-6; FRUS, 1942, 4: 561-65; Sumner Welles to FDR, 12 February 1942, OF 3500 Arabia, FDR Papers; J. H. Shullaw to P. Alling, 5

November 1942, DOS 890F.61A/72;   US Agricultural Mission to Saudi Arabia, report no. 1, 1 June 1942, DOS 890F.61A/33, RG 59.   The mission also included Albert L. Wathen, chief engineer of the Bureau of Indian Affairs, and J. G. Hamilton, agronomist in the Soil Conservation Service.

36. Wallace Stegner, Discovery! The Search for Arabian Oil (Beirut: Middle East Export Press, 1971), pp. 169-71; J. Moose to Secretary, 22 July 1943, DOS 890F.61A/107, RG 59; FRUS, 1943, 4: 861, 863-66. Also see Moose to Department, 22 July 1943, DOS 890F.6113/1, RG 59; Carleton S. Coon, "Operation Bultiste: Promoting Industrial Development in Saudi Arabia," in H. Teaf and P. Franck, eds., Hands Across Frontiers: Case Studies in Technical Cooperation (Ithaca, N.Y.: Cornell University Press, 1955), pp. 349-50; Anderson, Aramco, pp. 111-12.

37. Twitchell, Arabia, p. 30; John Dawson to F. Winant, 3 August 1944, DOS 890F.61A/8-344;   Max Wasserman to R. Sanger, 1 November 1944, DOS 890F.61A/11-144;   Landis to Acheson, "American Policy in Arabia," DOS 800.24/8-3044, RG 59; FRUS, 1945, 8: 879, 907-8, 912, 931-32, 952-53; Howarth, Desert King, p. 201; Van der Meulen, Wells of Ibn Saud, pp. 213-14.

38. Memoranda, P. McGuire, 3 and 7 November 1944, DOS 890F.51/11-344, 11-744;   NEA memo to G. Merriam, P. Alling, W. Murray, 10 July 1943, DOS 890F.51/7-1043; Memo of conversation, "Conference on Nature of a Financial Institution to Assist the Saudi Government," 27 November 1944, DOS 890F.51/11-2744; J. Byrnes to E. Collado, 8 August 1945, DOS 890F.51/8-745;   Memo, McGuire to W. Thorp, 14 September 1945, DOS 890F.51/9-1445; Memo, W. Murray to Secretary, 1 December 1944, DOS 890F.51/12-144;   Murray to Secretary, 20 December 1944, DOS 890F.51/12-2044; Memo, E. Collado to W. Clayton, 1 January 1945, DOS 890F.51/ 1-145; P. McGuire to E. Collado, 12 February 1945, DOS 890F.51/2-1245, RG 59.

39. Memo, W. D. Whittemore (Eximbank), 10 April 1945, DOS 890F.51/4-1045; J. Grew to W. Eddy, 18 June 1945, DOS 890F.51/6-1845;   Eddy to Secretary, 23 June 1945, DOS 890F.51/6-2345;   Grew to Eddy, 27 June 1945, DOS 890F.51/6-2745; Memo of conversation, G. Merriam, P. McGuire, L. Henderson, 18 July 1945, DOS 890F.51/7-1845;   Byrnes to Collado, 8 August 1945, DOS 890F.51/8-745, RG 59; FRUS, 1945, 8: 960, 973-74, 975 note, 981-83.

40. Coon, "Operation Bultiste," pp. 315, 330-31; Baram, Department of State in Middle East, pp. 210-14; Arabian American Oil Company, Handbook for American Employees, vol. 1 (Aramco, 1952), pp. 43-46; Stegner, Discovery, pp. 171-73, 178; Richard Finnie, Bechtel in Arab Lands (San Francisco: Bechtel Corp., 1958), pp. 7, 33; Congressional Group Report, American Petroleum Interests in Foreign Countries, 15 October 1945, pp. 286-87.

41. Stegner, Discovery, p. 181; Van der Meulen, Wells of Ibn Saud, pp. 145-46; Shullaw to Secretary, 10 March 1943, DOS 890F.6363/49;   Eddy to Merriam, 17 June 1944, DOS 890F.6363/6-1744, RG 59. Most of the information on Aramco's

operations in Saudi Arabia during the 1940s has come from the oil company itself.

42. Congressional Report, <u>American Petroleum Interests</u>, p. 286; Coon, "Operation Bultiste," p. 316; Stegner, <u>Discovery</u>, p. 168.

43. Stegner, <u>Discovery</u>, pp. 167-68; Van der Meulen, <u>Wells of Ibn Saud</u>, pp. 143-44.

44. Van der Meulen, <u>Wells of Ibn Saud</u>, pp. 145-48; Stegner, <u>Discovery</u>, pp. 174-75. For a different analysis of Aramco and Saudi Arabia, see Anderson, <u>Aramco</u>.

45. Sheikh Mohammad Iqbal, <u>Emergence of Saudi Arabia: A Political Study of King Abd al-Aziz ibn Saud, 1901-1952</u> (Srinager Kashmir: Sandiyah Publishers, 1977), pp. 250-51; Richard Sanger, "Ibn Saud's Program for Arabia," <u>Middle East Journal</u> 1 (April 1947): 180, 183-90; J. Rives Childs to Secretary, 6 August 1946, DOS 890F.51/8-646;   Childs to Secretary, 1 March 1948, DOS 890F.50/3-148;   Donald Bergus to Secretary, 21 March 1949, DOS 800.50TA/3-2149; Childs to Secretary, 13 June 1949, DOS 890F.50/6-1349;   A. W. Shaw (Bechtel) to Sanger, 1 July 1949, DOS 890F.50/7-149, RG 59.

46. <u>FRUS, 1946</u>, 7: 22-23, 26;   <u>FRUS, 1947</u>, 5: 553; Memo, P. McGuire to Ness, 25 September 1946, DOS 890F.51/9-2546, RG 59; Sanger, "Ibn Saud's Program," p. 190.

47. Memo of conversation, Fuad Hamza, L. Henderson, R. Sanger, 17 January 1947, DOS 890F.51/1-1747;   Childs to Secretary, 6 August 1946, DOS 890F.51/8-646;   Childs to Secretary, 24 February 1947, DOS 890F.51/2-2447, RG 59; Roger Davies, "Annual Economic Review, 1946," 1 March 1947, Folder 850 Confidential, Entry 59A543, Post Records Dhahran, RG 84; <u>FRUS, 1947</u>, 5: 1329-35, 738 note 1; <u>FRUS, 1946</u>, 7: 739-41, 746-47, 750.

48. <u>FRUS, 1948</u>, 5: 226 note 3, 238-42, 241 note 5, 226-27.

49. J. Rives Childs to Secretary, 13 June 1949, DOS 890F.50/6-1349; Bergus to Secretary, 21 March and 2 July 1949, DOS 800.50TA/3-2149, 6-1349, RG 59; <u>FRUS, 1949</u>, 6: 161-70, 1573, 1587-88, 1600; NAC Minutes, Meeting 141, 8 November 1949, Records of NAC, Treasury, RG 56, U.S. National Archives, Washington, D.C.; UN, <u>Review of Economic Conditions in Middle East, 1949-50</u>, p. 76.

50. <u>FRUS, 1947</u>, 5: 662-63; <u>FRUS, 1948</u>, 5: 249-50.

51. "Middle East Operations Report Released by Arabian American," <u>Oil and Gas Journal</u> 48 (13 October 1949): 69; Aramco, <u>Report of Operations to the Saudi Arab Government, 1949</u>, pp. 12-13; Sanger, "Ibn Saud's Program," p. 182; UN, <u>Review of Economic Conditions in Middle East, 1949-50</u>, p. 63; David H. Finnie, <u>Desert Enterprise: The Middle East Oil Industry in its Local Environment</u> (Cambridge, Mass.: Harvard University Press, 1958), pp. 109-11; Van der Meulen, <u>Wells of Ibn Saud</u>, pp. 193-94.

52. Coon, "Operation Bultiste," pp. 322-27; "Middle East Operations Report," p.69; Aramco, Report of Operations, p. 18; FRUS, 1948, 5: 40; Finnie, Desert Enterprise, pp. 161-68; Michael Cheney, Big Oil Man from Arabia (New York: Ballantine Books, 1948), p. 280. For a profile of a Saudi Arab who prospered under AIDD auspices, see "A Saudi's Stake in US Banking," New York Times, 19 October 1980.

53. A. W. Shaw (Bechtel) to R. Sanger, 1 July 1949, copy of "Summary of Activities of Bechtel Interests for the Saudi Arab Government, July 1946 to April 1949," DOS 890F.50/7-149; D. Bergus to Secretary, 21 March 1949, DOS 800.50TA/3-2149; Hill to Secretary, 17 October 1949, DOS 890F.50/10-1749, RG 59.

54. Van der Meulen, Wells of Ibn Saud, pp. 198-200, 208, 213-18, 250-52; Cheney, Big Oil Man, pp. 36, 208; Niblock, "Social Structure and the Development of the Saudi Arabian Political System," pp. 100-101. For an analysis of oil production's impact on economic development, see Fred Halliday, Iran: Dictatorship and Development (Middlesex: Penguin, 1979), pp. 138-72. An excellent brief review of Saudi Arabia's political economy is Helen Lackner's A House Built on Sand: A Political Economy of Saudi Arabia (London: Ithaca Press, 1978), pp. 135-39, 147, 185-87, 216.

55. Sophie A. Udin, ed., The Palestine Year Book, vol. 1, 1944-45 (Washington, D.C.: Zionist Organization of America, 1945), pp. 147, 169; Robert R. Nathan, Oscar Gass, and Daniel Creamer, Palestine: Problems and Promise--An Economic Survey (Washington, D.C.: Public Affairs Press, 1946), pp. 117-27, 148, 150-52, 196-201, 213-14, 217, 220-22, 231.

56. Baram, Department of State in Middle East, pp. 298-307.

57. PEC, Annual Reports of PEC, 1940-1945 (New York: PEC, 1942-1945). Also see David Resnick, "The Palestine Economic Corporation," in Udin, ed., Palestine Year Book, pp. 444-45; Harry Schneiderman, ed., American Jewish Year Book, 1944-45, vol. 46 (Philadelphia: The Jewish Publication Society of America, 1944), p. 455; John Simons, ed., Who's Who in American Jewry, vol. 3 (New York: National News Association, 1938).

58. Abraham Dickenstein, "AMPAL-The American Palestine Trading Corporation," in Udin, ed., Palestine Year Book, pp. 448-49; American Jewish Year Books, 1944-45 and 1948-49, vols. 46 and 50 (Philadelphia: 1944, 1949).

59. Saul Spiro, "Zionist Organization of America," pp. 374-83; Judith Epstein, "Hadassah," pp. 384-88; Morris Rothenberg, "Jewish National Fund," pp. 425-27; Robert Szold and Sanford Schwarz, "American Interests in Palestine," pp. 361-62, in Udin, ed., Palestine Year Book.

60. Eli Ginzberg to Louis Bean, includes letter by M. H. Blinken, 6 October 1943, Subject File 1923-53, Palestine, Louis Bean Papers, FDR Library, Hyde Park, N.Y.; Current

Biography, 1941 (New York: H.   W.   Wilson, 1941), pp. 604-5; Henry A. Wallace, The Price of Vision: The Diary   of Henry A. Wallace, 1942-1946,   ed.   John   Morton Blum   (Boston: Houghton Mifflin, 1973), p. 264.

61.   Memo of conversation, State   Department and   ZOA, 13 July   1945,   DOS   867N.50/7-1345;   Memo   of   conversation in London,   12   and   14   April   1944,   DOS   740.0011   Stettinius Mission/132;   Memo of   conversation, R. Nathan and members of NEA, 10 May 1944, DOS 867N.50/29;   L.   Pinkerton to Secretary, 14 June   1944, DOS   867N.50/30;   Memo of conversation, Nathan and G. Merriam, 20 June 1944,   DOS FW   867N.50/34, RG   59;   R. Nathan to   H. Hopkins,   7 August and 7 September 1944, Hopkins to Halifax,   12 September,   Halifax to   Hopkins, 15 September, and Nathan   to Hopkins,   16 September 1944, "Palestine" folder, Group 24, Harry Hopkins Papers, FDR Library, Hyde   Park, N.Y.; Nathan et al., Palestine, pp. v-viii.

62.   Nathan to Secretary, 3 October 1945, DOS 867N.50/10-345, RG 59;   Nathan et al., Palestine, pp. 3-15,   398-99, 425-26, 486-87, 547-49, 593-94, 632-34.

63.   Walter   C.   Lowdermilk,   Palestine: Land of Promise (New York: Harper & Brothers, 1944), pp. 2-3, 10, 25, 169-78. Lowdermilk   statement   to   National   Conference   on Palestine, Washington, D.C., 9 March 1944 in Palestine Can   Take Millions (London: The Jewish Agency for Palestine, 1944), pp. 17, 19; Lowdermilk,   "Hope for the Middle East," in Christian Palestine Committee,   Problems   of   the   Middle   East   (New   York: NYU Conference, 1947), pp. 4, 7-9.

64.   James B. Hays, TVA on   the   Jordan: Proposals for Irrigation   and   Hydroelectric   Development   in   Palestine (Washington, D.C.:   Public Affairs Press,   1948), introduction by Lowdermilk,   pp. vii-ix and 1-16;   S. Schwartz, "Blueprint and Vision: The Jordan Valley Authority," The   Palestine Year Book,   1945-46,   vol.   2   (New   York: ZOA, 1946), pp. 86-91; Lowdermilk,   "Hope for the   Middle East,"   pp. 10-11;   Memo of conversation between British and State Department officers, 29 December 1944, DOS 867N.6461/12-2944, RG 59.

65.   Alfred Bonne, "The State of Israel: A   Great Enter-prise   of   Reconstruction,"   and "Foreign Investment in Pales-tine," in The Palestine Economist, Annual, 1948:   A Review of Palestine   Economy,   (Jerusalem: 1948),   pp.   11-12, 14,   54; Nadav Halevi and Ruth   Klinov-Malul, The   Economic Development of Israel (New York: Praeger, 1968), pp. 31, 34-39, 43, 45-46;   A. B. Magil, Israel in Crisis (New   York: International Publishers, 1950);   Alex   Rubner, The Economy of Israel: A Critical Account of the First Ten   Years (New   York: Praeger, 1960), pp. 18-22.

66.   Eleanora   W.   Schoenebaum,   ed., Political Profiles: The Truman Years (New York: Facts on File,   1978), pp. 409-10; FRUS, 1946, 7: 583 note, 583-84, 619, 644-45, 672.

67.   Nahum   Goldman,   Louis   Lipsky, Abba Silver, Stephen Wise to Harry Truman,   14   June   1946,   OF 204 Misc.,   Truman Papers;   FRUS, 1947,   5: 1090-94;   Memo, W. C. Sauer, "Pales-tine Economic Corporation,"   20   June 1947,   and memo,   Ness to

Henderson, 25 June 1947, DOS 867N.51/6-2047; Memo, Henderson to Ness, 1 July 1947, DOS 867N.51/7-147, RG 59.

68. Memo, G. Merriam to L. Henderson, 31 December 1947, DOS 867N.51/12-3147, RG 59; FRUS, 1947, 7: 1317.

69. FRUS, 1948, 5: 1169-71; James G. McDonald, My Mission in Israel, 1948-1951 (New York: Simon and Schuster, 1951), pp. 12-13; Baram, Department of State in the Middle East, pp. 276-307.

70. FRUS, 1948, 5: 1042-43, 1051, 1104-5, 1120-21, 1170, 1261-62, 1300-1, 1306.

71. Ibid., pp. 1313, 1391, 1346; John Snetsinger, Truman, the Jewish Vote and the Creation of Israel (Stanford, Calif.: Hoover Institution Press, 1974), pp. 117, 120-21. The department rationalized this change in policy by declaring that conditions in Israel and the surrounding area were now conducive for economic development. See, FRUS, 1948, 5: 1468-69, 1514.

72. FRUS, 1948, 5: 1633-34, 1677-78.

73. Ibid., 1679 note 5; FRUS, 1949, 6: 647, 681; NAC Minutes, Meeting 117, 17 January 1949, Records of NAC, Office of Secretary of Treasury, RG 56.

74. Memo of conversation, members of Israeli Mission to US and NEA and department economic officers, 23 February 1949, DOS 867N.51/2-2349, RG 59.

75. FRUS, 1949, 6: 964, 1062, 1110, 1236, 1311-13, 1329-32, 1388-89, 1455-56.

76. Halevi and Klinov-Malul, Economic Development of Israel, p. 163; FRUS, 1949, 6: 1433-34; FRUS, 1948, 5: 1170.

77. Galal Amin, The Modernization of Poverty: A Study in the Political Economy of Growth in Nine Arab Countries, 1945-1970 (Leiden: E. J. Brill, 1974), pp. 4-24.

78. E. Crocker to Secretary, 5 August 1949, includes memo of conversation with Iraqi Foreign Minister Fadhil Jamali, 28 July 1949, DOS 890G.51/8-549, RG 59.

Epilogue:
The United States
and Third World Development

The 1940s offered the shapers of America's policies the opportunity to install an integrated international economic and political order. Such an order was anchored in traditional American values and policies that stretched back to the birth of the nation. Economic depression in the 1930s and global conflagration in the 1940s intensified the need for a systematic and rational world order and reinforced the demand for American hegemony in the capitalist world-economy.

American imperial state and capitalist class leaders viewed the economic development of the periphery as a crucial element in the expansion of the capitalist world-economy. President Franklin Roosevelt evoked these sentiments in 1943 when he announced that the United States would seek to raise the standards of poor, agrarian nations without hurting the economies of the rich, industrialized states. America's "own pocketbook" and safety demanded some movement toward world development. Between 1942 and 1945, imperial state bureaucrats--in the State Department, the Bureau of the Budget, the Board of Economic Warfare, the Office of Inter-American Affairs, and the Commerce Department--began to outline an American foreign economic development policy.

America's economic policy for the Middle East and other Third World areas revolved around the achievement of an integrated world economy in which private enterprise and capital, free trade, technical aid, and export goods would help poor, agrarian nations to develop according to the doctrine of comparative advantage. State Department officials avoided domestic debates concerning economic development so long as the local governments in the periphery did not wander far from agricultural development, moderate social reform, and cautious industrialization policies. These policies adhered to the American concept of development and, therefore, could be rewarded with American technical and limited financial assistance. During the war, however, few Third World countries reaped these rewards.

In the Arab East, American support for development in Saudi Arabia and Palestine transcended diplomatic rhetoric. Securing and developing Arabian oil--important for the war effort and postwar reconstruction--demanded active American participation in Saudi economic development. Private American companies and the U.S. government did their best to comply

with King Ibn Saud's wartime requests for aid. In the case of
Palestine, the American government refrained from commenting
on, much less aiding in, that country's development. On the
other hand, private American businesses and Zionist organizations contributed heavily to the development of Jewish Palestine.   Saudi Arabia and Palestine received the greatest
amounts of private American capital that flowed into the Arab
East.
     Throughout the periphery, nascent bourgeois classes hoped
to achieve substantial economic progress in the postwar
period. They counted on the United States to fulfill the
promises of Roosevelt's four freedoms, the principles of the
Atlantic Charter, and the charter of the United Nations. Even
during the war, however, it was clear that the United States
and the other capitalist core nations differed with the Third
World over economic development. American officials believed
that through the free play of market forces the periphery
would specialize in the production of raw materials and agricultural goods. If allowed to operate unhindered, the forces
of free trade and comparative advantage would increase national production and raise living standards.   Both nationalist
economic policies and special Western aid would be unnecessary.
     Anti-Western nationalism in the newly independent coun-
tries of the Third World, Communist opposition to American
hegemonic plans, severe economic dislocation in Europe and
Asia, and a fiscally conservative and protectionist Congress,
all threatened the imperial state and capitalist class goal of
an integrated, American-dominated capitalist world-economy in
the immediate postwar years. Despite these obstacles, American leaders maintained that the economic recovery of war-torn
industrial societies, the establishment of multilateral trade,
and currency convertibility were the keys to achieving Pax
Americana--the internationalizing of American capitalism and
corporatism.
     European and Japanese economic recovery depended on the
development of the periphery. Larger markets and new sources
of raw materials in the periphery would aid reconstruction by
easing the dollar crisis. During the late 1940s, American
leaders supplied massive economic aid to Europe, while arguing
that Third World development would both accompany and result
from European recovery. Development depended not on special
aid to the poor nations, but on special assistance to Europe,
on the revival of international trade, and on unhampered currency exchange. The imperial state and corporate sector could
accelerate Third World development by extending technical aid
and commercial loans. But the ultimate development of the
periphery, according to American officials, hinged on those
regions' ability to grow within the capitalist world-system
and to create conditions conducive to the expansion of private
and public core capital, goods, technology, and knowledge.
These principles formed the basis of American initiated, sponsored, and dominated institutions and programs--from the World
Bank and the International Monetary Fund, to the Marshall
Plan, the International Trade Organization, and Point Four.
     America's global economic policies encountered domestic
and foreign obstacles. Congress grudgingly extended economic
assistance to underdeveloped nations. Special domestic agricultural and manufacturing interest groups possessed enough
power to chip away at the practice--if not the ideal--of trade

liberalization. Such was the case with American import quotas
on Egyptian cotton.   Under   these   restraints, administration
officials limited the size and the number of reconstruction
and development aid programs. In the case of the Arab East,
State Department officers rejected proposals and requests for
substantial development loans to Arab states. As the Cold War
intensified in the late 1940s, however, administration aid
programs increasingly became wrapped in a Cold War rhetoric
that Congress found more palatable.   The Truman Doctrine,
Marshall Plan, and Point Four were all deemed essential to
protect the free world from Communism. As Louis Bean had
foreseen in 1944, the American people and Congress would
approve a government foreign aid program based primarily on
perceptions of national security needs rather than economic
benefits. Threats to the nation's physical safety aroused the
public and Congress more than a ledger of economic advantages
accruing to America's capitalist class.
     Political   instability   and   economic   nationalism in the
periphery hindered American economic policies.   American
officials refused to consider economic aid for the Arab East
until the Palestinian issue was resolved.   The Arab-Israeli
conflict temporarily obstructed aid to Saudi Arabia, although
this made little difference because massive private investment
helped to develop Saudi oil resources. Large private American
contributions also flowed into Israel.   By 1949 the Eximbank
had begun loans to aid Israeli development--despite State
Department opposition.
     Arab East countries complained about American loans to
Israel.   They criticized the United States for linking an
Arab-Israeli agreement to economic development aid for the
region.   These attacks constituted one part of a larger Third
World assault on American development assistance. Underdeveloped countries accused the United States of a preoccupation
with European and Japanese reconstruction to the detriment of
the periphery. Leaders in the Arab East and elsewhere desired
their own Marshall Plans. Caught in contradictory arguments,
poor nations wanted finance capital for industrialization and
agricultural improvements, yet feared the imperialist effects
of foreign capital.   Other Third World demands included
monetary and trade concessions from the core, solutions to
blocked foreign balances and the dollar gap, and technology
suited to local conditions. Most ruling and bourgeois classes
in the periphery accepted the basic conditions of the capitalist world-economy; what they sought were temporary exclusions
from its rules and special economic assistance from the United
States or institutions under American control.   As the 1940s
ended, countries in the Third World intensified their campaign
for these items in the ECOSOC and other international forums.
     Despite criticisms and pressures from the periphery, the
imperial state remained committed to its traditional capitalist development framework. "Landmark" programs such as Point
Four added nothing new either to America's conceptualization
of development or to tactical/strategic policies aimed at
achieving development.   Free trade, comparative advantage,
private enterprise, and private capital continued to comprise
the conventional wisdom.   Any serious attempt to reform or
abandon these principles constituted a direct threat to America's imperial state and capitalist class elite. No ruling
class worthy of the name accepts changes to its rules without
massive and sustained pressure from indigenous and/or external

nonelite classes. Some domestic and foreign forces supplied
such pressure during the postwar era--for example, working
classes in both the United States and periphery.   But America's ruling elites weathered these attacks.   Imperial state
policymakers increasingly countered with the holy crusade
against Communism.   National and international red scares,
Cold War hysteria, and so on, allowed the quashing of internal
and external challenges.   In this atmosphere U.S. economic
development policy was safe from any sustained, serious, or
critical analysis.

GRAY AND ROCKEFELLER REPORTS

Two significant reports on the United States and world
economic development appeared in 1950 and 1951.   In early
1950, President Truman asked former Secretary of the Army
Gordon Gray to study post-Marshall Plan relations between the
United States and Europe.   According to Edward Mason, Gray's
deputy, this investigation naturally led to spending "a lot of
time writing about and thinking about the newly emerging
problems of the less developed world."(1) The Gray committee
identified Third World problems and the policies that could
achieve economic development.
Gray defined development as increasing production for
both domestic and foreign consumption. By increasing exports,
poor nations could expand their ability to obtain vital goods
from abroad.   At the same time, the United States, Western
Europe, and Japan would receive needed raw materials.   Underdeveloped countries had to improve agricultural and mineral
output and expand facilities in light industry--that is, the
production of consumer goods and the refining or processing of
primary goods.   There also was a need to expand public
services such as transportation, communications, health care,
education, power, and irrigation.(2)
The Gray committee conceded that Third World development
was "a more complicated and long-range process than that
involved in expediting recovery in well developed countries."
An American aid program, therefore, had to stimulate private
investment in the periphery, extend some public financial aid,
and provide technical help.   Private investment remained the
"most desirable method of development."   But international
tensions, Third World nations' fear of exploitation, political
instability, currency exchange problems, private corporations'
fear of government controls and expropriation, and the long-
term and low-yield nature of development projects, all inhibited the flow of private capital to underdeveloped states.
The Gray committee recommended that the United States counteract these obstacles by negotiating investment treaties. These
would standardize the status of foreign investors, promote
private investment through tax incentives, increase technical
aid, and guarantee against nonconvertibility and expropriation.   Even with these measures, however, private investment
could not shoulder the entire burden of financing development.(3)
"An effective foreign policy," argued the committee,
"must thus have at its command adequate funds available for
public capital assistance in the underdeveloped areas" in
order to supplement private investment, construct basic
service facilities not attractive to private capital, and

assist in financing strategic raw material production. The World Bank and Eximbank--the chief financial institutions working in the periphery--had to push for sound development projects and extend funds on a commercial basis. In a break with past policies, the Gray committee recommended that the United States not tie development loans to American exports because loans would take a circuitous route home. Peripheral countries could use loans to buy goods from Europe and Japan, which could then use the dollars to purchase American capital goods. In another break with past policies, the report contended that technical aid could be "most productive only when used as an adjunct to or implemented by programs supplying capital funds." The committee also recommended the extension of a small number of development grants to further the production of strategic raw materials needed by the United States and to strengthen strategically located Third World nations.(4)

The Gray report concluded that the United States had "long been concerned with material progress of the peoples of the underdeveloped areas, both as an end in itself and as means to the development of stable, democratic societies." Material progress depended on bringing the peripheral areas "increasingly into a network of international trade." To achieve this the United States had to reduce its import barriers, thus allowing other nations to increase their dollar earnings. Less developed countries had to end their discriminatory trade practices and exchange controls. President Truman received these recommendations in mid-November 1950.(5)

Truman found that the Gray report reinforced his conviction that a campaign of world economic development was "vital to the attainment of our goal of an expanding world economy and to the building of the security of the free world." In late November, Truman selected Nelson Rockefeller to head the International Development Advisory Board (IDAB). The board, which represented the basic corporatist elements in society-- capital, labor, and agriculture--had the task of formulating specific plans for carrying out the objectives of the Gray report. Rockefeller and his hand picked staff clearly dominated the advisory board and shaped the board's final report issued in the early spring of 1951.(6)

In the atmosphere of the Korean War, the IDAB viewed Third World development as a vital part of America's "defense mobilization." The United States faced the challenge of "economic development versus economic subversion." Soviet rulers sought to "chop off country after country, to leave us in isolation." In such a situation, economic development and defense were inseparable. Like the Gray report, the Rockefeller report pointed out America's growing dependence on Third World raw materials. The board also recognized the periphery's reliance on American exports, capital, and technology. Although focusing on the strategic importance of underdeveloped countries to the United States, the IDAB carefully explained that "even if there was no threat of aggression in the world or no danger of subversion," America would have a vital interest in "the world-wide task of economic and social development." American and West European economic expansion depended on the expanding economies of the underdeveloped areas.(7)

Rockefeller and his staff viewed economic development as revolving around free trade, private enterprise, private

property, and democratic institutions.   The IDAB argued that
economic development would lead non-Western underdeveloped
societies into the path of American liberal capitalism.   The
American concept of economic development acknowledged the need
for some degree of equity within the periphery, but not
between the periphery and the core.   Ideally, American policymakers sought to create relatively prosperous nations in which
wealth was distributed fairly enough to make those nations
stable.   In practice, the United States supported any regime,
regardless of its commitment to socioeconomic or political
equality, so long as it found its proper niche in the American
dominated capitalist world-system.   American leaders neither
tried nor desired to achieve an equitable distribution of
international wealth (or power).   The goal was an absolute
increase in international wealth rather than a fair distribution of that wealth.

     The Rockefeller report outlined several sources for
financing development.   Whenever possible, local capital had
to be encouraged to participate with American investments.
The board recommended the creation of a new International
Development Authority to finance a portion of the cost of
vital public works in poor countries.   Stimulating the flow of
private investment from the United States and Europe to the
Third World and channeling local savings of peripheral areas
into productive investment, however, continued to overshadow
international public finance in importance.   Expanding the
outflow of private investment required American tax incentives, bilateral tax and commercial treaties, underwriting the
transfer risk on foreign dollar obligations, creating a new
agency of the World Bank to serve private enterprise, and a
special officer to encourage the maximum and most effective
use of private enterprise.(8)

     Rockefeller pushed the IDAB to accept the idea of a new
imperial state agency to centralize and unify the major foreign economic activities of the government.   The proposed
Overseas Economic Administration (OEA) would support defense
in Europe; preserve the economic stability of the periphery;
supply the Third World with essential goods; initiate, on a
cooperative basis, national and regional development programs
for the poor; and stimulate world food production.   Emphasizing regional programs as the only "intelligent" way to meet
development problems, the advisory board envisioned regional
organizations for Africa, Europe, Latin America, South Asia,
East Asia, and the Near East.   Each division would stress expanded food production (e.g., turn the Tigris-Euphrates Valley
into the "bread basket" for the Arab East); land reform; and
developing and extracting a region's raw materials.(9)

     Nelson Rockefeller believed that the OEA would efficient-
ly coordinate a complex policy for world economic development.
But the OEA concept also reflected Rockefeller's desire to
become the tsar for America's international economic policies.   The proposed agency was to be a global successor to the
regional Economic Cooperation Administration, which oversaw
European recovery.   Like the BEW during World War II, the OEA
raised questions about who in the imperial state would control
foreign economic programs and strategies.   Once again, as it
had done during the war, the Department of State refused to
surrender its bureaucratic prerogatives (e.g., control of the
Point Four program) to an interloper.   Rockefeller also met
resistance from fellow finance capitalist and imperial state

policymaker W. Averell Harriman.   The latter favored a more
military-oriented economic aid program to replace the fading
ERP.   President Truman settled the conflict by requesting
congressional appropriations for a Mutual Security Administration and by naming Harriman as its director.(10)
     The inability of Rockefeller to secure his own fiefdom in
the imperial state did not lessen the significance of the IDAB
report.   Like the Gray report before it, the Rockefeller report emphasized the strategic location and resources of underdeveloped countries. National defense increasingly became the
ostensible motivating force behind aid for the Third World
nations.   As Sino-Soviet economic overtures to peripheral
nations increased in the 1950s, imperial state efforts to aid
those areas also quickened.   As former president of the
Eximbank Warren Pierson noted in 1953, "while barricading the
front door of the Russian house, we should not overlook the
back." The Gray and Rockefeller reports also began the movement toward a soft loan and grant program for the underdeveloped world.   Whereas in the late 1940s and early 1950s,
American officials opposed the establishment of a UN agency to
distribute grants and soft loans for economic development, by
the late 1950s government officials had convinced Congress to
support two soft loan institutions--the Development Loan Fund
and the International Development Association.(11)
     During the 1950s American leaders continued to emphasize
the need for peripheral countries to create the conditions for
successful development--for example, land and financial reforms and improvements in social overhead capital. Following
these reforms, peripheral states could proceed to modernize
and expand agricultural and raw material production. United
States policymakers sought to use private investments, commercial loans, and public grants and soft loans to move underdeveloped nations in this direction. Collaborating classes in
the Third World nations recognized the need to create an economic infrastructure and to improve primary goods production,
but they also sought industrialization as a means of gener-
ating more income and stabilizing earnings.(12)
     The underdeveloped countries of the Arab East and other
regions maintained their demands for foreign capital and
technology during the 1950s.   Together with other peripheral
nations, the Arab states successfully pushed for the creation
of a Special UN Fund for Economic Development in 1957. By the
early 1960s, the special fund was financing several development schemes in the Arab East. Technical aid also flowed into
the area under Point Four and the UN technical assistance
program.   Sino-Soviet economic aid gradually entered the
region.   Between 1954 and 1964, Sino-Soviet bloc nations
advanced a total of $1.7 billion in aid to Egypt, Iraq, and
Syria. American aid to the same three countries during the
1954-64 period yielded $1 billion. Soviet-American competi-
tion in the development of the Arab East was evident in the
financing of the Aswan High Dam.   In July 1956 Secretary of
State John Foster Dulles hoped to expose "empty Soviet
promises by an abrupt withdrawal of the American offer to
finance" the dam in Egypt.   Dulles' action not only led to
eventual Soviet funding for the project, but also resulted in
Egyptian President Gamal Abdul Nasser's nationalization of the
Suez Canal and the subsequent Suez crisis.(13)
     While playing Cold War games with the Soviet Union in the
Arab East, the United States continued its public and private

economic aid to Israel.   Between 1948 and 1955, U.S. government aid to Israel amounted to $367 million, compared to $163
million for all the Arab states. Approximately two-thirds of
the $2.5 billion that Israel received from foreign countries
between 1948 and 1957 came from the United States in the form
of grants-in-aid, loans, donations, and private investments.
During its first decade, Israel achieved economic development
through foreign capital transfers--the bulk of which came from
the United States. Arab countries believed that with similar
amounts of capital they too would experience economic growth.
Speaking before the General Assembly in 1960, Nasser described
the international community's responsibility to redress the
economic disparity among nations.(14)

A NEW INTERNATIONAL ECONOMIC ORDER?

In the 1960s, underdeveloped nations strengthened their
mutual ties. In September 1960 the first association of raw
material producers was formed--the Organization of Petroleum
Exporting Countries (OPEC). Four years later, at the first UN
Conference on Trade and Development (UNCTAD), underdeveloped
countries formed the Group of 77. These groups did not concentrate on issues such as the preconditions of development,
but rather on the "international rules and arrangements" that
exacerbated international economic inequality. Third World
nations directly attacked the international economic system
that the United States had established during the 1940s.(15)
In an attempt to defuse the explosive issue of reforming
the capitalist world-economy in favor of the poor nations, the
United States supported a pseudo-New Deal for the periphery--
that is, increased public economic and technical aid for the
Third World. In 1960 the UN declared the First Development
Decade. A year later, with much fanfare, the United States
announced the Alliance for Progress, which promised to promote
Latin American economic development. At the first UNCTAD in
1964 the United States and other core states agreed to direct
1 percent of their national incomes toward developing the
periphery. Despite these pronouncements the 1960s witnessed a
decline rather than an increase in the proportion of core
countries' GNP going to poor nations. American aid to underdeveloped countries--as a percentage of GNP--decreased over
the decade, from 0.53 percent in 1960 to 0.33 percent in
1969.(16)
Throughout the 1960s the aid that the United States
extended to underdeveloped nations continued to push those
nations in the direction of free enterprise, reliance on
market mechanisms, protection of private property, and an open
door for American multinational corporations. As in the 1940s
and the 1950s, American economic assistance was designed to
create relatively stable nations with markets, raw materials,
and inexpensive labor open to the United States and other
capitalist core nations.(17)
Although experiencing minor changes in the 1950s and
1960s, the relative positions of the core and periphery on the
issue of economic development remained remarkably static until
the mid-1970s. In the early 1970s the Bretton Woods international monetary system collapsed as global capitalist competition intensified and inflation and stagnation simultaneously
afflicted the capitalist world-system--especially the United

States.   The imposition of the Arab oil embargo exacerbated deepening economic problems in the capitalist core. Developed nations, which had long been dependent on the resources of the underdeveloped world, became abruptly aware of the extent of that dependence.   Multinational corporations wielded enormous power in the world-economy. But, perhaps most important, 30 years of Western-conceived economic development policies had clearly failed to close the gap between rich and poor.   Of course this had never been the objective of the hegemonic United States. But even on an absolute scale, the under- developed nations, as a whole, did not advance. As two astute political economists observed: "Acute poverty, chronic unemployment, and endemic undernourishment continued or even worsened in most Third World countries, while their economic dependence on the metropolitan countries increased and was even extended into new areas."(18)

Despite its few oil-rich countries, the Arab East was typical of underdeveloped regions during the 1960s and 1970s. Excluding oil development, the Arab East underwent relatively little industrial development during the two decades. By the early 1970s only Israel and Egypt had at least a quarter of their gross domestic product (GDP) originating in the indus- trial sector--37 percent for Israel and 28 percent for Egypt. In Lebanon one-third of all workers--those employed in various services--accounted for about two-thirds of the total national product.   Overall the Middle East was still predominantly agricultural with approximately 55 percent of its people living in rural areas and drawing the bulk of their livelihood from the soil. Nowhere in the Arab states did the manufactur- ing and oil industries employ more than 15 percent of the working population. "The two sectors which still occupy by far the greatest part of labor are those where low productivi- ty and disguised unemployment are most in evidence: agricul- ture and services." Oil production in Saudi Arabia, Iraq, and the smaller Persian Gulf states created an unequal distribu- tion of income in the region. In 1974, for example, Arab oil exporting countries had a gross national income per capita of $2,000, while all other Arab East states had a GNP per capita of $286. While the oil producing countries sought to unite against the Western oil buyers, the oil-less states of the Arab East sought to unite with the oil producers in order to secure development capital.(19)

In the late 1960s and early 1970s the peripheral nations consolidated their demands for a new order.   The Third World presented its design for a New International Economic Order (NIEO) at the Sixth Special Session of the UN General Assembly in late 1974.   The NIEO called for a modified redistribution of wealth in favor of the poor, agrarian nations.(20) Third World nations planned to use their control of oil and other valuable raw materials as bargaining tools.

The initial American response to the NIEO was swift and predictable.   Secretary of State Henry Kissinger praised the existing global economic order as "a common enterprise," and attacked the idea of redistributing wealth. The United States rejected the basis of the NIEO--the argument that the princi- pal cause of Third World poverty was external rather internal. The U.S. ambassador to the UN, Daniel Moynihan, in eloquent hyperbole, argued that widespread government mismanagement, corruption, and inefficiency in the poor countries were more responsible for those nations' underdevelopment than American

capitalism. Treasury Secretary William Simon chastised the
Third World for bowing to the "false gods" of expropriation,
indexation, and cartelization. Free and private markets were
the best protectors of scarce resources. "We are firmly
committed," declared Simon, "to the belief that the best model
for economic prosperity is a system which unites freedom of
commerce with freedom of the individual."(21)

The imperial state and capitalist class feared the
substance of NIEO reforms. But even more frightening to
America's ruling class was the sight of a developing solidarity among Third World nations; the possibility that diverse
nations of the periphery had begun to "collectively perceive a
common interest against the North." At the Seventh Special
Session of the UN General Assembly in the fall of 1975,
imperial state officials took a more conciliatory position
toward the demands of the Third World in a conscious effort to
break the Group of 77. American officials advanced the vision
of "global efficiency" and a "new interdependence" between
core and periphery. At the same time, however, they emphasized the "separateness of the Southern states" and refused to
negotiate with them collectively. The United States and other
core nations sought to meet some of the development needs of
selected Third World countries while maintaining the existing
economic order. Imperial state officials proposed limited
reforms of the international system with the aim of achieving
efficiency and stability. The United States hoped to mollify
the demands of the more important developing nations--espe-
cially those in the semiperiphery--by seeking "communities of
interest" between developed and underdeveloped worlds.(22)

As the decade came to a close, tension continued between
core and periphery. At the fifth UNCTAD in the spring of
1979, divisions within the Third World became apparent. The
splits between OPEC and non-OPEC developing countries, socialist and neo-capitalist developing nations, and advanced-
developing and least-developing countries allowed the United
States and other core nations to ignore the call for the NIEO.
A Council on Foreign Relations study on the Middle East, for
example, pointed out that the cleavage between petroleum-rich
and petroleum-poor Arab states would make it impossible for
those countries to "develop a cohesive, cooperative, regional
development strategy or a collective bargaining position in
relation" to the capitalist core.(23)

The United States pushed for its traditional goal of
integrating the periphery into the capitalist world-economy
and creating a "global community." Imperial state officials
in the late 1970s made some concessions to selected poor
nations--most coming in the form of increased development aid
programs, commodity agreements, and modified preferential
tariffs. But as Secretary of State Cyrus Vance noted in March
1979, "the developing countries themselves bear the major
burden" for development. American assistance to the poor
nations would include bringing those states "more fully into
the world trading system"; implementing "new codes and tariff
reductions in multilateral trade negotiations"; reaching a
"common understanding of the responsibilities of both governments and corporations to create a better environment for
international investment and the flow of technology"; and
finding ways to assure an appropriate role for the periphery
in international economic institutions.(24)

The imperial state's brief leaning toward a global New Deal died out as the lingering crisis of the capitalist world-economy intensified in the late 1970s. Although some members of the imperial state-capitalist class elite, such as World Bank president Robert McNamara, advocated the continuation of a global welfare state in the early 1980s, there was a clear movement away from this position. The administration of Ronald Reagan rejected basic New Deal policies at home and abroad. Both before and during the International Meeting on Cooperation and Development at Cancun, Mexico, in October 1981, Reagan, Secretary of State Alexander Haig, and Treasury Secretary Donald Regan reiterated the importance of the "magic" free market, private enterprise, and private capital in the development of the Third World. The Reagan administration totally ignored the recommendations of the Independent Commission on International Development Issues (the Brandt Commission)--which called for globalized Keynesianism. In the midst of a staggering Third World debt crisis, the Reagan administration refused to expand concessional aid or to explicitly write off bank debts. Instead, imperial state and finance capitalists insisted that the Third World pursue austerity programs (especially in the sphere of social welfare programs and price controls); liberal trade policies; and market-oriented, open-door economies geared to export promotion.(25)

Such policies are familiar and forge yet another link in the chain of American policy toward Third World development--a chain that stretches back to World War II and before. Historically, free trade, comparative advantage, the private market, private capital, private enterprise, and private property formed the foundation of American economic development policy toward the periphery. Through these forces American leaders attempted to manage international capitalism. They sought to avoid radical political alternatives--both at home and abroad. American rhetoric emphasized the interdependence and mutually beneficial nature of a liberal capitalist world order. This order maximized the economic and political power of the dominant classes in the United States, other core states, and the periphery. It also brought about an expanded global economic pie. But by its very nature that liberal capitalist order maintained and exacerbated global economic and political inequality. The attempt to internationalize American capitalism and corporatism and the consequent efforts to rationalize the place of the periphery in that liberal capitalist order inevitably fueled growing nationalist and revolutionary forces in the periphery. This presented imperial state policymakers with the ultimate contradiction. Postwar American development policies aimed at fostering international political and economic stability--because these were preconditions for the maintenance of the capitalist world-economy. But political and economic instability were inherent in a capitalist world-system based on unequal and uneven development. The inability to close the gap between rich and poor nations was and is inherent in the capitalist world-economy. American policy was doomed to fail even in the attempt to bridge that gap during the postwar era.

NOTES

1. Transcript, Edward S. Mason Oral History Interview, Harry Truman Library, Independence, Mo., 17 July 1973, pp. 38-39.

2. Gordon Gray, Report to the President on Foreign Economic Policies, 10 November 1950 (Washington, D.C.: U.S. Government Printing Office, December 1950), pp. 19, 21, 49-50, 56-57, 59-60.

3. Ibid., pp. 72, 61-63.

4. Ibid., pp. 63-72.

5. Ibid., pp. 49-50, 75-78, 93-94.

6. Partners in Progress: A Report to the President by the International Development Advisory Board, March 1951 (Washington: U.S. Government Printing Office), p. 89. The IDAB's members included Rockefeller, Robert P. Daniel (president of Virginia State College), Harvey S. Firestone, Jr. (chairman of Firestone Tire & Rubber, Co.), James W. Gerard (politician, diplomat, lawyer), John A. Hannah (president of Michigan State College--agricultural expert), Lewis G. Hines (representative of AFL), Jacob F. Potofsky (member of CIO Executive Board), Margaret A. Hickey (lawyer, educator), Clarence Poe (editor of Progressive Farmer), Charles L. Wheeler (corporate executive, director of National Federation of American Shipping), John L. Savage (civil engineer), and Thomas Parran (health educator). Folder: "Point Four Program: Minutes, Memos, and Reports, Nov. 29-30, 1950," Subject File, Box 24, Papers of Lewis G. Hines, Manuscript Division, Library of Congress, Washington, D.C.

7. Partners in Progress, pp. 1, 4-5, 11, 43, 51.

8. Ibid., pp. 11, 52, 73-74. Rockefeller's call for a special IBRD agency to stimulate private investment was enacted in 1955 with the creation of the International Finance Corporation.

9. Ibid., pp. 12, 16-18, 23, 25, 29, 34, 43, 54-55, 71-72.

10. Department of State, Foreign Relations of the United States, 1951, vol. 1, pp. 278-80, 339-40, 1652-57; Peter Collier and D. Horowitz, The Rockefellers: An American Dynasty (New York: Holt, Rinehart and Winston, 1976), pp. 266-70; Joe Alex Morris, Nelson Rockefeller: A Biography (New York: Harper & Brothers, 1960), pp. 273-80.

11. Fred L. Block, The Origins of International Economic Disorder: A Study of United States International Monetary Policy from World War II to the Present (Berkeley: University of California Press, 1977), pp. 99-108, 114-15, 134-37; Joyce Kolko and Gabriel Kolko, The Limits of Power: The World and United States Foreign Policy, 1945-1954 (New York: Harper & Row, 1972), pp. 471-72; Harry Magdoff, The Age of Imperial-

ism: The Economics of United States Foreign Policy (New York:
Monthly Review Press, 1969), pp. 122-23; Burton I. Kaufman,
"The U.S. Response to the Soviet Economic Offensive of the
1950s," Diplomatic History 2 (Spring 1978): 153-65 (quote);
David Baldwin, Economic Development and American Foreign
Policy, 1943-1962 (Chicago: University of Chicago Press,
1966), pp. 88-95.

    12. Wilbur   F.   Monroe,   The   New   Internationalism:
Strategy and Initiatives for United States Foreign Economic
Policy (Lexington, Mass.:   Lexington Books, 1976), pp. 180-81.

    13. Mohamed El-Hadi Afifi, The Arabs and the United
Nations (London: Longmans, Green, 1964), pp. 127-40, 159-65;
G. A. Amin, The Modernization of Poverty: A Study in the
Political Economy of Growth in Nine Arab Countries, 1945-1970
(Leiden: E. J. Brill, 1974), p. 9;   Townsend Hoopes, The
Devil and John Foster Dulles (Boston: Little Brown, 1973),
pp. 329-32, 338-44; John Donovan, ed., US and Soviet Policy
in the Middle East, 1945-56 (New York: Facts on File, 1972),
pp. 152-58, 215-17.

    14. Galina Nikitina, The State of Israel: A Historical,
Economic and Political Study (Moscow: Progress Publishers,
1973), pp. 201-5, 209, 270, 273;   David Horowitz, The Enigma
of Economic Growth: A Case Study of Israel (New York:
Praeger, 1972), pp. 11, 49-53;   Afifi, Arabs and the United
Nations, pp. 165-68.

    15. Monroe, New Internationalism, pp. 180-81; Karl P.
Sauvant and Hajo Hasenpflug, eds., The New International
Economic Order: Confrontation or Cooperation between North
and South? (Boulder, Colo.: Westview Press, 1977), pp. 4-10.

    16. Sauvant and Hasenpflug, eds., New International
Economic Order, pp. 4-10; Judith Hart, Aid and Liberation: A
Socialist Study of Aid Policies (London: Victor Gollancz,
1973), pp. 30-32, 222;   Peter G. Peterson, The United States
in the Changing World Economy, vol. 2, Statistical Background
Material (Washington, D.C.: U.S. Government Printing Office,
1971), pp. 50-52.

    17. Teresa Hayter, Aid as Imperialism (Middlesex:
Penguin, 1971), pp. 9, 87-98, 150-52.

    18. Sauvant and Hasenpflug, eds., New International Eco-
nomic Order, pp. xvii, 98;   Keith Griffith and Azizur Rahman
Khan, "Poverty in the Third World: Ugly Facts and Fancy
Models," World Development 6, no. 3 (1978): 299.   See also
Bernard D. Nossiter, The Global Struggle for More: Third
World Conflicts with Rich Nations (New York: Harper & Row,
1987).

    19. Amin, Modernization of Poverty, pp. 16-17, 23; Z.
Y. Hershlag, The Economic Structure of the Middle East
(Leiden: E. J. Brill, 1975), pp. 38-41, 80, 82, 84-85, 299-
307; Yousef A. Sayigh, The Economies of the Arab World:
Development Since 1945 (London: Croom Helm, 1978), pp. 665-
67, 670-71.

20. Sauvant and Hasenpflug, eds., New International Economic Order, pp. 39-62, 85-96, 98-103. Third World demands included commodity agreements to regulate prices and quantities of primary goods, orientation of the international monetary system toward the needs of the developing world, production cartels along the lines of OPEC, linkage of export prices in the poor countries to the prices for imports, preferential trade treatment, recognition of developing nations' permanent sovereignty over their natural resources, promotion of industrial development in poor nations, and transfer of advanced technology to the periphery on preferential terms.

21. Sauvant and Hasenpflug, eds., New International Economic Order, pp. 63-81, 101-3; Alfred Eckes, A Search for Solvency: Bretton Woods and the International Monetary System, 1941-1971 (Austin: University of Texas Press, 1975), pp. 275-77.

22. William D. Graf, "Anti-Brandt: A Critique of Northwestern Prescriptions for World Order," in R. Miliband and J. Saville, eds., The Socialist Register, 1981 (London: The Merlin Press, 1981), p. 25; Sauvant and Hasenpflug, eds., New International Economic Order, pp. 108-14.

23. John Waterbury and Ragaei El Mallakh, The Middle East in the Coming Decade: From Wellhead to Well-Being? (New York: CFR, McGraw Hill, 1978), pp. 21-26; "Less Developed More Divided," Time, 18 June 1979, pp. 57-58. For critiques of the NIEO, see Jimoh Omo-Fadaka, "The Mirage of NIEO: Reflections on a Third World Dystopia," Alternatives 8 (Spring 1983): 543-50; Ibrahim M. Samater, "From 'Growth' to 'Basic Needs': The Evolution of Development Theory," Monthly Review 36 (October 1984): 1-13; and Robert Cox, "Ideologies and the New International Economic Order: Reflections on Some Recent Literature," International Organization 33 (Spring 1979): 257-302.

24. Department of State (hereafter DOS), Bureau of Public Affairs, The Secretary of State, "America's Commitment to Third World Economic Development," 30 March 1979, pp. 1-7; DOS, Bureau of Public Affairs, "United States Prosperity and the Developing Countries," GIST, August 1978.

25. New York Times, 21 June 1981, pp. 1, 16; 22 September 1981, p. 6; 30 September 1981, p. 44; 15 October 1981, p. 4; 20 October 1981, p. 6; 22 October 1981, p. 4; 23 October 1981, pp. 1, 8; 24 October 1981, p. 4; Graf, "Anti-Brandt," pp. 20-46.

Appendix

Whatever the definition or measurement of economic development, the countries of the Arab East during the 1940s would
fall into the category of "underdeveloped." A variety of
studies, using different specifications, have come to this
conclusion.(1) But to classify all Arab East states as underdeveloped obscures important differences among them. The following brief analysis suggests the relative development of the
states in the region during the period under study. Chapter
Five selects representative cases for closer examination.

Seven countries of the Arab East for which data are
available have been included in this analysis. Each country
is ranked according to its relative position with reference to
a particular "indicator" of socioeconomic development. The 11
indicators are:

1. Estimated per capita annual income in dollars in
1949. A common indicator of economic development.

2. Agriculture as a percentage of national income in
the early 1950s. The more developed a nation, the
more diversified its economic structure and the less
agriculture will contribute to national income.

3. Percentage of population engaged in agriculture.
An indicator of the level of agricultural
mechanization.

4. Total commercial energy consumption in 1950 in
kilograms of coal equivalent per capita. An
indicator of the level of industrial technology.

5. Total number of radio receivers per 1,000
inhabitants in 1950. Crude indicator of level of
communications development.

6. Inhabitants per physician in mid-1950s.
Indicator of health care.

7. Infant mortality rate--the number of deaths under one year of age per 1,000 live births in 1950. One of the best measures of sanitation and nutrition; closely correlated with general levels of socioeconomic development.

8. Unadjusted school enrollment ratio for primary and secondary schools in 1955. Measure of education.

9. Value of number one export as percentage of total exports. Indicates degree of dependency on certain exports. Identifies nations that export a single crop or mineral.

10. Government expenditures on social services and public works as percentage of total government spending. Includes spending on development projects.

11. Percentage of population living in cities of 100,000 or more in early 1950s. Measure of urbanization.

These indicators have been drawn from a number of studies dealing with economic underdevelopment.(2) Each country is ranked with a number from one (most developed) to seven (least developed). The final ranking score is determined by adding up the rankings for the various indicators and dividing by the number of indicators. These data are presented in the following pages.(3) A figure presents the findings as a continuum of economic development in the Arab East during the 1940s.

ARAB EAST ECONOMIC DEVELOPMENT

INDICATOR	EGYPT	IRAQ	LEBANON	ISRAEL
1. Income	121 (3)*	85 (5)	125 (2)	389 (1)
2. Agriculture/ National Income	40.4 (6)	22** (5)	19.7 (3)	12.4 (1)
3. Population in Agriculture	67 (3)	80 (5)	50 (2)	15 (1)
4. Energy Consumption	251 (3)	141 (5)	375 (2)	556 (1)
5. Radio Receivers	13 (4)	6 (5)	30 (2)	122 (1)
6. Inhabitants per Physician	2900 (3)	5300 (5)	1200 (2)	450 (1)
7. Infant Mortality	129.6 (4)	97.3 (3)	NA	39.4 (1)
8. School Enrollment Ratio	29 (4)	19 (6)	38 (2)	71 (1)
9. Chief Export/ Total Exports	80.1 [raw cotton] (5)	80.9 [crude oil] (6)	24.3 [wool] (2)	42.3 [citrus crops] (4)
10. Expenditures on Social Services	32 (4)	22 (6)	40 (3)	50 (1)
11. Population in Cities	19.1 (4)	20.7 (3)	17.2 (5)	40.8 (1)
TOTAL RANKING SCORE [indicators]	43 [11]	53 [11]	25 [10]	14 [11]
FINAL DEVELOPMENT RANKING	3.9	4.8	2.5	1.3

---

* Comparative ranking is in parentheses.
** Percentage of Gross Domestic Product.

ARAB EAST ECONOMIC DEVELOPMENT (continued)

INDICATOR	SAUDI ARABIA	SYRIA	JORDAN
1. Income	38 (7)	100 (4)	60 (6)
2. Agriculture/ National Income	14 (2)	45 (7)	39.5 (5)
3. Population in Agriculture	NA	75 (4)	NA
4. Energy Consumption	164 (4)	98 (6)	72 (7)
5. Radio Receivers	2 (6)	15 (3)	2 (6)
6. Inhabitants per Physician	30,200 (7)	3600 (4)	7200 (6)
7. Infant Mortality	NA	40.1 (2)	NA
8. School Enrollment Ratio	3 (7)	29 (4)	34 (3)
9. Chief Export/ Total Exports	90.0 [crude oil] (7)	38.0 [raw cotton] (3)	23.2 [vegetables] (1)
10. Expenditures on Social Services	26 (5)	41 (2)	15 (7)
11. Population in Cities	8.4 (7)	31.5 (2)	14.8 (6)
TOTAL RANKING SCORE [indicators]	52 [9]	41 [11]	47 [9]
FINAL DEVELOPMENT RANKING	5.8	3.7	5.2

CONTINUUM OF ECONOMIC DEVELOPMENT IN THE ARAB EAST

MOST DEVELOPED   LEAST DEVELOPED

ISRAEL   LEBANON   SYRIA   EGYPT   IRAQ JORDAN   SAUDI ARABIA

NOTES

1. Galal A. Amin, <u>The Modernization of Poverty: A Study in the Political Economy of Growth in Nine Arab Countries, 1945-1970</u> (Leiden: E.   J. Brill, 1974); Z. Y. Hershlag, <u>The Economic Structure of the Middle East</u> (Leiden: E. J. Brill, 1975);   Kurt Grumwald and J. O. Ronall, <u>Industrialization in the Middle East</u> (Westport, Conn.:   Greenwood Press, 1960); Yusif A. Sayigh, <u>The Economies of the Arab World: Development Since 1945</u> (London: Croom Helm, 1978);   Sayigh, <u>The Determinants of Arab Economic Development</u> (New York: St. Martin's Press, 1978); Alfred Bonne, <u>State and Economics in the Middle East: A Society in Transition</u> (London: Routledge & Kegan Paul, 1955).

2. UN, Research Institute for Social Development, <u>Contents and Measurements of Socioeconomic Development</u> (New York: Praeger, 1972); Simon Kuznets, <u>Modern Economic Growth: Rate, Structure and Spread</u> (New Haven, Conn.:   Yale University Press, 1966);   Carmelo Mesa-Lago, "A Continuum for Global Comparision," in C. Mesa-Lago and C. Beck, eds., <u>Comparative Socialist Systems: Essays on Politics and Economics</u> (Pittsburgh: University of Pittsburgh Center for International Studies, 1975), pp. 92-102; Jacques Delacroix and Charles C. Ragin, "Structural Blockage: A Cross-National Study of Economic Dependency, State Efficacy, and Underdevelopment," <u>American Journal of Sociology</u> 86 (May 1981): 1311-47; Kurt Finsterbusch, "Recent Rank Ordering of Nations in Terms of Level and Rate of Development," <u>Studies in Comparative International Development</u> 8 (Spring 1973): 52-70;   Charles Taylor and M. Hudson, <u>World Handbook of Political and Social Indicators</u>, 2d ed. (New Haven, Conn.: Yale University Press, 1972).

3. Data are drawn from: UN, Statistical Office, <u>Demographic Yearbook, 1948</u> and <u>1955</u> (New York: UN, 1949, 1955);   U.S., Department of State, <u>Data Book: Near East and Independent Africa</u> (Office of Intelligence Research, May 1951); David Horowitz, <u>The Enigma of Economic Growth: A Case Study of Israel</u> (New York: Praeger, 1972); Sayigh, <u>Economies of the Arab World</u>;   UN, Department of Economic and Social Affairs, <u>World Energy Supplies, 1950-1974</u> (New York: UN, 1976);   World Health Organization, <u>Annual Epidemiological and</u>

Vital Statistics, 1957 (Geneva: WHO,   1960);   UNESCO,
Statistical Yearbook, 1963 (Paris: UN,   1964);   Galal Amin,
Modernization of Poverty; Grunwald and Ronall, Industrializa-
tion in Middle East;   UN, Statistical Office, Yearbook of
International Trade Statistics, 1953-55 (New York: UN, 1954-
56) and Statistics of National Income and Expenditures (New
York: UN, September 1955 and May 1956);   International
Monetary Fund, Balance of Payments Yearbook, 1947-53, 1950-54
(Washington, D.C.:   IMF, 1954, 1957);   Hershlag, Economic
Structure of Middle East; UN, Department of Economic Affairs,
Review of Economic Conditions in the Middle East, 1951-52,
Supplement to World Economic Report (New York: UN, March
1953) and Review of Economic Conditions in the Middle East,
Supplement to World Economic Report, 1949-50 (New York: UN,
March 1950);   UN, Economic Developments in Middle East, 1945-
54 (New York: UN, 1955).

Select Bibliography

PRIMARY MATERIALS

United States, National Archives, Washington, D.C.

Foreign Economic Administration, Record Group 169: Bureau of Areas; Economic Programs--Foreign Development Staff; Office of Administrator--Records Analysis

Foreign Service Posts Records, Record Group 84: Cairo Post Records; Dhahran Post Records; United States Mission to UN, Records of US Mission

Interdepartmental and Intradepartmental Committees (Department of State), Record Group 353: Economic Committees; Executive Committee on Economic Foreign Policy

Office of the Secretary of the Treasury, Record Group 56: Records of the National Advisory Council on International Monetary and Financial Policies

State Department Records, Record Group 59: Records of Harley A. Notter, 1939-45; Records of Policy Planning Staff; State Department Decimal File, 1940-44, 1945-49

Private Papers and Manuscript Collections

Acheson, Dean. Papers. Harry S. Truman Library, Independence, Missouri.

American Federation of Labor. Papers. Wisconsin State Historical Society, Madison, Wisconsin.

Baruch, Bernard M. Papers. Seeley G. Mudd Manuscript Library, Princeton University, Princeton, New Jersey.

Bean, Louis H. Papers. Franklin D. Roosevelt Library, Hyde Park, New York.

Becker, Nathan M. Oral History Interview. Harry S. Truman Library, Independence, Missouri.

Berle, Adolf A. Papers. Franklin D. Roosevelt Library, Hyde Park, New York.

Bohan, Merwin L. Oral History Interview. Harry S. Truman Library, Independence, Missouri.

Chicago Council on Foreign Relations. Papers. Department of Special Collections, University of Illinois at Chicago Library, Chicago, Illinois.

Clapp, Gordon R. Papers. Harry S. Truman Library, Independence, Missouri.

Clarke, Philip Ream. Papers. Department of Special Collections, University of Illinois at Chicago Library, Chicago, Illinois.

Clayton, William. Papers. Harry S. Truman Library, Independence, Missouri.

Clayton-Thorp Files. Harry S. Truman Library, Independence, Missouri.

Clifford, Clark M. Papers. Harry S. Truman Library, Independence, Missouri.

Cope, Elmer F. Papers. Microfilm edition. Ohio Historical Society, Columbus, Ohio.

Cox, Oscar. Papers. Franklin D. Roosevelt Library, Hyde Park, New York.

Culbertson, William S. Papers. Manuscript Division, Library of Congress, Washington, D.C.

Forrestal, James V. Diaries. Seeley G. Mudd Manuscript Library, Princeton University, Princeton, New Jersey.

Goldenweiser, Emanuel. Papers. Manuscript Division, Library of Congress, Washington, D.C.

Griffis, Stanton. Papers. Harry S. Truman Library, Independence, Missouri.

Henderson, Loy. Oral History Interview. Harry S. Truman Library, Independence, Missouri.

Hines, Lewis G. Papers. Manuscript Division, Library of Congress, Washington, D.C.

Hopkins, Harry. Papers. Franklin D. Roosevelt Library, Hyde Park, New York.

Howard, Harry N. Oral History Interview. Harry S. Truman Library, Independence, Missouri.

Hull, Cordell. Papers. Manuscript Division, Library of Congress, Washington, D.C.

Landis, James M. Papers. Manuscript Division, Library of Congress, Washington, D.C.

Long, Breckinridge. Papers. Manuscript Division, Library of Congress, Washington, D.C.

Lubin, Isador. Papers. Franklin D. Roosevelt Library, Hyde Park, New York.

Mason, Edward S. Oral History Interview. Harry S. Truman Library, Independence, Missouri.

Merchant, Livingston T. Papers. Seeley G. Mudd Manuscript Library, Princeton University, Princeton, New Jersey.

Morgenthau, Henry. Papers. Franklin D. Roosevelt Library, Hyde Park, New York.

Paul, Arthur. Papers. Harry S. Truman Library, Independence, Missouri.

Roosevelt, Franklin D. Papers. Franklin D. Roosevelt Library, Hyde Park, New York.

Ruml, Beardsley. Papers. Department of Special Collections, University of Chicago Library, Chicago, Illinois.

Salant, Walter S. Papers. Harry S. Truman Library, Independence, Missouri.

Satterthwaite, Joseph C. Oral History Interview. Harry S. Truman Library, Independence, Missouri.

Smith, Harold D. Papers. Franklin D. Roosevelt Library, Hyde Park, New York.

Smith, Dr. R. Burr. Oral History Interview. Harry S. Truman Library, Independence, Missouri.

Truman, Harry S. Papers. Harry S. Truman Library, Independence, Missouri.
Wallace, Henry A.   Papers. Franklin D. Roosevelt Library, Hyde Park, New York.

GOVERNMENT DOCUMENTS

League of Nations

Delegation on Economic Depressions. Economic Stability in the Post-War World: The Conditions of Prosperity After the Transition from War to Peace. Geneva: 1945.
Economic and Financial Committee. Report to the Council on the Work of the 1943 Joint Session. Geneva: 1944.
_____. Preliminary Investigation into Measures of a National or International Character for Raising the Standard of Living. Geneva: 1938.
Report of Special Committee to League. The Development of International Co-Operation in Economic and Social Affairs. 22 August 1939.

United Nations

Department of Economic Affairs. Economic Development in Selected Countries: Plans, Programmes, and Agencies. Lake Success, N.Y.: UN, October 1947.
_____. Methods of Financing Economic Development in Under-Developed Countries. Lake Success, N.Y.: UN, 1949.
_____. Relative Prices of Exports and Imports of Under-Developed Countries: A Study of post-war terms of trade between underdeveloped and industrialized countries. Lake Success, N.Y.: UN, December 1949.
_____. Review of Economic Conditions in the Middle East, Supplement to World Economic Report, 1949-50. New York: UN, 1951.
_____. Review of Economic Conditions in the Middle East 1951-52, Supplement to World Economic Report. New York: UN, 1953.
Department of Economic and Social Affairs. Economic Developments in the Middle East, 1945 to 1954, Supplement to World Economic Report, 1953-54. New York: UN, 1955.
Economic and Social Council. Official Records, 2nd-4th Years, 1947-1949. Lake Success, N.Y.: 1948. Geneva: 1949.
_____. Report of the Ad Hoc Committee for the Middle East, Supplement no. 4. Lake Success, N.Y.: 1949.
_____. Report of the Second Session of the Sub-Commission on Economic Development, Supplement 11A. New York: 1948.
_____. Report of the Third Session of the Sub-Commission on Economic Development, Supplement 11B. New York: 1949.
_____. Resolutions adopted by ECOSOC, 3rd session, 1 September to 10 December 1946. Lake Success, N.Y.: 1947.
_____. Sub-Commission on Economic Development, Summary Record of Meetings, March-April 1949. New York: 1949.
Information Office. Documents of the United Nations Conference of International Organizations, San Francisco, 1945.

Vol. 3, <u>Dumbarton Oaks Proposals, Comments and Proposed Amendments</u>. New York: 1945.

_____. <u>Yearbooks of the United Nations, 1946-49</u>. New York: 1947, 1949, 1950.

Secretary-General. <u>Technical Assistance for Economic Development</u>. Lake Success, N.Y.: May 1949.

United Nations. "First Interim Report of the UN Economic Survey Mission for the Middle East," Doc. A/1106, <u>Ad Hoc Political Committee, Annex, vol. 1, 1949</u>. New York: 1949.

_____. <u>Report of the 1st session of the Preparatory Committee of the UN Conference on Trade and Employment</u>. London: 1946.

_____. <u>Report of the 2nd session of the Preparatory Committee of the UN Conference on Trade and Employment</u>. Geneva: 1947.

United States

Congress, House of Representatives. <u>Postwar Economic Policy and Planning</u>. Report 1527, part 2, 79th Congress, 2d session, 1946.

_____. <u>Report of Activities of the National Advisory Council on International Monetary and Financial Problems</u>. Document 365, 80th Congress, 1st session, 1947.

_____. <u>United States Foreign Policy for a Post-War Recovery Program, Hearings before the Committee on Foreign Affairs</u>. 80th Congress, 1st and 2d sessions, 1949.

Congress, Senate. <u>International Petroleum Cartel: Staff Report of the Federal Trade Commission, Select Committee on Small Business, Subcommittee on Monopoly</u>. 82nd Congress, 1952.

_____. <u>Monopoly and Cartels: Hearings before a Subcommittee of the Select Committee on Small Business</u>. Part I, 82nd Congress, 2d session, 1952.

Department of Commerce. <u>Foreign Aid by the United States Government, 1940-1951</u>. A supplement to the <u>Survey of Current Business</u>. Washington, D.C.: 1952.

_____. <u>Foreign Commerce Weekly</u>. 1942-1950.

_____. <u>Foreign Commerce Yearbook, 1948</u>. Washington, D.C.: 1950.

Department of State. <u>Bulletin</u>. 1942-1950.

_____. <u>Foreign Relations of the United States, 1941-1950</u>.

_____. <u>Point Four: Cooperative Program for Aid in the Development of Economically Underdeveloped Areas</u>. Washington, D.C.: 1950.

_____. <u>Proceedings and Documents of United Nations Monetary and Financial Conference</u>. Bretton Woods, July 1944. Washington, D.C.: 1948.

_____. <u>Proceedings of the International Civil Aviation Conference</u>. Chicago, 1 November-7 December 1944. Washington, D.C.: 1948.

Gray, Gordon. <u>Report to the President on Foreign Economic Policies</u>. Washington, D.C.: 1950.

Notter, Harley A. <u>Postwar Foreign Policy Preparation, 1939-1945</u>. Washington, D.C.: 1949.

Rockefeller, Nelson. <u>Partners in Progress: A Report to the President by the International Development Board</u>. Washington, D.C.: 1951.

JOURNALS

Business Week. 1942-1950.
L'Egypte Contemporaine. 1943-1951.
Fortune. 1940-1950.
Great Britain and the East. 1941-1949.
The Oil and Gas Journal. 1942-1950.

SELECTED SECONDARY SOURCES

Bibliographies

The American Economic Association. Index of Economic Jour-
    nals, 1925-1939, 1940-1949, 1950-1959. Homewood, Ill.:
    Richard D. Irwin, 1961, 1962.
American University of Beirut. A Selected and Annotated
    Bibliography of Economic Literature on the Arabic
    Speaking Countries of the Middle East, 1938-1952, 1953-
    1965. Beirut: AUB, Economic Research Institute, 1954,
    1967.
Atiyeh, George N. The Contemporary Middle East, 1948-1973: A
    Selective and Annotated Bibliography. Boston: G. K.
    Hall, 1975.
Burns, Richard Dean, ed. Guide to American Foreign Relations
    since 1700. Santa Barbara, Calif.: ABC-Clio, 1983.
Field, Norman S., ed. League of Nations and United Nations
    Monthly List of Selected Articles--Cumulative 1920-1970:
    Economic Questions, Economic Conditions, 1920-1955.
    Dobbs Ferry, N.Y.: Oceana Publications, 1973.
Hazelwood, Arthur. The Economics of Development: An Anno-
    tated List of Books and Articles Published 1958-1962.
    London: Oxford University Press, 1964.
Pearson, J. D. Index Islamicus, 1906-1955; Supplements 1956-
    1975. Cambridge: W. Heffer & Sons, 1958-75.
Powelson, John P. A Select Bibliography on Economic Develop-
    ment with Annotations. Boulder, Colo.: Westview Press,
    1979.

Autobiographies, Memoirs, Letters

Acheson, Dean. Present at the Creation: My Years in the
    State Department. New York: W. W. Norton, 1969.
Berle, Beatrice B., and Travis B. Jacobs, eds. Navigating the
    Rapids, 1918-1971: From the Papers of Adolf A. Berle.
    New York: Harcourt Brace Jovanovich, 1973.
Campbell, Thomas M., and George C. Herring, eds. The Diaries
    of Edward R. Stettinius, Jr., 1943-1946. New York: New
    Viewpoints, 1975.
Dobney, Frederick J., ed. Selected Papers of Will Clayton.
    Baltimore: Johns Hopkins Press, 1971.
Hull, Cordell. The Memoirs of Cordell Hull. London: Hodder
    & Stoughton, 1948.
Millis, Walter, ed. The Forrestal Diaries. New York: Viking
    Press, 1951.
Truman, Harry. Memoirs: Years of Trial and Hope. Garden
    City, N.Y.: Doubleday, 1956.

Economic Development

Amin, Samir. <u>Accumulation on a World Scale: A Critique of the Theory of Underdevelopment</u>.   New York: Monthly Review Press, 1974.

Arndt, H. W. <u>The Rise and Fall of Economic Growth: A Study in Contemporary Thought</u>.   Melbourne: Longman Cheshire, 1978.

Asher, Robert, Walter M. Kotschnig, and William A. Brown, Jr. <u>The United Nations and Economic and Social Co-Operation</u>. Washington, D.C.: The Brookings Institution, 1957.

Baran, Paul A. <u>The Political Economy of Growth</u>.   New York: Monthly Review Press, 1962.

Barratt Brown, Michael. <u>The Economics of Imperialism</u>. Middlesex: Penguin, 1974.

Bean, Louis. "International Industrialization and Per Capita Income."   <u>Studies in Income and Wealth</u>, vol. 8. New York: National Bureau of Economic Research, 1946.

Behrman, Jere R. "Development Economics." <u>Modern Economic Thought</u>.   Edited by Sidney Weintraub. Philadelphia: University of Pennsylvania Press, 1977.

Clairmonte, Frederick. <u>Economic Liberalism and Underdevelopment: Studies in the Disintegration of an Idea</u>. Bombay: Asia Publishing House, 1960.

Clark, Colin. <u>Conditions of Economic Progress</u>.   New York: MacMillan, 1940.

Dobb, Maurice.   <u>Economic Growth and Underdevelopment</u>. New York: International Publishers, 1963.

Emmanuel, Arghiri. <u>Unequal Exchange: A Study of the Imperialism of Trade</u>. New York: Monthly Review Press, 1972.

Finer, Herman.   <u>The T.V.A. Lessons for International Application</u>. Montreal: ILO, 1944.

Frank, Andre Gunder. <u>Dependent Accumulation and Underdevelopment</u>. New York: Monthly Review Press, 1979.

Griffin, Keith.   <u>International Inequality and National Poverty</u>. New York: Holmes & Meier Publishers, 1978.

Gupta, Partha Sarathi. <u>Imperialism and the British Labour Movement, 1914-1964</u>. London: The Macmillan Press, 1975.

Hart, Judith. <u>Aid and Liberation: A Socialist Study of Aid Policies</u>. London: Victor Gollancz, Ltd., 1973.

Hayter, Teresa. <u>Aid as Imperialism</u>.   Middlesex: Penguin, 1971.

Higgott, Richard A.   <u>Political Development Theory: The Contemporary Debate</u>. London: Croom Helm, 1983.

Hirschman, Albert O. "The Rise and Decline of Development Economics." <u>The Theory and Experience of Economic Development: Essays in Honor of Sir W. Arthur Lewis</u>. Edited by Mark Gersovitz et al. London: George Allen & Unwin, 1982.

_____. <u>A Bias for Hope: Essays on Development and Latin America</u>. New Haven: Yale University Press, 1971.

Hobson, J. A. <u>Imperialism: A Study</u>. New York: James Pott, 1902.

Kemp, Tom. <u>Historical Patterns of Industrialization</u>. London: Longman, 1978.

Lorwin, Lewis L. <u>The Postwar Plans of the United Nations</u>. New York: Twentieth Century Fund, 1943.

Luxemburg, Rosa. <u>The Accumulation of Capital</u>. Translated by

Agnes Swarzchild.   New Haven, Conn.:   Yale University
    Press, 1951 (1913).
Machlup, Fritz. A History of Thought on Economic Integration.
    New York: Columbia University Press, 1977.
_____.   Essays in Economic Semantics.   New York: New York
    University Press, 1975.
Mandelbaum, K.   The Industrialization of Backward Areas.
    Oxford: Basil Blackwell, 1945.
Myrdal, Gunnar.   An International Economy: Problems and
    Prospects. New York: Harper & Row, 1956.
_____. Development and Under-Development: A Note on the
    Mechanism of National and International Economic Inequal-
    ity. Cairo: National Bank of Egypt, 1956.
Rosenstein Rodan, P. N.   "The International Development of
    Economically Backward Areas."   International Affairs 20
    (April 1944): 157-65.
Rothschild, K. W. "The Small Nation and World Trade."   The
    Economic Journal 54 (April 1944): 26-40.
Staley, Eugene.   World Economic Development: Effects on
    Advanced Industrial Countries. Montreal: ILO, 1944.
Sutcliffe, R. B.   Industry and Underdevelopment.   London:
    Addison-Wesley, 1971.
Trimberger, Ellen Kay. "World Systems Analysis: The Problem
    of Unequal Development." Theory and Society 8 (1979):
    127-37.
Warriner, Doreen.   Economics of Peasant Farming. London:
    Oxford University Press, 1939.

United States and World-Economy

"The American Challenge." The Economist 143 (18 July 1942):
    66-67.
Baily, Samuel L.   The United States and the Development of
    South America, 1945-1975.   New York: New Viewpoints,
    1976.
Baldwin, David.   Economic Development and American Foreign
    Policy, 1943-1962.   Chicago: University of Chicago
    Press, 1966.
Berman, Edward H.   The Influence of the Carnegie, Ford, and
    Rockefeller Foundations on American Foreign Policy: The
    Ideology of Philanthropy. Albany, N.Y.: State Univer-
    sity of New York Press, 1983.
Block, Fred L. The Origins of International Economic Disor-
    der: A Study of United States International Monetary
    Policy from World War II to the Present.   Berkeley:
    University of California Press, 1977.
Borden, William S.   The Pacific Alliance: United States
    Foreign Economic Policy and Japanese Trade Recovery,
    1947-1955.   Madison: University of Wisconsin Press,
    1984.
Butler, H. "The American Approach to Reconstruction." Agenda
    1 (April 1942): 97-107.
Campbell, Thomas M.   Masquerade Peace: America's UN Policy,
    1944-1945. Tallahassee: Florida State University Press,
    1973.
Condliffe, J. B.   Agenda for a Postwar World. New York: W.
    W. Norton, 1942.
Council on Foreign Relations.   Studies of American Interests
    in the War and the Peace. 1940-1944.

Cox, Robert W. "Social Forces, States and World Orders: Beyond International Relations Theory." Millennium: Journal of International Studies, 10, no. 2 (1981): 126-55.

Elliot, William Y., et al. The Political Economy of American Foreign Policy: Its Concepts, Strategy, and Limits. New York: Henry Holt, 1955.

Gardner, Lloyd C. Economic Aspects of New Deal Diplomacy. Boston: Beacon Press, 1971.

_____. Architects of Illusion: Men and Ideas in American Foreign Policy, 1941-1949. Chicago: Quadrangle Books, 1970.

Gardner, Richard N. Sterling-Dollar Diplomacy: Anglo-American Collaboration in the Reconstruction of Multilateral Trade. Oxford: Clarendon Press, 1956.

Hansen, Alvin H. After the War--Full Employment. National Resources Planning Board, February 1943.

Harris, Seymour E., ed. Postwar Economic Problems. New York: McGraw-Hill, 1943.

Hays, Samuel P., ed. The Beginning of American Aid to Southeast Asia: The Griffin Mission of 1950. Lexington, Mass.: Heath Lexington Books, 1971.

Hogan, Michael J. "American Marshall Planners and the Search for a European Neocapitalism." American Historical Review 90 (February 1985): 44-72.

_____. "Revival and Reform: America's Twentieth-Century Search for a New Economic Order Abroad." Diplomatic History 8 (Fall 1984): 287-310.

Hyde, Louis K. The United States and the United Nations: Promoting the Public Welfare--Examples of American Cooperation, 1945-1955. New York: Carnegie Endowment for International Peace, Manhattan Publishing, 1960.

Kaufman, Burton I. "The United States Response to the Soviet Economic Offensive of the 1950s." Diplomatic History, 2 (Spring 1978): 153-65.

Kolko, Gabriel. The Politics of War: The World and United States Foreign Policy, 1943-1945. New York: Random House, 1968.

Kolko, Joyce, and Gabriel Kolko. The Limits of Power: The World and United States Foreign Policy, 1945-1954. New York: Harper & Row, 1972.

Lipson, Charles. Standing Guard: Protecting Foreign Capital in the Nineteenth and Twentieth Centuries. Berkeley: University of California Press, 1985.

Louis, William Roger. Imperialism at Bay: The United States and the Decolonization of the British Empire, 1941-1945. New York: Oxford University Press, 1978.

McCormick, Thomas J. "'Every System Needs a Center Sometimes': An Essay on Hegemony and Modern American Foreign Policy." Redefining the Past: Essays in Diplomatic History in Honor of William Appleman Williams. Edited by Lloyd C. Gardner. Corvallis, Ore.: Oregon State University Press, 1986.

_____. "Drift or Mastery? A Corporatist Synthesis for American Diplomatic History." Reviews in American History 10 (December 1982): 318-30.

Packenham, Robert A. Liberal America and the Third World: Political Development Ideas in Foreign Aid and Social Science. Princeton, N.J.: Princeton University Press, 1973.

Petras, James. Class, State, and Power in the Third World:
    With Case Studies on Class Conflict in Latin America.
    Montclair, NJ: Allanheld, Osmun & Publishers, 1981.
Rabe, Stephen G. "The Elusive Conference: United States
    Economic Relations with Latin America, 1945-1952."
    Diplomatic History 2 (Summer 1978):   279-94.
Schriftgiesser, Karl. Business and Public Policy: The Role
    of the Committee for Economic Development, 1942-1967.
    Englewood Cliffs, N.J.: Prentice-Hall, 1967.
Shoup, Laurence H., and William Minter. Imperial Brain Trust:
    The Council on Foreign Relations and United States
    Foreign Policy. New York: Monthly Review Press, 1977.
Thorp, Willard. Trade, Aid, or What?   Baltimore: Johns
    Hopkins Press, 1954.
Wallace, Henry A. Sixty Million Jobs. New York: Simon &
    Schuster, 1945.
Wilcox, Clair.   A Charter for World Trade.   New York:
    Macmillan, 1949.
Wilkins, Mira.   The Maturing of Multinational Enterprise:
    American Business Abroad from 1914 to 1970. Cambridge,
    Mass.: Harvard University Press, 1974.

Middle East

Amin, Galal A. The Modernization of Poverty: A Study in the
    Political Economy of Growth in Nine Arab Countries, 1945-
    1970. Leiden: E. J. Brill, 1974.
Anderson, Irvine H.   Aramco, the United States and Saudi
    Arabia: A Study of the Dynamics of Foreign Oil Policy,
    1933-1950. Princeton, N.J.: Princeton University Press,
    1981.
Baer, Gabriel. Population and Society in the Arab East.
    Translated by Hanna Szoke. New York: Praeger, 1964.
Baram, Phillip J. The Department of State in the Middle East,
    1919-1945. Philadelphia: University of Pennsylvania
    Press, 1978.
Bonne, Alfred. State and Economics in the Middle East: A
    Society in Transition. London: Routledge & Kegan Paul,
    1955.
Bryson, Thomas A. Seeds of Mideast Crisis: The United States
    Diplomatic Role in the Middle East During World War II.
    Jefferson, N.C.: McFarland, 1981.
Cooke, Hedley V. Challenge and Response in the Middle East:
    The Quest for Prosperity, 1919-1951. New York: Harper &
    Brothers, 1952.
DeNovo, John A. "The Culbertson Economic Mission and Anglo-
    American Tensions in the Middle East, 1944-1945." The
    Journal of American History 63 (March 1977): 913-36.
_____. American Interests and Policies in the Middle East,
    1900-1939. Minneapolis: University of Minnesota Press,
    1963.
Godfried, Nathan. "Economic Development and Regionalism:
    United States Foreign Relations in the Middle East, 1942-
    1949." Journal of Contemporary History 22 (July 1987):
    481-500.
Halevi, Nadav, and Ruth Klinov-Malul. The Economic Develop-
    ment of Israel. New York: Praeger, 1968.
Hanifi, M. J. Islam and the Transformation of Culture. New
    York: Asia Publishing House, 1970.

Hays, James B. _TVA on the Jordan: Proposals for Irrigation and Hydro-Electric Development in Palestine_. Washington, D.C.: Public Affairs Press, 1948.

Hershlag, Z. Y. _The Economic Structure of the Middle East_. Leiden: E. J. Brill, 1975.

Hourani, Albert. _Arabic Thought in the Liberal Age, 1789-1939_. London: Oxford University Press, 1962.

Hussein, Mahoud. _Class Conflict in Egypt, 1945-1970_.   New York: Monthly Review Press, 1973.

Issawi, Charles. _Egypt at Mid-Century: An Economic Survey_. London: Oxford University Press, 1954.

Kermani, Taghi T. _Economic Development in Action: Theories, Problems, and Procedures as Applied in the Middle East_. Cleveland: World Publishing, 1967.

Kitchen, Helen A., ed. _Americans and the Middle East: Partners in the Next Decade_. Washington, D.C.: Middle East Institute, 1950.

Lackner, Helen. _A House Built on Sand: A Political Economy of Saudi Arabia_. London: Ithaca Press, 1978.

Louis, William Roger. _The British Empire in the Middle East, 1945-1951: Arab Nationalism, the United States, and Postwar Imperialism_. New York: Oxford University Press, 1984.

Lowdermilk, Walter. _Palestine: Land of Promise_.   New York: Harper & Brothers, 1944.

MacDonald, Robert W. _The League of Arab States: A Study in the Dynamics of Regional Organization_.   Princeton, N.J.: Princeton University Press, 1965.

Meyer, Albert J. "Economic Thought and Its Application and Methodology in the Middle East." _Middle East Economic Papers_ (1956): 66-74.

Miller, Aaron D. _Search for Security: Saudi Arabian Oil and American Foreign Policy, 1939-1949_.   Chapel Hill: University of North Carolina Press, 1980.

Musrey, Alfred G. _An Arab Common Market: A Study in Inter-Arab Trade Relations, 1920-1967_.   New York: Praeger, 1969.

Nathan, Robert, Gass Oscar, and Daniel Creamer. _Palestine: Problems and Promise--An Economic Study_.   Washington, D.C.: Public Affairs Press, 1946.

Niblock, Tim. _State, Society and Economy in Saudi Arabia_. London: Croom Helm, 1982.

_____, ed. _Social and Economic Development in the Arab Gulf_. London: Croom Helm, 1980.

Rodinson, Maxime. _Islam and Capitalism_.   Translated by Brian Pearce. London: Allen Lane, 1974.

Rubner, Alex. _The Economy of Israel: A Critical Account of the First Ten Years_. New York: Praeger, 1960.

Sachar, Howard M. _A History of Israel: From the Rise of Zionism to Our Time_. New York: Alfred A. Knopf, 1976.

_____. _Europe Leaves the Middle East, 1936-1954_.   New York: Alfred A. Knopf, 1972.

Safran, Nadav. _Israel: The Embattled Ally_.   Cambridge, Mass.: Harvard University Press, 1981.

Sayigh, Yusif A. _The Determinants of Arab Economic Development_. New York: St. Martin's Press, 1978.

Terry, Janice J. _The Wafd, 1919-1952:   Cornerstone of Egyptian Political Power_.   London: Third World Centre, 1982.

Tignor, Robert L.   State, Private Enterprise, and Economic
    Change in Egypt, 1918-1952. Princeton, N.J.: Princeton
    University Press, 1984.
Turner, Bryan S.   Marx and the End of Orientalism. London:
    George Allen & Unwin, 1978.
Warriner, Doreen.   Land and Poverty in the Middle East.
    London: Royal Institute of International Affairs, 1948.
Wilmington, Martin. The Middle East Supply Centre. Edited by
    Laurence Evans. Albany: State University of New York
    Press, 1971.

Index

Acheson, Dean, 124, 125, 128; attacks BEW, 37; on criteria for IBRD loans, 48; on economic approach to Arab East conflicts, 136, 137; on the open door and productionism, 39; wary of aid to Jewish Palestine, 169-70

Africa: Communism in, 73; European participation in development of, 70; private U.S. aid for, 72-73

Al Kharj Reclamation Project, 160

American Economic Mission to the Middle East (AEMME). See Landis, James M.

American Federation of Labor (AFL): conflict with labor movements in periphery, 73; and corporatism, 3-4, 74; Free Trade Union Committee, 73; and H. W. Fraser, 74; and improving working conditions in Third World, 30-31; on ITO, 84; on Point Four, 107; on protectionism, 68; and Serafino Romualdi, 73-74; on Subcommission on Economic Development, 75; support for imperial state's development policy, 73

Arab East: 15, 134, 187; economic development of: indigenous approaches to, 149-50; in 1940s, 201-3; in 1950s, 191-92; in 1960s-70s, 193. See also names of specific countries

Arabian American Oil Company (Aramco): development activities in Saudi Arabia, 159-62, 164-65; operations constitute junior Marshall Plan, 132

Arab-Israeli conflict: obstacle to ERP, 131; obstructs economic development, 138, 150

Atlantic Charter, 28-29, 47

Australia, 46, 50-51, 79, 81

Autarky, 34, 65

Bean, Louis H., 40; on aid programs and security threat rationale, 43, 187; background of, 42; critiques Hull-Acheson Report, 42-43; on industrialization in periphery, 42; recommendations of, for Third World development, 43

Berle, Adolf A., 47; on British and Russian imperialism in Middle East, 123; on U.S. hegemony, 39; on integration and regionalism, 85 n.2; on productionism, 39

Blocked sterling balances: in Arab East, 124-25, 153, 154; issue at Bretton Woods, 48

Board of Economic Warfare (BEW): and Third World development, 36-37; vehicle of New Deal liberals, 36-37

Bretton Woods Conference: discussion of Third World economic development at, 47-49; stabilize capitalist world-economy, 97

Bureau of the Budget. See Smith, Harold D.; Bean, Louis H.

Capitalism. See Capitalist mode of production

Capitalist class, U.S., 3; components of, 7; and control of means of production, 6; and imperial state, 8; views on Third World development, 29-30

Capitalist mode of production: bourgeois theory of, 23 n.44; and corporatism, 4; defined, 2; global, 5; inequality in, 2; role of the state in, 2-3

Capitalist world-economy: achieving integration of, 62; the core in, 5; defined, 5-6; early theory of, 13; the periphery in, 5; the semiperiphery in, 5-6; the state in, 6; unequal and uneven development in, 6

Chapultepec Conference: economic development issue at, 49-50; Latin America confronts U.S. at, 50, 73

Clapp, Gordon R., and Economic Survey Mission to Middle East, 136-37

Clayton, Will, 31, 68, 86 n.10; on American hegemony, 32, 65, 97-98; at Chapultepec Conference, 49; concentrates on Europe and Asia, 128; and ITO, 82; and liberal capitalism and corporatism, 64; on Marshall Plan for Latin America, 69-70; opposes BEW activities in Third World, 37; on reconstruction and development, 65; on regionalism and free trade, 66; on U.S. need for economic expansion abroad, 32

Clifford, Clark, 131

Collado, Emilio: background of, 41, 77; criticizes Subcommission on Economic Development, 77, 78

Committee for Economic Development (CED), 47; on economic nationalism, 84; on ITO, 83-84; linked capitalist class and imperial state, 31; on regionalism, 65; on Third World economic development, 31-32; vote on ITO issue, 95 n.83

Communism: containment of, and economic development of Third World, 70, 73; threat of, as rationale for aid programs, 187; and U.S. hegemony, 109-10

Comparative advantage, fallacy of, 119-20 n.54

Conciliation Commission for Palestine (CCP), 136

Congress of Industrial Organizations (CIO), 73, 107. See also American Federation of Labor

Core: defined, 5; dependence on the periphery, 193

Core-periphery: conflicts in, 9-10; and persistent gap in, 192-93

Corporate liberals: on Point Four, 106; reject international welfare capitalism,

112-13; on the state's role in new world order, 64; tactical battle with New Deal liberals, 36-37, 43-44, 52; views of, reflected in Hull-Acheson Report, 42

Corporatism: and capitalism, 4; defined, 3-4; illusions of, 4; and organizations, 31; and U.S. commitment to expansion, 5

Council on Foreign Relations (CFR), 31-33, 50. See also Hansen, Alvin H.; Staley, Eugene

Culbertson, William S., 122, 124, 125, 127

Dollar Diplomacy, 97

Dollar Gap: defined, 67; and developing the Third World, 69; in the Middle East, 124-25, 131; and reciprocal trade agreements, 68; solutions to, 67-68

Economic development: Arab East perceptions of, 149-50; and autarky, 13; criticism of capitalist theory of, 14-15; debate over, 1; defined, 10-11; economists define, 12-15; and free trade and comparative advantage, 11-12; indicators of, 199-200; myth and reality of, in U.S., 15-16; and nationalism, 10; and social revolution, 10; Third World vision of, 110; U.S. model of, 16; U.S. perceptions of, 11, 18; use of state controls in, 30; Western capitalist theories of, 12-14

Economic development, Third World: and containment of Communism, 70; component of U.S. hegemony, 110; contribution to reconstruction, 62, 68; different visions of, 110-11; and the dollar gap, 69; ECEFP defines sound development, 40; and

Europe, 69, 70; free trade as the key to, 111; responsibility for, 28; ruling elites of periphery view, 51, 113; as seen by U.S. corporate and state elite, 51-52, 112-13; Third World theories of, 15

Economic nationalism: and economic development, 10; of Egypt and U.S. concern with, 152, 154, 155; ITO contained elements of, 83

Economic and Social Council, UN (ECOSOC): criticized by Third World, 76; establishment of, 51; origins of, in 1930s, 61 n.88; regional economic commissions of, 78-80; and U.S. technical assistance policy, 109. See also Subcommission on Economic Development

Economic Survey Mission. See Clapp, Gordon R.

Egypt, 151-57, 201, 203; barter and bilateral trade of, 154; bourgeoisie of, 153, 157; at Bretton Woods, 48; criticism of ECOSOC, 76; desired U.S. economic aid, 153-54; on economic development, 151; on Marshall Plan for Middle East, 155; National Bank of, 154, 155, 156; nationalists of, wary of private U.S. capital, 155; an open door in, 155-56; and Point Four, 156; Stanton Griffis in, 154-55; and Suez Crisis, 191; U.S. aid to, 156; U.S. concern with industrialization in, 152

European Recovery Program (ERP), and Arab East, 130-33

Executive Committee on Economic Foreign Policy (ECEFP), 40; and April 1945 Report on Middle East, 121-28

Export-Import Bank, U.S. (Eximbank): credits to Egypt, 153; as instrument of U.S. foreign policy, 100; loans to Jewish Palestine and Israel, 169-72; loans to Saudi Arabia, 160-61; and Middle East economic development, 100-101; role in development of Third World, 100-101; State Department interferes with, 100-101

Financing economic development, 96-102

Foreign investment: CED rejects ITO provisions on, 84; for peripheral development, 33, 35, 96-97, 114 n.4; Third World wary of, 77, 97

Fortune: on dangers of protectionism, 68, 84; on U.S. role in economic development of Third World, 29, 30, 70-71

Gray, Gordon, Report on Economic Development, 188-89

Great Britain: blocked sterling balances of, 48; developed colonies, 44-45; formulates regional approach to Middle East development, 125-26, 128-29; and hegemony, 6; and Ibn Saud, 158; at ILO Convention, 46; on importance of Third World development, 45; relations with U.S. on Third World development, 45; and Richard Clarke memorandum, 45, 46

Griffis, Stanton, activities in Egypt, 154-55

Hakim, George, 78, 108, 134

Hansen, Alvin H., and analysis of Third World development, 33-34

Hawkins, Harry, 42, 46

Hegemony, U.S., 109; committed to liberal capitalist framework, 187-88; and Communist threat, 109; defined, 6; dependent on uneven and unequal development, 112; forms of, 8; institutions of, 97-98; obstacles to, 186-87; responsible for reconstruction and development, 70-71; and Third World development, 34; in twentieth century, 6-7

Henderson, Loy: ignores Arab masses, 128; and loans to Jewish Palestine, 170; protects vital interests in Arab East, 171. See also Near Eastern Affairs, Division of

Hoffman, Paul, 31, 35, 47

Hoover, Calvin B., and study for CED, 31-32

Hull, Cordell, 51; on BEW, 37, 39; on reciprocal trade and Third World development, 18

Hull-Acheson Committee: members of, 41, 58 n.56; report of world development, 41-43

Ibn Saud: and economic development, 158-59, 162-63; U.S. perceptions of, 158. See also Saudi Arabia

Imperial state: defined, 7; and rules of the game, 8

Imperial state, U.S.: conception of underdevelopment, 8-9; and irreconciliable and negotiable conflicts with periphery, 62-63; and necessity of Third World development, 46; plans to bridge gap between rich and poor, 9; rejects global New Deal, 195; and rules of the game, 8; seeks to undermine NIEO, 194

Import substitution, 35

India: and blocked sterling balances, 48; at Bretton Woods, 48-49; economists of, 15; at ILO Convention, 46; and protectionism, 46, 81

Industrialization of Third World: Hansen and Staley on, 33-34; ITO Charter protects, 82; under U.S. guidance, 30, 33, 34-35, 36

International Bank for Reconstruction and Development (IBRD): competition with Eximbank, 100-101; debate at Bretton Woods over, 48; and IMF as institutions of U.S. hegemony, 97-98; lending policy of, criticized, 101; loans in the Middle East, 99-100; role in Third World development, 98-100; philosophy on Third World development, 99

International Basic Economy Corporation (IBEC), and aid to Latin American economic development, 71-72. See also Rockefeller, Nelson

International Development Advisory Board (IDAB), 189-91, 196 n.6

International development authority, 28, 33, 35, 77, 190

International Labor Organization, Convention of, 46-47

International Monetary Fund (IMF), role in Third World development, 98

International Trade Organization (ITO): CED rejects investment provisions of, 84; and European recovery, 66; Fortune reverses position on, 84; imperial concessions regarding, 81-82; imperial state-capitalist class debate on, 82-84; origins of, 80-81; protectionism as issue in, 81

Israel, 171-73, 191-92, 201, 203. See also Palestine, Jewish

Jewish Agency, 135, 169-70

Jordan Valley Authority (JVA), 168-69

Kennan, George, 69, 70

Kirk, Alexander C., 123, 127, 151-52, 158

Landis, James M., 125; and aid to Ibn Saud, 159; on al Kharj project, 160; conflict with State Department, 127; on expanded economic relations with Egypt, 151-52; on MESC, 124, 126; on regional approach, 126-27; and role in Middle East Company, 89 n.29, 152-53; views on Egypt and Britain, 152

Latin America: and Chapultepec Conference, 49-50; economist of, 15; and European reconstruction, 69-70; on hemispheric Marshall Plan, 69; Regional Economic Commission for, 79-80, 93 n.68; and U.S. economic aid, 47, 49-50

League of Arab States, 80, 148 n.56

Lebanon: critiques U.S. economic development policy, 173-74; laissez-faire and open door capitalism in, 76. See also Hakim, George; Malik, Charles

Lend lease, article seven of, 29, 46

Liberal capitalism, 111, 127-28, 119-20 n.54

Liberia, 72-73

List, Friedrich, 12, 14

Lombardo Toledano, Vicente, critiques core capitalist development policies, 47, 50, 73

Lowdermilk, Walter C., 135, 168-69

McGuire, Paul, 159, 160

Malik, Charles: background of, 76-77; on economic development programs, 76-77, 149; on regional economic commissions, 79

Marshall, George, 128, 171

Marshall Plan: and European integration, 66; for Latin America, 69-70; for Middle East, 132, 155, 164; for Third World, 110, 132. See also ERP

Middle East: British regional approach in, 128-29; and great powers, 122-23; IBRD activities in, 99-100; and Point Four, 108; regional economic commission for, 79-80; U.S. discussion of financing development in, 123-24; pre-World War II U.S. interests in, 121

Middle East Supply Centre (MESC), 93 n.66, 124, 126

Nathan, Robert R., 89 n.29, 135, 167, 169; Palestine economic study by, 167-68

National Association of Manufacturers, 82-83, 105-6

National City Bank, 97

National Foreign Trade Council, 83, 96

Near Eastern Affairs, Division of (NEA), 124, 128; and financial aid to Saudi Arabia, 160-61; raises Communist specter in Jewish Palestine, 170

New Deal liberals: advocate global TVAs, 112; corporatism and reforms of, 4; on Point Four, 106; tactical debate with corporate liberals, 43-44, 52; on Third World economic development, 33-37

New International Economic Order (NIEO), 192-94, 198 n.20

Oil development: and Arab East, 132-33; as component of ERP, 130-33; crude and refined oil prices in, 132-33; no link to larger economy, 165; and Saudi Arabia, 157; U.S. interest in Arab East, 122

Palestine: dual socioeconomic structures in, 166; private U.S. studies of, 167-69

Palestine Economic Corporation (PEC), 166-67, 170

Palestine, Jewish, 134-37, 166-71; activities of private U.S. firms in, 166-67; as center for Arab East economic development, 134-36; Jewish Agency asks aid for, 169-70; role of state in, 169

Palestinian refugees, and Arab East development, 136-37

Pentagon Talks, 1947: and Anglo-American consensus, 138; background to, 128-29; issue of economic development at, 129-30

Periphery: bourgeoisie in, 186; collaborating classes of, 63; core conflict with, 62-63, 192, 193; defined, 5; foreign investment in, 69; and Group of 77, 192,

194; U.S. direct private investments in, 97; U.S. fears solidarity in, 194

Point Four Program, 187; AFL and CIO views on, 107; corporate liberals analyze, 106; and Egypt, 156; imperial state development of, 103-5; legislation on, 107-8; New Deal liberals support, 106; origins of, 102; and Nelson Rockefeller, 106-7; and Saudi Arabia, 164; self-interest as universal principle in, 104; and U.S. business, 105-6

Policy formation organizations, 7, 31. See also Committee for Economic Development; Council on Foreign Relations

Policy Planning Staff (PPS), 69, 70

Political economy, defined, 1-2

Polk, Judd, 163, 165

Productionism, 34, 39; and corporatism, 3-4; and debate over ITO, 81-84; U.S. policy of, 67, 153-54

Reconstruction, European and Asian: and Arab East oil, 138; as function of trade and capital flow, 64; importance of markets for, 69; and Third World economic development, 62, 69, 186

Regionalism: and autarky, 65; Will Clayton on, 66; IDAB report analyzes, 190; and UN regional economic commissions, 78-80; U.S. view of Arab East, 78-80, 126-28, 138-39, 148 n.56

Rockefeller, Nelson: ambition to guide U.S. foreign economic policies, 190-91; analysis of Third World underdevelopment, 38-39; and CED, 38; committed to

U.S. hegemony, 71; enthusiasm for Point Four, 106-7; and IDAB report, 189-91; interest in Latin American development, 37-39, 71-72; and Henry A. Wallace, 37

Rockefeller Foundation, 32, 38

Roosevelt, Franklin D., 37, 185; and Third World economic development, 40, 41

Ruml, Beardsley, 70, 71, 74, 83

Saudi Arabia, 157-66, 202, 203; al Kharj project in, 160; and Aramco, 161-62, 164-65; Bechtel International Corporation in, 165; economic development in, 159, 165; and oil production, 157, 163; and Point Four, 164; U.S. interests in, 157, 163

Schumpeter, Joseph, 10, 12

Semiperiphery, 5-6, 194

Smith, Harold D., 40-41

Soviet Union: and aid to Third World, 191; autarky of, 13, 34; and ECOSOC, 74, 77; and Jewish Palestine, 170-71; and membership on ECOSOC commissions, 80, 93 n.68; as model for Arab East development, 124; posed danger in Middle East, 122-23

Staley, Eugene, and analysis of Third World development, 34-35

State, the, 2-3, 6

State Department, U.S.: attacks JVA plan, 169; avoids Palestine controversy, 166, 167; and barter trade of Egypt, 154; and capital aid to Arab East, 127-28; on Clapp mission, 137; and CFR, 50; on loans to

Israel, 170-72, 184 n.71; opposes regional economic commissions in Third World, 78-80; pressure on Israel, 172; and regional approach to Middle East, 126-27; sees danger of Israeli expansionism, 171; solutions to dollar gap, 67-68; and Subcommission on Economic Development, 75; and technical assistance for Arab East, 133-34; and Third World economic development, 39-40, 185; unsympathetic to Zionism, 135, 174

Stettinius, Edward R.: and Chapultepec Conference, 50; on development and Communism in Africa, 73; and Liberia, 72-73

Subcommission on Economic Development, ECOSOC: Beardsley Ruml served on, 74; membership of, 74; reports of, 74-75, 77; State Department critiques reports of, 75, 78; State Department seeks to dismantle, 75, 78

Technical assistance: AFL and CIO views on, 107; for Arab East, 134; Henry R. Luce observation on, 107; Third World objects to core program on, 108-9; and UN, 102, 108-9; U.S. theory of, 102; U.S. wartime agencies' programs of, 38-39. See also Point Four Program

Tennessee Valley Authority (TVA), 36, 37; global, 112; and Middle East, 152; as model for JVA, 168-69;

Third World: and collaborator classes, 10; economic demands of, 198 n.20; and rate of development, 110-11; suspicious of private foreign capital, 77, 97

Thornburg, Max, 134

Thorp, Willard, 82; defends U.S. economic development policies, 76, 78; role in Point Four, 103

Truman, Harry S.: and loan to Israel, 171-72; and military aid program, 191; and Point Four, 102; requests studies on reconstruction and development, 188, 189

Twitchell, Karl, 158, 179 n.28

Underdevelopment: Arab East view of, 15; theories of, 14-15; U.S. perceptions of and solutions to, 9-10

Unequal exchange, 6, 111-12

United Nations (UN), 78, 102, 192

United Nations Special Committee on Palestine (UNSCOP), 135

United States: Arab criticism of, 187; attitude toward League of Arab States, 148 n.56; capital in Arab East oil, 132-33; commitment to foreign economic expansion, 4-5, 16; corporatism in, 4; design for a new international order, 64; development policy toward Arab East, 173-74; economic development of, 16-17; and economic mission of Gordon Clapp, 137; effort to achieve global integration, 65; Eximbank as policy instrument of, 100-101; foreign economic aid and security threats, 43, 68; foreign policy goals of, 8; goals in Middle East, 121-23; opposes regionalism in Arab East, 138-39; policy interests in Saudi Arabia, 157; potential Arab East markets for, 141 n.15; private investments in periphery, 97; relations with Third World, 9-10; response to NIEO, 193-94; Third World economic development policies of, 9, 16-18, 194-95

Wallace, Henry A.: battle a-gainst corporate liberals, 36-37; on Third World economic development, 35-36, 60 n.74

Wilson, Woodrow, 16-17

World Bank. See International Bank for Reconstruction and Development

---

About the Author

Nathan Godfried received his doctorate from the University of Wisconsin-Madison and has taught at Northwestern University. He has published articles on American foreign relations, Third World economic development, and broadcasting history. Godfried is Assistant Professor of History at Hiram College in Hiram, Ohio.